Agriculture and the Confederacy

CIVIL WAR AMERICA
Peter S. Carmichael, Caroline E. Janney,
and Aaron Sheehan-Dean, *editors*

This landmark series interprets broadly the history and culture of the Civil War era through the long nineteenth century and beyond. Drawing on diverse approaches and methods, the series publishes historical works that explore all aspects of the war, biographies of leading commanders, and tactical and campaign studies, along with select editions of primary sources. Together, these books shed new light on an era that remains central to our understanding of American and world history.

R. DOUGLAS HURT

Agriculture and the Confederacy

Policy, Productivity, and Power in the Civil War South

The University of North Carolina Press
Chapel Hill

© 2015 The University of North Carolina Press
All rights reserved

Set in Swift Neue and Clarendon by codeMantra
Manufactured in the United States of America

The paper in this book meets the guidelines for permanence and
durability of the Committee on Production Guidelines for Book
Longevity of the Council on Library Resources.

The University of North Carolina Press has been a member of
the Green Press Initiative since 2003.

Library of Congress Cataloging-in-Publication Data
Hurt, R. Douglas.
Agriculture and the Confederacy : policy, productivity,
and power in the Civil War South / R. Douglas Hurt.
   pages cm. — (Civil War America)
Includes bibliographical references and index.
ISBN 978-1-4696-2000-8 (paperback : alkaline paper) —
ISBN 978-1-4696-2001-5 (e-book)
1. Agriculture — Southern States — History — 19th century.
2. Agriculture — Economic aspects — Southern States — History — 19th
century. 3. Confederate States of America — Economic policy.
4. Confederate States of America — Politics and government.
5. United States — History — Civil War, 1861–1865. I. Title.
S445.H87 2015
338.10975 — dc23
2014030080

THIS BOOK WAS DIGITALLY PRINTED

For Mary Ellen, Adlai, Austin, Rachel, and Erin

Contents

Acknowledgments *xi*

Introduction 1

ONE. Southern Optimism 11

TWO. Confederate Apprehension 51

THREE. Western Troubles 91

FOUR. Eastern Realities 115

FIVE. Western Losses 163

SIX. Eastern Hard Times 191

SEVEN. Western Collapse 222

EIGHT. Last Things 243

Epilogue 275

Appendix:
Agricultural Prices, 1860 291

Notes 297

Bibliography 327

Index 343

Maps and Tables

MAPS

1. Major Crops of the Confederate States of America, 1861 12

2. Cotton Production, 1859 18

TABLES

1. Land and Slave Valuations, by Owner, for Sandy Creek District, North Carolina, 1863 148

2. Agricultural Prices, Athens, Georgia, and Confederate Government, March 1, 1865 249

3. Tax Valuations of Slaves in Georgia, by Age, 1865 257

Acknowledgments

I am grateful for the assistance that I received from a number of archivists at many institutions. Dale L. Couch at the Georgia State Archives and Library, John McClure at the Virginia Historical Society, Ann Watson and Grady Howell at the Mississippi Department of Archives and History, Jim Holmberg at the Filson Historical Society, and Mattie Abraham at the Special Collections in the Mitchell Library at Mississippi State University gave generously of their time and identified important collections for my research. I am appreciative as well for the assistance that I received at the Southern Historical Collection at the University of North Carolina at Chapel Hill, Library of Virginia, Tennessee State Library and Archives, Indiana Historical Society, and Newberry Library.

Larry Mykytiuk, History Librarian, Bert Chapman, Government Information, Political Science, and Economics Librarian, Cindy Yeoman, Reference Librarian, and Dot Lanzalotto, Head of the Interlibrary Loan Office at Purdue University found elusive sources skillfully and expeditiously. In addition, David Cambron, Rachel Steely, Carla Hostetler, Richard Moss, and Richard Collins assisted my research with considerable skill and efficiency. Caroline Janney, Frank Lambert, Nancy Gabin, and Michael Morrison, my colleagues in the Department of History at Purdue University, helped answer difficult questions and suggested pertinent sources that I might otherwise have overlooked. Kayla M. Flamm at the University of Missouri prepared the crop map for the Confederate States of America. Sara Morris at the University of Kansas provided excellent leads about collections relating to agriculture during the Civil War. Nancy Cramer helped prepare the manuscript. Thanks to all.

Agriculture
and the
Confederacy

Introduction

On the eve of the Civil War southerners considered cotton to be king, but below the Mason-Dixon Line "agriculture," primarily based on slavery – and collectively constituted from the major commercial crops of cotton, tobacco, rice, and sugar – more correctly deserved that sobriquet. Indeed, agriculture created the basis for southern prosperity. Small, diversified farms throughout the region raised a variety of crops to feed their owners' families and provide enough surplus for market to enable them to purchase things both needed and desired for daily life. Across the antebellum South, these farmers practiced an increasingly commercial agriculture while meeting most of the region's food needs. The Upper South produced a surplus of wheat, tobacco, cattle, horses, mules, and hogs. Farmers in Georgia, Alabama, and Florida raised cattle for southern markets. Plantations in South Carolina and Georgia provided rice for the world, a commodity that supported a rich planter class and an extensive slave population. Cotton farmers and planters from South Carolina to Texas and north to Arkansas and western Tennessee produced most of the world's cotton, and the staple was the leading export of the United States. Louisiana planters supplied the nation with sugar and molasses, the former a commodity that few people believed they could live without and the latter a product that served as an important food ration for slaves. Across the region southerners raised large corn crops each year, which they ground into meal for bread and fed to their hogs for fattening.

In the South most farmers and planters, the latter of whom I define as holding at least 500 acres and twenty slaves, not only believed their way of life and the institution of slavery was superior to northern farming and agricultural labor; they also contended that northerners did not appreciate and value southern contributions to the national economy. Moreover, southerners assumed that northerners would soon pay a high price for their false assumptions about the driving force of the American economy. Indeed, they knew that God smiled on the South in ways that he did not on the North, that their agriculture prospered as a result, and that it would do so forever. The North needed the South, but the soon-to-be declared Confederate States of America did not need northern agriculture to survive, an optimism that soon proved false.

This study traces the decline and fall of southern agriculture during the Civil War. Specifically, I discuss agriculture in the Confederacy as an element of power, a term that southerners used and understood in relation to agriculture, similar to military power on land and at sea. I discuss agriculture as power by tracing the most important aspects of production, transportation, labor, finance, and politics, as well as the effects of military raids, impressments, and seizures by both Confederate and Union armies, among other considerations, on farmers and planters. I also discuss Confederate agriculture in relation to the provision of food and forage to civilians and soldiers and to the war's effects on food prices. My approach is to survey agriculture in the Eastern and Western Confederacy in separate chapters on an annual basis to show progressive disintegration. Although this approach will provide the reader with a sense of the major issues and developments during each year of the war, I intentionally use some topical repetition between chapters, such as the impressment of commodities, the destruction of farms, and the growth of trade across enemy lines, as well as the increasing animosity of southern farmers toward the Confederate government. By so doing, my intent is to show the cumulative deterioration of southern agriculture, with most of the region ultimately relegated to subsistence farming. I discuss agriculture only as it relates to the war. I do not, for example, include agricultural organizations, fairs, soil improvement, plant breeding, or seed selection. Fundamentally, the history of agriculture in the Confederate states is a story about food and cotton production and government policy. What southern farmers and planters produced and what the public and soldiers did or did not eat – as determined by the vagaries of the conflict, crop and animal diseases, and weather – contributed to the war's outcome.

Southerners considered agriculture a fundamental strength that would enable them to win the war. Even before the conflict began, southerners considered agriculture a wartime tool that they incorrectly thought they commanded. Southerners believed they had the productive capacity to wage war and lure Great Britain into the conflict. They did not believe the Confederacy could be starved into submission or that Britain would permit its textile factories to close if southern cotton was cut off.

The South possessed agricultural power, and it intended to use it to gain independence.

This study is the first book on southern agriculture during the Civil War since Paul Wallace Gates published *Agriculture and the Civil War* in 1965. Gates surveyed agriculture in both the North and South. Although he discussed agriculture as it related to the war in both regions, much of his study dealt with farming practices and agricultural policies not directly related to the war, such as livestock breeding, the creation of the Department of Agriculture, and passage of the Homestead Act. Moreover, a large secondary literature has been published since Gates's study that requires synthesis, although the journal literature is scattered and far from comprehensive. In 1994 John Solomon Otto published *Southern Agriculture during the Civil War Era, 1860–1880*. He focused on production, though, and only one chapter was on the Civil War. I did not want my approach to replicate the work of either Gates or Otto. Instead, I consider southern agriculture and the provision of food to civilians and soldiers on an annual basis. By tracing the major issues and developments each year, this study—when read along with military histories, which often are chronological—will give the reader a better understanding of the war's annual complexities.

Even before secession, southerners believed that their agricultural trade in the form of cotton and food (including grain, cattle, hogs, and other provisions) would sustain an independent nation. The military superiority of committed men, bolstered by a sound defensive strategy and a strong agricultural sector, would lead to success on the battlefield and to independence. While some northerners expected Confederate armies to collapse before Union might, others believed that southerners would sue for peace when they got hungry. Southerners mocked the assumption that they raised only cotton and a sprinkling of tobacco, rice, and sugarcane.

Early in the war southerners turned to the 1850 census as explained by agricultural editors to challenge the northern belief that the Confederacy would soon be starved into submission when the war choked off southern trade with northern markets. Statistics did not lie. History favored Confederate agriculture, many southerners believed. Looking back on a decade of prosperity and fortified with the Census of 1850, they argued that their agricultural superiority had become readily apparent. The South produced more breadstuffs and provisions than the North or Northwest. By calculating production according to market value, a comparison that every farmer sensitive to the thickness of his wallet understood, the 1850 census reported southern grain production at $307.3 million, while northern grain production tallied $306.3 million. Livestock slaughter in the South totaled $54.3 million, while the North's was $56.9 million — which, southerners said, meant their region was "almost as rich" as the North. Overall, total southern agricultural production by value was $528.5 million, close to the North's $541.6 million. Southerners considered this lesser amount qualitatively superior because the Confederacy had fewer people to feed: its population was only 12 million to the North's 20 million. Boston alone bought $2.5 million worth of slave-state-produced flour, $1.2 million worth of corn, and $500,000 worth of rice annually; in all, New England spent some $50 million on provisions from the South. Confederates, as a result, did not believe their "sharp Yankee brothers" could starve the Confederacy into submission. Given these agricultural facts, one Confederate observed, "It is very evident that somebody is a fool." Moreover, the South produced 4 million bales of cotton worth $200 million in cash on the European market, and the North used 1 million bales of southern cotton annually. For Confederate observers, northerners had a peculiar sense of southern dependency. If southerners produced only 3 million bales for the European market and devoted their efforts to producing more grain and meat, a long war would ensue, to the detriment of the North. The result would be starvation not for the South but for the North. Moreover, a long blockade would enable southerners to develop a more diverse economy and emerge, perhaps a decade later, even stronger and richer than before the war.[1]

In the end, the Confederacy would suffer privation. Food shortages caused by marching armies, logistical breakdowns, and bad weather brought hunger and want, often necessitating relief efforts for the poor. By the end of the war many southerners feared imminent starvation, but such a calamity had never occurred to them earlier. While southern farmers could keep people from starving, they did not have the capacity to keep all civilians well fed or to help the army and the government win the war militarily or diplomatically. In the end, Confederate agricultural power crumbled. It rose again from the proverbial ashes, when planters established an impoverishing one-crop commercial system that differed little from the prewar years (minus slavery, of course). This return to southern economic prominence would come only later, after Reconstruction, and at great cost.

This history, then, is the story of optimism, decline, and the near collapse of Confederate agriculture based on a host of war-driven causes — disrupted production due to fighting armies; insufficient transportation; inadequate bureaucracy to create, administer, and enforce agricultural policy for the good of the nation; notions of states' rights and personal independence that hindered agricultural organization; and the collapse of slavery, among others. In the end, one should not be surprised that southern agriculture failed to lead the Confederate States of America to victory; rather, the surprise is that its farmers fed the population as well as they did for as long as they did under rapidly deteriorating conditions.

I divide this study into the Eastern and Western Confederacy. Although farmers shared many of the same concerns across this new southern nation, those Confederates east of the Appalachians and west of the mountains had particular concerns that merit attention. The Sea Islands of South Carolina and Georgia and the tidal-flow coastal plain permitted a prosperous plantation economy based on rice. In the Piedmont of Virginia and North Carolina, tobacco farmers pursued an agricultural year that lasted from fourteen to sixteen months or more. Farmers in Georgia struggled with the temptation to produce cotton rather than grain and were ever hopeful for a short war. Livestock raisers in western Virginia and Florida and Georgia dealt with market problems influenced not only by war but also by terrain, distance, and limited railroad transportation. West of the Appalachians cotton farmers across the Black Belt yearned to produce cotton but planted more grain instead. The cattle and tobacco country of Tennessee became transformed into wheat and corn fields. Farmers in the rich floodplain of the Mississippi River, known as the Delta, struggled to switch from cotton to grain and always looked downriver to markets in New Orleans or upriver to Memphis and the world beyond, while sugar planters experienced nearly complete destruction of their agricultural economy.

In the Confederate States of America, distinctive geography and the environment dictated where and when certain crops could be raised. Cotton did not grow well in the wet, humid, sugar country where some planters attempted to raise it. But cotton planters in the Western Confederacy regained northern markets sooner than did eastern planters because Union armies opened the Mississippi River corridor, while Union and Confederate armies locked in deadly combat prevented a similar free flow of agricultural commodities northward through Virginia. Moreover, while livestock producers in Texas raised an abundance of poor-quality animals, they were too isolated to help western, let alone eastern, armies and consumers. Each region struggled to manage an ever increasing number of freedmen and -women. Labor plans in the Eastern and Western Confederacy developed, if not ad hoc, at least piecemeal, based on the whims of regional commanders and local needs, and they were increasingly influenced by Federal agents, usually from the Treasury and War departments.

In the Eastern Confederacy the major interstate railroad lines ran from Atlanta to Macon, Savannah, and Charleston, as well as to Charlotte, Wilmington, and Raleigh, before reaching Petersburg and Richmond. In the Western Confederacy the lines primarily ran north and south, from Corinth to Meridian, Mississippi, and Mobile, Alabama, or from Jackson to New Orleans. In each section the few railroads linked farmers, usually cotton producers, with commercial markets. Few lines existed to provide efficient local and regional transportation of agricultural commodities. As a result, Tennessee grain could not easily reach eastern markets, and Virginia, Georgia, and Florida cattle could not easily reach civilians and soldiers in the Western Confederacy. Texas beeves came to western markets on the hoof.[2]

Although railroad tracks totaled 31,168 miles nationwide in 1860, only 8,783 miles of track crossed the South. Virginia led the Confederacy with 1,800 miles of track, and agricultural commodities often reached market by river and the Chesapeake, especially for local trade. Georgia and South Carolina trailed with 1,400 and 1,000 miles, respectively, while North Carolina had only 900 miles of track—all relatively serviceable mileage but not in wartime, when men, materiel, and food and forage had to be transported. In contrast, only 797 miles of railroad track served farmers in Mississippi, while Louisiana farmers and planters had access to a meager 328 miles of track. Tennessee, however, had 1,284 miles by 1861. The Appalachians dictated southwest to northeast railroad traffic, while the railroad lines in the Western Confederacy remained primarily local and scattered. By the Civil War, the South's railroads were too few in number to meet the wartime needs of the army and farmers, the proverbial case of too little too late. No railroad *system* existed in the Confederacy when the war began. Rail lines were often piecemeal or incomplete and without uniform gauge. All these shortcomings meant agricultural shipments from the Western to the Eastern Confederacy were difficult at best. In terms of railroad communication alone, the Eastern and Western Confederacy remained distant from one another and nearly unreachable. For the shipment of agricultural commodities and livestock, farmers and planters in each region relied on their own markets rather than an integrated, national marketing system. In addition, in the Western Confederacy the river trade ran south to the Gulf of Mexico or to the Mississippi River. In the east the rivers that supported the freighting of agricultural provisions flowed into the Atlantic and the Chesapeake. Geographically, then, the rivers also divided the agriculture of the Eastern and Western Confederacy, particularly when farmers were trying to transport commodities to major markets.[3]

The division of the Confederate States of America into eastern and western regions makes sense not only for these reasons but also because Richmond recognized this regional division. In November 1862, the Confederate government appointed General Joseph E. Johnston "plenary" commander of the Department of the West, including responsibility for the armies in East and Middle Tennessee and Mississippi. This department was generally known as the Western Department. By viewing Confederate agriculture in its eastern and western regions, my intent is to help readers make meaningful generalizations, often location based, from specific experiences.[4]

Overall, then, I stress the power of southern agriculture when the war began and its ultimate failure to help the seceding states win independence. In addition, I analyze agriculture in the Confederate States of America as it related directly to the war — that is, in the ways that men and women, black and white, contributed to farming during the conflict and the ways the war affected them and their new nation. I have listened to the voices of the people who lived the agricultural experience — and they were a majority.

In 1860, the South had a population of approximately 9.1 million, of which 5.4 million were white (59.9 percent of the population), 3.5 million were slaves (38.7 percent of the population), and nearly 133,000 were free blacks (1.5 percent of the population). Whites owned 549,071 farms and plantations. The Federal government did not count the number of people living on farms until 1920, but it recommended estimating five to six people per farm in the South. Based on that calculation, approximately 2.7 to 3.2 million whites, or as much as 59 percent of the white population, lived on farms and plantations on the eve of the Civil War.[5]

I use many voices to emphasize the commitment of southerners to farming, their concern about the decline of agriculture across the Confederacy, and their despondency when it collapsed. I extend my study of southern agriculture to include agricultural activities in Union-occupied areas before the conclusion of the war. In addition, I discuss the rise in farm and food prices in relation to their effect on the people who lived in the Confederacy and depended on agriculture. Moreover, I evaluate the decline and fall of the slave labor system, which primarily was an agricultural labor system, and I reflect on the significance of its collapse for southern agriculture, remembering, however, that nearly 75 percent of the white population did not own slaves. Last, I survey the rise of a new agricultural labor system that depended on the continued subservience of the freedpeople. My intent is to show the racial and economic relationships of whites and African Americans in Confederate agriculture. I also intend to suggest similarities as well as differences between the Eastern and Western Confederacy. Although government policy, transportation problems, impressment, and raiding affected farmers throughout the Confederacy in similar ways, details make a difference, particularly when comparing the effects of the war on farmers and planters in both regions. The Eastern and Western Confederacy, in short, experienced distinct problems, particularly in relation to slave labor and the occupation of the plantations. At the same time, the regional similarities merit consideration for the light they shed on the daily lives and problems of farmers and planters across the Confederacy.[6]

A few words about farm and food prices are merited. Often farm and wholesale prices are indistinguishable. I relied on account books, diaries, and letters as well as newspapers to determine them, but farm and food prices listed in the weekly issue of the major newspapers were often commercial wholesale prices, and publishers did not list the prices of all agricultural produce. But even if it is not possible to precisely attribute every agricultural or food price for farmers, planters, and consumers, the figures cited will give the reader a close approximation of the economic issues that farmers and planters confronted throughout the war. Moreover, greed and government policy as well as supply and demand often determined agricultural and food prices. In addition, the South is a big region, and eleven states constituted the Confederacy. Consequently, agricultural production as well as farm and food prices varied widely across the South during the war. Some of the agricultural prices noted in the text can be compared to prewar 1860 prices listed in the Appendix. Such comparisons will show the rapid increase in agricultural and food prices during the war, the former benefiting farmers, at least early in the war, and the latter proving a burden to civilian consumers.

Finally, I have crafted the narrative on a yearly basis to show change, if not in real time, at least as a topical and chronological timeline. It is far too easy to make sweeping generalizations about agriculture that apply to the entire region. It is more difficult, but equally important, to analyze agricultural problems and change with as much immediacy as possible to better understand the experience of the men and women who lived on the farms and plantations as well as those who depended on others for food on a daily basis. By this means, I believe the reader will be best able to learn about the significance of agriculture to the Confederacy.

This timeline, then, shows that in 1861 southern farmers and planters were confident that agriculture would help the South gain independence. Agricultural prices held firm, and farmers responded to Confederate and state government requests to plant more corn and raise more hogs and forgo a cotton crop. Southerners believed they could feed themselves. The cotton embargo would force Great Britain into a war that would be short. In the meantime the Confederate government would purchase food for the army, and farmers and planters would reap great profits from the sale of their produce at civilian markets. The South had the agricultural power to sustain independence. It did not need northern meat, grain, and dairy products. The abundant agricultural production of the Old Northwest would flow to the sterile Northeast now that the profitable southern market had closed. Northern farmers would not be able to adjust production and marketing before the war ended, and Yankee civilians and soldiers would suffer for it. Agricultural weakness would be an Achilles' heel for the North.

In the second year of the war, southern farmers and planters remained optimistic that agricultural prices would remain high and that they could adequately supply civilians and soldiers. They continued to believe in the agricultural power of the South. By the end of the year, however, hunger and privation nagged at people in some towns and cities across the region. Southern farmers now complained about the Confederate cotton reduction program. The Union's capture of New Orleans severely damaged agriculture and the institution of slavery in the Southwest. Confederate impressments of agricultural commodities at less than free-market prices angered farmers and planters. Increasingly, they expressed animosity toward the Confederate government for its policies that led to inflation, depreciating currency, and fixed prices for agricultural provisions. They also criticized the government's failure to address their concerns about the safety of their slaves as Union forces pressed at the northern and western peripheries of the Confederacy.

In 1863, southerners realized that their agricultural power was not as strong and enduring as they had originally believed. Food shortages spread and provoked rioting in some cities—the most significant one in Richmond. The impressment of agricultural commodities escalated. Southern farmers, desperate for markets and cash, increasingly traded across enemy lines. Hunger spread through more areas, particularly where armies marched. Confederate tithing policy broke down due to farmer opposition, and the tax-in-kind policy infuriated them. White southern women increasingly worked in the fields as conscription took more men into the army. The slave market remained active, except where threatened by Union armies, but slave owners began worrying about their investments. The year ended with growing desperation and want.

By 1864, labor shortages hurt agricultural production, as did creeping Union forces, and food prices escalated. Farmers now hid provisions from impressment officers, and they willingly refused Confederate money for the sale of their produce. They also criticized the new Confederate currency issue. Conscription further hindered agricultural production. Hoping for higher prices, many farmers withheld their produce from civilian markets. Others traded with the enemy. Greed, loyalty, and self-interest as well as patriotism ruled the actions of many farmers and planters. Slave owners increasingly moved their bondsmen and -women to perceived safe areas, but prices remained high. Some planters in the Southwest hired freedpeople to work their plantations under Federal oversight. General Philip Sheridan's army ransacked farms in the Shenandoah Valley, and General William Tecumseh Sherman pillaged farms and plantations across Georgia and into the Carolinas. By December southerners realized that their agricultural power had failed. The slave labor system had essentially crumbled, and many civilians and soldiers went hungry. Southern agriculture neared collapse in many areas, and farmers looked to the North for markets and money.

In 1865 southern agriculture as a bountiful, commercial, and profitable enterprise was over. The barter economy in the countryside expanded for want of sound money. Hunger prevailed in many cities. Few crops had been planted by April. Slavery ended and sharecropping emerged, but the switch brought little change to plantation operations, particularly for cotton and sugarcane. Across the South farmers and planters turned from the production of grain, especially corn, to their old staple of cotton. By the end of 1865 the South struggled to rise above the wartime destruction of property, slavery, and markets. The resurrection of southern agriculture would not come soon.

CHAPTER ONE

Southern Optimism

"The year opens full of troubles to the once United States," wrote an Alabama farmer. As the fateful year of 1861 began, many southerners worried about the possibilities of war and disunion and anxiously awaited the course of events. Farmers hoped for the best politically but feared the worst as the South moved irrepressibly toward civil war. In Virginia the new year brought sunshine and snow, the first brightening the spirit and the second bringing soil moisture for the spring crops. Farmers considered both a good omen. Across the South as they went about the rhythm of the season, killing hogs, packing pork, making bacon, splitting fence rails, and stripping tobacco, agricultural life differed little from the past. Daniel W. Cobb, a farmer and slave owner in Southampton County, Virginia, had his hands working in the fields cutting corn and cotton stalks and burning brush along the ditches and fences to prepare his land for plowing and planting and to improve its appearance. His bondsmen thrashed cowpeas for seed, built fences, and plowed while slave women followed planting cotton and corn. In mid-January he sold 3,735 pounds of cotton from his fall crop for 11 cents per pound, 2 cents less than the average price of 13 cents on the New York market, but a consistently low price in this range since the mid-1820s, which scarcely paid his expenses. Cobb did not expect the price to rise soon.[1]

Overall, however, farmers and planters remained optimistic. They considered agriculture another form of southern power that would command national and international respect and recognition if war could not be averted. The creation of a new nation would be good for agriculture. In January one southerner wrote, "The absurdity of our importing Hay from Maine, Irish potatoes from Nova Scotia, Apples from Massachusetts, Butter and Cheese from New York; Flour and Pork from Ohio, and Beef from Illinois, is apparent at a glance.... Let us at least show the world that we are AGRICULTURALLY

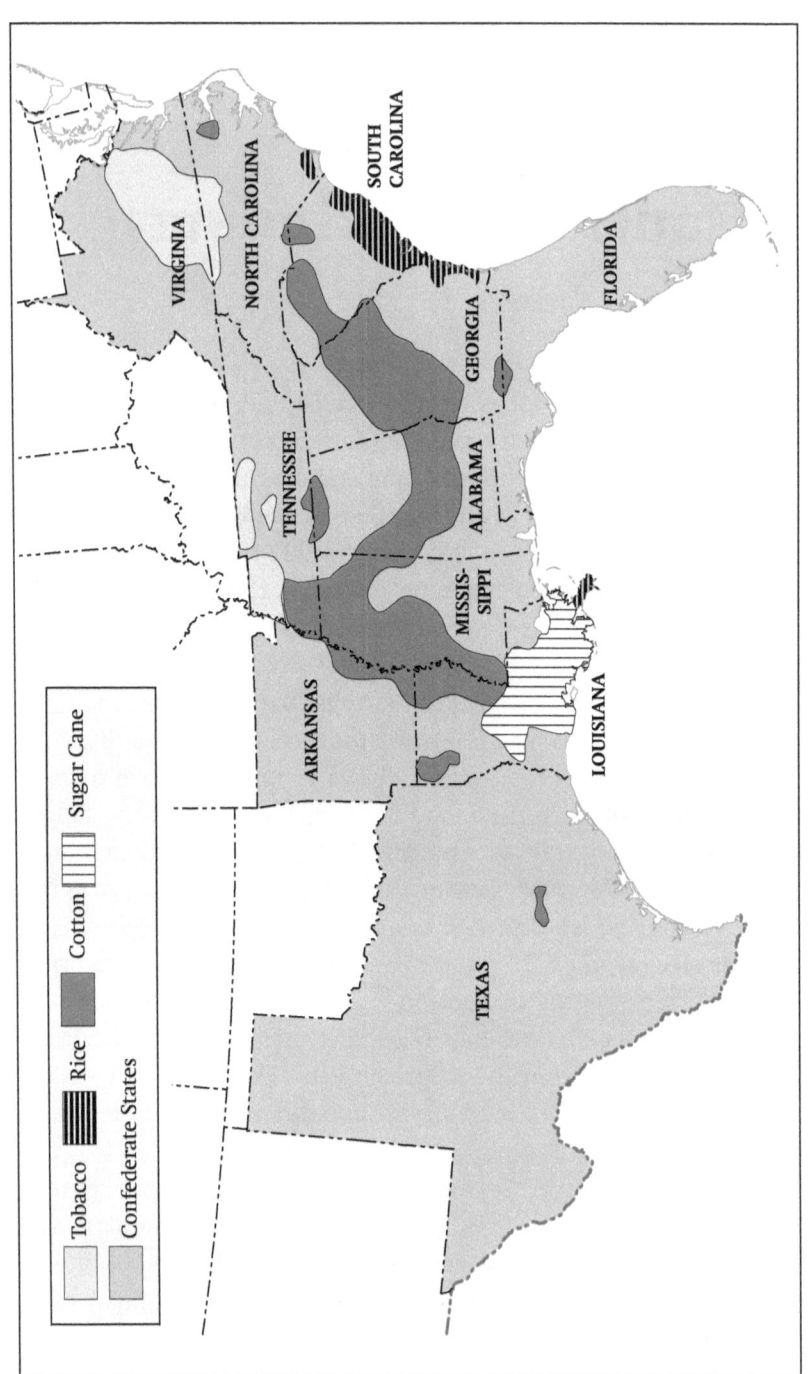

MAP 1. Major Crops of the Confederate States of America, 1861. Map prepared by Kayla M. Flamm.

INDEPENDENT." War would mean an end to dependency on northern food supplies. Agriculture and its product, food, would help win the war.²

In New Orleans, 217,834 bales of cotton awaited shipment and prices ranged from 7½ cents to 11½ cents per pound, and dealers and shippers conducted "considerable business." A thousand hogsheads of sugar, 1,500 barrels of molasses, and 13,743 hogsheads of tobacco also awaited loading on the ships moored along the landing. Ample supplies of corn and flour and some 2,400 sacks of oats had arrived from St. Louis, all offered at good prices for merchants and farmers. In Jefferson City, Texas, cattle sold for $14 to $35 per head. Nearly wild or "piney woods hogs" brought 5 cents per pound while hogs fattened with corn sold for 6½ to 7½ cents per pound. Overall, agricultural prices remained consistent with the previous year (see Appendix), but the volume of sales brought money into merchants' and farmers' pockets.³

Agricultural abundance, not scarcity, seemed only a niggling problem. A report from Texas indicated that the "prairies swarm with fat beeves," and cattlemen worried about declining prices from oversupply. Even so, good rains "cheered" Texas farmers and planters who prepared to seed cotton and looked forward to an "abundant harvest" of wheat. In February and March, Mississippi planter James Allen had ten plows and twenty-four mules breaking ground for corn and cotton, and his field hands followed with hoes and bags of seed. In all, they planted 220 acres of corn and 566 acres of cotton. For Allen and planters like him, the spring of 1861 seemed a time for business as usual.⁴

Yet, while spring brought another planting season, it now had a new urgency because nearly everyone across the South sensed the certainty of war, and southerners were optimistic about their prospects on the battlefield. Committed farmers and planters dedicated to increasing the production of grain, vegetables, meat, and fodder in a bountiful land would feed the armies while meeting the food needs of the civilian population. Southerners treated rumors that the North would win any war between the sections by starving them into submission as ludicrous. One Texan spoke for all southerners when he said, "If we make plenty to eat, both breadstuffs and meat, we cannot suffer." The South could not lose.⁵

By early March, a little more than a month before P. G. T. Beauregard's artillery fired on Fort Sumter in Charleston's harbor, the record-breaking cotton crop of 1860 had been tallied. Everyone agreed that it had been "extraordinary," with 4,675,000 bales picked, including 52,413 bales of long-staple Sea Island cotton that averaged 33 cents per pound for $118 per 350-pound bale, a total value alone of $6,184,754. British and European manufacturers of fine lace and muslin purchased virtually the entire Sea Island crop, as they had during previous years. Short-staple cotton averaged 11 cents per pound, a low but necessarily acceptable price given the lack of alternatives. In Atlanta yellow corn brought 90 cents per bushel and white corn a nickel more, but on the Richmond market corn sold for as low as 60 cents per bushel and cotton 9 to 12½ cents per pound, while wheat brought from $1.35 to $1.55 per bushel – prices little changed from the past few months. Agricultural and food prices soon would vary widely across the South depending on crop conditions, transportation, supply, hoarding, and speculation as well as military activities and the vagaries of the weather.[6]

On April 12, the day of the southern attack on Fort Sumter, agricultural prices held firm. In Mississippi, planter Robert B. Alexander reported that people in town greeted the news with "great rejoicing." Few if any farmers or consumers thought about panic buying or hoarding, which always increased farm prices in wartime. A week later agricultural prices remained steady or increased slightly except for a decline in tobacco attributed to "a want of confidence in buyers to purchase in the present unsettled condition of the country," as sales lagged on the Richmond market. "There is little or nothing doing," one observer reported, "owing to the excitement prevailing throughout the country." At the same time, 1,250 bales of cotton sold in New Orleans in a single day, with the price increasing to 12 cents per pound. Southerners, however, felt secure knowing that their farms produced abundant food and fiber while reports circulated from Washington, D.C., that the city suffered from a "great scarcity" of corn and other provisions. No one feared that the food supply would fail for soldiers or citizens. One Georgian contended, "We can feed our army twelve months without buying a dollar's worth."[7]

Others, however, saw the looming danger of a long war. A Union blockade of the Atlantic and Gulf coasts, closure of the Mississippi River, and the presence of northern armies stifling agricultural trade would end any southern reliance on northern breadstuffs, forage, and livestock to feed urban and slave populations. Northern flour, packed pork, butter, eggs, hay, mules, horses, and farm equipment that southerners relied upon to help meet their food needs would no longer move south, and Confederates would suffer from this loss of trade. Patriotic optimism about the power of Confederate agriculture could change sharply from theory to reality. One Virginian urged farmers and planters to seed large crops because "we must depend on ourselves, and may have no other source of supply but our own soil." He foresaw high prices for "everything eatable," during the next twelve to eighteen months. His prediction proved true, but he underestimated the duration of the war. Even so, Virginians could see a bit of the future based on escalating food prices resulting from fears of a blockade. Those who had money and access to food began stocking supplies, an act that some called senseless hoarding.[8]

Still, the spring crops looked more than encouraging. Georgia and Alabama farmers anticipated an "abundant" wheat crop and admired "good stands of corn." One Texan remarked that "the wheat crop is very promising; times getting a little easier." Across the South "unusual quantities of grain" had been planted. In middle Tennessee farmers anticipated the best wheat crop since 1855, while Arkansas farmers considered it the largest crop in acreage and the best quality ever planted. In Tennessee the General Assembly asked farmers "to devote the breadth of arable land in the State to the culture of grain and grass." Many southerners were uncertain whether northerners and international traders would obey the impending blockade of the coasts and rivers. Northern pork, grain, and other agricultural products might still reach southern markets. But southerners also believed that "hereafter our supplies will be raised at home." The southern agricultural landscape could meet all military and civilian needs with proper development and adjustment, such as planting cotton lands with corn. Some Virginia observers even considered the early blockade of the James River beneficial because the strawberry crop stayed home rather than heading to traditional northern markets, and Virginians enjoyed the "luxury" of a plentiful crop. One Georgian reported that the North could never starve the South into submission, and remarked that if the northerners were not careful they would be "on their knees to us for bread."[9]

On April 29, President Jefferson Davis informed the Congress in Montgomery that "a bounteous Providence cheers us with the promise of abundant crops. The fields of grain which will within a few weeks be ready for the sickle give assurance of the amplest supply of food for man; whilst the corn, cotton, and other staple productions of our soil afford abundant proof that up to this period the season has been propitious." When Virginia governor John Letcher issued a proclamation prohibiting the export of flour to northern cities, southerners believed that northerners would pay a high price in hunger for their folly of driving the South from the Union.[10]

One observer cautioned that "this revolution will cost us some sacrifice," but in the heady days of spring, optimism prevailed over such views amid the excitement of war. Few planters, farmers, or other southerners with independence on their minds saw a "dark uncertain future" or the possibility of anything but better days once freed from northern oppression. Yet cautiousness became recognizable by late April. One Georgian observed, "No one is speculating in land, or negroes, or any other species of property." Farmers paid their debts and took an optimistic but wait-and-see approach to the future. In the meantime, they planted more corn. Agricultural advisers who spoke through the newspapers urged farmers to plant corn because the grain and meat trade with the Northwest via the Mississippi River would be cut off by northern armies. At the same time, Confederate soldiers would require great quantities of meat. The result would be high prices for corn, pork, and beef. "Everything that can be eaten will bring high prices and ready cash," one contemporary noted, and he urged farm families to raise chickens and turkeys and to make butter because those commodities, too, would produce good profits. Southern farmers could be prosperous and patriotic. From Louisiana came the boast that the South could produce all of the breadstuffs, beef, and pork that it needed. Agriculturally speaking, the South was already independent.[11]

By May the corn crop began to sprout in Virginia, and rice and cotton broke through the soil in the Carolinas, leading one observer to report that the "vast" cotton fields in South Carolina had mostly been planted in corn. By mid-May the Georgia wheat crop neared its harvest, and the corn crop had begun to silk and tassel. Southerners remained convinced that the region's agricultural capacity would prevail, so rich were the lands, so productive were the plantations and farms, and so committed were farmers across the South to meeting civilian and military needs for the war effort. While some realized that the times were now "critical," they had enough confidence in the Confederate army and their own productive ability to continue planting cotton even though the Union blockade and Confederate policy closed all but a few domestic markets. Cotton had always meant consistent, dependable money in the bank, and even when southerners needed corn, wheat, pork, beef, and other agricultural products, many farmers and planters would not totally abandon this crop.[12]

In late May, Union forces gave no sign that they possessed the organization, strength, and leadership to bring a quick end to the war. Although General George B. McClellan issued overblown reports about his success against Confederate forces near Grafton and Beverly in western

Virginia, few southerners worried about a northern invasion, which, they believed, their armies would squelch in a heartbeat. While McClellan drafted reports to enhance his career, Virginia farmers sold more cattle on the Richmond market than the butchers needed; the price declined to $4.25 per hundredweight, and the demand for hogs remained limited at $.07 per pound. In North Carolina, Piedmont farmers received 12½ cents per pound for their bacon, a good price not driven by shortage. In Tennessee, beef brought an acceptable $.05 per pound, while eggs sold for $.20 a dozen, chickens $.15 each, and butter $.15 per pound. Farmers marketed hay for $1 per hundredweight. In Jefferson County, Mississippi, one farmer reported that the corn and sweet potato crops looked "good" and the cotton "tolerable well." Mississippi farmers continued to sell corn at $1 per bushel, pork at $26, and flour at $12 per barrel respectively. Abundance seemed normal and certain, and food and agricultural prices consistent and reasonable. A bountiful agricultural sector would ensure independence and enable southerners to "combat tyranny to the bitter end." Reports of Yankee soldiers shooting cattle, stealing horses, destroying wheat crops, and impressing slaves in attacks from Hampton to Warwick Court House in Virginia caused less concern for the losses to the farmers who experienced the raids than anger about the "brute force" levied against civilians.[13]

By May the blockade of the Mississippi River had halted shipments of northern flour and corn, and these provisions had become scarce in some locations, increasing prices. Soon flour brought $15 per barrel and corn $2.50 per bushel in Hardin County, Texas. Spring rains, however, gave farmers the confidence that they would soon harvest a three-year surplus of wheat. Despite the annoyance of the blockade, southern farmers and planters considered themselves the chosen people of God, who gave them signs of his blessings. After a good and timely rain, one Tennessee farmer wrote, "Providence has smiled on us, has thwarted the designs of a sectional majority in their intentions of starving the southern people into submission." The agriculture of the Confederacy was too powerful for that outcome. Texas optimists also considered the blockade beneficial to farmers who sold their wheat to local millers, who in turn hauled flour to the coast, where residents now ate bread made from wheat raised in Texas instead of flour from Illinois. "Hurrah for the blockade!" one Texan wrote. "Nobody hurt." Another contended that if farmers learned to provide their own seed potatoes and garden seeds, they could become even more independent of the North. In this sense the blockade could be "truly a blessing to Texas, ultimately."[14]

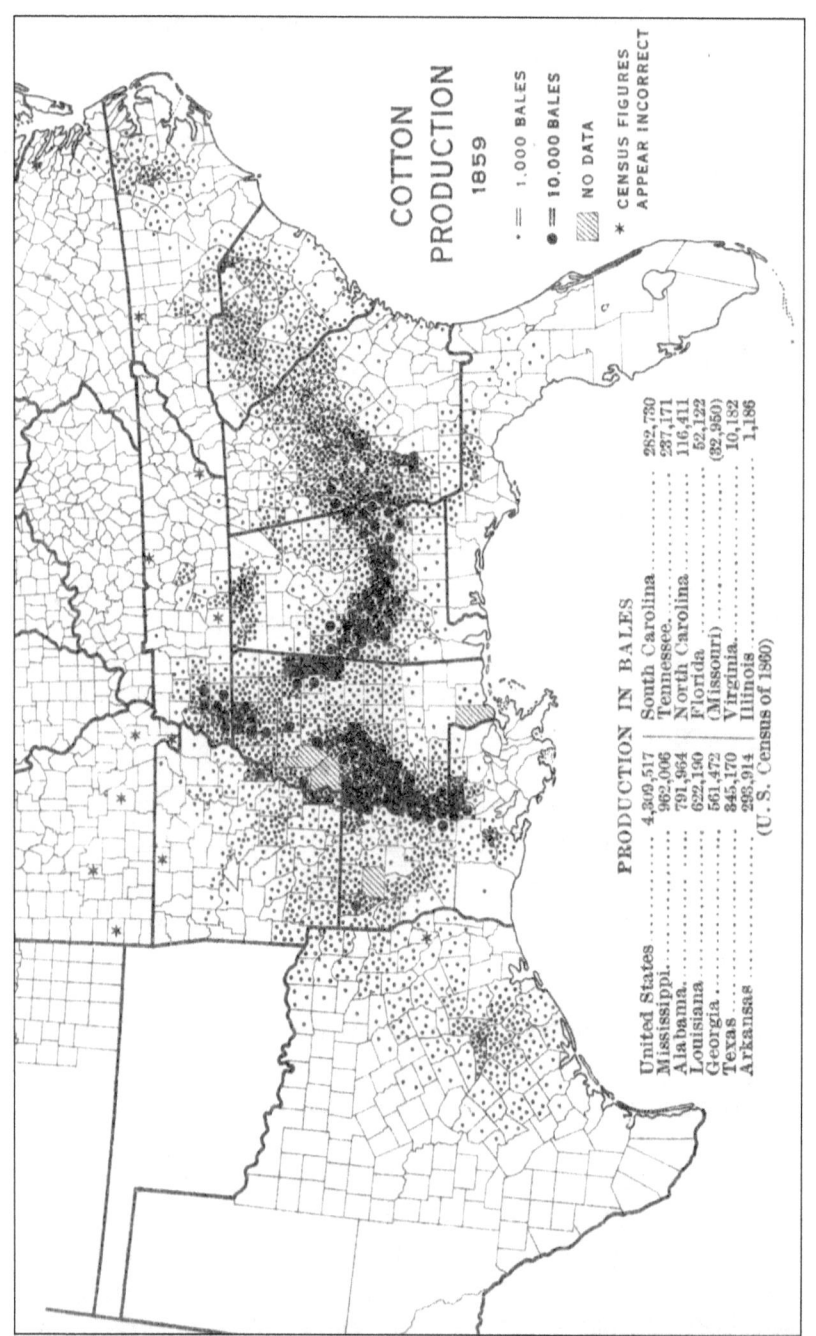

MAP 2. Cotton Production, 1859. From O. C. Stein and O. E. Baker, *Atlas of American Agriculture*, part V, section A: *Cotton*. Washington, D.C.: Government Printing Office, 1918.

SOUTHERNERS KNEW THAT COTTON WAS "King" for their economy. They also believed that it gave them considerable diplomatic leverage, even power. From the plantations and farms came "white gold," which created a global network of trade and European dependence on southern agriculture. By 1860 slaves cultivated approximately two-thirds of the world's cotton in the South. William Lowndes Yancey, a "fire-eater" secessionist from Georgia, had told northerners not long before the South declared independence that "England needs our cotton and must have it." Southerners intended to pursue a free, international trade policy that would serve its diplomatic, political, and economic interests, but when President Lincoln imposed a blockade on southern trade after the bombardment of Fort Sumter, the Confederate Congress retaliated by prohibiting trade with the North and by prohibiting the export of cotton except through Confederate ports or Matamoros, Mexico. The threat of a complete southern embargo of its cotton became clear. The *Charleston Mercury* asserted to Great Britain, "The cards are in our hands and we intend to play them out to the bankruptcy of every cotton factory in Great Britain and France or the acknowledgment of our independence."[15]

The British proclamation of neutrality worried Lincoln and his advisers because, according to international law, such a declaration permitted trade with the Confederacy. Trade would prolong the war, during which time British cotton reserves might become depleted, forcing Britain to break the Union blockade to get the needed fiber for its manufacturers. Cotton became the agricultural anvil upon which diplomatic policies for the Union and Confederacy would be forged. At the same time, the Union blockade of the Atlantic and Gulf coasts proved porous. Blockade-runners brought luxury goods that sold at high prices, but they did not contribute significantly to the sale of cotton or other agricultural commodities. Overall, the Union blockade did not prevent a Confederate cotton trade with Europe, and the Confederacy did not make an effort to run the blockade with ships laden with cotton. The fiber was worth more for its diplomatic value in southern warehouses and barns than as income generated from international sales. Blockade-runners proved skillful risk takers who sometimes provided cargo space for the government, but neither they nor the Union blockade significantly affected Confederate cotton sales abroad. The blockade proved more effective in preventing the customary trade of northern agricultural commodities, particularly via the Mississippi River, to consumers in the South, both black and white. As the conflict wore on, then, Union armies contributed more to stifling Confederate agricultural trade than the Union navy and the blockade. Moreover, the Confederate government never prohibited cotton's export, and it never made the international cotton trade an economic issue for pursuit at all costs.[16]

While the Union blockade and reciprocal trade ban took effect, southerners waited for imminent British, French, and Russian recognition to ensure cotton supplies for their textile mills. British diplomat Robert Bunch informed his government that southerners had an almost "unrivaled conviction" that Great Britain would "make any sacrifice, even of principle or of honor to prevent the stoppage of the supply of cotton." One North Carolina woman mocked the blockade, saying that "the English will sweep Lincoln's navies away like dust." Confederates would learn in time with considerable disappointment that British foreign policy depended on more than maintaining an uninterrupted and unlimited supply of southern cotton, because the British valued peace with the United States more than the Confederate cotton trade.[17]

Still, Great Britain and France held out the possibility of diplomatic recognition, in part, by proclaiming neutrality, which granted belligerent status to the Confederacy and which further encouraged southern hopes for recognition. While the Confederate Congress and President Davis dallied, a group of merchants and planters gathered in New Orleans and proposed to hold all cotton inland until Lincoln lifted the blockade. Planters and cotton brokers in Georgia and South Carolina followed suit. Although some planters held their cotton from market, they expected their economic coercion to bring diplomatic fruit. British textile mill owners, however, had abundant reserves in storage from the previous crop year, and they met their needs by acquiring additional cotton from Britain's colonies or smuggling it from the South.[18]

DESPITE SOME EARLY APPREHENSIONS ABOUT cotton production, by June, the South's agricultural abundance seemed beyond question; nevertheless, the Confederate government lacked money to finance a war that everyone still hoped would soon end. Besides levying property and income taxes, the government also developed several revenue-raising plans that fell directly on farmers and planters. On May 16, the Confederate Congress passed the Produce Loan Act, authorizing the Treasury Department to issue bonds at 8 percent interest to raise $50 million, which it increased to $100 million on August 19. Essentially, farmers and planters subscribed to the produce loan program by consigning cotton, wheat, corn, and other provisions to the government. Government officials believed that farmers would benefit from the loan because their crops would sell at market rates and they would not have to deal with middlemen whom they believed cheated them on prices paid upon sale. Farmers would deliver their crop to a railroad depot, where government agents would arrange to ship the crop once all subscriptions for the area had been delivered. Then, the surplus commodities consigned to the government would be transported and held in Confederate-controlled warehouses and systematically sold at a fixed date at home or abroad. The proceeds, less all handling charges, would be paid in specie to the government, which would issue twenty-year bonds at 8 percent interest, based on the income earned, from the sales to the producers. Government cotton would then establish a basis for credit abroad, and this would enable the Confederacy to acquire needed supplies without having to pay in specie. Farmers and planters also would get government bonds at a high interest rate for investing in the Confederate States of America. Theoretically, the government would resell the cotton on the international market at a 50 percent markup, or no sale would be made.[19]

On paper, the produce loan program made sense to enable the government to purchase crops, particularly cotton, with bonds. All other agricultural commodities could easily be sold at home. In the beginning, many southern cotton farmers and planters supported the produce loan. By June, Confederate agents circulated through cotton country signing subscription contracts with farmers. They offered to take a quarter to half of the bales that a planter expected to produce in the autumn. Some farmers also subscribed grain, tobacco, sugar, molasses, rice, and wheat.[20]

Success depended on the quick lifting of the blockade, at least by the end of the year, so that the government could sell the subscribed cotton abroad. Confederate farmers and planters, however, needed money – that is, Treasury notes that would circulate as currency. Moreover, merchants and cotton factors who had advanced credit on the next crop before the war began had a prior claim to it, although the Produce Loan Act now gave it to the government. One merchant in Panola County, Mississippi, stated the problem succinctly when he wrote to the Treasury Department, "I am determined, as far as possible, not to do anything that will interfere with the loan of the Confederate States; but money or cotton I must have." Southern agriculture depended on credit, and farmers, planters, and merchants needed money, not bonds, to pay their debts.[21]

In June a report circulated from Montgomery that Alabama planters would subscribe 700,000 bales, which supposedly proved "the patriotism of a generous and liberal people who love their country more than gold." On July 4, a group of cotton planters gathered at Macon, Georgia, and voiced support for the produce loan program. At this Cotton Planters Convention, leaders resolved that planters should pledge half of their crop for the loan. Although the cotton producers preferred that the government purchase their crop outright with currency, they believed that it should use the cotton acquired to establish credit for purchases abroad. Many farmers and planters, however, ultimately preferred to hold their cotton and other produce to sell it when and where they could make the most profit. By late July, a Montgomery trader agreed to accept Confederate bonds for the sales of his slaves, and a city editor believed Confederate bonds would soon be used to pay debts and "to a great extent become currency of the country." The power of agriculture seemed clear to most cotton planters and farmers.[22]

Not all planters at the Macon convention believed the plan would work, given the blockade and the complex credit transactions involved with shipping cotton to international markets. Others contended that the Confederate cotton purchase program would be a "financial blunder, a social canker, a political monster," because other farmers would be taxed to pay for debts incurred for what some called a "gigantic cotton speculation." Some farmers argued that agricultural loans were the proper business of state governments and banks, not the central government, upon whom people might easily become dependent. Many farmers and planters warned that if the government bought cotton, it would create an expensive, costly bureaucracy.[23]

Moreover, while many southerners could see the wisdom of such a policy for cotton, not everyone believed that it would work for food commodities. The editor of the *Richmond Daily Examiner* did not think the government should be in the business of serving as a "huge commission house for the purchase and storage of wheat, corn, oats, hay, beef, and pork." Cotton and tobacco were different, because cotton as well as a considerable portion of the tobacco crop could only be sold abroad, and planters and farmers could not sell it internationally themselves. In New Orleans an observer suggested raising money by imposing an export tax of $2 per bale on cotton and taxing cultivated land at 25 cents per acre and uncultivated land at 5 cents per acre rather than accept the government's produce loan program for cotton. New Orleans cotton factors urged planters to store their cotton until the blockade ended instead of shipping it to them. They did not have sufficient storage facilities or markets for the fiber. This policy also would remove the temptation for seizure by Union forces as well as help reduce the chances of a catastrophic fire.[24]

Jefferson Davis believed that the cotton subscriptions to the produce loan program would exceed $50 million and the army would be supplied by the consignment of other agricultural products. Despite early support, however, the loan revenue plan quickly collapsed. Patriotic enthusiasm and practical execution were two different things. Although the cotton planters in Adams County, Mississippi, had subscribed 22,000 bales valued at nearly $1 million by mid-September, and although a government agent charged with acquiring the cotton through the produce loan program operated in nearly every county in the Confederacy, subscriptions lagged.[25]

Thomas S. Dabney, commissioner of the Treasury, complained that the voluntary cotton produce loan failed because only small-scale producers supported it. He charged that farmers and planters who produced from 1 to 300 bales attended recruitment meetings and generally subscribed half of their crop, while the large-scale planters who produced thousands of pounds usually offered only a few hundred bales. Dabney recommended that the government purchase the entire cotton crop by mandate at the rate of 10 cents per pound payable in Treasury notes – that is, paper money. Cotton producers would store their bales at home and deliver them on call by the government for sale to cover various expenses. Congress did not accept his plan, but some cotton agents believed the loan program at least gave planters the opportunity to show a measure of symbolic patriotism by subscribing their cotton.[26]

By September cotton prices had fallen nearly 25 percent from June, when many cotton pledges had been made, while the general price index rose 27 percent. The planters who had subscribed cotton lost considerable money, at least on paper, given the absence of an international and domestic market. Moreover, the Confederate government and the northern blockade of southern ports discouraged trading with the enemy. By the end of the year planters and farmers had subscribed only 417,000 bales of cotton, 5,000 bushels of wheat, 1,000 hogsheads of tobacco, 270,000 bushels of rice, 1,000 hogsheads of sugar and molasses, and $1 million in other produce. Most of the subscribed commodities went uncollected because farmers and planters saw prices increase rapidly, and they refused to deliver their subscriptions and take bonds in payment. They instead preferred to sell their provisions for higher prices on the open market.[27]

Still, the Confederate officials who designed the produce loan policy assumed that the British and French governments would pay a fair price when their ships were loaded from government warehouses at Confederate ports. The British and French navies would then protect their merchant fleets and ensure the delivery of cotton to their textile manufacturers. Confederate officials believed the laws of war permitted belligerents to trade with neutral nations; belligerent powers could not capture neutral ships. This cash-and-carry plan seemed to meet the needs of the European textile manufacturers and southern planters as well as the Confederate government. Because British and French textile manufacturers depended on southern cotton to keep their mills operating and their workers employed, southerners reasoned that Britain and France would soon enter the war to guarantee their cotton supply. By so doing they would sustain a prosperous economy while preventing social unrest at home. The South would benefit because southern agriculturists would find a ready market for their cotton. The Confederate loan program also seemed to ensure that the sale of cotton between governments would keep private citizens from making arrangements on their own and thus would head off international entanglements. Moreover, the demand for cotton and tobacco was "illimitable" because both commodities stored well and could be exchanged for specie. Credit based on these commodities was essentially as good as credit based on metallic money. The logic of this plan seemed so simple and reasonable that it had to be true.[28]

Secretary of the Treasury Christopher G. Memminger supported the cotton loan program, but he noted that the government could not regulate the time of sale or the price. He urged farmers to await a good price before they authorized the sale of their subscribed cotton, and he affirmed that the government did not have the authority to lend money to farmers. Planters, however, needed a circulating currency to meet their expenses and pay their debts and taxes. They depended on cotton for "food and raiment," and they needed foreign markets for an income. With Congress unwilling to provide direct relief in the form of loans (whereby the government would take a lien on the crop or purchase it with a negotiable currency), farmers and planters suffered increasing financial strain by fall. Until the government sold their cotton, they could not be paid in bonds for their subscriptions. In the meantime their cotton remained in storage. By late 1861, then, farmers and planters generally wanted the government to intervene in the form of direct purchase, guaranteed higher prices, and loans at favorable rates.[29]

Essentially, the produce loan program failed from the beginning, although no one knew it at the time, because it lacked any enforcement mechanism. The Confederate government never established a Department of Agriculture to help create and administer agricultural policy. Government officials were too sensitive to states' rights and individual freedom of action to require farmers and planters to follow any government policy—whether it be the produce loan program; mandatory reduction of cotton acreage planted; forced burning of cotton to keep it from the enemy or to create a controlled shortage for diplomatic purposes; or the acceptance of government-established prices for military purchases of provisions. The call for voluntary participation in the cotton loan program gave farmers alternatives. Soon after announcement of the program, cotton planters "burdened" the Produce Loan Office with letters bemoaning their need for money. These planters, hoping to gain some advantage from the program, sought government loans to enable them to meet operating costs and promised "large additions" to their subscriptions if they received government financing for their operations.[30]

By the time government officials realized that voluntary participation in agricultural programs and policies did not work effectively or sufficiently to meet government goals, it was too late. The creation and administration of Confederate agricultural policy required planning, a carefully designed system, and order. Above all, it required a professional bureaucracy dedicated to the task at hand. Confederate agriculture had no centralized, planned, efficient direction and organization. Yet, farmers and planters only wanted an agricultural policy that benefited them individually rather than collectively for the good of the nation. Self-interest on the farms and plantations often superseded the desire for an agricultural policy designed to benefit the Confederacy.[31]

As a result, the states sometimes attempted their own agricultural policy to aid the war effort. In November, the Mississippi legislature approved an Agricultural and Mechanical Committee to which all matters pertaining to agriculture would be referred. Observers believed the committee would be "very useful to our wise planters and mechanics, and facilitate wise legislation for their benefit." Beyond this generality of purpose, no specifics were forthcoming.[32]

Some critics believed the government had made a grave financial mistake if it thought the cotton loan program would provide planters with a market and "relieve the cotton growers from the embarrassments of the blockade." Rather than embark on a costly, government-controlled program, the editor of the *Richmond Daily Examiner* advised that "the planter can well afford to be patient, at least, for a season." The cotton program would make the Confederate government a large-scale cotton factor. Once such a program began, the government could easily remain in agriculture and expand its influence into the lives of farmers and planters and burden the nation with debt for agricultural programs. For some Confederates, the potential for government agricultural regulation seemed clear and dangerous.[33]

Although the produce loan program included tobacco, many growers in the Piedmont remained out of harm's way during the first year and in some cases for the duration of the war, and they were not always enthused about participating in the program. Bright or yellow leaf tobacco had been particularly important to Virginia farmers before the war, and demand remained high. Although the price declined as farmers dumped their previous year's crop on the market in spring 1861, fearing a collapse if war came, the price held relatively steady. Despite state and central government calls to forgo tobacco planting, soldiers considered the staple a necessity and civilians discovered, if they had not already, that it was an agricultural commodity that they could not easily do without. In fact, the more tobacco a person used the more he wanted, no matter the government wartime policy. Although production decreased in 1861, tobacco had proven to be a reliable, profitable cash crop with a ready market, and farmers did not give it up entirely if they could avoid it. Besides, they could raise a small patch of tobacco and still cultivate wheat, corn, and oats. Tobacco meant money, wartime or not, and farmers did not want government interfering with this cash crop.[34]

Without strong central direction of the agricultural economy, then, the states necessarily acted independently. In the autumn, banks in Georgia began extending loans to planters for operating expenses and to pay state and Confederate taxes. In Savannah, the Mechanics Savings and Loan Association granted "small cash advances to meet emergencies." It provided loans at the rate of 5 cents per pound on cotton of middling quality delivered in bales to warehouses in Macon and Griffin. The bank would maintain possession of the cotton until the blockade ended and the planters could sell their fiber and repay the loan, less 7 percent interest, payment of a 2½ percent commission, and the covering of warehouse expenses and insurance fees. Whether any cotton planter would have made a profit on his crop with such a loan repayment obligation will never be known, but the important point is that Georgia state banks, not the Confederate government, provided loans to cotton farmers to help them meet operating expenses in the absence of a market for their crop.[35]

While the government attempted to make the produce loan program work, farmers and planters responded to the lack of currency by demanding immediate government aid. The planters proposed two alternatives: the Treasury should purchase the entire cotton crop or advance planters 5 cents per pound on a projected harvest until they marketed their crop and paid off the loan. Treasury Secretary Memminger, however, rejected both proposals because the Confederate Constitution did not permit lending money for relief and because such a plan would encourage farmers and planters to raise cotton rather than convert their acreage to corn and other grains. Instead the government authorized the printing of $20 million of Treasury notes in small denominations on May 16 and another $100 million on August 19. The government issued this paper currency through banks. These Confederate notes were backed only by public faith in the government, not gold or silver. Proponents argued that people should accept these notes at face value as a circulating currency, because if the Confederacy lost the war they would lose more than their currency and bonds, so they might as well support the government. Although the government never made the notes legal tender backed by specie, people had little choice but to use them as a matter of necessity. Inflation and a corresponding devaluation of the currency, not surprisingly, quickly occurred. Farmers and planters complained that Confederate currency became increasingly worthless, but they needed it to pay debts and taxes on slaves, cattle, horses, and mules as well as meet operational and living expenses.[36]

ON MAY 21 THE CONFEDERATE Congress voted to block the trade of cotton to the North except through southern ports or across the Rio Grande to Mexico. Its intention was to keep the fiber from northern manufacturers and traders who would sell it to British and French textile manufacturers, or use it for domestic production. On August 2 the government extended this trade prohibition to tobacco, sugar, rice, and molasses. Five weeks later, President Lincoln also prohibited all trade with the Confederacy except by permit issued by the secretary of the Treasury. Lincoln's edict remained in force until Memphis fell on June 6, 1862, but farmers, merchants, and speculators in the Upper South soon discovered that they could cross Union lines relatively easily and sell their farm produce for Federal dollars. Indeed, while the Union forcefully imposed a blockade on Confederate ports, it proved less insistent on the strict observation of trade prohibitions across Union lines, if it could be accomplished safely and profitably, particularly for cotton.[37]

Confederate cotton producers needed money and northern textile manufacturers needed cotton, and, in areas under Union occupation, trade naturally developed no matter whether the planters took loyalty oaths (although that pledge eased trade considerably). In August, Union secretary of the Treasury Salmon P. Chase ventured that "the best thing to be done ... is to ... let commerce follow the flag." By so doing northerners could trade with southerners in occupied areas if they received a license from the U.S. Treasury Department. Planters could receive money and needed supplies under this policy. During the first year of the war, however, little trade in cotton occurred because the areas occupied first did not support extensive cotton production.[38]

Still, by early July, more than 8,000 cotton bales moved up the Mississippi River from Memphis to northern buyers. Confederate farmers, planters, and traders who made the initial sales demanded payment in gold or silver specie, which they could spend once back in Confederate territory. U.S. Treasury notes or "greenbacks" would cause suspicion. General Ulysses S. Grant, however, required these farmers and speculators to accept state or Federal paper money when offered because it was legal tender in the North. Farmers who refused Federal currency would be arrested and their produce – cotton, grain, or livestock – confiscated. Trading across lines quickly increased the price of cotton to 60 cents per pound in the West. Farmers who sold their cotton and corn on the Memphis market might want southern independence, but many wanted Union cash even more.[39]

As Union soldiers captured more territory, trade across Federal lines increased, particularly in cotton. Both northern and southern speculators and Confederate farmers benefited from trading across lines; profit trumped politics on the southern farm front throughout the Civil War as farmers, planters, and speculators pursued their own ends. Although provisions also crossed southern lines and eventually aided the Confederate army, Lincoln believed that this trade benefited northern manufacturers and helped weaken the loyalty of southern farmers for their cause.[40]

SLAVE-PRODUCED COTTON SERVED AS THE foundation of southern economic power. Confederate officials, merchants, and planters believed that cotton would give legitimacy to the newly proclaimed nation because of Great Britain's dependency on the fiber for its own economic growth. Southerners owned approximately 4 million slaves worth $2 billion to $4 billion; the average value of a prime male field hand was

$1,800. Confederate farmers and planters thus believed they possessed the agricultural labor force to maintain a strong cotton economy despite the loss of the northern textile markets. This agricultural power, they contended, would translate into diplomatic power and cause Great Britain and France to enter the war to secure the fiber their manufacturers needed. It also might pressure northern manufacturers, financiers, shippers, and "Cotton Whigs" to demand an end to the war for their own economic purposes, because both regions needed the other. Businessmen and workers as well as farmers and planters depended on slave-produced cotton. Any interruption of the cotton supply would gain the Confederacy new friends and strengthen old ones. Cotton was king. It was agricultural, diplomatic, and economic power, and southerners knew it.[41]

Confederate agriculture in relation to slave-produced cotton caused the North and Europe to take the new nation seriously. Rather than antagonize the British and French with a formal cotton embargo, the Confederate government chose to let the states impose restrictions on cotton planting and trade to create a shortage of fiber that would invite British and French intervention. Yet the cotton crops of 1859 and 1860 had been huge, and European textile manufacturers had purchased 3.5 million and 3 million bales, respectively, during those years. When the war began British textile manufacturers had more than 1 million bales of cotton on hand. They did not experience a shortage until summer, and the volume of cotton in British possession did not compel it to grant immediate recognition of Confederate independence because it used the opportunity to sell down its surplus textiles, and it looked to India and Egypt for access to new sources of supply. Great Britain and France needed southern cotton less than the Confederate government, farmers, and planters needed them.[42]

Many farmers and planters had already seeded much of the cotton crop when the war began, and they did not want to plow it under and replace it with corn and wheat. But they were uncertain about what to do with it. In the West some planters believed they should produce as usual and send their cotton bales to New Orleans for shipment abroad by blockade-runners, or they wanted it held in storage. Others contended that such a policy would ensure capture by the Union navy and lead to considerable financial loss. Some argued that cotton should not be ginned but stored raw on plantations. As long as it could not be sent to European textile manufactures because of the blockade, the price would rise when the war soon ended. Eventually, planters would capitalize on pent up demand and high market prices from their cotton held in storage. Yet others maintained that cotton stored in warehouses would depreciate prices and warned that a large surplus at war's end would flood the international market and drive prices still lower.[43]

Planters hedged their bets and planted cotton. One Louisiana soldier reported that a common subject of discussion was "planting or not planting cotton" and that the officers with whom he served divided over the subject. He urged his father to plant as much cotton as possible. In Mississippi one Warren County planter used most of his 120 slaves to pick 98,000 pounds of cotton from 566 acres for approximately 173 pounds per acre. This harvest produced 245 bales that averaged 400 pounds each. A significant reduction in the crop would not come until Union forces occupied large areas of Louisiana, Tennessee, Arkansas, and Mississippi, and farmers and planters made a concerted effort to plant crops other than cotton. In the meantime, while many farmers and planters debated whether to plant cotton, they believed they could easily feed the people of the region. By comparison, farmers in the Old Northwest would soon have to provision New England, where agriculture on unproductive, rocky lands was in decline. In July the editor of the *Charleston Mercury* aptly noted that "agriculture supports war" and that southerners essentially were an agricultural people, steeled by hard work for the task at hand.[44]

Many farmers, such as those near Winchester, Virginia, also had completed planting their grain crops when the war began. As the Confederate government called up the state militias and as farmers joined the army, many believed they would be home for the fall harvest. By July, however, they knew that they had been too optimistic. They had not returned to reap the wheat crop and their harvest of the autumn corn crop seemed unlikely. Julia Chase of Winchester thought that the farm boys in uniform who milled about the town were "thinking probably their wheat was of more consequence to them than fighting." The older farmers who remained at home now worried about a scarcity of labor if the war continued much longer. The presence of Joseph Johnston's army strained their resources, and impressments of food and fodder quickly became a burden. Moreover, as Confederate soldiers built defensive works they ripped out fencing. Army control of the Winchester and Potomac Railroad limited or prevented the shipment of provisions from other areas, and the price of food rose rapidly. Sugar disappeared from merchants' shelves, and consumers began to grind rye and mix it with coffee to make it last longer. Most civilians hoped that Johnston's army would soon leave.[45]

Nevertheless, Jefferson Davis believed the military and agricultural power of the Confederacy was still sound in midsummer. When Confederate soldiers routed Union troops at Manassas (Bull Run to northerners), southerners believed the battle proved the superiority of the Confederate army, and southern farmers went about their business confident of their safety. (The Union's capture of Fort Hatteras, Fort Macon, Fort Beaufort, and Elizabeth City along the Outer Banks and Pamlico Sound in North Carolina should have given them pause, as General Winfield Scott's Anaconda Plan began its squeeze.) Instead, Confederates believed that British recognition would be forthcoming. Southerners thought that after the battle of Manassas, Confederate military and agricultural power could not help but force the issue.[46]

At the same time, the grain harvest had been abundant, perhaps even capable of supplying flour for the next two years. "Cotton, sugar, and tobacco forming the surplus production of our agriculture, and furnishing the basis of our commercial exchanges, present the most cheering promise," President Davis wrote, "and a kind Providence has smiled on the labor which extracts the teeming wealth of our soil in all portions of the Confederacy." An Alabama planter agreed, confiding in his diary that "the South will rejoice in plenty of food. God is good to us." Hunger and want still seemed beyond comprehension. In Macon, corn brought $1 per bushel and cotton 15 cents to 17 cents per pound, prices that farmers and planters considered fair. Sacrifices remained small as many farmers now at government request used their corn to make meal and pork rather than whiskey. This agricultural change prevented one Virginia farmer from giving his wheat cutters whiskey during the day because he could not get it, a wartime condition that both he and his harvest workers regretted. Still, the wheat crop brought $1 per bushel in the James River area. By August only the government purchase of beef on the Richmond market kept the price from falling below $3.75 per hundredweight because the 196 head of cattle offered for sale flooded the market.[47]

By late summer, food and agricultural problems were becoming apparent. On August 31, a soldier in Randolph County, Virginia, complained that "our fare is bread and mutton or beef – rice and tea or coffee, a little brown sugar. We have been out of butter and potatoes for some time – and now are pretty short of sugar, coffee, and salt." Little did he know that except for cornmeal for bread and salt pork for meat, most of these foods would soon disappear from his diet. Another soldier in the Thirteenth Virginia Infantry complained that the food was "such as our negroes would refuse to eat, fat and tough — badly cooked and not clean ... beef and heavy bread ... washed down by a black liquid dignified with the name of coffee." Problems of supply and production became increasingly troublesome.[48]

Southern farmers now understood that the government needed them to produce as much food and forage as possible and that it would buy much of their produce. One South Carolinian urged farmers to cut and bale their tall grass because the Quartermaster's Department would purchase it: hay, he wrote, was "indispensable to any army." The war had almost immediately, then, created a market for a host of agricultural commodities, and the government served as a major buyer. At the same time, however, Union forces began attacking and occupying some areas. By mid-September farmers in Hardy County, Virginia, had lost an estimated $30,000 in cattle, horses, and sheep to Federal troops. In a letter to President Davis, they asked the army to protect their beef, pork, and corn for the sake of the Confederacy. These farmers along the South Branch of the Potomac River had a long tradition of raising corn, cattle, and hogs. If they did not receive military protection, they contended, they could only supply the army with several thousand cattle and hogs, and they would not be able to feed themselves.[49]

Moreover, the vagaries of weather and marching armies soon affected one area of the South but not another, usually for ill. In Alabama, wet autumn weather followed a dry summer, damaging the quality and quantity of the crops. One farmer had planted 287 acres with corn and harvested only 17 bushels per acre when he had expected double that amount. Given the unpredictability of the weather and the blockade, he believed that planters and farmers had to produce more food. Despite the "troubles and hard times" the war would enable the South to become self-sufficient, and a self-sufficient people would be an independent people with an economy soundly resting on a bountiful agriculture.[50]

By autumn, however, much of the braggadocio about the capabilities of southern farmers and planters who would ensure victory began to wane. For those who watched the markets subtle changes had begun to occur. Great disparity existed for agricultural prices due to the proximity of military engagements and marching armies as well as transportation. Corn, for example, sold as low as 4 cents per bushel in South Alabama. By November, the price had risen to 70 cents per bushel on the Richmond market, up a nickel since April, while cornmeal rose 10 cents to 85 cents per bushel due to high demand. The price of cornmeal also rose to 95 cents to $1 per bushel in New Orleans by mid-November. Wheat reached

$1.15 per bushel and increased to $2 per bushel on the Mobile market. Wartime demand had begun to force agricultural prices upward.[51]

Farmers, of course, enjoyed high prices. War is good for them unless an enemy army marches through or fights in their fields or kills them or their sons. Farmers and planters made money during the first year of the war, but price increases indicated growing shortages. In Atlanta, by late autumn bacon had become "very scarce" and other cuts of pork limited or unavailable. Earlier, flour rose to as much as $9 per hundred-pound barrel, up from $6.25 in April. In Richmond flour trended upward and brought from $4.25 to $7.25 per hundredweight, but steady prices since April with the summer milling coming to market. In Atlanta flour reached more than $11 per barrel by December amid rumors that speculators were attempting to control the market for wheat, flour, and salt, the latter of which was essential for preserving pork at slaughter time and which increased to $15 per sack. One critic remarked that some buyers "with their patriotism are endeavoring to speculate upon the necessities of the country."[52]

By late autumn, then, agricultural prices generally had risen since the war began, all to the benefit of the farmer who had commodities to sell and whose fields the armies of either side had not trampled, foraged, or pillaged and where slaves had not been lured away by sympathetic Union officers or, depending on perspective, taken or given refuge as in northern and eastern Virginia and Tennessee. By November, however, high agricultural prices brought increasing criticism that farmers charged as much as 200 percent to 400 percent more for their produce than before the war, despite the fact that their costs had not increased and they had produced abundant harvests. In Richmond, corn rose from 65 cents per bushel in April to 70 cents per bushel in November, while the price of butter increased from 10 to 20 cents per pound depending on quality to 45 to 50 cents per pound during that same period. Flour also rose from $6.50 to as much as $8.50 per hundred-pound barrel, equal to high prices in early spring before the harvest of the wheat crop. In early December one observer noted a drove of sixty-three hogs headed for Richmond, which, at 31 cents per pound, was worth between $3,000 and $4,000. In the early spring those hogs would have brought 7 cents per pound. The earnings for raising hogs in wartime had become substantial, if farmers could get their swine to market, a routine task that became increasingly difficult.[53]

More problems were obvious. Some agricultural observers did not believe that sufficient pork could be packed to meet military and civilian requirements because of the insufficiency of hogs. The South needed time to convert from cotton to corn to produce sufficient pork now that it could not rely on Kentucky, Missouri, western Virginia, and the Old Northwest. Whether southern farmers would have enough time to breed and raise more hogs became a concern. One observer noted that unless Kentucky and Missouri could be freed from the "vandals of the north, the planters will suffer for the want of it." Already pork had reached 14 cents per pound — that is, $14 per hundredweight in Atlanta, good for farmers but bad for consumers.[54]

Other problems developed as well. By December, the army decided that if Federal forces threatened the coastal area of South Carolina, the rice planters would be directed to destroy their grain and other crops as a "military Necessity." If the planters did not destroy their crops, the army would do it for them and remove their slaves by force, if necessary. In the rice area, the Confederates, then, planned their own scorched-earth policy, and the rice planters would bear the brunt of it. With more than two-thirds of South Carolina's rice produced along the tidal-flow rivers, the crop became a strategic target for the North and potentially easy pickings, since the rice was stored on the plantations. The Confederate commanding officer of the First Military District warned that the loss of this area "would be disastrous in many ways should our enemies ever succeed in possessing themselves of so large an amount of provisions, particularly valuable to them for reasons too numerous to mention." This fear was not unfounded. By mid-December Union forces occupied Ladies Island, South Carolina, and proceeded to collect the cotton from the plantations as well as in the deserted portions of the state; they then ginned and baled it for transport north. The planters could not sustain labor-intensive agriculture as slaves fled and because Federal naval units also quickly occupied Port Royal and Beaufort, South Carolina, and prevented the export of rice from Charleston. Although the planters continued to raise some rice with a diminished labor force, they increasingly emphasized other food crops.[55]

In the Western Confederacy the sugar country hugged the narrow portions of land between the rivers and swamps in southern Louisiana. The plantations fronted the rivers, which enabled the planters to ship their hogsheads of sugar to New Orleans for sale at the levee and transshipment to eastern markets and customers in the Upper Mississippi and Ohio River valleys. Sugar dominated agriculture below Baton Rouge, where approximately 1,300 farms and plantations with 139,000 slaves raised sugarcane on the "coast" southward from the mouth of the Red River on the Mississippi. Here, the average sugar planter owned 75 slaves, but planters in the parishes adjoining the Mississippi River each held nearly 100 slaves.[56]

Most Louisiana sugar planters opposed secession because their plantations were productive and profitable. They wanted slavery and Union. Northerners provided an important market, and sugar and molasses always brought high prices. In 1861, the sugar planters produced a record sugar crop of 459,410 hogsheads with little interference from the war, but the bumper crop depressed prices and the closure of the Mississippi River soon terminated trade. In Memphis commission merchants urged planters to avoid the depressed New Orleans market and ship their sugar by rail to Memphis, but the military need for the railroads prevented that commerce. In New Orleans sugar held steady at 7 to 8½ cents per pound, but by September the sugar crop was so large that planters did not know what to do with it. This crop was the last made exclusively with slave labor.[57]

As farmers and planters made adjustments to their crops, the summer grains fell to the scythe and reapers. Larger-scale wheat farmers used horse-powered threshing machines, but many farmers and slaves relied on flails for "whipping out" the grains of wheat and rye. Near Union City, Tennessee, some farmers used mowers to cut clover, and the machines did "nice work." Hardware dealers such as Rousset and Genin in New Orleans sold improved Peacock plows along with the traditional favorite Carey or King plows. They also sold a "general assortment of Plantation Implements" to meet individual needs. The Southern Agricultural Implement Factory in Jackson, Mississippi, made plows with steel points, wagons, and other agricultural equipment. By the end of the year, however, the blockade ended the shipment of northern-made agricultural equipment to the South, and stocks of agricultural tools and implements had declined significantly despite continuing strong demand. Some entrepreneurs attempted to establish their own factories to manufacture corn shellers, wheat fans, and other implements. Although the ultimate success or failure of these endeavors lay in the future, one editor believed that "this is the way to make the Confederacy really independent."[58]

SOUTHERNERS HAD RELIED ON NORTHERN pork in the form of bacon and salted meat packed in barrels to sustain the protein needs of the white and black populations. Across the region, however, farmers raised hogs that were not pure bred or upbred animals but rather were near wild rooters that forged in the cornfields and woods for food. Because they were not systematically fattened with corn, they produced little meat and lard. One observer called them "bony, snake-headed, hairy wild beasts." Georgia and Tennessee farmers raised the most hogs in the Confederacy, but once the Union blockaded the Mississippi River, slave owners could not provide the traditional three pounds of pork, usually bacon, per slave weekly. When hog cholera devastated herds in Mississippi and Alabama and anthrax struck in the latter state as well, some farmers stopped raising hogs, which further worsened the growing meat shortage in the South. At the same time, the price of salt rose, reaching $7 per barrel in Richmond by September and $15 per sack in Atlanta by November – prices that threatened to limit the pork-packing season. A Virginia newspaper editor reported that "there is an outcry against the scarcity of salt," and farmers worried about their ability to preserve their hog crop. "Without salt what will become of the negroes?" a northern editor wondered. Hunger among slaves and whites would be "a most effective motive of ill-feeling and dissatisfaction." With two hogs weighing 200 pounds each bringing about $32 total, roughly the equivalent of a 400-pound bale of cotton, and produced at 25 percent less cost, planters would surely see the value in raising hogs rather than cotton. Or so some southerners believed.[59]

The supply of beef also became an immediate problem. In 1861 farmers in the Upper South, particularly the Shenandoah Valley, provided most of the beef cattle for the Eastern Confederacy, although Texas raised more cattle than any other southern state. Texas had more cattle than Georgia, Alabama, Mississippi, and Louisiana combined. In the Eastern Confederacy beef cattle usually weighed between 400 to 600 pounds dressed, and they had a reputation for being "scrubby" and small enough to warrant being called "pony cattle." Georgia farmers produced a large number of beef cattle, second only to Texas, but northerners who saw those cattle considered them "lean and bony-rumped." The few dairy cows raised produced little milk due to poor breeding, feeding, and care.[60]

Texas cattle, customarily called longhorns, had little meat, which consumers considered poor in quality. Texas cattle did not fatten easily or at all on grass, and cattle raisers did not attempt to feed them corn before sale and slaughter. Although longhorns produced tough meat and little of it per animal, the cattle raised elsewhere in the South proved to be hardly better. Planters with large acreage had preferred growing cotton because it earned more money than cattle. A large-scale cattle producer raised no more than 100 head and sold his beeves on a local market, where butchers processed the animals into various cuts for consumers in towns and cities. The rich soil of the Black Belt primarily produced cotton, not cattle.[61]

Planters raised more hogs than cattle because they reproduced quickly and provided considerable meat with little effort on the part of the planters. They let their hogs range in the woods and, if progressive, fattened them with corn near slaughter time. Cattle took about four years to raise from birth to slaughter, while several good hogs could produce as much meat annually as one good steer after a few years. In the hills and mountains of the Appalachians, farmers raised some cattle for subsistence and local markets, but these efforts remained small scale. At the outset of the war, then, livestock raising did not substantially contribute to southern agriculture. Southerners did not eat much beef. When the fighting commenced, the Confederate armies and civilian population necessarily looked to Texas, and to a lesser extent Florida, for beef.[62]

Texas livestock raisers relied on markets in Louisiana and Mississippi. By 1861, New Orleans received more than 50,000 head of cattle annually from west of the Sabine River in Texas. With the beef supply cut off from the Old Northwest, the Confederacy needed beef from the Lone Star State. In New Orleans beef prices quickly escalated and ranged between $30 and $50 per head, depending on supply, compared with the $10 to $15 per head before the war. Cattle raisers hurried to take advantage of these high wartime prices. Government agents also bought Texas cattle for the army and drove the longhorns to Confederate stockyards at New Iberia, Louisiana. In November, when word spread about the construction of an "immense" slaughterhouse in Alexandria, Louisiana, capable of processing 40,000 Texas cattle during the winter for the army, supply seemed more than adequate for demand. But when butchers in Alexandria increased the price of beef and pork from 8 to 10 cents per pound, the local editor considered it "extortion upon the public." Soon consumers would consider this price cheap, and they would not see it again during the war.[63]

By late December many Texas cattle producers sold their beeves to buyers in Jefferson at $18 to $20 per head for slaughter and shipment down the Red River to the New Orleans market. In Dallas, however, beef was in "horrible abundance" and brought only 4 cents per pound, and one resident reported "no danger of starving." Most southerners would have agreed with a farmer near Marshall, Texas, who wrote, "We have the most self-sustaining country in the world." No one considered the slightest possibility of "subjugation." Texas livestock raisers also drove a large number of cattle to Mexico, but the commanding officer of the Department of Texas believed these cattle would be resold to support the U.S. Army in New Mexico. The Confederacy needed trade with Mexico, he believed, but not if it ultimately benefited the North. Far from the scene of battle, Texas cattlemen proved more loyal to their bank accounts than to the Confederacy, and Texans worried little, if at all, about the resale of their cattle northward from Mexico.[64]

When the war began farmers and planters were also well supplied with horses and mules that they bought from Kentucky, Tennessee, Missouri, and western Virginia. The number of horses and mules available for draft power, however, quickly declined because the army needed these animals. Cavalrymen and mounted officers furnished their own horses, while the army purchased horses and mules for the artillery and teamsters. The Quartermaster's Department preferred to buy horses in the Shenandoah Valley or North Carolina. Throughout 1861 farmers and planters had a sufficient surplus of horses and mules to meet the army's transportation needs as well as cavalry requirements, and they enjoyed receiving high prices for their animals. Soon, however, the procurement of horses for the army would become a burden.[65]

In the meantime, southern farmers sold their poorest horses and mules to the army. General John B. McGruder complained that his artillery horses were "almost without exception worthless" and "nothing but the *vilest refuse* has been sent here." The Quartermaster's Department also had great difficulty procuring adequate grain and forage. By the end of the year the army did not have and would not have the horses and mules that it needed, in part, because farmers began refusing to sell them for depreciated Confederate currency. As a result, the army had no resort but to impress the horses and mules that it needed, which left farmers unhappy and often without sufficient draft power to meet their needs.[66]

NOT ALL PLANTERS FLED WITH their slaves before the invading Union armies, and many slaves escaped or remained behind. Nor did the U.S. government have a plan to manage deserted property, particularly abandoned slaves. Gradually, however, the Federal government developed a policy to control slave labor for the benefit of agricultural production and their own subsistence. Some Unionists suggested the confiscation of plantations and the use of the freedpeople or contrabands to operate those properties for the production of cotton, corn, and other food and forage.

In November the U.S. Supreme Court significantly aided the development of a policy for the use of plantations and slaves by Federal forces. It held that plantations fell under the administration of the Federal government by the right of the "sovereign belligerent." This decision upheld international law providing that all enemy property, including land, could be confiscated and that civil wars were governed by this principle. Consequently, a sovereign belligerent had the right to confiscate the property of a subject belligerent. This also meant that it could use confiscated plantations to employ freedmen and -women. Military authorities, however, had the responsibility to administer the work of the freedpeople on the confiscated plantations, but they did not at first have a specific policy to accomplish this task. Moreover, the War Department had responsibility for more women and children than men because they usually remained on the plantations while the men fled to Union lines and went to work on fortifications or at various camps.[67]

In November on the recently captured island of Beaufort, South Carolina, the War Department planned to pay wages to the freedpeople whose masters had abandoned them. The department expected that Yankee supervisors would direct them in the planting of the next crop. General William Tecumseh Sherman also had orders to secure the corn and rice crops and to ship the cotton and grain not needed by the army and freedpeople to New York City. When Union soldiers captured Port Royal, South Carolina, the rice planters abandoned the plantations and fled inland, and rice production ceased. They also left behind about 10,000 slaves who came under Union management on the plantations.[68]

When many planters abandoned the lowlands in the autumn of 1861, one planter who did not leave complained that "they have fled like sheep leaving all their property in the hands of the enemy, many without even a change of clothes. No man had the courage to burn his cotton or his house before he left – and with one or two exceptions scarcely a negro has been saved." Yet the flight of planters and the employment or management of the freedpeople on occupied plantations were not the only agricultural labor problems for southerners. Many men who enlisted when the war began left wives and children to operate the farm or plantation, the latter of which usually included a number of slaves. Had they not had confidence in their wives' ability to manage crops, livestock, and slaves, many young farmers probably would not have been so eager to enlist. In 1861, one in every four men who signed up left a wife and children at home, and most of these men were farmers. One in three volunteers owned slaves or lived with family members who owned bondsmen, thereby making their departure for the army burdensome for the women left behind. In October 1861, a farmer's wife in Georgia wrote to her soldier husband in Virginia that "I am overseeing a little more. . . . [The slaves] don't respect [the overseer] half as much as they do me." Her husband told her that he could not run the farm from a distance and wrote, "You'll have to get along almost by yourself so you must be man and woman both while the war lasts."[69]

During the war's first year, white women in South Carolina could be seen in the fields fixing fences, plowing, and cultivating cotton lands during the spring and picking cotton late in the summer and early autumn. In Mississippi, white women tended their kitchen gardens, but they avoided fieldwork if possible and instead supervised crop production by family members, neighbors, and friends as well as slaves, at least for now. Mississippi's 31,000 plantation owners had the luxury of using approximately 436,700 slaves, often directed by white women when the war began. Across the South by the end of the year, the women best able to meet their farm responsibilities were those with teenage and other children capable of work; women from families who could provide help; those who had a labor support network; and plantation women.[70]

Slavery, of course, was primarily agricultural, and the year began as usual with slave owners hiring out their unneeded bondsmen and women – that is, surplus slaves to generate additional income. In early January male field hands in Virginia hired for $105 per year and for $1.50 per day in Mississippi at the end of the year. Slaves did all kinds of agricultural labor, but picking cotton was one of the most important. Planters and farmers had accepted as a natural law the belief that only slaves could produce cotton because free white workers could not labor in the hot southern sun, but even then some whites worried about them. Kate Stone, the twenty-year-old daughter of a plantation owner near Vicksburg, reported in late July that "the Negroes are sick and by the dozen have been all summer. . . . Now that they are pulling fodder, it will put many more on the sick list. It is such hard work." Even so, planters believed they had developed the institution to a nearly perfect condition. Representative H. H. Hill of Georgia affirmed that belief, telling southerners that they were not only an agricultural but also a people who had a "peculiar system of agricultural labor."[71]

Slave prices remained high and demand consistent when the war began. Virginians alone held 511,154 slaves valued at nearly $400 million, and the bondsmen were often worth more than the lands on which they labored. One-third of Virginia's white population of 1 million depended on slaves, primarily for agricultural labor. Farmers and planters earned some $10 million annually from the sale of surplus slaves to other states, especially Louisiana and Mississippi, while those who remained in Virginia produced some $8 million in tobacco and another $8 million in wheat and flour. Their labor in the cotton and corn fields, among other activities, added $2 million to the state's agricultural economy. The taxation of slaves also greatly swelled state coffers. In South Carolina the annual levy was $1.60 per head.[72]

In Louisiana the hot, humid climate made the raising of cane and the production of sugar hard, brutal work, and some contemporaries estimated the average life of a male adult field hand in cane country at seven years. As a result, New Orleans became a booming slave market, and slave owners in the Upper South, particularly Virginia and Missouri, customarily sold their surplus and recalcitrant slaves on that market. Demand kept prices high with prime male field hands bringing $1,800 to $3,000 on the New Orleans market. Given this investment, plantation owners often preferred to hire Irish workers to clear the land and dig drainage ditches and canals. This work could easily break one's health or cause death. One planter remarked that clearing land for sugarcane was "death on niggers and mules." If a slave died doing such work the financial loss would be considerable, but if an Irishman died he was only an Irishman who could be easily and cheaply replaced. One planter put it succinctly: "It was much better to have the Irish do it, who cost nothing to the planter, if they died, than to use up good field hands in such severe employment." During the grinding season when the juice was pressed from the cane, planters often hired white locals and paid "Cajun" farmers by the day to help with the processing into sugar and molasses.[73]

By late June, however, the sale of bondsmen ended on the Richmond market for the lack of buyers and slaves. When two males ages twenty-three and twenty-five brought only $795 and $815 respectively and a woman of undetermined age $320, buyers no doubt wanted to see what the war meant for them in terms of slave ownership, and they had reason to be apprehensive. Prime male and female field hands easily brought from $1,000 to $1,500, so this price decline proved significant. Moreover, in August, George W. Adair, editor of the *Southern Confederacy* in Atlanta, wrote that "this is a war to abolish slavery." Everyone knew that the war portended ominous possibilities for agriculture and its "peculiar" labor system, but southerners treated northern reports of increasing slave runaways as "grossly erroneous." Slave owners had invested considerable capital in their workforce, the loss of which they believed would be catastrophic. By late August, Virginia slave owners reported an increasing but undetermined number of men and women fleeing to Union lines. In the meantime, slave owners went about their business as usual or at least as much as possible, buying and hiring slaves with the intent of making money from their agricultural labor. In Mississippi, planters expected their female slaves to pick at least 55 pounds and most males 100 pounds of cotton per day depending on their master's need to secure the crop.[74]

Although slave owners often had a personal attachment to their slaves, those relationships did not equal an owner's monetary investment in his bondsmen and -women. In July a Tennessee slave owner lamented the loss of "Old Aunt Lucy." This "faithful servant" cared for the family, white and black, for forty years and "died much regretted." Perceptions, of course, differ in the eye of the beholder, none more so than when some men and women own others. Where white planters and farmers considered their black servants faithful members of the family, the coming of the Civil War fostered increased anxiety, concern, and even fear on the part of slave owners. In March, Robert H. Cantrell, a farmer in Madison County, Tennessee, observed that "negroes are becoming more and more difficult to manage." He considered whippings a necessary punishment for insubordination and to encourage fieldwork.[75]

BY AUTUMN AGRICULTURAL PRICES HAD inflated beyond the ability of the government to procure food and forage at reasonable rates, because Confederate currency had already lost considerable value. As agricultural prices increased for reasons of supply and demand as well as an inflation of the currency supply, farmers became reluctant to sell their provisions to the military. Consequently, the quartermaster general and the commissary general persuaded Secretary of War James A. Seddon to grant them impressment powers. Impressment officers had the authority to seize food and forage if farmers and planters refused to sell at government rather than free market prices. These agents, however, had to show written authority, provide receipts, and make payment on the spot. But if farmers refused to sell, the agents could take what they needed and provide a receipt for payment later. The impressment of food and forage seemed a fair way to acquire needed provisions, but farmers objected when government authorities paid less than market prices for impressed provisions and forage. In October, Confederate officials impressed 4,500 pounds of pork in Louisiana and paid $40 per barrel. Yet on the open market, farmers received $45 per barrel, and the price discrepancy caused considerable hard feelings.[76]

As impressment and agricultural and food prices increased due to inadequate production and distribution problems, consumers accused farmers of gouging them by hoarding their produce and restraining trade to gain still higher prices. The farmers and planters, in turn, argued that high food prices resulted from speculators who tried to corner the market on provisions, salt, and other commodities, and they reminded consumers that they had operational and transportation costs for production and sales. In Texas, Senator Louis T. Wigfall called farmers extortionists. For him high prices and cheap money made farmers "cheap" men and speculators at best. By late autumn the price increases attributed to hoarding and speculation encouraged the Alabama legislature to pass an Act to Suppress Monopolies, and Governor Andrew Barry Moore approved it. This legislation authorized the courts to impose a fine or imprisonment for anyone who attempted to corner the market in livestock or any other agricultural commodity with the intent to create a scarcity and drive up prices. Soon thereafter Florida, Mississippi, and Georgia passed similar legislation. In December the Mississippi legislature also attempted to prevent speculators and merchants from attempting to corner the market for livestock and "victuals." Anyone found guilty of "unreasonable" speculation could be fined $1,000 or sentenced to one year in the county jail or both. This legislation indicated increasing problems with agricultural production and supply. Yet these regulations proved difficult to enforce and farmers and speculators continued to exacerbate the problems of scarcity and high food prices. Within a year, this legislation had become dead letters.[77]

Yet, many southerners still contended that Louisiana planters produced more sugar than residents could consume while Texas farmers and planters raised more wheat, corn, cattle, and hogs than the public needed. Some rashly believed that southerners could burn all of their cotton and not suffer a financial loss. One Alabama planter, however, complained that the blockade had increased food prices. Bacon brought as much as 25 cents per pound. A month later, Union forces had surrounded Nashville and prevented farmers from reaching the city market. One Tennessee farmer wrote, "Everyday approaches nearer a state of DESPERATION. Surrounded, nothing is permitted to go in or out, everything is becoming scarce and enormously high." In November Governor Zeb Vance of North Carolina attempted to keep needed food supplies at home by prohibiting speculators from exporting bacon, pork, beef, cornmeal, flour, and potatoes, among other food goods. At the same time, the Confederate government had rented a large slaughterhouse near Clarksville, Tennessee, where hogs and cattle would be received during the packing season for processing into meat for the army. By so doing, the government would provide a local market for farmers and save on the purchase of meat by avoiding price-gouging slaughterhouses.[78]

Food shortages now occurred in some areas. In Georgia, the state legislature blamed speculators and passed legislation prohibiting them from charging more than a 60 percent price increase from the previous April for wheat, flour, bacon, lard, and salt. Even so, the editor of the *Natchez Weekly Courier* still believed that the river blockade hurt northern wheat farmers more than it did southerners, and they would not recover their loss of trade and profit for years after the war ended. An "unprecedented" Texas wheat crop gave additional proof of the Confederacy's agricultural power and its destined independence. Indeed, by early autumn the editor in Natchez believed the blockade was good for the Confederacy because its farmers had produced enough breadstuffs, cattle, and hogs, and their "new direction" away from cotton production would provide even greater surpluses of food and forage in the future. Some Mississippians believed that northern farmers in the Union army fought only to open the blockade so that wheat and other agricultural products from the Old Northwest could, once again, reach southern markets. In Jackson the editor of the *Weekly Mississippian* wrote, "Here we see the real motives governing our foes. They will lose their markets if we become an independent nation."[79]

Still, by November food shortages had developed in some urban areas. City and government officials responded by encouraging the opening of free markets where farmers would bring some of their surplus provisions to help feed the needy. Flour brought $12.75 per barrel in New Orleans, up $2.50 from October, and $14 per barrel in Mobile. In New Orleans the mayor fixed the price of bread based on the quality of the grain with a 12-ounce loaf baked from second quality No. 2 flour at 5 cents per loaf. Pork brought $45 per barrel retail, which cost $13.25 in April. Salt cost $12 per sack in Macon, Georgia, up from $1.25 in the spring. The chances for a large pork-packing season remained grim.[80]

The early optimism of farmers and planters had begun to fade. In South Carolina one farmer complained that "it is a truth indisputable that money can not be had, there is no goods or property that man can produce, that will bring cash, for the plain reason there is no money in the country, the whole base of our system is credit." A North Carolinian farmer agreed, confiding in his diary that he and his neighbors had experienced a "great want of money" and that his Confederate tax of $18.20 proved burdensome and annoying. A Virginia farmer concluded that land remained "better than any bank note or Confederate note. The Confederacy may fail, banks destroyed, our slaves may be liberated and property confiscated," he wrote, "but our lands will be the last thing wrested from us." His forethought proved prophetic. Another believed that farmers could make the most money by planting small grains. A month later wheat brought $1.60 per bushel in Georgia, a price highly beneficial to farmers but less than desirable for consumers wanting flour and bread.[81]

Still, some optimists remained confident and clung to the hope that the war would be won by January 1, 1862, the Confederacy would be recognized by the European powers, and the soldiers would be home for spring planting. If the war ended soon, farmers and planters would need cotton to sell. Any crop reduction would hurt their prospects. Farmers and planters seemed able to provide an adequate food supply, and the blockade did not seem to matter. The New Orleans *Crescent*, however, now reported that flour was advancing to "famine figures. Each succeeding day is attended with an advance of 25 cents per barrel," because the wheat crop had proved insufficient to provide the needed flour.[82]

By autumn the Confederacy continued to discourage cotton sales to prevent it from being shipped through the blockade for the benefit of textile manufacturers in Great Britain and France, which would make intervention less likely if they had access to cotton. Deprivation of cotton — that is, economic coercion — would encourage diplomatic recognition. Louisiana governor Thomas O. Moore ordered that no cotton be brought to New Orleans after October 10, and ruled that the government would seize all ships attempting to export cotton. As a result, along with a short crop due to heavy rains during the summer, the receipts in New Orleans from September 1 to December 19 totaled only 4,992 bales, a decline of 149,641 bales from that same period in 1860. Some southerners, however, such as Mary Chesnut, a privileged and acid-tongued observer of Confederate life, did not believe that the cotton embargo would bring Great Britain into the war on behalf of the South because "England had never been governed by a noise from below. The[y] will not care if five million manufacturers starve." She was correct.[83]

Even so, by November, the Mississippi legislature lamented the "studied neglect of mixed husbandry heretofore, and too much engrossment in the production of cotton," and it urged planters to reduce their cotton acreage for 1862 by 75 percent, to plant grain and forage crops, and to raise more livestock. The legislators also asked the planters to form associations to promote their acreage reduction and to "pledge their word of honor" not to exceed planting by one quarter of their previous cotton crop. On December 14, with a large cotton crop harvested and no market available, and with the possible shortage of food becoming apparent, Governor John J. Pettus urged the legislature to place such a high tax on cotton that planters would not seed a crop for 1862. Southern planters, however, were too independent-minded to accept such state control over their agricultural activities.[84]

In December one Tennessee farmer reflected on events, noting that "this year on the whole has been one of plenty. Crops throughout the country fine. Corn crop good, grain crop abundant." One South Carolina farmer worried not at all, because he had raised large crops of corn, potatoes, peas, turnips, and "provender." He had enough to feed his family and some surplus to sell until conditions returned to normal. Late in the year, Thomas J. Hudson, a Mississippi cotton planter, contended that the South, or at least Mississippi, had the "best soil, climate, season, and labor" and could meet all wartime adversities. With part of the 1860 cotton crop still unsold and with the 1861 crop piling up in barns and warehouses, he urged his fellow planters to divert 25 percent of their slave labor from the production of cotton, sugar, and tobacco for the cultivation of food crops. By so doing, he maintained, "we can be independent of the world for food." Southern agricultural power remained strong in the minds of many who believed that "by decreasing the quantity of cotton, tobacco and sugar but little, we can raise abundant supplies of food." But the reduction of cotton, sugar, and tobacco for replacement with food crops took more effort in Mississippi and across the South than a mere reallocation of 25 percent of the labor force from the production of staple crops.[85]

Late in the year a desperate Mississippi legislature attempted to deal with the lack of currency on the state level. It passed the Cotton Loan Act, which "created" a state currency. The act authorized the legislature to issue $5 million in Treasury notes in denominations from $1 to $100 that state banks would lend against cotton produced. The notes or currency would be loaned to farmers and planters in advance of their cotton crop to help them meet expenses until harvest. The loan rate could not exceed 5 cents per pound, and the act required farmers and planters to hold their cotton, with the penalty of imprisonment or payment of double indemnity on the amount of the loan if they still sold it before the government called for it. In the meantime they could use the notes for expenses and taxes. The bank would secure the loan with a lien on the crop. This cotton could be sold only upon the governor's approval. Although these notes also depreciated, they held their value better than did Confederate notes, and Mississippi farmers preferred them, at least for a while. In Mississippi the state banks also attempted to limit the amount of cotton sent to market by restricting credit and thereby encouraging a cotton shortage until international sales and high prices benefited the Confederacy. In addition, the state legislature authorized the banks to issue shares that farmers and planters could purchase with cotton based on the assigned value of $125 per bale. The bank directors would sell the cotton when the blockade ended, benefiting producers and bank alike.[86]

Still, many planters believed that the war would soon end or at least the blockade would be broken. If not, the British would intervene and her merchant ships would be loading cotton in southern ports by spring. When a rumor spread in late December that England would soon join the war against the United States to guarantee the supply of cotton for its textile industry, agricultural prices declined substantially with wheat buyers in Nashville demanding a 25-cent reduction in the price per bushel as farmers began marketing their surplus grain in anticipation of returning to cotton production. Some feared that their agricultural prosperity might soon end. Still, when the first calendar year of the war ended, agricultural prices in the West remained high. Cotton planters and farmers, however, suffered from over production, no market, and low prices, but grain and livestock producers enjoyed high prices. Southern planters and farmers had substantially increased their acreage of corn, wheat, and potatoes. In eight states (Alabama, Florida, Georgia, Louisiana, Mississippi, North Carolina, South Carolina, and Virginia), the acreage in these three crops had increased to 13.9 million acres from 10.6 million acres in 1860. Farmers and planters also had increased their production of wheat from 24 million to 45 million bushels, their corn from 196 million to 330 million bushels, and their potatoes from 36 million to 50 million bushels. Yet many soldiers and civilians went hungry because farmers and planters could not meet civilian and military demand for food now that the Mississippi River and the Atlantic and Gulf coasts were under a tightening blockade. Moreover, by late December the army's demand for pork exceeded supply, and transportation, distribution, and Federal seizures created a meat shortage for the Confederacy that worsened during the war.[87]

Confederate cotton policy had failed to bring the northern economy to a halt and to enlist Great Britain and France as fellow revolutionaries. Still, southerners remained confident that a policy of cotton denial would eventually help win the war because it was a powerful component of southern agriculture. Yet more discipline was required, and southern agricultural policy changed from buying to burning surplus cotton, particularly those stocks in danger of capture, and to reduce planting by 50 percent to 75 percent in 1862. In Georgia, the legislature limited the planting of cotton for the next year to three acres per hand, subject to a $500 fine for violations. In Hancock and Clark counties, some planters agreed to plant only one and a half acres per hand, but others such as former Secretary of State Robert Toombs scoffed at the idea that government — state or national — could restrict planters' agricultural freedom in any way. One observer believed that if the planters organized and refused to accept a price for cotton below a minimum or floor price, they could end speculation and the price would increase to 12½ cents per pound. Cooperative organization such as this would not come until the 1880s. In the meantime, speculators bought cotton at a low price with the intent to store it until the war ended, when they believed British and European buyers would pay high prices. At best Congress, state governments, and editors could only urge planters and farmers to make corn king instead of cotton.[88]

The Georgia legislature also attempted to provide some monetary relief by creating the Cotton Planters Bank of Georgia, which was to award loans on cotton if insured. Governor Joseph E. Brown recommended that bankers loan planters two-thirds the value of the cotton crop stored in warehouses. This policy would work only if the government released the cotton that it held under the produce loan agreement, which it did not do. In Mississippi some believed that the state legislature should prohibit the growing of another cotton crop to force farmers and planters to raise food crops. Still others argued that government, central or state, could not prevent farmers from planting cotton by law but that they had a "great *moral* obligation" to stop planting it for the good of the nation. No one could agree about a cotton policy that would benefit the Confederacy as well as farmers and planters.[89]

Indeed, by the end of the year, the 1861 cotton crop had no foreign market except that which passed through the blockade or across the Rio Grande to Mexico. Texas planters and farmers found some outlet for their fiber with Mexican cotton buyers who purchased about 40,000 bales at the low price of 9 cents per pound. Through the autumn, Texas planters in the San Antonio area sent their cotton by wagon to the coast where light-draft, blockade-runners negotiating the shallow bays and bayous loaded it for sale in Mexico or New York, where it brought 22 to 23 cents per pound.[90]

While President Davis praised farmers and planters for a year of abundant production, careful observers knew that planters had raised too much cotton while expecting a lifting of the blockade. By the end of the year cotton farmers and planters still hesitated to make a "radical" change in crop production. Yet, with the price of wheat increasing by more than 33 percent since September, some argued that farmers could make both a substantial profit and aid the war effort. If the war lasted another year, agricultural reformers believed, wheat prices would reach as high as $3 per bushel. If southern planters and farmers seeded wheat the North could never starve the South into submission.[91]

WHEN THE WAR BEGAN THE agricultural power of the Confederate states seemed obvious, even overwhelming. The seceding states produced all of the rice and sugar and most of the sweet potatoes, peas, and beans in the United States. They also grew more corn than the free states, as well as major wheat crops. The draft and food animals on the farms and plantations seemed adequate for daily needs. Cotton lands could be converted for human food and forage. Any cotton grown would meet the needs of southern manufactures for the production of clothing, and it could be traded for provisions and held as a lure for foreign intervention. The slave population would till the fields and produce the necessary food crops and livestock for the civilian and military populations. Given the South's intent to fight a defensive war, the region's agricultural power seemed invincible.

Yet by the end of the year, the military and civilian populations had taxed the productive ability of farmers and planters to their capacity, if not beyond. Moreover, much of the food crop production involved perishable vegetables that could not be easily and swiftly transported on an inadequate railroad system. Farmers did not produce wheat, corn, and fodder in sufficient quantities to support a long war. Most of the beef cattle grazed west of the Mississippi River in distant Texas. The loss of Missouri, Kentucky, and Maryland quickly reduced food and feed grains as well as meat, particularly from beef cattle and hogs – perhaps as much as one-third of the grains and livestock needed in the slave states. The loss of the border states to the Union before the war began meant that the Confederate armies could not be adequately supplied from the very beginning.

Soon the soldiers were eating a monotonous diet of beef, bacon, cornmeal, and flour; given the inadequacy of the railroads, much of the meat spoiled before it reached the troops. Food prices rose in the cities, particularly in the Upper South and especially Virginia, where Union armies threatened and Confederate armies camped. Hunger became a grim problem in some areas. In Warren County, Mississippi, a planter remarked that "an unmarked hog is in danger now days, in fact so is a marked one." Salted pork brought $45 per barrel in Natchez but little reached the market.[92]

At the same time, Union forces entered the fringes of the Confederacy and inflicted considerable damage to southern farms. In October a Union soldier reported that between Fairfax County, Virginia, and Washington, D.C., the country was "in a sorry condition, the fences all burned up, the houses deserted, the crops annihilated, and everything showing the footprint of war." Many southerners also had learned that Confederate soldiers showed little respect for their property: they took corn, livestock, and vegetables, and burned fence rails for fuel, particularly in northern Virginia, because the railroads and teamsters could not always meet the army's supply needs. One Georgian who had fought at Manassas told his wife, "Let me always if I must do it fight for Georgia outside her limits." The pillaging of farmers and planters on Confederate soil by its own men embarrassed many soldiers. In Florida the army had impressed or otherwise purchased hundreds of horses, which one observer considered counterproductive because the affected farmers had insufficient draft power to plow, cultivate, and harvest their crops. By the end of the year farmers and planters in the areas where the armies met and marched had learned they would pay a price that they had not reckoned on for independence.[93]

Few southerners had given much thought to these agricultural problems in the heady days when sentiment for war and independence was growing. They would have been well served had they listened to the editor of the *Southern Cultivator* who, in January, warned that the southern states did not have sufficient grain and livestock to feed its population without northern imports before the next crops could be harvested. Southerners had emphasized cotton rather than food and forage crops. As a result, he wrote, "never were a people suddenly over-taken by an emergency in a worse state of preparation . . . than the people of the South at this moment; and if it comes to the worst, who shall feel it fearfully." His words still rang true in December.[94]

The new year loomed ominously for southern farmers and planters.

CHAPTER TWO

Confederate Apprehension

By January 1862, southerners understood the importance of agriculture to winning the war as never before. Planters and farmers remained optimistic that the new year would bring continued high prices and the sufficient production of grain, hogs, and beef to supply civilian and military needs. The editor of the *Southern Cultivator* told his readers, "*Corn* makes bread and bacon and poultry and beef, and fat horses and mules. . . . It will feed our armies and help vanquish our foes." Few doubted the agricultural power of the South and the certainty that it would help win the war. Still, hunger and privation while not all pervasive had begun to nag at some southerners in the cities and towns across the region, which prompted the editor to remind his readers that "this war is to be fought out as much with the plow as with the sword."[1]

Despite their optimism when 1862 arrived farmers and planters carried over their arguments about the benefits and liabilities of the government cotton purchasing or loan program. Advocates believed that it would help alleviate the surplus and eventually put cash in the pockets of planters and farmers as well as help finance the war, if the government could sell it on a cash-and-carry basis to neutral nations. Opponents continued to view the program as a costly, bureaucratic, governmental interference in their lives that denied them freedom of action and opened the door to other agricultural regulations by the central government.[2]

In January, Secretary of the Treasury Christopher G. Memminger began receiving reports that some planters were selling cotton that they had consigned to the government under the Produce Loan acts of August 19 and December 19, 1861. Congress attempted to solve this problem by giving the Treasury Department authorization to pay farmers and planters for their cotton at the time of subscription with 8 percent bonds instead of payment in bonds when the government sold it. Still, the government paid less than farmers received on the open market,

[51]

in part, because government cotton upon sale often suffered from poor handling and storage, which damaged the fiber and reduced the price. At the same time, cotton producers wanted more money for their crop. Not until May 21 did produce loan agents receive detailed instructions about accepting subscriptions in-kind from farmers and planters. The agents now had orders to emphasize the subscription of cotton at market prices because government officials still believed the fiber could be sold to Great Britain and France and that those nations would necessarily break the blockade to get it. The new directive not only continued the payment policy in 8 percent bonds but also permitted planters to sell their subscribed cotton on their own and to pay the government for the amount promised.[3]

Cotton producers still complained that cotton prices paid by the government were too low and differed from state to state. James Dunwoody Brownson DeBow, chief commissioner of the Produce Loan Office, responded that the prices offered on the public market were "determined by the relative safety of the article from the torch of the enemy." When some cotton producers refused to subscribe unless the government paid in negotiable Treasury notes rather than nonnegotiable bonds, Secretary Memminger had no alternative but to instruct his agents to make their purchases with bonds as far as practicable. Whenever farmers refused to accept bonds, they were authorized to make payment with cash, provided it did not exceed more than one-half of the total cost. The cotton producers accepted this compromise and subscribed a considerable amount of cotton that they had stored on their plantations. They would continue to sell their cotton to the government as long as the government could pay with sound money.[4]

Planters and farmers also struggled over their decision to plant cotton. Part of their ambivalence about whether to plant cotton revolved around the institution of slavery. In Atlanta the editor of the *Southern Confederacy* put the matter succinctly, noting that the "real question at issue" involving the war was slavery. Some Georgia cotton planters believed that cotton production was essential because they needed a high-value crop to earn a livelihood. They knew that abandonment of cotton posed a major risk if the war did not end quickly. Cotton paid debts, particularly those owed to cotton factors who marketed their crop, established lines of credit for them, and furnished a host of necessities and luxuries from distant cities that they could not purchase locally. They also needed cotton to keep their slaves busy all year. Grain crops required only four months of labor from seed time to harvest in the Lower South after which their slaves would be unemployed if they did not raise cotton. "Can the farmer afford to keep his negroes, horses and other capital idle and 'eating their heads off' for the balance of the season?" one asked. A total prohibition of cotton planting would not yield a "good effect," but instead be "productive of evil." Sensible agriculture during this difficult time, it seemed, mandated planting food crops large enough to produce a surplus; it also seemed to require the seeding of as much cotton as planters' slaves could cultivate, which meant at least a "moderate" cotton crop.[5]

However, everyone — planters, farmers, and city people — agreed that a large corn crop had to be raised as a matter of "great military and political necessity." One contemporary correctly observed, "We are cut off from the provision markets of the Northwest, upon which we have been in the habit of relying, no other resource is now left to us but self-dependence — the industry, patriotism and good sense of our own agriculturalists." He believed that independence depended more on southern farmers than Confederate soldiers. Still, corn, wheat, and other cereal crops sold at "famine prices," and the "fabulous prices" charged for beef and pork caused increasing concern. One southerner thought the high cost of bread and meat was nothing less than "scandalous." As a result, poor families had begun to suffer "distress and destitution," a situation made worse by the fact that so many husbands, sons, and brothers were serving in the army and could not increase the agricultural production of their farms. Yet, if agricultural production increased, some hoped the food needs of the South could be met and prices might begin to fall. While many planters and farmers supported increased production for patriotic reasons, they enjoyed their income from high farm prices, and they hoped that their prosperity would continue.[6]

The Edgefield, Georgia, *Advertiser* urged farmers to remember that "*we are not only a blockaded but a block-headed people*," given their reluctance in 1861 to plow up their cotton crop and reseed their lands in corn and wheat. The editor told his readers, "If the planters of the South are wise, they will act upon the presumption (unless some event shall show the contrary before planting-time) that the blockade will not be raised this year, or even the next. It is prudence, at any rate, to prepare for the worst." Farmers should plant their acres in corn and wheat and seed only the amount of cotton that would not interfere with their other farming operations. Still, some planters were reluctant to reduce their cotton crop or to plant none at all, contending that cotton was their only cash crop. But they failed to take into account that cotton brought only the current price of 5 or 6 cents per pound and would not pay many debts.[7]

Some, in true farmer fashion, saw ways to hedge their bets: if they planted cotton, they could profit from the mistakes of other planters who abided by government wishes and reduced their cotton crop. Many supporters of cotton reduction proposals, however, urged planters to forgo a cotton crop to restore their land and to keep the supply limited so the price would increase with demand when the war ended. In Georgia, many planters pledged not to plant a full cotton crop, and they recommended seeding only enough cotton to preserve the seed and to produce fiber sufficient for family clothing. They also promised to plant more grain and report all distillers to the government.[8]

Most farmers and planters cooperated for the good of the nation and substantially reduced their cotton production, because little grain and a long war meant defeat. One planter's daughter noted that they decided to reduce their cotton crop from 300 acres to 40 acres at planting time in March. Another planter near Ebenezville, South Carolina, reported that "very little" cotton had been planted in his neighborhood. In July he welcomed instead the wheat crop, which he thought should give farmers reason to ask the "exorbitant" price of $3 per bushel, but which to his surprise rose to $5 per bushel in November. One traveler heading from Corinth, Mississippi, to Mobile, Alabama, reported that planters had substantially reduced their cotton crop and that while she saw cornfields everywhere, she observed few acres of cotton. Indeed, the efforts to reduce the cotton crop proved successful, because it fell dramatically from 4.5 million bales in 1861 to 1.5 million bales in 1862. As a result, cotton prices increased from 13 cents per pound to 31 cents per pound on the New York City market, which made many planters wistful. But many farmers considered those who did not reduce cotton production as "unwise," "disloyal," "traitorous," and "insane."[9]

General Robert Toombs was one of those outcasts. He had planted a large cotton crop on his plantation in southwestern Georgia along the Chattahoochee River. Others followed his example, even though most Georgia planters had substantially reduced their spring plantings or seeded no cotton at all. As a result, the committees of public safety in Cuthbert and Eufaula charged that Toombs was influenced "more by avarice than patriotism," and asked him to remove his slaves from the cotton fields and dispatch them to the committee for defense work along the river. Toombs, who was not known for humility, shot back that "my property, as long as I live, shall never be subject to the orders of those cowardly miscreants, the Committee of Public Safety of Randolph County and Eufaula. You may rob me in my absence, but you cannot intimidate me." Toombs believed a planter could do as he pleased no matter the political or military situation. "Producers have nothing to do with morality," he wrote. Farmers have always been an independent people, even in wartime, and they usually make decisions based on their pocketbook. However, with wheat at $2.50 per bushel on some markets in June, up from $1.50 in March, many southerners thought that planters like Toombs could make good money by changing farming practices without compulsion, all for the Confederacy's benefit, but for some planters agricultural traditions proved too difficult to change.[10]

From across the South calls also came for planters and farmers to burn their cotton and tobacco to prevent its seizure by northern armies. Otherwise, the cotton and tobacco would be sold on the international market to the detriment of the South. This fear became widespread. In late February cotton factors in Augusta made arrangements to move 100,000 bales into the interior because they believed the city might soon be attacked. At a meeting of planters in Richmond, one attendee remarked, "We have been taught to believe that England and France was dependent on this staple [cotton], and that they would come and get it. Why do they not come?" Some now thought that the only solution for the cotton problem was for the Confederate government to purchase the entire crop and burn it. Either way, they argued, the planters and farmers would lose their crops. If northern soldiers seized their cotton, it would be used against the South diplomatically and economically, but if the Confederacy won the war the government would surely pay cotton producers for their losses. Better, then, to burn it and take their chances with victory than gamble and lose it to seizure by northern troops as contraband. Only spring planting season would tell what individual cotton planters and farmers had decided.[11]

On April 4, Congress passed a joint resolution urging farmers and planters to seed food crops rather than cotton and tobacco to prepare for "every emergency." A month later Congress responded to the plea for a cotton-burning policy by passing an ordinance authorizing the destruction of cotton, tobacco, and other property in the case of a military emergency; that is, if the crop was about to fall into the hands of the enemy. Congress did not provide for compensation, but optimists did not believe that more than 5 percent of the cotton crop was in danger of seizure. If farmers felt threatened, some contended, they should move their cotton and tobacco to storage facilities beyond the reach of northern soldiers, but many could not do so. In Pitt County, North Carolina, one planter destroyed 800 bales, which he valued at $32,000 or 10 cents per pound. Planters in other endangered counties also pledged to burn their cotton bales, and the army helped when planters needed assistance. By early April Confederate soldiers and planters had burned nearly all the cotton along the water courses in Washington, Pitt, and Martin counties. In late May, an Alabama planter reported "great destruction in burning cotton and other property to keep out of the enemys [sic] hands, never was their so much self-sacrifice before." Little did he know that even greater sacrifices by farmers and planters would be required and endured in the days ahead.[12]

Planters also did not realize that the burning of cotton in the spring of 1862 foreshadowed political and economic divisions among themselves. Cotton-burning would continue during the next two years. Some planters burned for patriotic reasons: they saw themselves as helping the cause by creating a shortage that would bring Great Britain into the war. Some planters burned cotton to keep it from Union forces. Others burned their cotton only under compulsion by Confederate forces. The reluctance to burn might be an economic decision to hold off destroying a valuable crop as long as possible, but some Confederates questioned the patriotism of those who did not voluntarily and enthusiastically burn their cotton. Division and animosity over orders and expectations for the planters to burn would intensify as the war lengthened.

In the spring other signs occurred that difficult days lay ahead. In early March the Confederate ironclad *Virginia* engaged five Union frigates at Hampton Roads off Norfolk, Virginia, where she made a shambles of the fleet. The next day, however, the Union ironclad *Monitor* joined the fray and drove the *Virginia* back to port. Scott's Anaconda Plan squeezed a bit tighter. A month later General McClellan's troops began debarking at Fort Monroe for his campaign up the peninsula between the York and James rivers with the intent to capture Richmond. On May 31, however, Confederate forces checked his advance. When Robert E. Lee replaced Joseph E. Johnston as commander of Confederate forces, McClellan had met his match, and Federal troops began retreating in late June. McClellan's Peninsula Campaign had failed despite Confederate blunders, and Richmond remained secure. Union forces remained inadequate for the task before them. Even so, Union and Confederate soldiers disrupted agriculture in the region, prevented farmers from marketing their produce, and contributed to the escalation of food prices in the capital city.[13]

ALTHOUGH PLANTERS AND FARMERS PLANNED to reduce their cotton crop substantially, perhaps due as much to the low price as to patriotism, Georgia governor Joseph E. Brown and other leaders did not trust them as the next planting season approached. He had good reason, because many farmers and planters still cultivated small cotton crops for sale to local manufacturers. In January one Alabama planter picked 17,511 pounds of the 1861 crop and sold it to a local factory for 10 to 12 cents per pound, and he planned to continue that practice. In the absence of a Confederate mandate, enforced by agents of the central government, the states necessarily had to act alone to achieve Richmond's desires for a smaller cotton crop. In November Governor Brown attempted to stop cotton production by urging the legislature to impose a heavy tax on all cotton produced beyond that necessary for domestic consumption. A substantial tax would make cotton production unprofitable for those who hoped the war would soon end so that they could sell their surplus fiber on the world market at high prices.[14]

Brown's recommendation came to naught, but late in the year the Georgia legislature prohibited planters from raising more than three acres of cotton per hand for workers between the ages of fifteen and fifty-five and three acres for each two hands under fifteen and over fifty-five years of age; violators would face a $500 fine. This legislation seemed necessary to increase food production, even though cotton planters and farmers had reduced the 1862 crop to only 60,000 bales while increasing corn production to 60 million bushels. In South Carolina the legislature also limited planting to three acres for short-staple cotton for prime field hands (those between the ages of fifteen and forty-five) and half that acreage for slaves between twelve and fifteen years old. Alabama taxed planters 10 cents per pound for all cotton produced above 2,500 pounds per hand. But Congress, fearing infringement on states' rights, never attempted to limit cotton production by law. All limitations resulted from state regulations or vigilante action, such as when forty women reportedly hoed out all the cotton plants they could find in Calhoun County, Georgia.[15]

By April, reports from Georgia, Louisiana, and Texas indicated that planters and farmers would not plant cotton except to produce fresh seed in hope that they could return to maximum production in 1863. If southern farmers and planters grew as much corn and produced as much meat as possible, the South would be safe, some argued. "If we make enough to eat and feed an army we will triumph," reported the editor of the *Southern Confederacy*. "If we don't," he warned, "we are whipped." The *Montgomery*

Advertiser held that if planters seeded cotton, southerners would be "conquered by starvation." Moreover, planters and farmers who emphasized food crops would find ready sales at high prices. The power of agriculture in wartime remained apparent to an increasing number of southerners, if they maintained discipline in their farming practices.[16]

Tobacco farmers fared better. Although the blockade ruined the international market, the price remained high with inferior lugs bringing $5.00 to $6.50 and good tobacco selling for $7.00 to $8.00 per lug in early February, up several dollars in each category since December. Some observers attributed this high price to speculators who purchased tobacco as an investment that would yield great profits once the Atlantic trade resumed. If planters could hold their crops, they would profit later. Some observers believed that tobacco investments were the safest after real estate because the price continued to increase. Even so, many tobacco planters voluntarily reduced their planting at the government's urging. In mid-June one Virginia planter reported to the secretary of war: "We planted full crops of corn for all our hands[,] our determination being to raise grain and meat. We have planted all our best lands in corn (no tobacco is planted with us)." In the fall when planters normally prepared for the harvest, an observer reported that "tobacco raising in Virginia during 1862 was affected by the same circumstances: like cotton, the crop hardly existed." He believed that not more than a fifteenth of the average crop had been planted and that "during the autumn when I went through the region formerly planted to tobacco, I looked in vain for those immense fields of green which one used to see everywhere: the long, yellow corn stalks had crowded out the broad green tobacco leaves."[17]

Governors, politicians, and editors also urged farmers and distillers to stop making corn whiskey as long as the war lasted. In March, Virginia became the first state to ban the distillation of whiskey from grain, although it relaxed the prohibition on October 1 to permit distillers to make it for medicinal purposes. Alabama also authorized the seizure of stills. North Carolina banned the distillation of whiskey from fruit, but the Confederate government had several large contracts with North Carolina farmers to produce corn whiskey for military medicinal purposes. On February 28 Georgia's Governor Brown by proclamation, effective March 15, prohibited distillers from operating and railroads from transporting whiskey. Several months later the Georgia legislature banned the distilling of whiskey, but in late November Brown approved a statute that permitted distillation for medicinal purposes. Distillers had to acquire a license, and the state would not permit the production of more than 1 million gallons annually. No distiller could operate closer than twenty miles to a railroad to ensure the shipment of grain, particularly corn, to millers, the army, and public markets. South Carolina also prohibited the distillation of whiskey from grain, with violators subject to a $10,000 fine and a year in jail, unless producers were acting under contract to the Confederacy to produce it for medicine.[18]

Farmers honored the laws prohibiting the distilling of whiskey more by the breach than by observance, because the price escalated and brought considerable income to those who made it. Equally important, Confederate policy that restricted the distillation of whiskey to increase the amount of corn and wheat available to feed people and livestock ran counter to economic and geographical reality, particularly in mountainous regions where the transport of corn in bulky grain sacks strapped over a mule or hauled by wagon to market proved difficult. Farmers could take more corn to distant markets in a jug or barrel than in a sack or wagon and receive a higher price for their product. In Virginia, farmers with their own still could make whiskey and sell it for $5 per gallon. In October one Georgia soldier advised his wife in a letter to "make all the corn (whiskey) you can."[19]

In addition to corn for meal and wheat for flour the army needed great quantities of meat, particularly pork, which could be easily preserved with salt, provided farmers raised the hogs and packers had enough salt to process them. By January 1862, the government contracted with several pork packing firms in Virginia to ensure a ready supply of meat for the armies. The government advanced the money needed to operate the packing houses so that bonded agents could purchase hogs from area farmers. These purchasing agents had instructions to pay from 6 to 8 cents per pound for hogs but offer more if "absolutely necessary," and prices soon ranged as high as 11½ cents per pound for live hogs. These agents received compensation of $500 per month. The packers also used agents to purchase beef at 3¼ to 4¼ cents per pound, that is, $3.25 to $4.00 per hundredweight. In addition, commanders in the field sent their own agents to purchase cattle so their men could have fresh beef, because it did not preserve adequately by salting or pickling. Usually army agents, often soldiers, paid with promissory notes – much to a farmer's chagrin. When Confederate commissary officers or soldiers impressed agricultural produce, they paid with paper money or offered a receipt; that is, a promise to pay in Confederate money at a later date. The government also authorized its agents to purchase flour at the rate of $1 per bushel for the wheat required to mill it. Farmers considered this price too low because flour brought high prices in the marketplace, and they complained vociferously about this purchasing policy.[20]

While southern farmers and planters contemplated planting cotton or corn, they also confronted an implement shortage because they had depended on northern manufacturers for their hand tools and equipment, which dealers sold across the region. Local foundries made limited quantities of basic implements and marketed them through hardware stores. In addition, blacksmiths crafted wrought-iron moldboards from cast iron, but many farmers preferred the standardized implements from northern manufacturers. Still, some small-scale implement manufacturers continued to operate. In Augusta, John and Thomas A. Bones made a variety of farm equipment from imported Swedish and British iron still in stock. Other firms specialized in plow making. The war, however, soon brought local, small-scale agricultural implement manufacturing to a halt. In January the American Hoe Company in Winsted, Georgia, announced that it would emphasize the production of sabers and bayonets at the expense of agricultural tools until the war ended.[21]

Thus, while farmers and planters received encouragement to plant more corn, forage, and other crops, their technology could not meet this challenge. Southerners had depended on northern implement manufacturers and often purchased plows and cultivators that could be cheaply and easily replaced if broken or abused by their field hands. With northern supplies cut off and with southern foundries and forges working at full capacity to produce military equipment, farmers and planters entered the second year of the war already needing new plows, scythes, corn shellers, and other implements. They quickly learned that they had to make do or to do without, a situation that would continue for the duration of the war. By the summer of 1862, broken and irreparable threshing machines sat idle as men beat the grain from the heads with flails and winnowed it with baskets and the wind, or with their fanning mills that remained operational. Still, the demand for manufactured implements, particularly plows, had been kept relatively low because some planters preferred to keep their hands busy hoeing weeds. Relying on human hands took longer than using shovel plows and other implements.[22]

INFLATION BECAME A SERIOUS PROBLEM as Confederate currency continued to deflate in value. By 1862, Confederate currency had become nearly worthless. In January, bankers discounted Confederate money by 20 percent when exchanged for gold. In March they discounted it by 95 percent in some areas. By April the value of a Confederate dollar had dropped 75 percent compared to the value of a gold dollar across the Eastern Confederacy, and by September 1 it exchanged at the rate of $2.50 for $1 in gold. As Confederate currency plunged in value, farmers withheld their produce and refused to sell it unless payment was made with specie rather than Confederate paper money. But little hard money circulated, and farmers often resorted to bartering for needed goods, such as shoes, clothing, equipment, and household items.[23]

By late July, many farmers had serious reservations about taking Confederate money for their crops and livestock. One Virginian complained that even in Richmond, some merchants had refused to take a $5 Confederate bill for any purchase when Union forces had been near the city a few weeks earlier. "With them," he wrote, "the success or defeat of the Confederate army either attracts or repels its currency, which fact shows that they are governed by a mercenary spirit, and have neither part nor lot in its ultimate independence." Farmers and produce merchants wanted good money, and they distrusted Confederate currency, particularly if Federal troops threatened to occupy their neighborhood.[24]

In Atlanta, the weakness of Confederate money kept agricultural prices high, with beef, pork, and mutton selling at 25 cents per pound, bacon at 50 cents per pound, and cabbage at $1 per head. Tomatoes and cucumbers brought 75 cents a dozen, chickens $1 a piece, eggs 85 cents per dozen, butter as much as $1 per pound, and wheat $3.50 per bushel by August. One observer called these prices "unaccountably high." Part of the problem, of course, was supply and demand. When McClellan's Army of the Potomac threatened Richmond during his Peninsula Campaign, considerable quantities of agricultural produce were needed to feed the defending Confederate troops and the civilian population. When the Union army retreated, an inflated currency supply kept prices high for consumers, but not always for farmers.[25]

McClellan's Peninsula Campaign, which was designed to lay siege to Richmond, had kept the farmers in Albemarle, Madison, Green, and neighboring counties from transporting their produce and driving their cattle to the Richmond market. With the failure of the Union campaign and the retreat of Federal soldiers, Virginia farmers hurried their cattle to city butchers, and a glut occurred with wholesale prices declining sharply. Butchers now paid only 5 to 9 cents per pound for beef cattle, but they continued to charge from 40 to 50 cents per pound, a practice that made them in the eyes of residents no better than "hucksters and other extortionists" who "in these times of public calamity and private distress [were], wringing money from the necessities of the people." While southerners argued about the currency problem, farmers watched, waited, and took their chances if sound Federal greenbacks could be acquired from the sale of provisions through the lines or to Federal troops who captured or passed through their neighborhoods.[26]

On May 20, the U.S. Congress attempted to prevent that trade by prohibiting Union army and navy officers from buying and selling cotton, but no law could prevent it given the profitability of trading with the enemy for the fiber. Secretary of the Treasury Salmon P. Chase remarked that among army officers as well as civilians, "the appetite for trade is eager and exacting." Although Chase could appoint special agents to buy and sell cotton on behalf of the Federal government, the profits ensured abuse of the system for personal gain. Chase continued to believe that the best policy was to let trade follow the flag. Usually, however, it went ahead of it if Confederate farmers and planters could access northern buyers who offered greenbacks for commodities, usually cotton. As a result, the internal cotton trade thrived to the benefit of northern speculators and southern farmers and planters on the periphery of the Confederacy.[27]

AGRICULTURAL PRICES INCREASED NOT ONLY because of scarcity and inflation but also because working people in the cities had wartime wages that provided considerable disposable income, at least for the moment. In February a South Carolina planter near Aiken noted that corn brought $1.10 per bushel and wheat $1.20 per bushel. Bacon earned 25 to 30 cents per pound, which along with the other agricultural prices had crept upward. In Charleston butter brought 50 to 60 cents per pound but he noted that "up here [the Aiken vicinity] it cannot be obtained at all. We are now doing without it." In mid-March a Richmond resident complained that beef and mutton cost 20 cents per pound and turkeys $3 each. He noted that the farmers near Hanover had the "conscience" to ask $3 per bushel for sweet potatoes. Only turnips seemed cheap. He believed the high food prices, which escalated from farmers to wholesalers to retailers, could only be attributed to the "extravagances" of the working class, which now made $100 doing what previously had earned $10. With money in their pockets from wartime industrial and related employment, consumers paid high prices for food. This resident suggested that "if in these flush times, poor people would practice some self denial, stint their bellys a little, and lay up their earnings, they would quickly find that 'produce' would shrink back to its old price." Farmers who enjoyed high prices were not sympathetic. Others suggested that if Congress compelled planters and farmers to seed corn instead of cotton — that is, regulate agriculture by law — then it should also fix the price of labor and merchandise. Farmers alone, they believed, should not be compelled to sacrifice for patriotic reasons.[28]

At the same time, recent military reverses in Kentucky and Tennessee caused "great excitement" on the agricultural markets. During March, bacon and bread rose to 33 cents per pound, and pork to 20 cents per pound in Atlanta. If the Confederate losses were not reversed, observers believed, bacon, lard, and grain would soon advance to "enormous prices" for consumers, to the benefit of farmers who had commodities to sell. Others considered Kentucky and Tennessee "dead letters" concerning the supply of wheat and meat. With corn and sweet potatoes as high as $1.15 per bushel, Irish potatoes at $3 per bushel, and bacon at "just whatever the conscience of a speculator will allow him to ask for it," the danger of hunger and starvation seemed more than a possibility. In Atlanta rice rose to 5 cents per pound as speculators made rapid purchases fearing that Union troops would soon overrun the coastal plantations. Southerners now became acutely aware that their reliance on northern foodstuffs had ended, and they worried about adequate food supplies. With agricultural commodities from the Old Northwest, Missouri, and parts of Tennessee (the granary of the South) cut off, and with the ports of North Carolina under Union control and Maryland held by Federal soldiers, food shortages, even starvation, might soon plague the region. One South Carolina planter succinctly stated the problem when he wrote that "without a large grain crop (if the war continues through the summer) we cannot feed our army, and certain defeat with all its attendant sacrifices follows famine."[29]

The loss of farmland for production in the West caused agricultural wholesale prices to rise as well. In Atlanta, by early April, wheat reached $2 per bushel, up a dollar per bushel since March, while corn brought as much as $1.30 per bushel, pork 22 cents per pound, bacon 36 cents per pound, butter 40 cents per pound, rice 6 cents per pound, and sugar as much as 18 cents per pound. Beef commanded 8 cents per pound, molasses 92 cents per gallon, and flour as much as $6.75 per barrel. Prices for these agricultural provisions had trended upward since January. In Mobile and New Orleans food prices had been fixed by martial law, largely due to the heavy use of the Memphis & Charleston Railroad by the army. When the troop movements were completed observers believed that the flow of food products from the Southwest would improve and grocery prices would decline. Until that happened food prices would remain high.[30]

By mid-April much of the country north of the James River in Virginia had been abandoned after the withdrawals of the Confederate army and the movement of slaves farther south. Other bondsmen had already fled to enemy lines. As a result, many farmers did not have sufficient labor to plant and harvest a crop with slave labor, and their sons had gone into the army. A similar situation occurred in the Virginia Tidewater and the Shenandoah Valley, all of which meant a diminished wheat crop for 1862. With a high troop concentration near Richmond and the railroads unable to supply wheat to the flour millers in the city because of army needs for that transportation, speculators began purchasing flour to corner the market. In response residents anticipated the invocation of martial law to ensure adequate food supplies from farmers at fair prices, because, in the words of one resident, "enormous evils require extraordinary remedies." But some argued that the best way for farmers to foil speculators was to produce bountiful crops; the surplus would then lead to lower prices for city people. Most farmers preferred maximum prices.[31]

Southern farmers had great difficulty resisting the high prices that speculators offered for their commodities. Individual farmers could not keep food prices from rising by refusing to sell to speculators, and they understandably wanted to secure their share of wartime prices and markets. Farmers charged that they, too, paid high wartime costs for salt, "negro shoes," and clothing, usually at double peacetime prices. One Georgia farmer argued that if agricultural prices were proportional to products that a farmer needed for daily living, corn would bring $3.00 per bushel, wheat $4.50 per bushel, and bacon 40 cents per pound. He believed that farmers had done more to support the war effort than anyone else. He also contended that cotton factors – who purchased the fiber and thereby encouraged cotton production, and who ran the blockade to gain "enormous profits" in Britain and France – should be hanged because they aided the northern war effort.[32]

By late April farmers brought less food into Richmond than earlier, and desperate shoppers sometimes endangered their sales. When a farmer brought two barrels of eggs to market, several female shoppers rushed his cart, pushing and shoving for a position to buy his eggs and nearly overturning the cart and making the sales impossible. In response he withdrew and sold his eggs to a military hospital to prevent a "serious riot" by the shoppers. Another farmer brought a load of chickens to the Richmond market but, upon learning that a military order fixed prices at 25 cents per chicken, retuned home saying that he would not sell until the price of sugar had been reduced. In the James River area, farmers sold bacon for 25 cents per pound, a price that they considered fair.[33]

The problem of high food and agricultural prices often resulted more from inadequate transportation than from lack of farm production. As a result, one Richmond resident contended, "There is great danger of famine in the South; of a sugar and molasses famine in the Atlantic States, of a salt and flour famine in the Gulf States." He also believed that "there is a great danger of salt and meat famine in eastern Virginia, even though the western portion of the State would be glad to exchange their superabundance of these articles for flour, coffee, nails, and a thousand minor articles, for many of which they are pinched." Farmers maintained that they should not be blamed for high food prices because they were productive. Rather, the government and the army, which controlled the railroads, created food hardships for the public. Consequently, "the quantity of eatables in the markets have grown suddenly small and most terribly less," reported another resident, who believed that "starvation stares us in the face." In Richmond in late April beef now sold at 50 cents per pound, and it was "tough at that," and farmers had been driven from the markets by government and military regulations. "If something is not done quickly," a resident wrote, "we shall all be at the tender mercy of the butchers." The food supply problems, however, were not as serious in other parts of the South. In Athens, Georgia, the merchants had abundantly stocked their shelves, but they charged high prices – bacon from 40 to 60 cents per pound, corn $1.25 per bushel, flour $12.00 to $15.00 per barrel. A year earlier bacon brought 10 to 12 cents per pound, corn 88 cents per bushel, and flour $6.25 to $8.25 per hundred pounds.[34]

By May agricultural prices had escalated in Richmond. Eggs brought 75 cents per dozen, butter $1.50 per pound, and beef as much as 50 cents per pound, while bacon sold for 35 cents per pound – prices that had increased during the past few months. Although these prices were wholesale, farmers profited from the increase. High agricultural prices, of course, indicated scarcity as much as farmers' profits. High agricultural prices existed across the South, but observers considered them "excessively high" only in a few areas, such as Richmond. Optimists still believed that farmers provided sufficient meat and wheat for flour and bread to meet the needs of the entire population. If the army stopped monopolizing the railroads, shortages would disappear and agricultural and food prices would decline. But, as one Virginian wrote, "If our people, for want of access to our abundant supplies of food, be starved, or if our army fail to be supplied with provisions, then will begin our real danger." Agricultural production was not the problem, he believed. Rather, an inadequate railroad system endangered the nation. Yet railroads alone were not responsible for all food shortages. Drought and crop disease, particularly rust in wheat, caused crop failure. By late May, a North Carolinian reported a "good deal" of rust in the wheat fields near Ashville; she hoped for the best on her farm. As a result of these problems one Alabama planter complained that "provisions are alarmingly high and becoming [sic] very scarce."[35]

The problems of high food prices and agricultural productivity, however, often depended on perspective. In May a South Carolina planter wrote, "These are terrible times." He had 1,200 cattle, hogs, horses, and mules to feed along with more than 300 slaves. Although he could sell bacon for 40 cents per pound and beef and mutton for 30 cents per pound, he had little to market because his slaves consumed most of the provisions that they raised. He also had to pay 25 cents per pound for sugar, up as much as 15 cents a pound since March, and $40 per sack of salt. In addition, he had sent the government a check for $12,500 for the sale of 10,000 bushels of corn for a produce loan, and he owed 200 bales of cotton. "These are indeed *hard times* & especially so on me," he wrote. Despite his complaints about prices, the planter sold his cotton to the government for $32,778.25 in November. Georgia farmers also welcomed wheat prices of $2 per bushel, which increased to $6 per bushel by late September, and they sold their beef cattle for $10 per hundredweight and their bacon for 25 cents per pound — but they lamented that these high prices were paid with Confederate currency.[36]

By the summer of 1862, the Confederacy confronted substantial agricultural and food distribution problems as prices escalated due either to limited production or inadequate transportation. In early June a Richmond resident complained about the cost of strawberries, eggs, and spring chickens that sold "at such exorbitant prices as to put them entirely beyond the reach of the mass of the people." Strawberries and "half-ripe cherries" brought 50 cents a quart, eggs a dollar per dozen, and "chickens the size of a partridge [were] considered sacrificed if sold for less than a dollar and a quarter." Cabbage brought a dollar per head and black berries as much as 75 cents per quart. In Atlanta heavy demand and limited supply drove the price of flour to $22 per barrel, up more than $10 since January, wheat rose to $3.50 per bushel, up nearly $2 per bushel in six months and corn held steady at $1.60 to $1.75 per bushel. Away from the cities, farm prices declined substantially because costs for transportation and middlemen did not add to the expenses for consumers. Even so, prices remained comparatively high. In the North Carolina Piedmont, farmers received $2.50 per bushel for wheat, $1.50 per bushel for corn, $1 per bushel for oats, and 30 cents per pound for bacon. Farmers could make money from these high prices, if they reached city markets.[37]

In Richmond, the "poorer classes" now began to suffer from insufficient food, and by mid-June food shortages had begun to worry many residents. Northern troops had cut the railroad to the east and north, and the Confederate government monopolized the lines south and west. Farmers and middlemen could not get agricultural produce to Richmond, and they needed the Richmond market to make money as much as its residents needed them for food. Increasingly, residents held the Confederate government responsible for food shortages. If it was going to clog the railroads by bringing troops and supplies into the city for its defenses, they wondered why the government could not transport adequate provisions for the civilian population. The solution seemed simple – add more freight cars to the troop trains. Davis responded that only the Danville railroad reached the city and that no extra cars existed, but he asked the Richmond City Council to study the problem – a suggestion that comforted no one.[38]

The failure of General George McClellan's Peninsula Campaign, however, eased agricultural supply problems as the Confederate army regained control of the area and permitted more commodities to enter the city via train. In early July chickens that had sold for $1.25 each now brought 60 cents apiece. Farmers sent more vegetables to market, and the prices declined to "reasonable" levels for Richmond residents. Prices for farm products, however, quickly increased again due to supply and demand. Fresh beef soon brought from 62 to 75 cents per pound, salt pork and ham $1 per pound, butter $1.50 to $2 per pound, eggs $1.25 to $1.50 per dozen, potatoes $16 per bushel, onions 25 cents each, and milk 25 cents per quart. Fresh pork and cheese were not available.[39]

The wheat harvest proved "miserable" in Virginia, and consumers worried about the availability and price of bread in the days ahead. In Richmond, vegetables were "plenty but dear." One resident, however, believed that market prices in this "age of extortion" were reasonable even though a vendor sold watermelons for $3 each and charged customers 10 cents to inspect them, which some called extortion. The food situation became worse whenever the army mess corps swept through markets before citizens had the opportunity to purchase the farmers' produce, and the public became increasingly critical of the army. As wholesale food prices rose in Richmond, the *New England Farmer* remarked that the "rebellion is expensive and terribly inconvenient."[40]

Planters and farmers did not oppose high prices, so long as they—and not just wholesalers—were reaping the benefit. On the Atlanta market, wheat brought $3.50 per bushel in July. In South Carolina the wheat harvest had been good, and farmers asked from $3.50 to $6 per bushel for Galo wheat, which caused one Columbia resident to remark that "very little flour will be ate at these figures by a large class of our citizens, especially soldiers' wives and children who have to depend upon buying their necessities." In Columbus, Georgia, a resident complained that "it would seem as if the poulterers charged a dime for every chirp." When chickens grew large enough to cackle or crow, he remarked, they cost $5 each, which made Sunday dinners expensive.[41]

By autumn wheat reached $4 per bushel, a hundred-pound sack of flour $25, corn $2 per bushel (up 80 cents), apples $6 per bushel, and Irish and sweet potatoes and onions $5 per bushel on the Richmond wholesale market. Brown sugar brought 65 cents per pound for an increase of 45 cents per pound since March. The tobacco market was "excited" with sales at $1.32 per pound. All farm commodities reportedly had an "advancing tendency." In Macon, Georgia, salt brought the exorbitant price of $145 per sack, which placed a severe hardship on farmers and planters planning on the winter hog slaughter to meet family, military, and consumer needs. In Atlanta wheat reached $6.50, then rose to $7 per bushel, while flour brought $40 to $44 per barrel and corn sold for $1.75 to $1.85 per bushel, up from a dollar per bushel in January. In Richmond vegetables and poultry were scarce. Merchants and speculators had scoured the countryside for thirty miles beyond the city, buying up butter at 75 cents per pound and selling it for $1.50 per pound. Farmers made money, but many consumers in the Eastern Confederacy became increasingly apprehensive about food prices and availability in the future.[42]

As agricultural and food prices escalated, the editor of the *Southern Confederacy* boldly argued that the joint problems of food shortages and high prices could be resolved only by resorting to authoritarianism—the government should regulate the agricultural economy. Without a comprehensive agricultural and food policy, many consumers, particularly urban residents, suffered increasing want, especially from the lack of flour. He recommended that farmers and millers only sell wheat and flour to consumers, and not to merchants or speculators. Farmers should meet their family needs but then under government compulsion sell their surplus wheat and flour at fixed prices. The editor understood, however, that an authoritarian government that intervened in and managed the agricultural and food economy would fail: city people could not reach farmers to make their purchases, and a struggling economy would open the door to further government regulations and directives. Yet by suggesting this solution, he showed that at least some southerners considered more government regulation, not less, necessary to keep people from going hungry. Proposals for government to fix prices received support in Richmond, where consumer food prices had become "exorbitant" with no "disposition to 'come down'" and which appeared to be on an "ascending scale."[43]

BY FEBRUARY 1862, UNION SOLDIERS began to have an effect on the Confederate food supply, at least in Virginia. Destruction of barns, livestock, and haystacks along with the seizure of provisions by Union soldiers became common experiences for farmers in northern Virginia. The war now brought problems for some farmers that they could not overcome, and these problems became increasingly troublesome across the Eastern Confederacy as Union forces swept through the countryside. Federal soldiers had burned the village of Frenchburg in Hampshire County, Virginia, and the barns and farmhouses in the vicinity. An observer reported, "At every turn dead hogs, cattle and horses, which have been wantonly shot, are found. . . . They seemed to have aimed to destroy every living thing." A planter in Fauquier County, Virginia, also reported the pillaging of Federal soldiers saying, "All day long the soldiers continue to destroy property. . . . Many hundreds of sheep, cattle and hogs & . . . poultry are destroyed. People generally are entirely stripped of subsistence." As a result, the food situation had become serious, one observer remarked, because "one-half of the people of this truly unfortunate country have been robbed to destitution & the other half have nothing to spare for their relief." During March, Union soldiers also seriously depleted the food supply for Winchester, Virginia, and the surrounding area. Foraging parties stripped the grain bins, hay mounds, and smokehouses and seldom left enough corn to plant. Union soldiers told farmers that "they did not intend that there should be any planting done this Spring." One wrote in his diary that "fifty or sixty wagons, perhaps more, have this morning passed down the hill laden with fence-rails and boards, young timber just cut, oats, corn, hay, straw, etc. taken from the farms in the vicinity."[44]

In April, Union Quartermaster General M. C. Meigs informed Secretary of War Edwin M. Stanton that Union cavalry had reported the Shenandoah Valley had "many good horses" the army needed because so many men lacked mounts. Meigs told Stanton that "a horse fit for military service is as much a military supply as a barrel of gunpowder, or a shot-gun, or rifle." U.S. Army regulations authorized the commanding general in enemy territory to levy military contributions in money or kind "when the wants of the Army absolutely require it." Meigs believed the needs of the army "absolutely required that a portion of its supplies should be drawn from those who, having caused the war, are now waging it against us." He asked for authorization to take not fewer than 1,500 horses from Shenandoah farmers for cavalry, artillery, and wagon service. If more could be taken without "too much interfering with agriculture," they should do it.[45]

Staunton agreed and ordered General Nathaniel Banks, commanding the Department of the Shenandoah, to take not fewer than 1,500 horses from valley farmers; that would mean "only horses absolutely needed for agriculture [would] be left in possession of persons believed to be disloyal." Officers who seized these horses had to give a receipt promising payment after the suppression of the rebellion and upon proof that the farmer had conducted himself from that date as a loyal citizen of the United States. Farmers loyal to the Union, however, should not have their horses taken. Banks did not oppose taking horses from Confederate farmers, but he notified General Lorenzo Thomas, adjutant general of the army in Washington, that he doubted that more than 300 horses could be found between Harpers Ferry and the most distant Union outposts in Virginia. Two armies had occupied the area, and they drew heavily on it for food, forage, and horses. Moreover, the Shenandoah Valley was wheat country, and farmers raised little hay that Union troops could confiscate. Plus, both Union and Confederate forces had already taken the best horses from valley farmers. This additional Union impressment, however, meant that Confederate farmers in the Shenandoah entered the spring with too few horses for the plowing season. Confederate Quartermaster General Abraham C. Meyers reported that across the Confederacy, so many horses had died in public service that the demand exceeded supply. Farmers could not furnish the needed animals, and western drovers could not get enough replacement horses and mules across the Mississippi River. Some Georgia planters and farmers had lost so many horses and mules by May that they used oxen to plow their fields.[46]

By summer the loss of Missouri, Kentucky, western and middle Tennessee, and trans-Allegheny Virginia removed the major producers of high-grade horses from Confederate supply, while inflation made those remaining more expensive in Confederate currency. Farmers in unoccupied areas could not meet the needs of the Quartermaster's Department for artillery and wagon horses. Cavalrymen who had to provide their own mounts also had difficulty finding adequate horses and paying for them. When Confederate or Union soldiers did not take a farmer's horse, the wartime free-market economy proved profitable. In August a Confederate cavalryman paid $675 for a horse in Virginia, and the transaction pleased both buyer and seller.[47]

Union foraging and impressment continued to limit the availability of food in the Winchester area because farmers feared the loss of their provisions if they tried to take their produce to town. In March, Laura Lee, a Winchester resident, complained that "we live principally on bacon, beans, rice, dried apples, and often bread." A month later another Winchester woman observed, "We are realizing now the privations of the war, more than we have ever done before; there is no market; I have not had a morsel of fresh meat in the house for a week, & I could not get either eggs or butter, & have had very little sugar." In early May her sister-in-law confided in her diary that "we are almost in a state of starvation here, no fresh meat for a fortnight and almost impossible to get eggs and butter, and what we do get at fabulous prices." While valley farms struggled with both Union and Confederate forces, fewer farmers brought their produce to the Richmond market, due to the number of pickets on the roads and the soldiers in the streets.[48]

Federal soldiers were not the only ones to blame for the decimation of agriculture in Virginia because secessionists "robbed" the farmers as unmercifully as Union soldiers. Confederate secretary of war George W. Randolph warned General Joseph E. Johnston that "I am instructed by the President to call to your attention to the habit in which many of the regiments have fallen of burning the fences near their encampments and bivouacs, and I must request that you issue orders requiring . . . Army Regulations to be executed. . . . Unless the destruction of fences can be arrested it will materially lessen the crop . . . and impair the power of the Government to subsist the Army." Of course, cold, wet soldiers, whether

Confederate or Union, gave no thought to farmers' ability to raise grain and livestock if they burned their fence rails. Personal, immediate comfort determined their actions, and fence rails proved excellent material for campfires. In Virginia so many farmers lost their fences to Confederate or Union soldiers that they dug ditches around their fields to prevent wagons from entering and hauling out loads of rails, corn, and forage. One Confederate officer compared his command to "an army worm leaving nothing at all standing." His soldiers "ran through gardens on the road devouring every particle of vegetables," and "wherever a cow or hog were found it was shot down & soon dispatched."[49]

In March the soldiers' food supply in northern Virginia became an increasingly serious matter, while the farmers upon whom they relied suffered when General Johnston retreated from the Manassas area to establish a new line south of the Rapidan. As his forces retreated, Johnston's men destroyed grain and abandoned more than a million pounds of meat — provisions that southern farmers and planters could not easily replenish. One of Johnston's officers lamented, "The destruction of stores of every kind was terrible." Before spring warmed into summer, another Confederate soldier observed that "the country passed over by our own army is totally destroyed & the most wanton damage frequently committed by our own men." He had seen "Stock *killed* by our half famished soldiers — crops trampled down & destroyed & famine for the next year staring the poor farmer in the face." Another observer reported that in northern Virginia, "the farmers are making preparations to plant and sow the same as ever, and it will be highly necessary, for the country is drained of everything eatable or that will feed horse flesh. Not a pig, cow, horse, or sheep or poultry of any kind, has been saved from the ravages of the Confederate government and the army."[50]

The new year also brought more impressments on southern farmers. In May Confederate soldiers took a wagon and four mules from a farmer near Tidewater, Virginia, and gave him a promissory note for $650. John Walker, the aggrieved farmer, complained without avail that the impressment was "abominable" and "outrageous." By the autumn food and forage shortages for the army had forced the War Department to intensify its impressment of provisions. Confederate farmers now found themselves besieged by frequent seizures, and impressment agents often waited along well-traveled roads and confiscated their produce and forage. In many areas, particularly near Richmond, farmers brought fewer cattle and other provisions to market and defied impressment officers.[51]

Secretary of War James A. Seddon attempted to ease the animosity and ensure either the sale of food and forage to the army or the impressment of those agricultural provisions at fair prices. Commissary General Lucius B. Northrop urged the creation of a fixed-price schedule that would give stability to farm prices across the Confederacy. Seddon agreed and established a commodity price schedule based on a five-year prewar average, plus a percentage ranging from 100 percent to 200 percent, to account for supply and demand. On December 6, 1862, the War Department published the agricultural price schedule, which required impressment officials to pay the listed prices at the time of acquisition, if possible, and to leave sufficient provisions for family subsistence. This order meant that impressment no longer served as an occasional method for the acquisition of food and forage for the army. Rather, it became a regular, systemic, nationwide policy for waging war and a government control mechanism for agricultural and food prices, at least on paper.[52]

In reality the impressment price schedule was doomed from the beginning because it did not account for local production, costs, and price differences. Most important, government prices remained considerably lower than market prices, and southern farmers and planters complained loudly and tried to avoid impressment officers – all to the benefit of their pocketbooks but to the detriment of the army. By mid-October they proved so successful at hiding provisions that General Lee authorized his commissary and quartermaster officers to impress food and forage if farmers and planters refused to sell at government prices, provided they gave certificates listing what they took (these certificates also served as promises to pay later).[53]

OTHER PROBLEMS BECAME EVIDENT BY the summer of 1862. In August Union general John Pope – commanding the newly created Army of Virginia, constituted from fragments drawn from the Shenandoah Valley and the Army of the Potomac – moved south to engage Lee's Army of Northern Virginia. They met a second time on the Bull Run River near Manassas, with another retreat for the Union army. Although the Confederacy remained intact, Lee began planning an offensive into the North, in part, to gain needed food provisions for his army. At the same time, disease and military impressments of horses not only had seriously depleted farms of draft power but also reduced further supply to the army from breeding. Some southerners urged farmers to stop breeding mules, although Virginia and Georgia farmers who had mules to sell received handsome prices ranging from about $140 to $175 each. Broodmares had become difficult to acquire and farmers, wagon drivers, and cavalrymen needed more horses. By late summer, while some farmers enjoyed high wartime prices, the cotton loan program received even harsher criticism than earlier. One Virginian believed that the loan program worked different in fact than theory because the government now required planters and farmers to keep the subscribed cotton on their own property to save storage costs. As a result, the government became nothing more than an agent or commission merchant for selling the staple. The cotton loan program still had not coerced Britain and France to break the blockade and purchase the fiber. Instead, the Confederate Congress seemed "incapable of rising above half way measures," and the loan program became nothing more than "red tape and a bureau." Some planters argued that if the government bought the cotton crop at 8 cents per pound, it could reap several hundred million dollars in profit by selling it on the international market at 28 cents per pound or more, a price that would enable payment of the entire Confederate debt after the war.[54]

Had the government followed that cotton loan plan as originally proposed, critics argued, cotton-burning and no-planting policies would have driven the price still higher and made foreign governments want the cotton even more, to the point they would intercede in the war to get it. These critics charged that the Confederate government did not have the will to purchase the cotton crop of 1861, and its foreign policy had been too weak to coerce other nations to intercede. The cotton loan program, then, did not benefit either planters or the government. At best, by summer it had become a failed agricultural program. In the meantime, the Union provided surplus grain and cotton to Britain and, although English workers suffered from want of adequate food and income, the British were not prepared to risk war for cotton. In this context, Union policy used the agricultural power of the North to help keep the British neutral.[55]

Drought became a problem as well. When the Virginia wheat crop fell short of expectations, Secretary of War George W. Randolph prohibited the export of flour from the state. Although military impressments of flour continued unabated, the army paid market prices to producers but only reimbursed speculators for their costs. In August an editor reported, "Virginia will be starved out in twelve months if the war continues in her territory." Many slaves had fled to Union lines, fewer acres had been planted, and fewer white men remained on the farms to perform the work. With approximately 300,000 Confederate soldiers in the state and an equal number of Union troops expected, some 600,000 to 1 million men and horses would soon be foraging across Virginia. "What will be left for citizens?" he asked. "A parched earth, a desolate country. . . . That is what awaits Virginians in the future." Many feared that his assessment was correct.[56]

Similar problems plagued Alabama, where, in mid-August, a planter wrote that "the earth is parched most distressingly, not enough will be made with even the best of seasons to give the people plenty, economy from the beginning, with every attention to root crops with winter pastures can alone save the stock and keep the people from suffering." He also confided in his diary that "the effects of the drought on the confederate states has been awful, the time has past [sic] to gain any thing from rain, scarcity and high prices must prevail, economy [sic] and effort should be the watch word of the people." In the North Carolina Piedmont, drought also kept the wheat, corn, and oat crops short. One farmer wrote, "A famine is feared among all classes, but more among those who have all to buy and nothing to sell." He believed that meat and bread soon would not be available at any price. "There is perhaps," he wrote, "nothing better calculated to humble a nation than famine and nothing better calculated to produce famine than war and short crops."[57]

THE CONFEDERATE CONSCRIPTION ACT OF April subjected all men from eighteen to thirty-five years of age to military service, but this draft did not meet the army's manpower needs and, in September, Congress passed the Second Conscription Act, which raised the draft age to forty-five. This legislation was followed on October 11 by an amendment that expanded the classes of exemptions. Collectively, this legislation caused considerable animosity among small-scale farmers who had left home and families for the army. They considered these acts nothing less than class legislation because it exempted one man per plantation – that is, an owner or overseer, who had responsibility for at least twenty slaves. Known variously as the "Twenty Slave Law," "Twenty-Negro Law," or "twenty negro clause" – or more colloquially and prejudicially, the "Twenty-Nigger Law" – it fostered animosity between small-scale farmers and planters for the remainder of the war, and the legislation further decreased the labor supply on small farms. As more men left their homes, production declined and farms fell into disrepair and weeds grew in once productive fields.[58]

This conscription legislation also meant that as the men in this age category left their farms for the army, their wives, in the absence of older male family members, necessarily confronted the problem of managing the farm. Nonslaveholding farm women sometimes hired a slave or relied on their children or nearby family members to help with the necessary work. Although their husbands frequently sent letters home with instructions concerning the operation of the farm, these women were really on their own. By late 1862 farm men in the army realized that their advice and communications were too infrequent to meet immediate needs for advice and direction. Confederate farm women now knew that they would have to rely on themselves to operate the farm. One Alabama farmer recognized this reality, writing to his wife that "I would be glad to come but I cant so you must make your own arrangements. . . . You can see what is needed better than I can and me not nowing [sic] how things is going on." White farm women with husbands gone also had to face the possibility that they would need to manage the farm indefinitely. One Alabama farmer told his wife that "if I never come back again . . . I want you to keep the land and such things as you need to raise your children the best you can . . . carry on your business as if you never expected me at home." If the family did not own slaves, many white women, then, began working in the fields for the first time. By the end of 1862, they had become farmers.[59]

Women left alone on plantations and farms with slaves but without overseers often had great difficulty compelling their bondsmen to do their accustomed work. Black women, of course, had always worked in the fields and white women, too, in the poorer families of small-scale farmers, but now their labor was particularly needed, and they entered the fields in uncustomary numbers. One Alabaman reported to Governor John Gill Shorter that during spring planting "Feemales" would soon be seen "between the handles of the plow." In July white women went into the wheat fields in Jefferson County, Virginia, to harvest an abundant crop, but observers reported that most of it would be lost for want of labor despite their work in the fields.[60]

By 1862 the war also brought planter women into agriculture as never before. Many plantation women hired overseers whose age kept them from the army, but in time these men left as the government steadily increased the age limits for conscription. Or, they relied on an older male neighbor for advice and assistance. Still, white farm and plantation women often assumed responsibility for directing the slave workforce by default in the absence of their husbands. By so doing, they became the great defenders of the institution. When their slaves grew increasingly restless as Union forces neared and as the war progressed, women slave owners or managers had little choice but to exercise their authority for the sake of agricultural production, maintenance of the institution, and the social order. Many women did not want to manage slaves, however, and some chose to rent out their bondsmen rather than direct them on the plantation. Other slave-owning women managed as best they could, knowing that their labor force differed significantly from that managed by their husbands, given the growing restlessness among their bondsmen for freedom. By 1862, then, the war brought social and economic change to farm and plantation women as they undertook agricultural work that until now had not been their domain.[61]

THE WAR DID NOT YET produce substantive change for the black agricultural workforce. In early January slave sales increased, and bondsmen and -women brought high prices. In Georgia, executors of estates sold slaves at City Hall Square in Atlanta at prices undiminished from the previous year. In Decatur, an estate sale brought $1,665 for a "plain field hand," while "second class" men, that is, men past their prime working years, usually older than twenty-five years of age, sold for $1,450 to $1,500. In DeKalb County, a twenty-five-year-old man, still considered a prime field hand, brought $1,400, while a teenage male sold for $1,601 and a twenty-two-year-old woman with a two-year-old child for $1,877. Buyers with good agricultural securities, such as land, received credit until Christmas, with the interest calculated from the day of sale if the first payment did not determine the day from which they paid interest on the loan.[62]

Optimism prevailed about slave prices. Auctioneers sold slaves at estate sales from courthouse steps, and private dealers maintained active slave markets. One North Carolina slaveholder boasted that he could sell a woman for $1,300 and two men for $1,000 each. He also sold male children at prices ranging from $40 to $200 each, and hired others out. He reported to a friend that "the impression prevails that after [the] war they will command fabulous prices – there seems no fear of losing them off the coast." In March a twenty-year-old woman sold for $900, while a sixteen-year-old girl brought $925 in Richmond. Prices declined by age after approximately thirty, and here a sixty-year-old man brought $415. In South Carolina slave prices remained steady with a number of mothers and small children as well as families on the auction block. In Charleston, however, prices had declined. A fifty-year-old woman and her sixteen-year-old daughter each brought $605. Family groups sold for an average of $400 to $450 each. Prime male and female field hands sold for only $700 to $800 each.[63]

In early July, despite increasing apprehension about the ability of southern farmers to meet the public need for grain, pork, and beef, slave prices held steady on the Atlanta market. At an estate sale a twenty-one-year-old woman with a child sold for $1,300 while a fourteen-year-old boy brought $1,540, a sixteen-year-old boy sold for $1,400, and a girl of fifteen brought $1,399. One five-year-old boy brought $575. These prices held firm through July and buyers believed that their labor investment would bring both immediate and future dividends. In the Abbeville District of South Carolina a thirty-year-old man sold for $900, a twenty-five year-old woman with a three-year-old child for $1,160, a nine-year-old boy for $600, a six-year-old girl for $425 and another for $600, a four-year-old girl for $250, and a thirty-five-year-old woman with a three-year-old child for $900. In Richmond fifty slaves sold for $34,670 for an average of $693.40. In that lot a twenty-two-year-old boy sold for $1,500 and an eighteen-year-old girl for $1,320. These prices were considerably higher than a decade earlier, when slaves in their early teens brought about $500 and prime field hands from eighteen to twenty-four years of age went for $800 to $900.[64]

In August, however, the price of slaves began to slip. Although some slaves sold at "sound prices," most did not bring the price that their owners desired. Many of the slaves sold at Atlanta's City Hall Square returned lower prices than comparable slaves a month earlier. Some owners refused to accept the prices offered and withdrew their slaves from the market. While believing that the institution remained secure, some observers speculated that the fighting near Richmond, the decline in tobacco prices, and Lincoln's impending Emancipation Proclamation might have caused the decline. This lack of confidence among slaveholders did not last long. In early September one Virginian wrote that "it would seem that Southern confidence in the perpetuation of the peculiar institution remains unshaken, judging from the recent sales of negroes in Richmond." Two "very likely" boys had been sold for $1,100, while other slaves, young and old, male and female, also brought good capital gains. "Prices have not been so regularly buoyant since the commencement of the war, especially in Virginia," one observer noted.[65]

Although field hands brought from $1,300 to $1,450 in Richmond during October, prices trended downward and varied by age and gender. One slave owner with a plantation along the James River sold a forty-six-year-old man for $1,000 and a thirty-six-year-old woman for $600, but a thirteen-year-old girl brought $1,250, an eight-year-old girl $650, a seven-year-old girl $500, and a four-year-old boy $250. He also sold another slave whom he listed as "Old Moses" for $350. Still, slave owners remained confident that their investment was secure. Despite the war, one Georgia woman wrote, "the servants appear content and doing their duty." Her "boys" were busy plowing and shearing sheep. In Georgia a farmer reported that "our negroes are doing tolerable well."[66]

Yet by October prices dropped due to overstocking, as owners from the upper counties of Virginia tried to sell their slaves to prevent a monetary loss if Union troops confiscated them as contraband. Some slave owners believed they needed to take their "negroes" farther south to get high prices. Other observers felt that the price decline resulted merely from the lack of buyers and speculators, not a "permanent diminution in the value of likely negroes," because "young and likely negroes of both sexes" still commanded "standard prices." Once the war ended, optimists believed, the counties where the slave population had been reduced by Union confiscations or slave-owner removals would repopulate, and high market prices would prevail.[67]

In early November the sale of a "young and likely negro man" for $1,600 and several women sixteen to twenty-two years of age for $1,500 in Richmond gave some hope for "buoyancy" because dealers from the Deep South had entered the market and kept prices high. In late November in the "sale rooms" of one Richmond dealer, a family of eight consisting of the mother and seven children – one in the mother's arms – sold for $5,100 and a second family consisting of the mother and four children brought $2,880. In the "auction rooms" of another slave dealer, a "likely boy" of fifteen years of age brought $1,480, a "common woman" and a girl $1,015, a "likely" sixteen-year-old girl $1,290, a woman with a boy and a girl $1,860, a woman and a boy $1,200, a "likely girl mulatto" $1,320, a "likely mulatto boy" age ten years $1,300, a woman with two "likely" children $1,900, and a "likely farm hand (man)" $1,010. At the end of December a report from Atlanta indicated that "the negro market still keeps active, at high prices." Slave prices on the Richmond market "advanced" where "likely" young girls brought from $1,250 to $1,400, "likely" boys, "farm hands," and plow boys brought $1,040 to $1,390, adult male "farm hands" brought $1,020 to $1,660 at the sale house of Messrs. Dickson, Hill and Company.[68]

Slave owners with surplus labor also continued the custom of hiring out their hands. In Virginia and North Carolina, owners offered a large number of slaves for hire at prices ranging from $50 to $80 per year for women and $75 to $100 for men. But a Florida planter hired out a boy for $400 per year, paid quarterly, an increase of $100 from 1861. He also had slaves in North Carolina, but by November he was discouraged: "Sometimes I think the chance of keeping them so small as hardly to justify the expense and trouble of sending for them." He also worried about the eventual application of the Emancipation Proclamation, which theoretically would free approximately 3.4 million slaves on January 1, 1863. Moreover, with Confederate money declining in value, one Alabama planter hired out a female slave in the fall for 55 bushels of corn, which had a value of approximately $1 per bushel. He also hired out a man for $10 per month, but the form of payment remains uncertain. In late 1862, the Confederate Ordnance Department in Macon, Georgia, hired eleven slaves from a Tennessee planter who had taken his bondsmen there to escape seizure by Federal forces. Another slave owner hired out thirteen slaves for $160 per hand for the year, with the Ordnance Department providing food, clothing, and medical attention. In the absence of agricultural productivity and profits, slave owners gained at least some income from hiring out their bondsmen, but at a further cost to southern agriculture.[69]

As the bondsmen and -women went about sowing, cutting wheat and clover, and performing other work according to the season, one Georgian wrote that "our negroes have been an element of strength in this struggle, in cultivating our fields, whilst our laboring white men have taken up arms in the cause of freedom." Although he did not see the irony in his statement, he believed without question that slavery strengthened southern agriculture in the fight for independence and that northerners were just now beginning to understand and appreciate this elemental truth. By August, however, a considerable number of slaves had fled through Union lines in northern Virginia, which had a "deplorable" effect on agriculture. Many sought Union lines at harvest time, and much of the wheat went uncut. The corn crop also suffered because field hands in the absence of white supervisors did not cultivate the crop, and the weeds choked the plants and diminished the yield.[70]

In July, the Congress of the United States struck at the institution of slavery with legislation titled "An Act to suppress insurrection, to punish treason and rebellion, to seize and confiscate the property of rebels, and for other purposes," which could only further limit the use of slaves for agriculture beneficial to the South. When President Lincoln signed the Confiscation Act on July 17, the principle of the right of the sovereign belligerent permitted the seizure of all Confederate property as a punishment for secession. Congress now declared that the slaves of anyone proved guilty of treason would be "declared and made free." In addition, slaves belonging to persons engaged in rebellion against the United States upon capture or desertion to Union lines or found in areas occupied by Union forces would be "deemed captives of war, and shall be forever free of their servitude, and not again held as slaves." Southerners could not help but realize that if the North won the war, their agricultural labor system was doomed. As a result, slave prices declined in some areas. Although slaves still sold at "sound prices," most did not hold the value that their owners desired.[71]

Other agricultural labor problems developed. On November 7, 1861, the Union navy captured Hilton Head and Bay Point, and the military immediately occupied the Sea Islands of South Carolina and took possession of several thousand slaves and a large cotton crop. A month later Secretary of the Treasury Salmon Chase sent Colonel William H. Reynolds to Beaufort as an agent of the Federal government to collect the cotton seized on the plantations and to ship it north for sale. The plantation bondsmen and -women were now in reality neither slave nor free, but they required food and many northerners questioned whether they could work for and by themselves to meet their own food needs. Cotton agents and textile manufactures also wanted a crop of long-staple Sea Island cotton.[72]

Secretary Chase sent Edward L. Pierce to report on the condition of the quasi-freed people and the state of the plantations on Port Royal. Pierce observed the freedmen and -women picking cotton for Reynolds at the rate of $1 per 400 pounds of unginned cotton delivered at the Port Royal landing. The pay for their labor came in the form of money, clothing, and provisions. In February 1862, Pierce reported that the black contrabands on the Sea Islands would cultivate cotton "with proper inducements." Pierce recommended the appointment of superintendents to manage the plantations and black labor force. Chase, with the approval of Secretary of War Stanton, then appointed Pierce to the position of general superintendent and director of All Persons Engaged in the Cultivation of Lands and the Employment of Blacks to assist military officials with the confiscation of abandoned property and the organization of freed labor for plantation agriculture. Pierce planned to use the freed black workers to cultivate food crops so that they could feed themselves and thereby limit the need for Federal assistance. He also wanted the freedpeople to raise cotton for northern manufacturers and for sale to Great Britain for diplomatic purposes. This revitalization of agriculture on the Sea Islands would pay the government for the cost of its labor experiment, and Pierce recruited northern farmers and missionary groups to supervise the black workers on the confiscated plantations. Each superintendent had responsibility for as many as six plantations and 500 freedmen and -women.[73]

On April 29, Stanton ordered General Rufus Saxton, commander of the Southern Department, to "take possession of all the plantations heretofore occupied by rebels, and take charge of the inhabitants remaining thereon within the department, or which the fortunes of war may hereafter bring into it." Saxton also had the authority to make "such rules and regulations for the cultivation of the land and for protection, employment, and government of the inhabitants as circumstances may seem to require." The plantation superintendents now answered to military authorities, although this policy merely sanctioned existing practices. Saxton did not make any immediate changes, and the contrabands or freedpeople continued to work on the plantations in gangs under the direction of superintendents for which they received a wage. They also were assigned "nigger fields," or private plots, which they were expected to cultivate for their own food needs.[74]

Under Saxton, Pierce and his superintendents soon managed 189 plantations and controlled 9,050 freedmen and -women. Field hands totaling 4,429 were assigned task work in the cotton fields by the superintendents. Their work routines and responsibilities, then, remained essentially unchanged from the days of slavery. However, Secretary Chase's plan to allot plantations among "loyal" blacks and to furnish plows, hoes, rakes, horses, mules, food, and clothing at government expense and to supervise their work raising cotton for the government caused some alarm. Critics of the plantation supervision at Port Royal believed the venture would cost the government $2 per pound of cotton. Others hoped that Chase would not, in the planter tradition, pledge the 1863 crop to finance the 1862 crop through New York bankers. The plantation superintendents also quickly learned that the differing needs of the Treasury and War departments caused difficulties that hindered them from organizing the freedmen and -women and reestablishing productive plantations on the Sea Islands. The army, for example, took the horses and mules from the plantations in the Port Royal District for its own use and left only the animals too old or sick to pull a plow. When Chase complained to Stanton, the secretary of war suggested that the Treasury Department purchase the needed horses and mules from the proceeds of the cotton sold at Port Royal.[75]

Similarly, in March, General John E. Wool, who commanded the Department of Virginia, appointed Charles B. Wilder as superintendent of negro affairs for the department and authorized him to appropriate all

Confederate land and cultivate it with freedmen and -women. Wilder placed each confiscated farm and plantation under the control of a white superintendent who had the responsibility to employ as many freedpeople as possible and to pay them wages monthly or at the end of the crop season. Black workers who opted for payment at the end of the crop year when the cotton, corn, or other crops reached market would, in the meantime, receive a small monthly wage for living expenses. This payment would be deducted from the total due when the crops were sold and the final payment made. Black workers also had the directive to raise vegetables for northern markets, and the secretary of war authorized free shipment of those provisions northward. Wool's system to employ contraband workers on the plantations, however, became expensive, and his plan to revitalize plantation agriculture in Virginia proved ineffective. It required new planning and leadership, but by that time the year ended.[76]

Naval authorities also attempted to establish a colony of freed slaves on St. Simons Island, Georgia. To make the freedmen and -women self-supporting, the navy ordered them to "procure" their living from the land and "to plant cotton and thus . . . become of use to themselves." By mid-April the former slaves had planted eighty acres of corn as well as fields of potatoes and beans. By July they had 300 acres of food crops under cultivation, and they had picked 25,000 pounds of long-staple cotton. This effort to restore agriculture on St. Simons, however, largely failed because the freedpeople "showed a great dislike to do the work they had been accustomed to." Commander S. W. Gordon attempted to encourage fieldwork by withholding their beef ration and by placing contrabands in irons when they did not work hard enough. For the freedpeople, plantation work seemed nothing less than a return to slavery. Federal officials would encounter similar problems across the plantation South as Union forces occupied Confederate territory. The reinstitution of agriculture by black workers on white-owned lands would require time, new policies, and social and economic adjustments.[77]

Still, Federal efforts to reestablish agriculture on St. Simons, Sopelo, St. Catherine's, and Ossabaw islands in Georgia achieved modest success. Under the direction of navy officials, the freedpeople planted subsistence crops on a collective and an individual basis and marketed their surplus vegetables and poultry for cash. In July the former slaves sold their agricultural produce to the navy on St. Simons at the scheduled rate of 4 cents per quart for milk, 65 cents per bushel for corn, 5 to 15 cents each for watermelons, 12 cents per dozen for eggs, 10 cents per peck for okra, 5 cents per peck for peas/beans,

50 cents per bushel for potatoes, 12 cents per chicken, and 13 cents each for cantaloupes, all considerably less than free-market prices but better than none at all. Periodically, the plantation superintendents distributed fish, bacon, and molasses to each family as well as paid $1 per acre for all cotton that had been planted for the Federal government before April.[78]

In August, the War Department issued a circular for the military superintendents responsible for confiscated or occupied plantations. It announced a pay schedule for work "done by negroes" on government lands. Blacks would be paid 25 cents per bushel for the corn raised but only after each worker contributed an unspecified amount to the army for the plantation's horses and mules. If these workers failed to produce enough corn on their "private patches" to meet their own food needs, they could take payment for their work in corn, as long as they had the means to store it. On Edisto Island, South Carolina, the freed blacks or refugees also earned $1 per acre for plowing and planting cowpeas, turnips, and potatoes for government use, 50 cents per acre for hoeing these crops, 30 cents per day for splitting eighty fence rails, 20 cents per day for cutting and gathering hay and cowpeas, 25 cents per day for gathering potatoes, and ½ cent per pound of cotton picked. The superintendents of the plantations had orders to provide their freedpeople or refugees with one pint of meal, a half pound of salt, four pounds of meat, two pounds of flour, and 100 crackers each month to supplement the food crops that they raised on their allocated patches.[79]

By September, 3,817 "effective" laborers planted 6,444 acres of corn and 1,407 acres of potatoes on the islands of Hilton Head, Port Royal, and St. Helena, which authorities believed would feed the black population. Pierce now believed that "the Negroes will work for a living." But only 3,384 acres of cotton had been planted, which returned about 90,000 pounds for an average of 26 pounds per acre; that compares poorly to the prewar average of 137 pounds per acre, although the discrepancy was due primarily to late planting, insects, and frost as well as poor seeds. Even so, by November the government reported that it obtained 3,500 bales of cotton, worth nearly $1 million (at 63 cents per pound based on 450-pound bales), from these workers on Port Royal, up from 2,000 bales the year before.[80]

In December Saxton attempted to improve the operation of the confiscated plantations and supervision of the black labor force by devising a new management plan. He based it on recommendations from his superintendents, and it harkened to the days of plantation management under slavery. Plantation superintendents now required their black workers to produce enough corn, potatoes, and other vegetables to meet their own needs and to cultivate sufficient corn for the plantation's mules and horses. The superintendents allotted land for that purpose on the basis of one and a half acres per hand. The superintendents also appointed a black plowman, who had the responsibility for all implements and draft animals, and paid him 30 cents per day. Although the black workers did not object to raising corn and potatoes, they balked at raising cotton for the Federal government because of its linkage to slavery. In fact, the former slaves had destroyed so many gins in 1861 that the cotton taken from the plantations had to be ginned in New York, thus losing the seed for the 1862 crop. General Saxton tried to encourage the black workers to cultivate cotton by paying them 25 cents per day for planting and cultivating and 2½ cents per pound for picking. A foreman similar to an overseer took responsibility for the daily operation of the plantation and management of the labor force. By late 1862, however, this government agriculture experiment had failed on the Sea Islands. The revival of agriculture with black labor would take time, and the army and its superintendents could not do it alone.[81]

While Union officials experimented with an agricultural labor system for black men and women on the confiscated plantations, the slave owners in Confederate territory confronted their own labor problems. By 1862, the planters along the Georgia coast had abandoned their rice fields. The presence of Union troops in North Carolina caused many slave owners to move their bondsmen to relatively safe areas in the Piedmont and the mountains. Some planters in that state took their slaves as far south as Florida. In January near McPhersonville, South Carolina, a planter reported that "our plantations are in ruin & wreck – no negroes but a few old and decrepid [sic]." In April the Confederate army further disrupted agriculture in South Carolina when it ordered all of the planters near the coast to take their slaves inland above the "line of defense." One witness to slave removal observed that "the negroes generally are very unwilling to go."[82]

The planters who moved their bondsmen used them for subsistence agriculture on interior lands, which they bought or rented, usually at high prices, or they hired out their slaves for railroad or military work, a practice that further reduced agricultural productivity. Although some rice planters sent their slaves back to the river plantations on a limited basis to plant and harvest a crop, they had difficulty keeping a cohesive workforce due to flight, and rice production remained comparatively limited. By late 1862, then, the Civil War had severely damaged this most prosperous agriculture in the Eastern Confederacy, an agriculture that had created vast wealth for a few planters. Further decline would follow.[83]

IN EARLY SEPTEMBER GENERAL LEE moved north with the intent to rout Union forces and encircle, or at least threaten, Washington. Federal troops under McClellan and led by Joseph Hooker and J. L. Reno blunted his invasion, and Lee took up a strong position near Sharpsburg, Maryland, on the banks of Antietam Creek. After hard fighting and heavy losses on both sides, Lee did not have sufficient strength to advance and withdrew on the 18th. The Union had repelled Lee's attack; whether it could do more to prevent a Confederate invasion remained to be seen. The defeat of the Army of Northern Virginia, however, gave southerners pause. Lee needed more men and appealed for a conscription law that soon took more farmers from their fields and further reduced agricultural production. Southerners could not defeat the Union unless northerners tired of the war and chose to end it. If they did not, the North would wear away at the Confederacy, and no southerner wanted a war of attrition.[84]

By early autumn, then, the agricultural power that most southerners believed would help win the war had substantially weakened. The grain-growing and agricultural-provisioning country stretching from the Potomac at Harpers Ferry to Memphis, Tennessee, had been exhausted of food supplies. The Confederate armies had consumed most of the agricultural produce in the central portion of that region, and northern and southern armies had taken the farm products on each end of that expanse. The most productive farming areas in North Carolina and along the Gulf Coast had been drained of food supplies as well.[85]

Everything edible bore a high price. Cattle brought $7 per hundredweight in southwestern Virginia, which served as the chief cattle raising area of the Upper South. Hay, which could not be sold for 50 cents per hundred pounds before the war, now brought $2 per hundredweight in the interior if it could be purchased at all. Eggs, which cost 3 cents per dozen in Boston, brought a dollar in Richmond. In Atlanta wheat reached $6 per bushel and flour $40 per barrel. In Charleston sugar brought 60 to 70 cents per pound, molasses $2.50 per gallon, and lard 50 cents per pound. One observer noted, "Every article of farm produce has gone up to these fabulous prices and the ready payment of these tempting rates has exhausted the farming regions of the South of their supplies." Farmers had made a great deal of money selling their produce, but they had sold so much of their surplus that they had few reserves. Only the planting of grain in the cotton regions of the Deep South would save the civilian and military populations from hunger and want. This region, however, could not meet the needs of the population for meat, and the supply would soon worsen now that Texas beef could not easily cross the Mississippi River because of the Federal gunboats, and with the railroad broken for cattle shipments from Texas. Only by capturing Kentucky could southerners obtain an adequate meat supply. Farmers in that state produced large numbers of cattle, hogs, horses, and mules, as well as food and forage in sufficient quantity to meet the civilian and military needs of the South. "The campaign in Kentucky," one contemporary wrote, "is not only for securing another State to the Confederacy, but for meat and bread." In September when Lee invaded Maryland, many southerners also believed that its farm produce would soon move to southern markets once Confederate forces captured the state. As a result, farm prices fell on the Richmond market. Bacon briefly declined to 60 cents per pound, but after the Confederate defeat and retreat at Antietam, farm prices again increased sharply.[86]

In the Shenandoah Valley, Confederate general William Nelson Pemberton reported that the country north of Winchester, Virginia, was "doubly desolate. Army after army has passed over it, and a cloud of locusts were hardly less destructive." When a rumor spread through Winchester that Pendleton's army would winter in the town, a resident could only say "God forbid it." She reported, "The country is barren in this portion" and "there will be some danger of a famine."[87]

Still, not everyone despaired. In the valley wheat farmers profited from the presence of the Confederate army, which in October agreed to purchase wheat for $1.50 per bushel, cornmeal for $2 per bushel, and flour for $8 per barrel from farmers. The soldiers hauled the grain to local mills, and the government provided the grain bags and flour barrels, and the price of flour fell by 40 cents per barrel. Yet sugar brought $2 per pound and hay cost from $25 to $30 per ton, and, in November, potatoes brought $8 per bushel—a jolting increase from $5 per bushel a few weeks earlier. In Winchester, Julia Chase reported that "no one seems to place much value upon the money now in circulation." In South Carolina one planter observed that "the Confederate Treasury notes have now taken the place of all bank bills and gold and silver are never seen." Farmers asked and received high prices in inflated Confederate currency, but they did not like it.[88]

In October Thomas Waddell, who lived in Staunton, Virginia, observed that the farmers in Augusta County had difficulty feeding the population.

"Provisions of all kinds scarce and prices high," he confided in his diary. Flour brought $14 per barrel, and "the extortion practiced by those who have anything to sell adds greatly to the hardship of the times." Waddell saw difficult days ahead because southerners had "more to fear from the scarcity of foodstuffs and clothing than from the Yankee armies." He wrote that "the drought continues unabated – the fields are perfectly barren – the wheat must perish soon. Farmers are unwilling to sell the produce they have on hand." He added, "Many persons who have money can scarcely procure necessary food, even this early in the Fall, usually the most abundant period of the year." By late autumn, then, farmers profited from high corn, grain, and pork prices if they had these provisions to sell.[89]

By early November, Commissary General Lucius B. Northrop estimated that the Virginia wheat crop averaged less than one-third the normal harvest. The Confederate government now impressed flour and paid $12 per barrel, but farmers who had their wheat ground at local mills could sell it for $24 per barrel on the commercial market. They groused about the inequity, and consumers complained that the railroads would not deliver it in a timely fashion because the army controlled the lines and privileged military traffic. At the same time, an editor in Staunton, Virginia, wrote that "the short crop of wheat and corn for the past year, the fatality that has attacked the hog crop; the waste super induced by large standing armies; the drought which has retarded the Fall operations of farmers getting their wheat sown . . . the presence of the enemy, and the demand made upon them by our Government, State and Confederate, will we fear, be manifest in a short supply of bread and meat next year." In South Carolina bacon and lard brought 60 cents and butter 75 cents per pound, respectively; flour sold for $30 per barrel and sorghum molasses for $2.50 per gallon – prices comparable across the Eastern Confederacy. Drought had ruined much of the corn crop. The future looked bleak, while the present was a time of "earnest self-denial."[90]

In early December corn became scarce in northern and central Georgia and some families suffered from the want of food. When a report circulated from Savannah that the army and people in the state faced the "peril of starvation," and that the grain supply would force the army to disband within eight months, southerners became increasingly worried. The Quartermaster's Department of General Bragg's army necessarily foraged farther to acquire food supplies: some detachments had to venture more than two hundred miles from their camps. Critics still maintained that more corn would be available for both civilians and the military if it was not used for distilling whiskey, which brought as much as $12 per gallon on the Atlanta market and $20 per gallon in Richmond. Many southerners had not given up the distillation of whiskey despite state prohibitions and congressional urgings because they preferred to convert their corn into a high valued product. Georgia's governor Brown so wanted to close down the distilleries to conserve grain for food that he urged farmers to inform on those who distilled whiskey from corn and other grains. By the end of the year, only the distilleries in Georgia that had government contracts to supply the military with whiskey for medicinal purposes could avoid seizure. At the same time, farmers in southern Alabama had harvested an abundant corn crop and willingly sold to anyone who would pay $12 per bushel. In Atlanta, flour brought $45 per barrel. Housekeepers wanted sugar but stood little chance of getting it. Tobacco farmers also profited from the military market and from sales through Union lines for greenbacks. Most southern farmers were patriotic, but all understood the value of hard money and knew that Union currency held its value while Confederate notes did not.[91]

Southerners had many reasons to be despondent by the end of the year, but they took heart with a major Confederate victory. In mid-December Generals Thomas J. Jackson, James Longstreet, D. H. Hill, and J. E. B. Stuart prevented Ambrose E. Burnside from crossing the Rappahannock and marching on Richmond. When Burnside attacked Confederate entrenchments near Fredericksburg and suffered 15,000 casualties, southerners rejoiced but few expected the North to give up. Fredericksburg provided hope, but more Yankee soldiers would come with the waning of winter and the renewal of spring planting time.[92]

In 1861 four of every nine southern men who enlisted were farmers. But by the end of 1862 those numbers had changed to three of every five soldiers after Congress in September passed the Second Conscription Act, which raised the draft age from thirty-five to forty-five years. But the army's inability to feed all of the men in that age group reduced the call to those ranging in ages from thirty-six to thirty-nine. Despite a growing agricultural labor problem, southern planters and farmers still met the overall food needs of the Confederacy. Nevertheless, the margin for error had become slim. Southern civilians and Confederate soldiers alike needed peace as their best defense against hunger.[93]

Many southerners still believed that the Confederacy had the agricultural ability—that is, the power—to meet the food needs of the military and civilian population. Although New Orleans and Nashville had fallen to the enemy and Union forces were nipping at the northern periphery and along the East Coast, planters and farmers had converted much of their cotton lands to grain and forage crops. Yet cholera had taken a toll on the hog crop. Railroad transportation for carrying food stuffs to city markets and consumers continued to worsen. Union soldiers had taken grain, livestock, and slaves and burned rail fences and cotton bales. Confederate forces did much the same.[94]

By the end of the year, wholesalers and retailers had come under increasing criticism, and some suffered physical violence for charging high prices. In December a group of women in Greenville, Alabama, attacked a railroad agent demanding "salt or blood," and a group of "regulators" raided a government depot at Bladenboro, North Carolina, and took sacks of corn and rice. In the Eastern Confederacy, the general price index rose from 193 in January to 686 in December (January–April 1861 = 100). High agricultural prices now meant little because of rampant inflation, and farmers increasingly refused Confederate money. So many Georgians suffered from want of food that the legislature purchased 97,000 bushels of corn and requested the railroads to ship it to distressed areas at half the normal rate. While some 800,000 to 1 million bushels of wheat had been shipped to Richmond annually before the war, that number was now only 250,000 to 300,000 bushels. The drop-off was even more serious because the white population had doubled and the city had become the supply center for the army. The continued enlistment of small-scale farmers took even more land out of production.[95]

Across the Eastern Confederacy, cotton planters grumbled about the Confederate loan program, but many had replaced cotton acreage with corn for the 1862 crop. Tobacco farmers profited from the military market and from some sales through Union lines for greenbacks. Rising prices, hoarding, and speculation as well as isolated food shortages raised the question of whether southerners had the will power to stay the course. Many southerners had now reached the conclusion that the war would not end soon and agricultural shortfalls would make a bad situation worse. The agricultural power of the South did not seem as dominant as it had in the spring of 1861. Earlier a Georgia farmer had asked, "When will war cease and the swords be beaten into plowshares?" No one knew the answer, and farmers and planters anticipated more hard times.[96]

CHAPTER THREE

Western Troubles

In the Western Confederacy many farmers and planters greeted the new year with optimism that faded to despair by December 1862. When the fighting began, the substantial expanse of the South and the absence of military engagements or the great movement of Confederate and Union soldiers meant that the war continued to benefit many western farmers. In the Texas wheat counties, farmers enjoyed the "easy circumstances" brought by the previous year's bountiful crop. Texas farmers believed the blockade of the Mississippi River had enlarged the demand for their wheat and flour, which enabled the establishment of local mills because the blockade prevented grain and flour from reaching the Confederate West via the Mississippi River from the north. Some farmers broke their land with gang plows manufactured in Dallas and used oxen for draft power to prepare the land for grain crops. Wheat farmers averaged twenty bushels per acre the year before, and they anticipated a large yield from this year's summer harvest. A Tennessee observer reported that "the people of the wheat country have very little cause to complain of the blockade, as [it] is scarcely known to them except by its benefits." By January 1862, however, the war had affected farmers and planters for both good and ill. In Mississippi one plantation woman sold "frying sized chickens" for 20 cents each and butter for 32½ cents per pound, all high prices. But her husband produced 100 bales of cotton, which brought only 8 cents per pound locally. She lamented that Texans sold their cotton to Mexico for good prices but that Mississippians could not reach that market.[1]

In mid-February another Mississippi planter reported that "our war news is awful." By April a Texan observed that wagonloads of baled cotton arrived daily in San Antonio with most destined for market in Mexico. In New Orleans the editor of the *Crescent* wrote, "It cannot be disguised that our bacon is running low. From whence and how is the stock or supply to be replenished? Fifty dollars for a barrel of pork, one dollar for a bushel of corn, fourteen dollars per barrel of flour." The threat of a Union occupation of the city no doubt kept farmers from marketing their produce because in Bienville, a parish in northern Louisiana, they had a surplus of bacon and corn.[2]

In early February General Ulysses S. Grant struck at Forts Henry and Donelson, eventually driving Confederate forces across the Cumberland River. With the fall of Fort Donelson, Admiral Andrew H. Foote quickly powered his gunboats up the Cumberland and Tennessee rivers into Alabama and wrecked General Albert Sidney Johnston's defense plan for east of the Mississippi River and, in late February, he evacuated Nashville, making it the first Confederate state capital to fall to Union control. The Union now controlled central Tennessee and its farms and plantations. In March Johnston struck Grant's forces at Pittsburg Landing on the Tennessee River near Shiloh Church. After hard fighting the Confederates took a defensive position at Corinth, Mississippi. When the shooting stopped, some 10,000 men from both sides lay dead. President Lincoln welcomed Grant's victory. Southerners, farmers and planters included, feared dark days ahead.[3]

They came quickly. In April Admiral David G. Farragut ran a flotilla of frigates, sloops, and gunboats over the sandbars at the mouth of the Mississippi River. After a hard fight passing Forts Jackson and St. Philip, the fleet sailed northward on the twisting river and took New Orleans. With the capture of the Crescent City, the Union controlled the largest and most important seaport in the Western Confederacy. Farmers who could reach the city could now sell their produce for greenbacks but the blockade also tightened and further discouraged British intervention. Confederate farmers might remain loyal, but in the vicinity of New Orleans they now tilled Union soil.[4]

Although most southerners, farmers included, were not yet totally at the mercy of northern armies, Union forces clearly threatened in the West, particularly in the Mississippi River Valley. Southerners worried that if New Orleans fell to the enemy, they would lose their source of sugar and molasses, the latter of which already brought $2 per gallon on some markets in the Eastern Confederacy. Agricultural observers urged farmers to plant more Chinese cane sorghum from which they could make sorghum molasses for cooking and to feed their slaves. Most farmers and planters heeded the call for more food production and reduced their cotton acreage substantially. In the Mississippi Delta slave women worked in the fields, "knocking down cotton stalks" and raking them into piles and burning the brush to help make plowing easier. The men followed with plows preparing the fields for corn and potatoes. Most planters, however, could not forgo all cotton planting. Huston Huling Parker, owner of a large plantation near Brandon in Rankin County, Mississippi, planted 150 acres. Others anticipated planting cotton, and they began sending more of their crop from 1861 to market in Natchez to make room for storage of the new crop. They eagerly anticipated the ending of the blockade. Some residents, however, urged them not to do it "under any circumstances" because they would endanger the city by inviting enemy attack to burn it and the city.[5]

At the same time, Confederate armies moved on cornmeal, salt pork, beans, and hay, and in Arkansas the latter two provisions were lacking. The chief quartermaster of the Trans-Mississippi District made an "appeal to the patriotism of all farmers" to raise prairie grass and other hay crops that they could deliver for sale to the army at various locations along the Memphis and Little Rock Railroad. The quartermaster also urged planters to put their slaves to work raising beans rather than cotton, which brought only 7½ cents per pound on the New Orleans market before the capture of the city (unlike peas, which fetched high cash prices). By June some planters could not sell it for 6 cents per pound. One Mississippi planter remarked, "We can rely upon no source of supply for the wants of the army, but ourselves." In the West as Union soldiers advanced, planters often burned their cotton as a matter of patriotism to keep it from falling into enemy hands or, if reluctant, government authorities burned it for them. In New Orleans authorities burned a large number of cotton bales in storage to keep it from capture as Federal authorities approached.[6]

Either way, cotton farmers and planters lost their crop, although optimists contended that those who burned their cotton to keep it from the enemy benefited because they "deprived the enemy of the enjoyment of rich plunder." Confederate soldiers also burned cotton for the same reason, and Union soldiers burned bales in retribution if the cotton could not be shipped north. In early May, Federal troops reportedly burned cotton in Louisiana whenever they found it. Rumors also circulated that between Memphis and New Orleans the work of burning cotton could be traced by the "ascending wreaths of smoke." But one Mississippi observer reported that cotton bales did not burn easily or quickly, and they had to be stirred like a log fire to keep them aflame. Properly tended cotton bales would burn for days.[7]

By early spring, as Confederate soldiers abandoned territory to Union forces, Mississippi cotton planters wanted the Confederate government to insure their claims for the loss of any cotton burned by its agents. They wanted a promise that they would receive the payment due for the cotton that they had sold to the government under the cotton loan program if Union forces confiscated or destroyed it. At the moment, they only held vouchers showing transfer of the cotton to the government. With their cotton in danger of destruction or confiscation, and in the absence of a government agricultural policy for wartime losses, they wanted assurance that they would be paid.[8]

Many attempted to hide their cotton and wait for peace. With New Orleans under attack, editors called for all planters and farmers to burn their cotton along the Mississippi and its tributaries to prevent confiscation. In Arkansas planters along the Red, Arkansas, White, and St. Francis rivers and the Mississippi River also prepared to burn their cotton, which they estimated at more than 100,000 bales. Most cotton planters, however, responded with reluctance and, on April 26, General Pierre G. T. Beauregard ordered General Earl Van Doren to burn all cotton within the reach of Union forces along the Mississippi River if the planters hesitated to do it. The Confederate officers had orders to keep an account of the number of bales destroyed pending future payment by the government. Because so many planters refused to burn their cotton without coercion, however, Louisiana organized cotton-burning committees, which had the authority to summon planters before them to prove they had burned or "otherwise destroyed" their cotton as ordered by Brigadier General M. L. Smith on May 28. Overseers usually appeared before the local cotton committees and received a certificate signed by the board members, who recognized that the planter's cotton had been destroyed and that legal action would not be pursued against him. In Louisiana rebel guerrillas received orders from military authorities to help the cause by burning cotton likely to fall into Union hands and to hang planters and farmers who resisted. Some planters began to consider the guerrillas more dangerous than Federal soldiers, and a few even praised Union soldiers for upholding "the principles of justice and civilization."[9]

When planters burned their cotton, they were not committing the fiber to the cotton loan program. By June some 500,000 bales had been destroyed in the Mississippi River Delta and another 300,000 bales in Arkansas alone. At the same time, Commodore Farragut's gunboats had passed the mouth of the Yazoo River on their way to lay siege to Vicksburg, and his men and supporting forces burned cotton along the Mississippi River. Below Vicksburg, Union forces torched an estimated 250,000 bales. One contemporary lamented, "Our agricultural power is diminished . . . by the loss of some of the richest domains in the South."[10]

As the cotton burned, farmers expressed outrage over the presumed privilege that President Jefferson Davis enjoyed. They were angered when a rumor spread from Mississippi that not a pound of cotton had been burned on the plantation of Davis and his brother Joe E. Davis near Vicksburg. Many cotton men expected their fellow planters to support the cause by denying the enemy an important agricultural commodity. In Tennessee rumors circulated that speculators were purchasing large quantities of cotton from planters and farmers with the intent to sell it to Federal forces when they arrived. The extensive amount of cotton in storage at Knoxville, the hotbed of Unionism in East Tennessee, indicated treason to some southerners. As a result, the army ordered the Western & Atlantic Railroad to suspend the shipment of cotton over its line until further notice and to refuse acceptance of cotton for storage at any depot or building along the road. If the planters and farmers kept their cotton at home, they might lose some money, but speculators could not use it for their own advantage while aiding the enemy. The loyalty, if not the patriotism, of some planters and farmers had begun to weaken depending on the proximity of northern forces and the potential to earn greenbacks for their agricultural commodities.[11]

Clearly, by the spring of 1862, some cotton farmers near Federal lines had begun to separate their feelings of self-interest from their sense of loyalty to the Confederate States of America. Already many cotton farmers and planters realized that neither the government in Richmond nor the Confederate armies could protect them, particularly the farther they lived from the Eastern Confederacy. Moreover, they may not have yet realized it, but the Federal government wanted to appease them with trade: it hoped to regain their allegiance, or at least their neutrality, through the exchange of cotton for badly needed sound currency.[12]

Lincoln had authorized trade with southerners in Union-controlled territory but not with farmers, planters, and speculators in states or areas still under Confederate control. All loyal citizens – at least those who testified as such – could trade cotton for northern goods and money, provided that they could provide evidence that they rightfully owned the fiber. Federal Treasury Department agents supervised this agricultural trade. In June, when Memphis fell to Union forces, the cotton trade began in earnest and advanced downriver with the army. Cotton planters may have equivocated early in the war, but their allegiance became shakier as the conflict dragged on. Without military protection their loyalty waned, particularly when northern agricultural markets beckoned. Agricultural self-interest and loyalty to the Confederacy increasingly became separate ideas, even needs, in the months ahead, especially in the Western Confederacy.[13]

The Confederate government did not have a consistent policy on the cotton trade with the Union. Jefferson Davis left the matter to the War Department and his generals, whose policies ranged from prohibition to assistance. Secretary of War James Seddon authorized licensed dealers and government agents to conduct trade to gain needed supplies for Confederate soldiers, but he prohibited the exchange of cotton and other agricultural goods, such as vegetables, eggs, and butter, by farmers, planters, and speculators. Nevertheless, farmers sold these provisions to Union forces because they needed the money. In this sense, loyalty to family superseded loyalty to the nation-state. Seddon did not, however, enforce his restrictions, and this failure made the War Department a complicit partner in illegal agricultural trade. The trade of provisions to the Union to benefit Confederate soldiers arguably indicated a merger of self-interest and national loyalty. Farmers and planters could benefit themselves and the Confederacy with this trade. Agricultural trade with the enemy, then, stemmed from complicated and sometimes conflicting motives arising out of necessity, opportunity, and loyalty – any one of which existed separately or which drove actions collectively.[14]

At the same time, the *Hinds County Gazette* in Mississippi urged planters to seed a "good deal" of cotton for the sole purpose of keeping their slaves employed, even if a successful crop drove the price down to 4 or 5 cents per pound. The editor of the *Weekly Mississippian* in Jackson disagreed, arguing that it would be "suicidal" for cotton growers to have two crops on hand when the war ended. Optimistically, he expected the war to end next year, and the 1861 and 1862 cotton crops would keep the price low for a long time. Slaves need not plant, cultivate, and pick cotton for the sake of keeping them busy. Rather, planters should "let" their slave women and children raise corn, potatoes, and hogs while the men were deployed elsewhere to build fortifications and to serve the army camps and on railroad labor details. Or, the editor argued that the slaves should work on the small-scale farms of the white owners who served in the army. "If the worst comes," he wrote, "give them arms to fight by the side of their masters," thereby showing the speed by which sensibility can give way to absurdity.[15]

In May cotton planters in captured portions of Mississippi, Arkansas, and Tennessee increasingly sold their cotton for greenbacks, which buyers transported north for resale to textile manufactures or shipment abroad. From Nashville an observer reported that "buyers are scouring the country in all directions as far as the protection of the Federal lines extend, and sometimes even further. *The planters are acting like men of practical sense, and are quick to trade.*" Cotton prices ranged from 16 to 17 cents per pound in specie or U.S. Treasury notes and brought 22 to 25 cents per pound in Tennessee currency. The planters were bankrupt. But seeing that the Federal government would not confiscate their land, they quickly expressed their desire to sell their cotton to northerners and return to the business of planting more cotton. After the fall of New Orleans, however, Louisiana governor Thomas O. Moore prohibited Louisiana farmers, planters, and factors from selling cotton to the enemy "under all circumstances." Cotton planters and farmers had much to lose by obeying his edict. When Union forces captured an area, they began collecting cotton for shipment to New Orleans. One Union soldier reported, "Cotton is king for the army [and it] is doing nothing else but gathering cotton."[16]

Yet, while planters and farmers wanted to sell their stored cotton to northern buyers, they were accused by neighbors, the Confederate army, and the government of being unpatriotic, even traitorous. Their dilemma worsened during the summer when speculators and northern agents from the captured cities of New Orleans, Memphis, and Nashville arrived in cotton areas with large quantities of Confederate currency that no longer had value in the Union-controlled territory. These speculators offered Confederate notes for cotton: they wanted to get rid of depreciating Confederate money while purchasing cotton in storage that they could sell on the northern market for greenbacks. The fall of New Orleans, Memphis, and other towns encouraged cotton farmers and planters to trade with Union agents.[17]

In midsummer Confederate authorities in Mississippi reportedly purchased cotton and burned the fiber to keep the planters from selling it through Union lines for greenbacks. Yet that summer thousands of bales of cotton and barrels of molasses and sugar were arriving in Memphis for reshipment to Louisville and other northern markets. In Nashville a resident reported that "large quantities of cotton pass through our streets daily. The planters have too much sense to burn their cotton, if they can help it." In Mississippi, farmers and planters alike had hid much of their cotton and now carefully but swiftly hauled it to market. When this cotton reached New York City, it sold for 44½ to 50½ cents per pound. The occupation of New Orleans and Memphis, then, permitted the legal reopening of the cotton markets, and many farmers and planters took advantage of the opportunity to sell their fiber. If they could get their cotton to market or at least to northern buyers, high prices and payment in greenbacks awaited them. With New Orleans factors paying an average price of $230 per bale for the 1862 crop, cotton farmers and planters earned immense profits.[18]

At the same time, Confederate editors and politicians urged western farmers and planters to seed corn rather than cotton but many saw the monetary possibilities in hedging their bets and profiting from the mistakes of others who abided by government wishes and reduced their cotton crop. These cotton producers still believed the war would end soon and the domestic and international market would pay high prices to those who had cotton to sell. In March the Arkansas legislature, not trusting farmers and planters to reduce their cotton acreage during spring planting, mandated that no one could plant more than two acres of cotton per hand, under penalty of a $500 to $5,000 fine. At the same time, a bill was pending in the Mississippi legislature that would allow each planter only three acres of cotton for each field hand; the measure also mandated that not more than five bales weighing 500 pounds each could be produced on those three acres or sold. Violators would face a fine of $1,000 and not less than twelve months imprisonment and forfeiture of their crop. A month later the governor asked Mississippi farmers not to plant more than one acre of cotton per hand and to seed the majority of their land to grain.[19]

Despite the efforts of Arkansas, Mississippi, and other states to limit the production of cotton, neither Louisiana nor Texas made any provision for decreasing the acreage planted as a matter of law. Robert H. Miller, a Confederate soldier from the "Flowery Mound" plantation along the Black River in Concordia Parish, Louisiana, wrote home: "I advise Pa to plant just as much cotton as he can cultivate, and these are my reasons, if $4/5$ of the planters fail to do so (as you suppose) the crop of that staple will be considerably smaller than it has been for years. If the Blockade is raised in six months from this time all the cotton now on hand will have been disposed of before the new crop comes to the market, but this new crop will bring more money than the last because of the shortness of the supply introduced by so many planters refusing to plant, or it will at least, bring as much as any crop ever did." If his father planted cotton, he could take advantage of those who did not by reaping a high price despite the war.[20]

The Confederate government did not mandate or allocate acreage reductions and abdicated the responsibility to the states. It then failed to create an efficient bureaucracy to enforce agricultural policy. Union commanders, meanwhile, encouraged planters to bring their cotton to them, for which they would receive payment in gold or greenbacks. In Jackson the editor of the *Weekly Mississippian* warned that the goal of their "magnanimity" was to weaken planter support for the Confederacy. Rather than sell cotton to northerners or let the Yankees confiscate it, he advised them to burn it. He also advocated the death penalty for any planter or farmer who sold cotton across Union lines, a punishment that would keep all cotton from the enemy and prevent "base and avaricious" men from selling out "their country." The cotton trade had to be stopped, the editor contended, for the good of the Confederacy. For many planters and farmers, however, the opportunity to make a wartime profit selling cotton trumped loyalty and patriotism.[21]

WHEN THE YEAR BEGAN FLOUR brought $9.95 to $11 per barrel in New Orleans, an increase from $4.55 to $5.45 a year earlier. Although buyers wanted corn, little reached the market. In late March corn brought $1.50 per bushel on the New Orleans market and $1 per bushel on local markets. The editor of the *Natchez Weekly Courier* contended that if the war continued farmers and planters would make more money from grain than from cotton and tobacco, and they would better serve the Confederacy by planting corn and wheat. In early April, just weeks before New Orleans fell to Union forces, the Confederate provost marshals in conjunction with the committees of public safety fixed the price of flour at $15 to $16 per barrel and corn at $1.25 per bushel. Some farmers and planters wanted $2.50 per bushel for wheat and corn, which prompted the editor of the *New Orleans Crescent* to suggest that President Davis declare martial law to keep agricultural and food prices under control. With corn selling in Shreveport for only 50 to 55 cents per bushel, the Committee of Safety encouraged farmers to sell their grain in New Orleans to help alleviate the food shortage. The New Orleans editor supported that suggestion, telling farmers and planters that "you have corn, you have hogs, you have cattle, send them to the city, the money is ready for all you may send, and at better prices than selling cotton at 12½ cents per pound, or even 15 cents; in fact $16 per barrel of flour is equivalent of 20 cents per lb. for cotton."[22]

As spring planting time approached, the Natchez editor reminded farmers in April "that if they wish a speedy termination of the war, and the speedy establishment of their independence, they must raise very large grain crops." Indeed, he wrote that "any people who have enough to eat . . . can not be conquered." Patriots planted grain, not cotton. "Let it be remembered," the editor continued, "that if you wish to grow rich, you must fill your corn cribs and granaries now, and be prepared to raise large crops of cotton when the blockade is raised." Moreover, the best protection against speculators was the production of surplus crops. Bluntly the editor told farmers that "you owe it as a solemn duty to God and your country – to your wives and children – to religion and liberty, to raise very large crops of provisions." Without agricultural power, the Confederacy would be lost.[23]

The plea for grain production was no idle alarm. Hunger stalked many families in Natchez and its surroundings because so many farmers had departed with the army. The situation had become so serious that residents wanting to eat were forced to pay inflated prices at an open market supplied by farmers and planters. (One spring morning, 105 families drew food supplies at this market.) Agricultural and food prices continued to increase, and in late March the editor of the *Natchez Weekly Courier* complained that residents paid $22 per barrel for flour while the army purchased it for $6.50 per barrel. Speculators and farmers reaped a profit in Confederate money on the open market, but farmers dreaded seeing impressment agents on their property. By April agricultural production also began to suffer in the Delta for want of labor. In Washington County, Mississippi, one resident reported that "there are only two young men left in our neighborhood and one of them . . . is lame and can't go [to war]."[24]

By midsummer Mississippi began to feel the effects of the blockade and war. In addition, rust had ruined the oats and damaged the wheat crop in many areas, and farmers cut it for fodder. The damaged grain meant that the "prospect for bread [was] very bad." One-third of the slaves had fled the plantations, and food shortages had become severe. A Confederate wrote Governor John J. Pettus saying, "We are now proving our loyalty by starvation – the tears of our women and the cries of our children for bread!" At Natchez, located in one of the most fertile and productive areas in the state, flour had disappeared from the market and even low-quality cornmeal brought high prices. Drought made matters worse and ruined the corn crop, which in turn reduced the amount of grain for hogs and cattle, which then decreased the amount of pork and beef available at slaughter time. In June, Mississippi farmers sold fodder in Jackson for $1.25 per hundredweight, a good price, but they soon paid $20 per bushel for salt to pack their pork. As a result, some Mississippians who had advocated secession now professed loyalty to the Union.[25]

Planters near Vicksburg had not by July been able to seed their crops, so dangerous was the countryside, and the Union army and Confederate guerrillas had confiscated so much food that residents had almost reached the "verge of starvation." One planter reported "provisions scarce at Vicksburg." He sold his cornmeal for $1 to $1.50 per bushel, but Vicksburg merchants raised the price to $2 to $2.50 per bushel. Farmers worried that their wagons would be "pressed" if they attempted to reach the city market. But a northerner remarked that Mississippians had corn and cotton to sell, and if they starved it was due to their "want of energy and loyalty." Still, by late summer a Mississippian reported that corn had largely replaced cotton, and he believed that "no fears need be entertained as to our ability to feed the armies of the Confederacy."[26]

Food prices by August had escalated so much in Arkansas that the provost marshal for that region fixed prices on "all eatables." Flour could not sell for more than $8.00 per hundred pounds, cornmeal $1.20 per bushel, eggs 20 cents per dozen, chickens $2.40 per dozen, and ham 30 cents per pound. Consumers supported this food policy, and beyond Arkansas others hoped that the provost marshals would do the same. Houston residents also favored military imposition of fixed prices for food because flour sold for $15.00 per hundred pounds, bacon 23 cents per pound, eggs 30 to 50 cents per dozen, and butter from 35 to 50 cents per pound – prices that they considered extortionate. Military authorities could not supervise or enforce price fixing policy such as that attempted in Arkansas, and agricultural and food prices brought all the market would bare.[27]

In San Antonio flour brought $40 per barrel and corn $2.50 per bushel during the summer. One resident attributed these high prices to the depreciation of Confederate currency and concluded that it was not worth more than "three bits on the dollar." On September 1, when flour reached $30 per barrel in Houston, an editor urged the public to stop buying flour and to use cornmeal for bread. With an estimated 2,000 wheat growers in Texas who had produced an abundant crop, he believed that high prices could only be attributed to greedy millers and merchants, and they needed regulation. The residents of Austin gave a "great hue and cry" because farmers asked $15 per barrel for a sack of flour and $1 per bushel for corn and barley. The farmers responded that these prices still did not permit them to get a plow sharpened or a wagon repaired, or to purchase items for the home because the merchants and tradesmen charged them even higher prices. The editor of the *Austin State Gazette* suggested that the authorities might have to impose martial law to keep the merchants and mechanics from gouging farmers and the public with unjustified prices. He believed that "as a class the farmers are now suffering more than any other from extortion."[28]

While wheat and corn supplies were dwindling, nearly 460,000 hogsheads of sugar sat on the New Orleans landing and in planters' storage facilities. Prices ranged from 2 and 4 cents per pound, depending on the grade, and the price of molasses ranged from 18 to 23 cents per gallon because the blockade of the Mississippi River kept these prices suppressed. In April the imminent fall of New Orleans encouraged cane growers to sell their sugar rather than to store it. They were hoping for a short conflict, Confederate victory, and high postwar prices. Seizure by Union troops would mean no profit at all. Soon, sugar planters sent their hogsheads up the Red River to Jefferson, Texas, and up the Ouachita River to markets in northern Louisiana and Arkansas. Houston and Beaumont, Texas, also provided a market for sugar and molasses. Later in September General Benjamin F. Butler conducted raids into the Lafourche region to confiscate sugar for shipment to northern refiners. Sugar planters had marketed their crops across the South, but war and the congestion of the railroads now forced them to sell their sugar in the towns and cities along rivers accessible to steamboats when Union forces were not nearby.[29]

In May the occupation of New Orleans ended Confederate control of the southernmost sugar parishes, prompting many planters to flee with their slaves to Texas. Some planters remained, however, and hoped for the best when Federal troops arrived. The captured sugar plantations quickly became refugee camps, and Union soldiers plundered and burned sugar mills, destroyed equipment, and impressed horses and mules. Along the lower Mississippi River cane fields sometimes became battlefields. Some cane planters still managed to ship sugar and molasses to Natchez by steamboat, where it bought 8 cents per pound and molasses $20 per barrel before Union gunboats closed the river to unlicensed traffic. Some planters also marketed their sugar and molasses by steamboat at Shreveport, but transportation costs made this venture unprofitable.[30]

Before Union forces captured New Orleans and the sugar parishes, the price of sugar fell and banks reduced the extension of credit upon which the planters depended to purchase food for their slaves until they could bring the crop to market as sugar and molasses. In 1862, they owed some $20 million to their factors in New Orleans. Their sharp reduction in spring planting made further financing impossible. Some planters turned to cotton and rice production as an alternative, but without much success. In late May, a reporter from Louisiana passed on the warnings of a resident that planters would not receive corn from the Northwest to feed their slaves and that the Union armies possessed large areas of the southern corn-producing states. The planters, the reporter wrote, had neglected their duty to raise corn instead of sugarcane, "although *at the outset* they were in favor of the most ultra measures." Now they raised only enough corn to meet their needs rather than those of the army. Their selfishness in planting sugarcane had created a great danger because "a week's lack of food would disband the whole Southern army." A cynical northerner noted that perhaps the sugar planters could foresee the end of the war and wanted to be ready with a large sugar crop for sale northward rather than get stuck with a surplus of low-valued corn. Perhaps so, but the 1862 crop produced only 87,000 hogsheads of sugar.[31]

BY 1862 TEXAS HAD BECOME the largest supplier of beef for the Western Confederacy. During the spring, commissary agents bought 200,000 cattle in Texas. Louisiana drovers loaded them onto boats or swam them across the Mississippi. Between the last week of July and the first two weeks of August, more than 20,000 cattle in herds ranging from 400 to 600 head made the crossing. These sales marked the peak of droving Texas longhorns to the New Orleans and Memphis markets, which by the summer were under Federal control. In November, however, a Richmond editor reported that 20,000 Texas cattle had crossed the Mississippi River destined for civilian and military markets in southeastern Louisiana and Mississippi. Along the way residents watched as hundreds of Texas longhorns passed through their towns. Congressman John A. Wilcox of Texas boasted that his state could "furnish the whole army with beef during the war, and charge nothing for it," provided the government would pay the droving expenses. Local slaughterhouses, such as the one in Alexandria, Louisiana, also packed large quantities of salt beef from Texas cattle. This cattle trade from Texas to Confederate territory east of the Mississippi River continued until Union soldiers and sailors took control of the river in the summer of 1863. By the end of the year, Union gunboats prevented most herds from reaching the east bank of the Mississippi River, although some drovers made the attempt as late as 1864.[32]

Meat packers processed Texas cattle in plants at Jefferson, Tyler, and Bonham, Texas, and helped supply Confederate soldiers in Missouri, Arkansas, and Indian Territory, although the supply never met the demand. The enlistment and later conscription of cowboys also hindered the raising of cattle in Texas. As a result, mostly old and young men remained to tend the herds, and their presence enabled many large-scale cattle ranches to continue operations. Congress provided a partial remedy to the draft law in October by exempting one stockman from conscription per 500 head of cattle on a ranch, but the stockman had to be exclusively engaged in cattle raising. Even so, the beef supply did not increase for the Confederacy because of Union control of the Mississippi River.[33]

At the same time, Union and Confederate armies impressed or simply took cattle from farmers east of the Mississippi River. In Tennessee, Union general Don Carlos Buell ordered his foraging parties to scour the countryside for all the cattle (beef and dairy), yearlings, and calves that they could "scrape up." But foraging for cattle proved no easy task because so few grazed in the countryside of the Western Confederacy. Southern Louisiana was an exception: planters in the sugar parishes produced a large number of cattle. Four sugar parishes sent approximately 30,000 head of cattle to markets along the coast and to New Orleans during the year. By late November, however, with New Orleans under Union control and Federal forces creeping farther into Confederate territory, one planter wrote, "Louisiana is lost — our only hope is to go West to Texas where beef is plentiful."[34]

IN THE WESTERN CONFEDERACY HUNGRY Confederate and Union cavalry and infantry took food and forage from farmers as a matter of right. These incursions onto the property of planters and farmers by both sides wreaked havoc on the agriculture of the Western Confederacy in the areas where the armies marched and fought. In April a planter's daughter in Washington County, Mississippi, complained that Yankee troops had raided their property, drank their buttermilk, and taken all of their mules and 186 slaves and "many plows." The men returned during the summer and stole their chickens. In July soldiers under General William Tecumseh Sherman's command destroyed many of the farms near Cold Water, Arkansas. His men overran the county, "stealing and destroying everything they could lay their hands on — not leaving a barrel of corn or a piece of meat." They killed every cow, hog, and sheep they saw and destroyed the growing crops by riding through them, and they took all of the horses and mules of value as well as more than two hundred slaves.[35]

Near Nashville, a planter complained that "the federals seem to think that the property of the Rebels or Secesh as they term us belongs to them and act accordingly. If horses or mules are wanted they go and get them."

He could have added "and slaves too." In September a planter near Baton Rouge reported that Yankees had taken thirty-eight "head of negroes," twenty-eight mules, and all of his wagons and cattle. He had a "tolerable crop of cane," which would make about 500 hogsheads of sugar, and a "very good" corn crop, but he expected Union soldiers to take all of it. He also estimated that Union troops had taken 600 slaves from his parish. Another Louisiana planter spoke for many when he said that his family members were "getting along as well as we can," but – between runaways and Union theft – he expected to lose all of his slaves unless he could move them to Texas.[36]

Horses, mules, corn, and forage remained in high demand by the Union army. In October near Nashville, a planter reported that the 95th and 106th Illinois Infantry had camped nearby and burned his cotton gin and killed his milk cows, hogs, and beef cattle, as well as those of other farmers throughout the area. When northern cavalry bivouacked on Confederate farms, he also complained they turned their horses loose "into fields of hay and grain to graze at will upon the cherished crops of the farmer in the vicinity." If the farmer attested that he was a Union man, his crops might be spared, or he might receive a note promising that the Federal government would pay for the damages. In November, he lamented that the 11th Illinois Cavalry had camped in his front yard. They had cut down his timber, burned his fence rails, occupied his stable, taken his mules and horses, cut his harnesses into little pieces, and destroyed his farming implements. In utter despair he attributed his loss to "chastisement" by God because southerners had "sinned greatly." In late October, a woman in Winchester, Tennessee, also reported that Union troops had taken "every fowl from the place except one or two old hens, which ran as if for dear life at the mere sight of blue britches."[37]

Near Bolivar, Tennessee, in late autumn teams from the 78th Ohio ventured thirteen miles from camp to find forage for their horses. One soldier reported that for miles around the town, "fields are laid bare; fences used up for fuel; corn crops long since appropriated; cotton fields half picked; and hundreds of acres of plain-land, upland, hill-side, and hollow still white with myriads of untouched and open bolls. . . . No horses, no mules, no cows, no calves, few hogs, no cabbage, no potatoes, apples, chickens – no nothing that is edible." Then he noted, "The secesh stole the cream, we drank the milk. They took first choice, and we appropriated the remainder." A Union officer confirmed that observation about middle Tennessee when he wrote, "This is a dreary, desolate, barren and deserted looking country." Near Holly Springs, Mississippi, a traveler reported seeing nearly endless cotton fields white with fiber but few people: farmers and planters had fled, taking their livestock and best slaves with them. Large cornfields that adjoined the cotton lands had gone unharvested. Only a few blacks remained who, to one secessionist, seemed "supremely happy."[38]

Union pillaging of farms and plantations had become so destructive that in early December, General Sherman in Mississippi issued General Orders No. 2, decreeing that "the indiscriminate and extensive plundering by our men calls for a summary and speedy change." Sherman opposed pillaging, but not the seizure of needed Confederate agricultural provisions. He ordered that quartermasters and commissaries of brigades could take only corn, fodder, livestock, meat, "or any species of subsistence store"; if the farmer or planter proved to be a loyal Unionist, the officers were to provide him with a receipt for later payment. Few Union soldiers paid much attention to the directive, particularly when they were hungry or feeling spiteful. Essentially, Sherman's order meant that agricultural products belonged to the United States, and its agents would take and distribute them as regular rations.[39]

Confederate "brigands" or guerrillas caused problems for farmers near Nashville, where they told farmers that they would confiscate their wagonloads of potatoes, vegetables, and fowl as well as apples, eggs, and other agricultural commodities if they attempted to market their produce in the Union-occupied city. As a result, food prices escalated. Housekeepers with money now began hoarding food, which made the acquisition of provisions more difficult for the poor. One resident suggested that the Union army send forage trains into the countryside so that traders could purchase agricultural products directly from the farmers under the protection of the military. At the same time, some farmers believed that if they made it to Union-controlled Nashville with their produce, the Federals would impress their grain, meat, butter, and other provisions, as well as wagons and teams, so they stayed home. Their absence did nothing to help Nashville's "famishing citizens." General Henry W. Halleck attempted to assure them that Union soldiers would not take agricultural produce, wagons, or horses belonging to farmers who were transporting their produce to the Nashville market. But farmers remained unconvinced, and only time and the strict enforcement of military policy would ease their fears and encourage them to take their commodities to the city. In the meantime, prices remained "exorbitantly high." By autumn many farmers and planters who occupied the lands where Confederate and Union armies marched saw little reason to invest the money, time, and labor needed to replant and split new rails for fences. Most Confederate farmers and planters remained patriots, but the yeomanry was demoralized.[40]

MISSISSIPPI PLANTERS REPORTED DURING THE spring that overseers were "scarce," and one hoped that his new man would "not need *as much overseeing* as his predecessor did." Planters, however, easily hired out their surplus labor, and slave prices held firm in the Western Confederacy into the spring. Even in Unionist East Tennessee, the price of slaves had not depreciated. In late March a twenty-year-old man sold for $1,500 and a woman with an eight-month-old child brought $1,180 while a lot of five slaves, gender unreported, sold for $5,000. Slave prices also remained high in Texas. High slave prices meant capital gains and income from the sale of surplus labor, but the war also jeopardized that investment in the Western Confederacy. In Tennessee, Louisiana, Mississippi, and Arkansas slave owners confronted the increasing problem of bondsmen fleeing to Union lines as Federal forces captured Confederate territory, which meant considerable loss of high-value property. They also struggled with the rapidly depreciating Confederate currency. In Mississippi one planter suffered arrest for refusing Confederate money for the sale of a slave.[41]

While the arrival of Union forces did not technically free the 139,000 slaves on the sugar plantations, planters made adjustments to the new labor conditions. Some abandoned their sugar plantations. Others planted cotton despite the absence of a market and an unsuitable climate in the lowlands. Some rented their plantations to those who had the capital for, and the interest in, planting crops. Other planters leased their lands under sharecropping-like conditions – the tenant received one-third of the crop and the owner two-thirds, with the tenant paying one-third of the expenses and taxes. Lessees, who agreed to pay half of the operating costs, received half of the sugar produced for the year. And some planters sent their slaves to Texas, where they hired the men out at the rate of $40 per month to cut and haul railroad ties and the women at $20 per month to do lighter work. Some were hired out to help coopers make flour barrels at the rate of $15 to $24 per week. Texas planters occasionally paid in cotton at the rate of 8 cents per pound. Other sugar planters hired their slaves to wheat farmers in Texas. By doing so they earned some income from the labor of their slaves and kept them from capture by Union forces. In Mississippi, planters also moved their slaves as far from the rivers as possible to protect them from Union raiding parties.[42]

When General Butler and Federal troops occupied New Orleans and took charge of the sugar country, planters saw the price of the staple plunge. The fall of New Orleans in the spring made the planters' problems of no markets and little credit far worse. Many slaves fled behind Federal lines. In July 1862 a Bayou Lafourche planter noted, "There has been a perfect stampede of the negroes on some places in this vicinity." When slaves remained on the sugar plantations they often refused to work. Land prices also declined, which further hurt planters' ability to borrow money.[43]

Although the flight of slaves from the sugar plantations angered the planters, confiscated slaves meant that the Union army had to feed, clothe, and shelter them as well as find them work. Some quasi-freedmen and -women could be put to work on various army details, but too many fled behind Union lines to accommodate all of them with employment by the army. Moreover, by the summer the Federal government still did not have a policy for dealing with fugitive slaves. In July the U.S. Congress, however, passed the second Confiscation Act and the Militia Act, which freed the slaves on the plantations where their masters had abandoned the land and authorized their employment for the military's benefit. Yet many slaveholders remained on their plantations and took the loyalty oath. These slaveholders wanted their property back so they could resume sugar and other agricultural production, and Butler had the legal responsibility to protect the property of loyal citizens.[44]

By autumn the labor supply problem had become serious and uncertain on the sugar plantations. General Butler responded to the dual problem—planters lacked sufficient labor to raise crops, and too many freed slaves had fled to Union lines to feed and clothe them—by devising a solution that existed in some similar form until after the war. In October, he provided the planters with labor and the freedmen and -women with protection from slavery. The de facto free men and women would be hired by loyal planters and lessees of abandoned plantations to work on their old plantations or other plantations of their choice, with all proceeds going to the Federal government. The freedpeople within Federal lines provided the labor at the rate paid of $1 per ten-hour day. He later applied this policy to other plantations in Louisiana. Butler also leased and sold some abandoned sugar plantations to speculators. If a planter took the oath of allegiance to the United States, he could continue operating his plantation and employ black men and women at the rate of $10 per month for able-bodied males, with women and children paid less for a month's work. Work consisted of ten-hour days, six days a week, for twenty-six days per month. The planters provided food, shelter, and other care and promised not to abuse their workers with corporal punishment. Butler's labor policy essentially made slavery a dead institution in the sugar region where it had not been politically declared illegal.[45]

On November 9, Butler issued General Orders No. 91 to help deal with the agricultural labor situation in Bayou Lafourche. The Lafourche Parish had many of the largest sugar plantations, some of which the owners had abandoned and on which remained thousands of freedpeople. With this order Butler attempted to revive the plantation economy, employ the freedmen and -women, and produce crops, especially sugar, for the Federal government. The order sequestered the plantations of disloyal owners and imposed the general's labor policy. In addition, it authorized a Sequestration Commission consisting of army officers to administer confiscated property, including slaves, and supervise the work on the plantations. Planters who had not borne arms against the Union since the fall of New Orleans and who took the oath of allegiance would have their property spared from confiscation. The Sequestration Commission rented the plantations of unrequited Confederates, often to northerners, thereby creating even more animosity. Some slave owners took their bondsmen and -women away rather than lose them to Butler's emancipation policy. This paid labor force, however, showed little inclination to bring the plantations back to full productivity, particularly for sugar, and the freed workers produced only 20 percent of the 1861 crop. This decline in sugar production, however, resulted from more factors than just low productivity by the freedpeople. When the year ended, only a few nominally loyal sugar plantations, whose owners had taken the oath of allegiance, remained in operation; instead, the majority hoped that with the retention of slavery they could return to the profitable production of sugar and molasses.[46]

In December General Nathaniel Banks succeeded Butler as commander of the Department of the Gulf, which constituted the Union-occupied portion of Louisiana south of the Red River. Banks wanted to get the freedpeople back on the plantations, and he expanded General Butler's provisional labor system. Even so, the management of plantations in Union-occupied areas and the supervision of the freedmen and -women developed differently in the West than it did in the Sea Islands in South Carolina under General Rufus Saxton. In the West, the Federal government did not have control of all the plantations because some continued to be occupied by the freedpeople, while others remained with Confederate owners who had not fled. General Banks confronted this agricultural labor problem as soon as he took command of the Department of the Gulf. The sugar planters, while grateful that the Federal government did not confiscate their lands, complained that the newly hired black labor force did not work as hard as slaves, and they could not use force to motivate them.[47]

BY NOVEMBER COTTON PLANTERS IN the Mississippi Valley had become disgruntled with the Confederate cotton purchase program. In Louisiana the government reportedly paid 13 cents per pound less than agents offered for cotton in Virginia and 8 cents less than they paid for cotton in Georgia and Alabama. The price difference resulted from transportation problems, but few planters accepted that explanation. Cotton planters in the lower Mississippi Valley believed the government should pay the highest market prices, reasoning that it was the fault of the Confederate army that their cotton was not safe from Federal confiscation. In Louisiana some government purchasing agents argued that all cotton acquired by the government had to be stored at least twelve miles from the Mississippi River. This regulation, they hoped, would keep farmers who lived close to the river from selling their crop to Federal or northern agents.[48]

Not all cotton farmers suffered. James Alcorn, a planter in Coahoma County, Mississippi, reported to his wife, who was living with her parents near Eutaw, Alabama, that he was sending her a wagonload of bacon, flour, sugar, and $1,050.75 of Federal money, $2,100 in gold, and $1,000 in Confederate currency. He had sold eighty bales of cotton for more than $12,000 in Memphis, and he hoped to sell another hundred bales for more than $15,000. He sold his cotton for 35 cents per pound in greenbacks. He could exchange some of the greenbacks for Confederate money for 30 to 40 cents on the dollar. When he went home, crossing through Union lines, he had a negotiable currency in Confederate-held territory, which he planned to invest in land, thereby paying for it with depreciated Confederate money rather than good Federal dollars. He smuggled his cotton to Memphis up the Mississippi River and reported, "The smuggling business has now become popular and people are beginning openly to trade." His planter friends were doing much the same. Federal dollars meant more than unequivocal allegiance to the Confederacy for many farmers and planters in the Western Confederacy.[49]

Alcorn also told his wife to purchase corn with Confederate money, as well as food for the slaves and forage for the horses and mules on her parent's plantation. The Federal dollars merited saving for the future because he believed the South was going to lose the war. "We will hope for the best, and prepare for the worst," he wrote. That preparation meant trading cotton to the enemy for all the profit it would bring in Federal dollars. And profit he made. In December he wrote, "I have been very busy hiding & selling cotton." He had marketed 111 bales and had $10,000 in greenbacks and $1,000 in gold. He still had 50 bales of old cotton and 40 bales of new but unginned fiber, which he hoped to sell for $20,000. "I am busy I assure you," he told his wife, "and am making my time count," by selling his cotton at 40 cents per pound.[50]

By early December, however, the summer drought meant failure of the corn crop in Mississippi, except in the bottomlands, and privation began to give way to hunger. One farmer complained to Governor Pettus that the farmers who cultivated corn in the river valleys had produced a "superabundance of corn," but they refused to sell it at a fair price. They commonly rejected $2.50 per bushel because the *"Demon spirit"* of speculation encouraged them to keep their crop off the market until they received $3.00 per bushel. Greed, he believed, harmed the Confederacy more than Yankee soldiers. This Mississippi farmer wanted the legislature to establish price controls to protect the poor and small-scale farmers from the more fortunate planters. Similarly, a Mississippi soldier reported to the governor that his wife could not afford corn at $3 per bushel on his soldier's salary of $11 per month, and he could not return home to help her with the farm. At the time, the army paid farmers $1 per bushel for corn when they needed or took it. Food prices had escalated beyond the ability of the poor to purchase it. Hunger began to touch many poor families in the towns and countryside alike. The soldier wrote, "In the name of God, I ask is this to be tolerated? Is this war to be carried on and the Government upheld at the expense of the Starvation of the Women and children?" During the coming winter the Mississippi state legislature appropriated $500,000 for food and other assistance for the indigent families of soldiers, most of whom were farm families.[51]

Many areas of the Western Confederacy now suffered from food problems, and prices continued to rise. In Houston, workers earned at best $3 per day, but bacon sold for 75 cents per pound, eggs for 75 cents per dozen, butter for $1 per pound, flour for $31 per barrel, cornmeal for $2.50 per bushel, and milk for 40 cents per quart – all prices that had increased since the war began, as they had across the Western Confederacy. Texas beef, however, remained plentiful at 30 cents per pound from the butcher. In Corpus Christi, flour sold for $40 per hundredweight, sugar commanded 75 cents per pound on Christmas Day, and shelled corn brought $8 per bushel, which reportedly gave farmers a profit of $2 per bushel. Merchants and residents hoped that these high prices would encourage farmers from the up-county to bring them their stock of provisions, all of which there was a "great scarcity" in the city. Although farmers enjoyed these high wartime prices, consumers complained that they could not make ends meet.[52]

As the year drew to a close drovers still managed to swim or transport a few hundred head of cattle across the Mississippi River, but that supply had seriously diminished since 1861. In December a farmer near Nashville killed forty-two hogs collectively weighing 6,620 pounds, and other farmers also pursued this wintertime activity. Army and civilian needs for meat, however, still exceeded supply. Editors and Confederate officials continued to urge planters and farmers to seed grain and raise livestock rather than plant cotton in the spring. The corn yield had tallied less than average across many areas, although it proved bountiful in southern Arkansas where one resident noted, "There is more corn in the Confederacy than its people can possibly consume." Hungry people in drought-stricken and heavily foraged areas could not appreciate his optimism.[53]

The growing absence of slave labor made the cultivation of cotton problematic. One Tennessee slave owner wrote that "most of my negroes are gone.... What the balance of the darkies will do remains to be seen." Federal-occupied Nashville proved a compelling lure. But small-scale farmers also had their own grievances about labor, particularly the exemption from conscription for planters who owned more than twenty slaves. One Mississippian wrote Governor Pettus complaining that the Twenty Negro Law was "the handle at which most of the malcontents grind." This law caused grievances to fester until the war ended among the farmers who did not own the required number of slaves for them to qualify for an exemption from the army.[54]

By late December, the key to agricultural prosperity in the Western Confederacy had become the northern market. A tobacco farmer near Clarksville, Tennessee, had been unable to sell his crop to Confederate buyers unless he accepted Confederate money. When Federal troops occupied his neighborhood and enabled him to safely transport his tobacco to Kentucky for sale, he received a high price of $20 per hundredweight and got $2,269.40 for 11,347 pounds or 20 cents per pound. He accepted payment in Kentucky money, however, rather than greenbacks because he and his neighbors still believed the Confederacy would win the war and bring Kentucky with them. Confederate farmers liked the high wartime prices, provided they could sell their produce for good, sound money—an outcome that became increasingly difficult to achieve when buyers paid with Confederate currency. In Murfreesboro, Tennessee, Confederate currency exchanged at the rate of three to one for greenbacks, another clear indication that southerners in the Western Confederacy were wavering in their support for independence.[55]

Agricultural prices had so escalated from lack of production and inflation that hunger prevailed in some areas of the Western Confederacy. In Arkansas military authorities continued to set food prices, but a lack of agricultural produce was not the essential problem. Rather, greed ruled the marketplace to the detriment of hungry people. Some planters were accused of refusing to sell foodstuffs unless they received their asking price, such as getting $4 per bushel of potatoes. If they did not get their price, they took their produce home. In Little Rock, residents called farmers, who sold cornmeal for $2 to $3 per bushel from their wagon beds, "extortioners." One observer noted, "There is . . . no established price for anything; everybody, even to the negroes, getting all they can." The sugar plantations suffered from neglect or abandonment. Drought had damaged grain crops, and hog cholera remained a threat across the region. Union foraging parties and Confederate impressments left farmers and planters with few provisions. Still, many farmers looked forward to spring when they hoped to plant large cotton crops if the war ended. In the meantime, the agricultural problems in the West meant shortages of corn for meal, hogs for bacon and salt meat, and flour for bread as well as little beef.[56]

In late December Confederate general Braxton Bragg engaged Union general William S. Rosecrans's forces along the Stones River near Murfreesboro, Tennessee. When the fighting ended Bragg withdrew to Chattanooga. Although Rosecrans did not pursue him, this Union victory gave the North another incremental piece of Confederate soil, and it bode ill for southern farmers and planters as well as soldiers in the Western Confederacy during the coming year.[57]

While Confederate and Union forces maneuvered, Robert H. Cantrell, a Tennessee planter, confided in his diary that his situation had become grim. "I was well fixed here before the war, even within the last six months but how different now. My place is a perfect waste. House burned down, fencing pretty well all burned, not an acre enclosed on the place, no hogs – about 130 killed. My cattle, except 2 milch cows killed; 1 mule & 3 good horses taken . . . my gin house & lint room greatly injured. . . . My harness run through the cutting knife. . . . Farming implements destroyed or burnt up." Foraging Union and Tennessee cavalry had taken at least 1,000 bushels of corn. Indeed, the war had cost him dearly. In despair he reflected, "I am at a loss what to do." Cantrell spoke for many farmers and planters in the Western Confederacy.[58]

CHAPTER FOUR

Eastern Realities

Southern farmers and planters greeted the arrival of 1863 with guarded optimism across the Eastern Confederacy. In mid-January Georgia farmers crowded the streets in Atlanta with their wagons hauling corn, fodder, hogs, peas, potatoes, and turkeys. Tobacco sold at "advanced prices," increasing 10 percent in one week. Corn whiskey brought $15 per gallon. One observer noted that fat hogs and "greasy speculators" both squealed and grunted "*ad libitum*." Eggs brought 75 cents per dozen and hams $1 per pound. Farmers who had commodities to sell received "enormous prices." Everyone wanted Irish potatoes, but the demand exceeded the supply. One local editor urged farmers to "drive up here with your North Carolina wagons loaded with them: you can get *apple* prices and more for 'taters." Milk cows, mules, horses, and beef cattle were in good demand. Only transportation problems caused by muddy roads and inadequate railroad service curtailed large transactions of farm commodities in the city markets. In eastern North Carolina, farmers prepared for the planting season. They, too, anticipated high prices due to scarcity because they could not meet the food needs of the army and the people and because speculators purchased commodities but held them from sale unless they received their asking price. An inflated currency also contributed to escalating agricultural and food prices.[1]

By the winter of 1863, however, the food supply problem became increasingly serious in North Carolina. In February a Raleigh resident reported, "Our market has been very barren for the last few days, and what is offered is held at such prices as to make the contemplation of a perfect torture." Cornmeal brought $4 per bushel, corn-fattened pork sold for 50 cents per pound, and turkeys brought from $5 to $8 per pair. "From sharks, speculators, extortioners, and other vermin and wild beasts," he wrote, "good Lord deliver us." Fresh meat had become a "luxury unknown," and roosters allegedly had stopped crowing in Fredericksburg,

Virginia, because they had been eaten. For the moment hungry southerners primarily blamed the military, which controlled their railroads, but in time they would blame farmers for high prices and inadequate supplies. One Mobile resident expressed a growing sentiment, saying "how in the name of God are the people to support this war. . . . How are the people to pay for the support of the war and its armies when, through stupid official orders, provisions are put at famine prices, and it requires more than all the earnings of the masses of them to buy meat and bread." In Charleston, bakers marked up the bread price to 25 cents for a half-pound loaf. Flour remained in short supply at $65 per barrel, which one resident considered "an enormous sin in the eyes of God."[2]

Southerners had rejected with considerable braggadocio the northern belief that the South could be starved into submission, but by spring 1863 some were less certain about the South's agricultural power. Farmers and planters often had commodities to sell, but depending on their location the market might not be southern. The region no longer had access to farm produce from Kentucky and Missouri, as well as from middle and western Tennessee and northwest Virginia (soon to be the new state of West Virginia). The Tidewater grain regions of Virginia and North Carolina had been lost to the North, which one contemporary believed had diminished the grain crops of southern farmers by one-third. Texas drovers also had increasing difficulty getting their cattle across the Mississippi River, and the Confederate meat supply declined by half. The substitution of grain for cotton by planters and farmers had partially offset these food losses, and grain seemed to be in "abundance" where armies did not fight and march. Although distribution of agricultural commodities remained a problem, large expanses of arable land lay unused and ready for farmers to make it productive. The agricultural potential and power of the South, many contended, only needed the "organization of a judicious and efficient system of distribution." For these southerners, speculators and the railroads had caused the food problems, not a lack of agricultural productivity. Some suggested the government nationalize the railroads to improve the distribution of farm commodities.[3]

In Atlanta prices were "greatly advanced" when the Emancipation Proclamation became operative on January 1. Tough beef brought 20 cents per pound but bacon, one resident reported, "we never see nor hear tell of." The sugar supply fell short of demand, and the price rose to 80 cents per pound for the best quality. Molasses brought $8 per gallon. The demand for wheat at $7 per bushel also exceeded supply and a price increase from $1.60. per bushel a year earlier. Farmers sold corn at $1.90 per bushel, up a dollar in a year, and wholesalers resold it for $2.25. Farmers also sold butter from their wagon beds for 75 cents per pound. Whiskey and peach brandy brought the "fabulous prices" of $15 and $18 per gallon, respectively. Farm prices increased farther north and closer to the Union armies. In early January, consumers paid 50 cents per pound for beef and $1.50 per pound for butter in Charleston. In Richmond corn brought $3.50 per bushel, an increase of 80 cents per bushel in a year. Butter brought $1.50 to $1.60, up from 30 cents per pound a year earlier and bacon sold for 75 cents to 80 cents per pound, an increase from 23 cents per pound in June 1862. The government purchased most of the wheat at $3.40 per bushel which officials hoped would prevent the price from escalating, although millers offered $3.55 per bushel.[4]

Tobacco farmers believed that only the fall of Richmond would prevent prices from advancing for all grades. One tobacco planter reported, "As heretofore, most of the fine shipping tobacco is being bought up by foreign merchants and their agents. If the war continues twelve months longer, foreigners and Jews will have possession of most of the real estate and all of the tobacco in Virginia." The leaf now brought $1.50 per pound. The profitable tobacco crop of 1862 that reached market the following February, however, brought more complaints that farmers should plant neither cotton nor tobacco. In the South man and beast alike needed food crops. The planters and farmers who raised cotton and tobacco increasingly had their patriotism questioned. One Virginian wrote, "The man who raises cotton and tobacco now is not only aiming a blow at the independence of his country, but at what, perhaps, he values more, his own interests. The only enemy we have to fear is the sacrifice of the common good to the individual. One more year of self denial and in all probability the South can return to the cultivation of its popular staples with safety and profit."[5]

Farmers and planters who made the decision to limit their cotton crop continued to express considerable animosity toward those who did not restrict their acreage according to state and socially acceptable standards. In the spring a correspondent of the *Savannah Republican* declared that anyone who planted cotton "deserves to be destroyed, or to have all his plantations and negroes ravaged and desolated, and himself fed upon corn cobs as long as he lives." Many planters in southwestern Georgia disagreed, however, arguing that they had produced an abundant corn crop the previous year at the government's urging, far more than could be transported to market or the army by the railroads. Some farmers already had planted the three acres of cotton allowed by law. Those who had not planted intended to do so, maintaining that it would be "unjust and unconstitutional" and "class legislation" against them if they could not plant cotton. In their own judgment they had produced enough corn, and this year many intended to plant cotton. Yet with some planters selling short-staple cotton for $1.07 per pound and long-staple cotton for $2 per pound in Charleston—crops that once brought only 16 cents to 18 cents per pound—the temptation to plant cotton instead of corn proved hard to resist.[6]

In early April President Jefferson Davis appealed to the patriotism of farmers and planters by urging them to raise food and forage and to "abstain" from planting tobacco and cotton and to provide an immediate supply of meat for the armies. The majority of planters and farmers supported the president's call for change. J. B. Jones, a clerk in the War Department, observed that "we are planting almost every acre in grain, to the exclusion of cotton and tobacco—resolved never to be *starved*, nor even feel a scarcity of provisions in future." The South's agricultural power still seemed sufficient to prevent hunger, certainly starvation, and to help win the war, provided that farmers and planters made immediate adjustments in their planting patterns.[7]

Those who did were wise to do so, because Confederate food needs increased when Union soldiers came again in force, striking for Chancellorsville. However, the Army of the Potomac, now under the leadership of General Joseph Hooker, proved inadequate to the task. After clashing with General Robert E. Lee's Army of Virginia on April 30, he withdrew a week later after losing more than 17,000 men. Despite the death of General Stonewall Jackson, Lee had taken bold risks and driven Hooker from the field. Once again Confederate military power prevailed. Whether Confederate agricultural power could endure remained to be seen.[8]

Although most planters reduced their cotton acreage and planted more corn, public and government officials did not trust them to act in the best interests of the Confederacy. A correspondent to the *London Times* saw the danger because the Confederacy needed food, not cotton or tobacco. He warned that there was "a tendency in the Cotton States to plant a greater breadth of their great staple, as also in Virginia to plant more tobacco than is consistent with the safety of the entire community." Indeed, too many planters and farmers still emphasized cotton, which they sold on local markets for manufacturing or held in reserve for the day when the international and northern markets reopened. The lack of a centralized, authoritative control of agriculture meant that the observance of farm policy remained a matter of state regulation or voluntary goodwill. Loyalty to wallets often came first.[9]

The South Carolina legislature, in the absence of action by the central government, prohibited anyone from planting more than three acres of short-staple and one and a half acres of long-staple cotton during the year for each hand owned or employed by them between the ages of fifteen and fifty-five. Two hands between fifty-five and sixty-five or between twelve and fifteen years of age could count as one hand for cultivating purposes. White, nonslaveholding farmers could plant cotton under the same restrictions. Violators were subject to a $500 fine for each acre planted above the number specified, with payment made to the district Soldiers' Board of Relief. The acreage allotment would be determined by the tax collector based on the number of slaves the planters reported for assessment. Slaveholders faced a $100 fine per slave for inaccurate reporting (this money also went to the Soldiers' Board of Relief).[10]

Governors Joseph E. Brown of Georgia, John G. Shorter of Alabama, and Zebulon B. Vance of North Carolina considered ways to reduce cotton production. Even General Braxton Bragg urged the government to mobilize agriculture on a wartime basis by prohibiting the planting of cotton and tobacco, by requiring planters and farmers to cultivate an allocated acreage for corn and other grains – and by government operation of plantations, essentially nationalizing agricultural production as a war measure. Commissary General L. B. Northrop favored the latter proposal. Congress, however, would only urge farmers and planters to "subordinate the hope of gain to the certain good of the country" by planting food crops rather than cotton and tobacco. It left land-use regulations on acreage and production allotments to the states.[11]

The states, however, responded with recommendations rather than regulations. In April a committee in the Georgia legislature advised farmers that they should not cultivate more than one and a half acres of cotton per hand. Half of the crop could be sold for commercial purposes and half used for home consumption. The committee members recognized the importance of providing cotton as well as provisions because people needed not only food but clothing. They agreed that cotton would enable the Confederacy to "raise the blockade of our ports, and relieve us from this direful war." The legislature, however, voted the bill down because it did not want to impose even this modest regulation on cotton planters. The editor of the *Southern Confederacy* in Atlanta did not believe that Georgia farmers would plant more than one- to three-quarter acres of cotton that spring because "the patriotism of the farmers is equal to their duty in any emergency." He did not believe that any cotton planting restrictions were necessary, and he urged farmers to raise as much cotton as possible after they grew enough food for their families, the public, and the military. He asserted, "Cotton is power. It is yet to be the most efficient weapon in achieving our independence, and the more we have of it the better. Plenty of provisions first – be certain of that; and then all the cotton that can be made. This should be our policy." Wartime production based on voluntarism rather than on efficient, enforceable government agricultural policy continued to weaken the Confederacy.[12]

The editor of the *Richmond Dispatch* urged farmers to plant corn, vegetables, and wheat rather than cotton. Food crops would help ensure independence, while cotton planted with the intent of gaining high profits from northern buyers if the war soon ended would make them the equivalent of Benedict Arnold. Too many planters, he believed, sought gold rather than independence, and the time had come for the government to develop a systematic and efficient food policy.[13]

A Virginian agreed and wrote that he was "pained" to learn that many planters prepared to cultivate tobacco. "We do not need more men in the army," he contended, "but rather the ability to feed them." The Confederacy could only depend on heaven and the "productive earth." The situation was clear. "No other friends have we; none other." Every foot of ground had to be planted because "every grain of the soil is a grain of gold." For him anyone who cultivated cotton and tobacco was a "public enemy" who would starve the defenders of his country. Then, with a call to all farmers and planters, he concluded, "Let us sacrifice selfishness and avarice . . . upon the altar of public good. Let us consecrate the soil to the support of the army and people. Let every man who does not fight, work to feed those who do."[14]

The detractors remained. A Virginia farmer serving the army wrote home telling his wife to raise tobacco. "I had rather had it [tobacco]," he wrote, "than Confederate bonds," because it was worth more than government securities. Another farmer agreed, saying that farmers should "make all the tobacco we can" because it was "bound to sell high." With tobacco prices ranging from $8 to $10 or more per lug, farmers pursued profits and independence, although they usually put their wallets first. Moreover, when quartermasters' agents arrived seeking food, they often left the tobacco alone – a decision that affirmed the value of raising it over food crops.[15]

While farmers and planters debated whether to plant cotton and tobacco, the food situation worsened in Richmond. "All kinds of fresh and cured meat now command in the market prices the like of which never were asked nor paid before," one observer reported. Until mid-February the *Richmond Daily Examiner*, in the words of its editor had stopped quoting market prices of provisions because that notification tended to "enhance them" and "alarm the community." But high prices had become "chronic and stationary," and he saw "no harm in letting the people know what they have to pay for a dinner." Indeed, high food prices had escalated with beef selling for 75 cents, pork for 90 cents, and bacon for $1.10 per pound respectively, or as much as the seller chose to charge, but considerably more since January. Irish potatoes brought $8 and sweet potatoes $10 per bushel, onions sold for $30, and apples for $40 to $50 per barrel, respectively. Other vegetables sold at high prices. Butter brought $1.75 and soon reached $3 per pound. Turkeys brought from $7 to $10 apiece, and chickens $2 each. These food prices had increased the cost of boarding in the city by 500 percent from the previous year. Richmond residents considered these prices "ridiculous," but "stern necessity" obligated consumers to pay them. Residents asked, "What next?" It seemed unimaginable that food prices and scarcity would increase and bring hunger and want to the nation's capital. Outside of Richmond, the price of forage also rose. In Southampton County, General James Longstreet's men foraged for grain and fodder, driving the price for corn to $20 per barrel and fodder to $3.50 per hundredweight. In Mobile, flour reached $73 per barrel in March.[16]

As food prices rose in areas where supply could not meet demand, quality declined rapidly. In Richmond, which was always taxed by the food needs of the Army of Northern Virginia and plagued by insufficient railroad transportation, food quality had reached a "miserable condition." One observer noted, "The beef when not entirely destitute of fat is grisly and jaundiced. The mutton looks like poor venison, red, blue, and stringy. The hogs are diminutive, with very long legs and noses." To make matters worse, he noted, "there is offered for sale a suspiciously large quantity of sausage meat. The less that is said about the probable components of this article of food the better," and he hoped that all of the horses that died about the city did not end up in some form on grocer's shelves and family dinner tables. Virginia farmers desperately wanted to send their produce to the Richmond market to reap high prices, but Confederate impressment officers made their efforts risky, if not impossible.[17]

As a result, one Richmond resident noted that "the truth is, we are in danger of famine amid plenty." The very existence of the nation had been jeopardized by the Commissary Department, he believed. Moreover, the food scarcity drove prices upward. Richmond's prices became the "rule of the country," further contributing to inflation in the Eastern Confederacy. One Alabama resident reminded farmers and planters that "there is a power to sustain your sons and brothers in the field, and it is expected of you. . . . Let the plowshare turn up every fertile yielding acre in your possession and plant therein corn and wheat – these alone." They were the Confederacy's "only salvation," while ensuring an "ample chance for profit." Cotton should only be planted for home consumption.[18]

In Atlanta grocers had taken sugar off the market, holding it until they could command prices above the 90 cents per pound as the Louisiana sugar plantations became increasingly threatened by Union forces. Consumers made a "great demand" for flour, cornmeal, and Irish potatoes, and they paid "advanced prices" for them. The city markets, however, had little of these food commodities. Wheat brought from $7 to $9 per bushel, and rice about the same price. In February near Asheville, North Carolina, a farmer's wife sold turkeys for $1.50 each, which satisfied both seller and buyer. Corn, however, remained scarce in the area and sold at "any price" but at least $2 per bushel.[19]

In early March the editor of the *Richmond Daily Examiner* warned planters not to depend on peace to decide what to plant in the spring. But because Confederate impressment agents usually paid them 50 percent below the market price, many planned to limit corn production to meet only their own needs. Robert Garlick Hill Kean, head of the Confederate Bureau of War, wrote that "the army will be starved and famine will ensue in the cities unless the Secretary changes his policy and buys in the market for the best price." Many people in Richmond needed food with supplies insufficient; with the railroads either unwilling or unable to transport food supplies; with much of the population employed by Confederate and state governments and unable to leave the city; with a large slave population working in the munitions and other war-related industries and hospitals; and with the army nearby. Outsiders formed an "immense population" and a "great city" on their own. Many government officials responsible for supplying the city could not manage the job because of incompetency, while others relied on confiscation "with too over bearing and sweeping a hand." Still, one North Carolina planter's wife contended that the food shortages in Virginia for the army resulted from failed *"management,"* not supply. She charged that the Quartermasters Department failed to "exert themselves" to find it. Her slaves had planted a large crop of Irish potatoes because of Army need and a high price, but she lamented that government buyers in her Halifax County neighborhood paid only $2 per bushel for wheat while civilian buyers paid $5 per bushel elsewhere. The government's low prices and inequity prevailed.[20]

In late March, Josiah Gorgas, chief of Confederate ordinance, reported a "deplorable state of the currency." Gold exchanged at the rate of five to one for Confederate dollars. With approximately $10 in paper now circulating for every $1 before the war, savvy farmers and planters could pay expensive prewar debts with cheap paper money. This increase in the currency supply, however, did not help consumers. As a result, flour reached $30 per barrel in Richmond. Butter brought $3 per pound and eggs $2 per dozen. Turkeys cost $15 each and beef $1.50 per pound. An employee in the War Department complained that his $3,000 salary would go about as far as $700 in 1860 because of these high prices. By October his salary equaled the prewar purchasing power of $300. Flour now reached $100 per 200-pound barrel. Richmond prices, however, did not always dictate farm prices everywhere in the Eastern Confederacy because local conditions affected consumer demand and prices, but they usually set the bar. In April farmers near Asheville, North Carolina, sold bacon for 75 cents per pound, corn for $4 to $6 per bushel – double and triple the price since February – and flour for 25 cents per pound. One farm woman called these prices "dear living to those who have to buy." In Columbia, South Carolina, farmers sold bacon for $1 per pound, and flour for $12.50 per hundredweight. Rice brought $9.25 per hundred pounds in Charleston where the "scarcity of food" led to apprehension. Bacon sold for $1 per pound and flour from $50 to $60 per barrel and soon reached $70 per barrel.[21]

Editors and government officials constantly responded to high agricultural and food prices by urging farmers to plant more corn. If peace came they could ship their surplus grain to European markets. If the war continued, the crop would be needed to make meal and pork. Surplus production would not be a problem. Yet, while loyalty and patriotism remained potent in 1863, farmers always favored profits over other considerations. In North Carolina some farmers refused to sell corn at $1 per bushel even though they could make a profit at that price. But much of the southern wheat crop had failed in 1862, and too many planters were still cultivating cotton. Flour, as a result, had escalated in price "beyond the reach of men of moderate means, and corn commands a price which is almost appalling to those who have not independent fortunes," the editor of the *Southern Cultivator* observed.[22]

To solve the supply and distribution problem, one observer recommended that the Confederate government collect all food commodities at a central location for systematic distribution, including supplies sent to the army. This procedure "would give the higher and more responsible class of officials control of them." Such a policy would not only ensure the provision of adequate food for the civilian population and army but would also lower the cost of living and ease the plight of women and children struggling with food shortages. Jefferson Davis and other Confederate officials did not respond, however, and the food supply and distribution problems continued to plague civilians and soldiers alike. Another Georgian complained about impressments, noting that "everything that man or beast can eat, scarce, enormously high, and will be as long as government agents seize anything. Country people will not bring in their eatables when they are thus abused."[23]

Others continued to urge farmers to plant more corn and less cotton. In mid-March the editor of the *Southern Confederacy* asked, "Every farmer and every body who has a patch of ground, to put his whole force and his whole breadth of land to raising corn, peas, beans, potatoes – anything that will make food for man and beast. Cotton is important, but food far more so. It will pay better than cotton." He reminded farmers that "whoever raises the most corn and meat will make the most money for the high price that can be obtained for cotton, it cannot equal that which corn and meat will bring." Then, he added, "If you love your country plant corn." Yet here was another call for voluntarism, rather than a government-directed agricultural policy that mandated grain production with guaranteed, but controlled, high prices while prohibiting production and penalizing farmers who raised cotton. Many southerners also thought that food problem would be resolved if the government would not conscript so many farmers.[24]

In Richmond an observer attributed food shortages and high prices to three abuses: government impressment of agricultural commodities at prices two-thirds below that paid by citizens; farmers and merchants holding back provisions for still higher prices; and poor transportation, particularly bad road conditions. He rightfully charged that had the government regulated agricultural and food prices and paid those same prices – that is, regulated its own purchases – prices would have been lower and supplies greater. Instead, the government let free-market prices escalate while it paid lower prices for food and forage. This two-price policy created considerable ill-will among consumers.[25]

Some Confederates, such as General Braxton Bragg and Commissary General L. B. Northrop, proposed other solutions. In April, they recommended to Secretary of War James A. Seddon that President Davis prohibit the cultivation of cotton and tobacco, require planters and farmers to plant an allocated acreage in grain and other crops in proportion to their holdings of land and slaves, authorize the government to take control of plantations where fields remained unplanted in grain, and employ slaves to raise such crops "as may be *deemed necessary*." Desperate agricultural and food conditions led to public demands for authoritarian government regulation and control far beyond the ability of the government to enforce or farmers and planters to abide.[26]

Still, spring brought optimism for many farmers. In Georgia the wheat crop near Milledgeville and Macon appeared "promising." Similar reports arrived from Selma, Alabama, where farmers anticipated an abundant harvest if a heavy frost did not damage the crop. Only inadequate railroad transportation "meddled with by the military" kept millions of bushels of corn and thousands of pounds of meat from market, all to the disadvantage of consumers and farmers alike. This problem indicated more than a lack of rolling stock. A military that meddled with railroad transportation meant that the Confederate government did not have organizational control of the lines. Miscommunications between government, railroads, and the army prevented a cohesive policy for transportation of agricultural provisions to civilians and soldiers alike. When wheat reached $7 per bushel on the Richmond market in early May, Virginia farmers anticipated a substantial income from their grain. Realists, however, saw no cause for optimism in the countryside. A Georgian wrote, "Food, particularly meat, is scarce. There is not enough meat in the Confederate States to feed the army and people; and bread is scarcer than many suppose." The Yankee threat to starve the South into submission now became the Confederacy's greatest danger for some southerners.[27]

By April, even the residents of prosperous Macon had begun to complain about the rise in food and agricultural prices and the corresponding inflation of the Confederate currency. As the blockade became increasingly effective, and as armies disrupted farming in various areas, both consumers and the military began to feel the pinch of inadequate food supplies. At the same time, some southerners attributed the increasing food scarcity to government agents who bid against the public for army provisions, which increased the price and decreased the food available on local markets. A report from Selma indicated that a merchant sold fourteen bacon hams for $918.76, which he considered a "big pile of money for these hard times." Then, upon reflection, he added, "Why it is almost the price of number one negro." In Lynchburg, Virginia, a farmer sold a sheep to a city butcher for $130, but the same animal would have brought only $5 or $6 a year earlier. A yoke of ordinary work oxen now commanded $800. One town dweller remarked, "When our country friends talk of the high prices of articles purchased from stores in town, doesn't it sound like the pot calling the kettle black?"[28]

As the capital of the Confederacy, Richmond was a showcase city. If the government could ensure that agricultural commodities could be brought safely into the city and "secured against the selfish designs of idiotic schemes of corrupt or conceited officials," farm provisions would soon flow into the town from every accessible area. The danger was clear, as one resident noted: "If Government induces the producers of grain and meat to bury it in the ground to keep it out of the way of its commissaries, the starvation of the army and subjugation of the country are certain events." Virginia farmers could and would meet the food needs of Richmond if the government stopped seizing grain and other commodities and paying low prices for it. Unless government agricultural and food policy changed, many Virginians believed, starvation and the collapse of the Confederacy seemed certain. The editor of the *Savannah Republican* told farmers and planters that "one grain of corn in the earth is as a bullet in the heart of a Yankee soldier; and a ridge of potatoes is worth any mile of breastwork from Vicksburg to the Rapahannock."[29]

Farmers in the Deep South experienced similar problems. One Georgian argued that Confederate agricultural policy should be founded on free-market principles. If farmers could grow what they pleased and as much as they pleased — and if they could use the railroads to ship their commodities and then could sell them at whatever price they could get — agricultural production would increase and food shortages would disappear. That would happen, however, only when the government bought goods in the marketplace, as individuals did, and paid a reasonable price for the commodity or food needed. As long as the government ignored the Constitution, which prohibited the seizure of property without paying a fair price, food shortages would continue. Moreover, if the government continued to seize crops and slaves for special work projects, farmers and planters could not produce enough grain and livestock to pay their taxes, let alone feed their families and city and military populations. If the government sent agents into the countryside to purchase agricultural commodities at fair market prices, and if farmers and planters delivered those commodities to local warehouses and distribution centers, Confederate agricultural policy would be based on system, order, and fairness. Farmers and planters would make money, the food needs of citizens and soldiers would be met, and the Constitution would be respected. Free-market principles and government organization in the agricultural sector, however, always worked better in theory than in practice, particularly in wartime.[30]

AS THE FOOD SUPPLY FOR Richmond became worse during the winter and early spring, the public criticized city, state, and national governments for their increasingly desperate situation. Ultimately, a group of women — their number was uncertain, but one press report estimated 3,000 were involved — led a looting spree where participants demanded food "at government prices." On April 3, the editor of the *Daily Examiner* wrote that the "so-called riot" on the previous day resulted when "a handful of prostitutes, professional thieves, Irish and Yankee hags, gallows-birds from all lands but our own, congregated in Richmond, with a woman huckster at their head, who buys veal at the toll gate for a hundred and sells the same for two hundred and fifty in the morning market." The editor did not believe that they wanted food but only to injure merchants whose wartime prices had escalated. He noted that "they broke open half a dozen shoe stores, hat stores, and tobacco houses, and robbed them of everything but bread, which was just the thing they wanted least." Instead of shooting "every wretch engaged at once," the authorities arrested them and brought them before a police court for fines.[31]

One Richmond resident admitted, "It cannot be denied that *want of bread* was at this time too fatally true, but the sufferers for food were not to be found in this mob of vicious men and lawless viragoes." Other observers also did not attribute the Richmond riot to hunger. Gorgas, the ordnance chief, wrote that on April 2, "their pretense was bread; but their motive really was license. Few of them have really felt want." He noted that "the President went down amongst them and said a few words to them telling them that the course they were pursuing was the one most likely to bring scarcity of food on the city." He contended that "it was a real women's riot, but as yet there is really little cause for one – there is scarcity, but little want." The Richmond riot, however, was the largest and most important demonstration for food in the South during the war.[32]

Some southerners thought that the Richmond "bread riot," or the "women's riot," had been instigated by emissaries of the Union government. "Plunder, theft, burglary and robbery, were the motives of these gangs; foreigners and Yankees the organizers of them," charged Edmund Ruffin, planter and irreconcilable secessionist. He believed that "the actors were mostly women, prostitutes & low foreigners, set on and encouraged by men of bad charter." Ruffin contended "that not one of these rioters was impelled to their criminal conduct by hunger or destitution." The demonstration that was first seen as a joke, however, soon became no laughing matter, particularly when one female leader demanded "bread or blood" and other participants threatened men and women alike with violence. The South always took care of its poor, some argued. If such a riot occurred again, a Richmond editor urged that it be ended with "immediate death." By blaming northerners for instigating the riot, Richmond leaders downplayed the seriousness of the food shortage in the city.[33]

News of the Richmond bread riot soon spread across Virginia and into the Deep South. Telegrams informed local newspapers that a "terrible" bread riot had occurred, fueled by "a great mob, consisting of three hundred women and between five and ten thousand men" who roamed the city ransacking stores, only to be quelled by force of arms. To the delight of northerners, the *New York Herald* reported that "three Thousand Armed Women attacked Government and Private Stores." The militia was called out to put down the bread riot but refused to go into the streets. Only an appeal and threat of death from President Davis supposedly calmed the "infuriated women" and restored the peace after he ordered a company of soldiers to fire on the demonstrators if they did not disburse. Although many women were subjected to fines and jail sentences for their participation in the riot, an astute Georgian noted that "even when hunger drives women to riot and violence, it is remarkable that they demand 'bread' and not 'peace.'"[34]

Women responded to high food prices not only as consumers but essentially as citizens of a nation that had broken its covenant to protect and care for them. They came not as supplicants but as soldiers' wives demanding their right to food. They had sacrificed sons, husbands, fathers, brothers, friends, and relatives for the cause of independence and the creation of a new nation. They, too, had sacrificed with care and want. As citizens, they demanded their right to food and sustenance unhindered by government and military bureaucracy. Although they did not have legal rights as citizens, they expressed their political views in the streets and gained some incremental improvements in Confederate food and relief policy at the state and national levels. That they had to resort to rioting is another indication of the government's failure to create and enforce an effective food and agricultural policy during the war years.[35]

Critics now believed that agricultural and food prices could be controlled only by government price fixing. With the government allegedly paying only one-third of the market price for farm produce, hoarding and hiding naturally occurred. Soon after the riot a rumor spread in Richmond that the army would confiscate the horses of country people when farmers brought their produce to town. As a result farmers had one more reason to hold on to their provisions, sell their produce locally, or store it rather than risk the loss of their horses.[36]

In hindsight, the Richmond bread riot resulted from numerous factors: the disruption of food production on the farms of northern Virginia; increased population due to refugees flooding into the city; the food needs of the Army of Northern Virginia; inadequate railroad transportation to ship food supplies from other states; a recent snowfall that hindered the movement of food into the city; speculators and farmers who kept provisions off the market while awaiting still higher prices; merchants who would not sell food at the prices that the government paid to farmers; and women who believed the government did not provide for them as soldiers' wives. The Richmond riot was not spontaneous but planned. Yet the city did not experience another bread riot until April 1865, because city officials improved the welfare system by enacting an ordinance for "the Relief of Poor Persons not in the Poor House" to enable them to acquire adequate food for free or reduced prices. An unintended consequence of the Richmond bread riot was that the city council appropriated $20,000 to establish free-food depots and appointed a committee to oversee the feeding of the deserving poor in each ward. The army also helped maintain law and order, in part, by placing cannon at major street intersections to intimidate the population.[37]

The riot was also important because it reflected a fundamental public response to the failure of government. The food riot, if it indicated anything, was a political response by an aggrieved public, primarily poor soldiers' wives. The bread riot in Richmond had political meaning. They were the public and political demands of Confederate women who demanded that government meet their basic needs as part of the social contract. They had experienced hunger, want, and separation from their husbands and family members, and they demanded protection and assistance from a government that claimed to represent them.

The Richmond women did not act alone. Others wanted state intervention to set and regulate food and agricultural prices. Demonstrations had occurred previously in Greenville, Alabama, in December 1862; in Bladenboro, North Carolina, in February 1863; in Atlanta, Salisbury, North Carolina, and Mobile, Alabama, in March; and in Petersburg, Virginia, in April. From February to late April 1863, women successfully used mob and organized violence to compel government action and satisfy immediate needs. They expressed the mass politics of direct action.[38]

In North Carolina, six weeks before food riots broke out in Salisbury, a group of women in Bladen County informed Governor Vance that they wanted corn at no more than $2 per bushel, and they would seize it whenever anyone charged more. They stated that "the time has come that we the common people has to hav [sic] bread or blood and we are bound boath [sic] men and women to hav it or die in the attempt." Much like the Regulators in 1760s North Carolina, they would force the government to do what it had been unable or unwilling to do—that is, meet their needs as citizens of the state and the Confederacy. And they would use violence if politicians failed to meet their needs. They also would take what they needed from merchants and planters (a vocal minority of women would, that is).[39]

By March food had become scare in some areas of North Carolina, with farm women and the elderly struggling to maintain adequate production. As hungry city people became more desperate, they began to take matters into their own hands, such as when a group of women who called themselves "Soldiers' Wives" marched into downtown Salisbury and demanded food from local merchants at government prices. Upon refusal, one woman reported that they forced their way in and "compelled them to give us something." They took from the merchants and a local Confederate depot and "succeeded in obtaining twenty three bbls of flour two sacks of salt and a half a bll of molasses and twenty dollars in money, which was equally divided among us." Residents supported this "female raid" against speculators who charged high prices for food.[40]

On April 8, a similar confrontation occurred in Greensboro, North Carolina. Governor Vance attempted to reason with the crowd by saying that "broken laws will give you no bread, but much sorrow; when forcible seizures have to be made to avert starvation, let it be done by your county or state agents." Two days later Governor Brown in Georgia received a report that a "lawless mob" was pillaging stores in Milledgeville, and neither the merchants nor city authorities could restore order. Brown responded by sending the Thirty-Third Regiment of the Georgia militia to the town to serve as a *posse comitatus*. Under the orders of the mayor, the militia was to suppress the rioting, recover the stolen property and restore it to its rightful owners, and arrest all women and men involved in the disturbance.[41]

In early April a group of women stole food at gunpoint in Clarke County, Alabama, where some, who had been eating cornbread for days, entered a store and asked the price of bacon. When the merchant replied that it cost $1.10 per pound, an argument ensued and the leader drew "a long navy repeater, and at the same time ordered the crowd to help themselves to what they liked, which they did accordingly, giving preference to the bacon, until they had taken . . . something like $200 worth." Norfolk, Virginia, also suffered a food shortage by late April, when some 700 families totaling approximately 3,000 people needed assistance, according to the *Baltimore Gazette*. Charitable groups working through the army sent 40 hogsheads of bacon, 150 barrels of flour, and gallons of molasses to the city merchants for distribution by a method that remains uncertain.[42]

With the Davis administration struggling to feed the army, the government now took one-tenth of all agricultural production and increased the draft age to forty-five. These harsher steps, as a result, took more men from the farms and worsened the plight of the civilian population, especially in areas threatened by Union forces. Hungry and aggrieved people are seldom silent and passive. The food riots were nothing less than raw, direct-action politics.[43]

In Atlanta, private citizens and city officials set up a relief fund for the poor. In Mobile the city council established the Citizens Relief Committee to secure food and sell it at reasonable prices to the needy and to even establish a free market for the poor. In Georgia the state legislature appropriated $2.5 million for food distribution to the destitute. It would increase that funding in the years ahead. Georgia and other states now transferred welfare responsibilities to the state legislature from the counties, but the Richmond government would not be part of it. Although the Confederate Congress and Davis called for farmers to plant food crops rather than cotton, military conditions often prevented them from expanding production and getting their food crops to market. In the end, however, the food riots brought only incremental change. In Richmond food prices remained high and provisions scarce, and the public, particularly those in need of assistance, disgruntled. The only people able to meet their food needs were farmers far removed from Union and Confederate armies and government impressment agents.[44]

Yet despite the food riots and relief efforts, many optimists throughout the Eastern Confederacy remained convinced that the North could never starve the South into submission; the South, one said, would win "by knife and fork what it cannot do with the sword!" Yet, these bread riots indicated that the agricultural power of the South had many weaknesses born of poor organization, nonexistent or insufficient restrictive policies, and inadequate coordination between military and civil authorities at a time when Union soldiers increasingly menaced farmers in northern Virginia. These problems would remain for the duration of the war.[45]

THE GOVERNMENT'S INABILITY to raise sufficient operating money from its tax policy and its produce loan program, along with rampant inflation, made the procurement of supplies difficult for the army. In addition, the unanticipated food shortages for the army during the winter of 1862–63 became severe. On April 24 Congress attempted to deal with its inability to resolve the army food shortages by passing a Tax-in-Kind Act (also called the tithe tax), and by so doing finally take some institutional responsibility for crafting agricultural policy. This legislation authorized a tax-in-kind to help the Subsistence Department acquire sufficient food and forage for the soldiers. This tax enabled farmers and planters to pay in food and forage rather than money. It would not be affected by inflation, speculation, impressment, or hoarding because each farmer would contribute his assessed tax from his subsistence stores. The law provided that at market time for each crop, the tax assessor would estimate the quantity of the commodities that the farmer owed the government. If a farmer disagreed with the assessment, local appraisers would determine the amount owed. Essentially, the act provided for an 8 percent tax on all agricultural products raised in 1862 that remained on a farm on July 1, 1863. It also levied a 10 percent tax-in-kind on all products raised in 1863. Each farmer would reserve sufficient food for his family, then provide one-tenth of his taxable field crops and one-tenth of his slaughtered hogs as bacon, all of which he would then transport to a government depot if one was within eight miles of his farm. The government would pay for the transportation of the tithed crops to depots situated at longer distances from his home and provide grain sacks and barrels for molasses. Farmers who did not deliver their tithe within two months of the appraisal would be subject to a 50 percent fine and to forced collection of the commodity in question.[46]

Section II of the act permitted farmers and planters to defer payment on the first 50 bushels of sweet and Irish potatoes, 100 bushels of corn, 50 bushels of wheat, and 20 bushels of peas or beans produced. Although this reserve supply of provisions was exempt, they had to pay a 10 percent tax-in-kind on all produce thereafter, such as corn, wheat, oats, Irish potatoes, sugar, and rice as well as hay, fodder, and cattle. The tax-in-kind also included cotton and tobacco. The tithed cotton had to be "ginned and packed in some secure manner," and the tobacco had to be "stripped and packed in boxes." The same delivery and penalty provisions of the act applied to cotton and tobacco planters. Produce loan agents took control of the cotton paid as the tax-in-kind and stored it in a safe, secure warehouse in a nearby town, on a plantation, or at a railroad depot where they weighed, marked, and tallied the bales. The tax-in-kind absolved farmers and planters of paying the progressive income tax of 1 percent to 15 percent of their net income from the land. However, they still had to pay income tax on the profits from the sale of beef cattle as well as a 1 percent property tax on the value of all cattle, horses, and mules not used for cultivation. Secretary of the Treasury Christopher G. Memminger and members of Congress believed the tax-in-kind would yield $130 million, or about one-third of the war expenditures, and would meet the food needs of the army while reducing government expenses.[47]

The War Department had overall responsibility for administering the tax-in-kind except for cotton, tobacco, and wool. Those three products were the responsibility of the Treasury Department, which intended to hold them for sale or export. Treasury agents also were responsible for visiting farms and plantations and determining the quality, quantity, and value of the commodities produced. They were to send tally lists to designated post quartermasters in each state. Post quartermasters then appointed agents to receive the provisions – that is, the tithe – at various collection depots and notified the farmer to deliver the produce. From there, the produce would be sent to issuing depots for distribution. Quartermaster agents often used slaves to load wagons with fodder and hay, while commissary agents employed whites to drive cattle to designated shipping points. In some cases farmers and planters could pay the tax in cash if conditions proved "impractical" and prevented them from hauling their commodities to a depot. Treasury Secretary Memminger hoped the tax-in-kind would reduce agricultural and food prices and decrease the need for the impressment of provisions for the army.[48]

Farmers and planters objected to the tax-in-kind, arguing that it prevented them from profitably marketing a considerable portion of their crops, and they called it "tyrannical," "unconstitutional," and "antirepublicanism." They contended that the tax permitted government agents to enter households, farms, and plantations to confront farmers, often women now home alone, about what they owed in the form of corn, cattle, bacon, and other provisions. They resented government regulation to the core. For most farmers and planters, the Confederacy had now become an intrusive state. Only surplus provisions were subject to collection, but government agents took as they pleased, which particularly hurt small-scale farmers. One North Carolina farmer called tax-in-kind agents "as grate enemys as the yankies."[49]

In North Carolina a group of farmers met in protest and labeled the tax "oppressive and a relic of barbarism, which alone [was] practiced in the worst despotisms." Basically, farmers and planters objected to the tax because they had to pay in high-valued crops rather than in low-valued Confederate currency. Essentially, the tax-in-kind was a sign that the Confederate government had retrogressed to a barter economy. In the end, the tax-in-kind increased food prices because it took more commodities off the market for the public, and consumers had more unspent money to buy food from merchants and farmers, which drove up inflation. The agricultural press also argued that farmers paid more taxes than anyone else, and that a direct tax on their profits would be more equitable. Farmers preferred to pay the tax-in-kind after they sold their products, that is, a tax on their profits. Many farmers and planters avoided paying that tax-in-kind, and the government could not create the bureaucracy in wartime to make it effective. Farmers and planters who lived near a railroad or army post soon learned that the tax assessors visited them most often because collection from them was easier than from those who lived in more isolated areas, particularly where poor roads prevailed. When government agents arrived on a farmer's premises, their attempts to collect the tax created even more animosity against the government. The tax-in-kind, however, gave the government the ability to collect agricultural commodities to redistribute as food to needy soldiers' wives, widows, and families.[50]

Southern farmers and planters wanted high prices and profits without government interference in their activities. They wanted to provide food and forage for the public and military but only from free-market sales, not by impressments at below market prices or by taxes of any kind. They knew that corn and meat would earn the most money and that the public and military needed large quantities of both commodities. They also understood that the future of the Confederacy depended on each farmer planting every "patch of ground." The editor of the *Southern Confederacy* agreed and urged, "If you love your country, plant corn. If you want to make money, plant corn and raise what pork you can." Cotton could wait for peace and independence. Rumors from Albany, Georgia, that 100,000 bushels of corn moldered in government storage facilities, the product of mismanagement and inadequate railroad transportation, raised further questions about the government's ability to acquire, store, and use agricultural provisions.[51]

Southerners did not doubt that their land and climate was well suited for diverse agriculture and that under normal circumstances, even allowing for drought, famine would not be a possibility. But the time was not normal. A large portion of Virginia had been ravaged by both northern and southern armies. Food was scarce, and many people were relegated to purchasing each day's food at a morning market. The Confederate government had worsened the problem by supplying the armies in Virginia from local supplies and impressing provisions and forage when they could not be acquired on the open market. Moreover, it shipped agricultural commodities produced in northern Virginia to other areas in the state, where contractors controlled the supplies and the profits. Still, famine and starvation had thus far been avoided due to the natural bounty of the land, the labor of its people (black and white) — and despite "the action of the most stupid commissariat that ever existed, operating during the most stupendous of all the wars ever known." In early May, peas reportedly sold for $5 per quart, equal to $160 per bushel in Lynchburg, Virginia, and a Savannah, Georgia, editor wrote that southerners had less to fear from northern generals than "general starvation." With a flourish of his pen equal to his alarm, he declared that "our farmers, every man, woman, and child that can wield a hoe can meet the latter in the field. If they can drive him from our midst, our brave soldiers will vanquish the others."[52]

Yet many farms in Virginia went unplowed and unplanted because thousands of slaves fled to Union lines or their masters took them farther south to prevent them from running away. Portions of the other slave states suffered a similar labor problem. A short crop following the partial failure of cereal crops the previous year, along with a scarcity of railroad transportation for the distribution of meat, grain, and forage, meant starvation by autumn in the minds of some. A northerner observed that with "the army every day eating away the insufficient supplies on hand, the prospect must indeed be one of terror." Still, optimists anticipated a good wheat crop, which, in June, looked "very fine" in Georgia. The governor of Alabama, however, saw the agriculture and food problems differently due to the Emancipation Proclamation alleging that "the enemy has called to his aid the terrible appliances of want and starvation, and is carrying out this savage and inhumane policy by the wholesale larceny of slaves, the seizure of provisions, and the destruction of agricultural implements."[53]

BY EARLY SUMMER OF 1863, many southerners still remained confident that they could not be starved into submission, and farmers continued to enjoy high prices. In Georgia's Etowah County, the previous corn crop sold for $2 per bushel, and "plenty" of it remained in storage. Near Eutaw, Alabama, reports indicated that the wheat crop was "maturing splendidly," that great quantities of potatoes, peanuts, and peas had been planted, and that the corn crop promised the best harvest in years, all of which the *Mobile Register* said proved the "humbug of scarcity." The Mobile editor proclaimed, "We have plenty to eat, and Heaven smiles upon us in the rich promise of abundant harvests." But in June beef sold for $1 and bacon $1.65 per pound respectively in Richmond. Common or "family" flour brought as much as $37 per barrel, cornmeal $12 per bushel, and pork $1.50 and butter $3 per pound respectively; chickens sold for $2.50 each, and eggs $1.50 per dozen. Sugar brought $1.60 per pound due to the capture of many plantations in Louisiana. Soon, watermelons from North Carolina reached the Richmond market and sold for $6 to $8 each primarily to speculators who intended a high markup at the grocery stores. Few vegetables reached the city market, in part, because drought stunted their growth, and one resident reported that "a single cabbage, merely the leaves, no head, sells for a dollar, and this suffices not for a dinner for my family." Oats brought $6, wheat $7, and corn $10 per bushel from the 1862 harvest, but almost everyone anticipated large crops in the coming weeks and months. Hay brought $12 per hundredweight and good summer rains and sunshine would enable multiple cuttings of grass for hay. The tobacco market in Richmond and Lynchburg, Virginia, remained lackluster, and prices ranged from $12 to $20 per lug depending on the quality of the leaf in storage from the previous autumn harvest, but the tobacco available appeared ample to meet all needs until the next crop reached market in the late fall. Optimism and uncertainty, then, prevailed for farmers and consumers alike as they entered the summer of 1863. Inadequate supply kept agricultural and food prices high. In early July the editor of the *Richmond Daily Examiner* wrote that "the second siege of Richmond may now be considered raised and lucrative prices await the dealers in meats and vegetables, and all kinds of produce from the country."[54]

His optimism proved unwarranted. In June, Lee launched a second invasion of the North, which culminated with the battle of Gettysburg fought between July 1 and July 3. Blocked by the Army of the Potomac under General George G. Meade, Lee withdrew after hard fighting and considerable loss of life on both sides. His defeat did not bode well for the Confederacy. It indicated that the North could not be defeated militarily. The war would go on, and farmers and planters, like Lee's soldiers, would have even greater demands placed on them.[55]

In late July an Alabama planter wrote, "The wheat crop is yielding finely and is much in demand at five and six dollars per bushel. Flour is sixty dollers a barrel. The currency is so expanded by large issues that a great depreciation has taken place. Gold is worth ten to one, every article is bringing enormous prices, some things from scarcity is beyond reason, horses from five hundred to one thousand. Cows and calves one fifty to two hundred. I paid about five hundred dollers for one barrel of sugar ... the whole usually cost about twenty-five dollars." Near Asheville, North Carolina, farmers got $6.50 per bushel of wheat and $25 per hundredweight for flour.[56]

By August flour sold for $45 per barrel in Richmond. But few farmers brought wheat flour to the Richmond market because, as one observer said, they "do not care to add to their ample stocks of Confederate Treasury notes." Some farmers thought that the Confederacy would "go down" during the winter. If it did, they would have large supplies of wheat and flour for Yankee buyers, who would pay with sound money. Soon rice reached 25 cents per pound, bacon brought $2.10 per pound, corn and cornmeal sold for $9 per bushel, and potatoes brought $6 per bushel. Millers paid a slightly lower price of $5 per bushel for wheat due to the arrival of newly harvested grain, although speculators paid farmers $6.50 per bushel and took the risk of impressment at lower prices. Low prices also prevailed for farmers when commissary agents impressed their produce. In South Carolina commissary officers seized beef at 25 cents per pound, bacon at 75 cents per pound, corn and oats at $2 per bushel, flour at $20 per barrel, pork at 35 cents per pound, hay at $1.50 per hundredweight, potatoes at $3 per bushel, and wheat at $3.50 per bushel. One South Carolina distillery bought peaches for $3 per bushel, which had cost only 40 cents per bushel in 1862, but it sold brandy for $25 to $30 per gallon. Farmers with fruit to sell could make money. In September peaches brought $6 per dozen from the wagon beds of farmers in Richmond, whereas before the war they sold for 5 cents each. Officials in the War Department were heartened by reports from Georgia that farmers would produce sufficient grain that would lower prices and provision the army and cavalry for the next twelve months. By late October, however, wheat brought $8 per bushel in some areas, while farmers received $10 per bushel for rye.[57]

By early August, farmers near Richmond were loudly complaining about Confederate soldiers stationed along the Mechanicsville Pike who robbed them of their produce as they made their way to market. Richmond residents feared that farmers would stop coming into the city and their food shortages would become worse. These farmers had already stopped hauling their wheat to market in anticipation of higher prices and because they feared seizure of their wagons on the roads by commissary officers. Speculators in the capital who had access to railroad transportation purchased hundreds of barrels of wheat for storage until "famine prices" ensured a high profit. One contemporary recommended sending speculators to the front lines, where they could be shot and bayoneted by the Yankees who they were assisting. Some critics urged the government to seize all barrels of flour in the possession of speculators to prevent them from hoarding it in warehouses. As a result, the demand for flour and ultimately bread exceeded the supply. Virginians believed that these food and agricultural problems would become worse.[58]

They were correct. By mid-August the prospects for a bountiful harvest had become less certain, at least in Henrico County, Virginia. There, farmers complained that "marauding soldiers" from the Confederate army had trampled, wasted, and destroyed thousands of dollars' worth of corn, fruit, and vegetables. These farmers primarily supplied the Richmond market. The Henrico farmers petitioned the secretary of war to provide military protection for their farms "from depredations from domestic invasion," but to no avail. Virginia wheat farmers also exchanged five bushels of wheat for one barrel of flour with the millers. The government paid them $25 per barrel, but they could sell it on the open market for $40 to $60 per barrel. Scarcity and the open market price for flour compelled at least one Richmond baker to close. Consumers and farmers alike now preferred exchange in-kind rather than sales for Confederate currency. One observer noted that if farmers sold their wheat for $5 per bushel, millers could supply the market with flour at $25 per barrel and all would be well, but if they held their crop for higher prices and the weevils or Yankees ruined or carried away the crop, flour prices would become "unprecedented" and "universal suffering" would prevail, including for farmers.[59]

In Richmond the demand grew for the state or central government to fix the price of meat and groceries in city markets. Government food prices would end extortion, many claimed. Only government regulation of food prices would save the citizenry from "much suffering and want" during the coming winter. With food on the Richmond market "alarmingly limited," and with farmers and merchants withholding provisions to drive prices still higher, bad days lay ahead. Some Richmond residents wanted the legislature to regulate food prices, but others argued that such regulation would prevent farmers from selling their provisions if they could not receive all the market would bear, and consumers would suffer even more. Farmers complained that butchers paid low prices for their cattle but gouged consumers for beef. Consumers also had begun to realize that suffering for want of food did not contribute to the war effort.[60]

BY JANUARY THE BEEF supply for the Army of Northern Virginia consisted of a few hundred scrawny cattle, which General Lee did not consider worth slaughtering unless they could be fattened for several months. Government purchasing agents also found livestock raisers increasingly reluctant to sell their cattle. In March, one Confederate officer reported from Oxford, Alabama, that he had found a considerable quantity of bacon in the vicinity, "some in the hands of speculators and some in the hands of wealthy planters, who like the speculators, are holding it up for prices much above the maximum established by the Secretary of War." He believed that if he received authorization to impress the needed meat that he could "secure many thousand pounds" of bacon in the area. He also had purchased 60 "good beef cattle" from nearby farmers, and he intended to drive 80 to 100 head to the army near Chattanooga. Moreover, he anticipated purchasing 100 to 400 head before the "grass beef" reached the market, meaning that he had acquired corn-fed cattle. In Georgia, however, the Commissary Department had difficulty acquiring beef cattle because the Army of Northern Virginia had taken most of the railroad cars to move troops and supplies. While farmers in southwest Georgia had "a good many beeves," they could not sell them to the army because delivery or shipment proved impossible. In Florida, farmers had an "abundance of cattle," but they were "indisposed" to sell them for Confederate currency. As a result, the prospect of feeding the Army of Tennessee seemed "quite gloomy."[61]

After Vicksburg fell on July 4, Union forces effectively prevented most of the Texas cattle from crossing the Mississippi. Texas cattle now remained essentially confined to grasslands west of the river. The army, then, also lost direct contact with Arkansas and western Louisiana, and Florida became the largest supplier of beef for the Eastern Confederacy. Joseph D. Locke, chief commissary officer in Georgia, estimated that Florida livestock raisers would need to ship at least 1,000 head of cattle per week to meet the beef needs of General Bragg's men at Charleston and those of General P. G. T. Beauregard in Tennessee. But Florida cattle raisers could not or would not meet that need, and in July soldiers in Lee's Army of Northern Virginia had their beef ration reduced to one-quarter pound per day, unless marching, which meant a half-pound ration. By August, the Commissary of Subsistence in Mobile had only thirty-four days of food, including bacon, salt pork, and beef for 20,000 men. Farmers in Georgia and South Carolina could not help because they had few cattle for sale. By December Lee had but a three-day supply of beef.[62]

In February Lee also experienced difficulty procuring adequate feed and forage for his cavalry and draft horses as well as replacing them when they wore out or died. Heavy draft horses for the artillery were particularly hard to find, because farmers usually did not willingly sell them or the army had already taken them. In April Lee wrote to General William N. Pendleton, his chief of artillery, saying, "The destruction of horses in the army is so great that I fear it will be impossible to supply our wants. There are not enough in the country." In mid-April Edmund Ruffin noted in his diary that in Richmond hay cost $25 per hundredweight. He added, "It seems to me that our country & cause are now, for the first time during the war, in great peril of defeat – & not from the enemy's arms, but from scarcity & high prices of provisions, & the impossibility of the government feeding the horses of the army, which is even much more difficult than to feed & support the men." Without corn and hay, "as might be expected, the horses are reduced very low in flesh & strength, & many are dying, & more failing entirely." The cavalry, artillery, and wagon teams could not perform even moderate service without feed and forage. Ruffin lamented that southern farmers had never raised many horses and mules and preferred to buy them from the western states. Overwork, battle, and disease, particularly glanders, had killed many, and now it was too late to breed and raise more for immediate needs. As a result, Lee and other army commanders never had enough horses and mules. "This alone," Ruffin observed, "is a very serious subject for gloomy anticipations."[63]

Diseased horses continued to hamper the army. Like diseases that plagued soldiers and took more lives than battle, microorganisms probably felled more horses and mules than shot and shell. The physical environment of heat, rain, mud, and cold as well as insufficient food helped wear out men and beast alike, but disease also proved a lurking enemy that arrived unseen. It brought sickness, incapacitation, and death, which, together with losses from battle, placed great demands on Confederate farmers for resupply.[64]

After Gettysburg Lee's horses were weak and worn out. With the corn crop not ready for harvest in Northern Virginia, and the railroads unable to deliver grain and forage from the South, Lee could provide only about one pound of corn per day per horse. While the general struggled to acquire and feed his horses, he created four "inspection districts" or "horse infirmaries" where artillery horses could be kept to supply the cavalry and wagon service. The first station operated by the Quartermaster Department began service in the fall of 1863. By December, however, glanders — an infectious disease that primarily afflicts horses — had become epidemic and soon spread across the inspection districts. Only slaughter of diseased animals would prevent glanders from spreading, but Lee needed all the horses that he could get, and he had little choice but to hope for the recovery of the sickened animals during a mounting death toll. Southern farmers could not make up those losses, and this further harmed Lee's ability to fend off the enemy. Virginia farmers also saw their horses become infected with glanders because the Confederate quartermaster contracted with local farmers to graze army horses and mules. As forage became nearly depleted, the Quartermaster Department for the Army of Northern Virginia sent its horses farther into the interior for rest and recuperation. This decision, however, spread the disease. Impressment agents often seized these horses for return to the army, while the horses of the farmers became diseased and often died before they could be sold or used for agricultural work.[65]

By early August Lee's army needed 1,000 bushels of grain per day for its artillery, cavalry, and wagon horses. Lee complained to President Davis that "some days we get a pound of corn per horse, and some days, none, some time our limit is 5 lbs. per day per horse." Receiving only three or four pounds of corn per day, artillery horses were not strong enough to perform heavy duty. In contrast, Union horses received ten pounds of grain per day. Virginia farmers could not provide the necessary corn, and the government bought corn in Georgia, Alabama, and South Carolina and transported it north to feed Lee's horses and mules. Yet the Confederate armies never had a sufficient number of horses, and as cavalry mounts wore out or died, they could not be replaced. Other armies across the Confederacy suffered similar shortages. A soldier in Georgia reported that few good horses could be found on the farms. One North Carolina farmer sold a "small horse" for $450, which his wife considered a "big price." By late autumn Union raids had taken a toll as well.[66]

In November a Union expedition left Limestone and Madison counties in Alabama "scoured and swept clean of horses and mules, cattle, sheep, poultry, hogs, meat and flour." When the soldiers departed they took 2,000 to 3,000 horses and mules for nearly all of the working stock, and "thoroughly stripped" the farms and plantations. This raid was the twenty-first of the year. These farmers were discouraged, because frequent Union raids had taken not only an economic but also a psychological toll. One observer wrote, "This time all has been swept off and our people feel as if it is useless to try to fix up again, even with old wagons, broken down mules and horses, as all may soon be taken by another raid. We have not enough now to haul and plough with. . . . Milch cows are worth as much or more valued than negroes." In Virginia farmers had a particularly hard time keeping their horses because Confederate soldiers took them unless they could be securely hidden, and some farmers now used oxen for plowing because of the equine shortage.[67]

IN NORTHERN VIRGINIA where Union cavalry ranged, farmers bombarded the Confederate War Department with complaints that they were doubly injured by the Federals taking their horses for fresh mounts and leaving their worn-down horses in exchange – and then have Confederate cavalry confiscate those horses, leaving the farmers without draft power for cultivating their crops. Confederate forces also impressed barrels of flour from nearby markets, further hurting farmers. Farmers complained "bitterly" that they were "about as harshly used, in this war, by one side as the other." In mid-March, John M. Daniel, editor of the *Richmond Daily Examiner*, contended that no issue concerned farmers and planters more than the impressment of their produce and livestock by the Commissary and Quartermaster departments. He warned that "if this business is not regulated on some satisfactory basis, the food of the country will be diminished in all the grain producing portions of the Confederacy by one-third." Too many farmers and planters hoarded and hid food. If Congress and the president did not provide a systematic and fair regulation of impressment with a "just compensation" and a commission to fix prices, he believed, "more cotton and tobacco [would] be cultivated in the South than was ever known before," because the government did not impress these commodities. Without regulation of impressment, farmers and planters would raise only enough food and forage crops to meet their own needs while they produced more cotton and tobacco to store until the war ended.[68]

Farmers across the Eastern Confederacy had similar complaints. In February corn reached $3.00 per bushel in Cherokee County, Georgia, but little reached the market because farmers did not want to risk impressment by commissary officers. As a result, families in the cities and towns experienced hunger, which prompted Governor Joseph Brown to write President Davis that "if this continues the rebellion in that section will grow, and the soldiers in service will desert to go to the relief of their suffering families." He urged the army to purchase corn in southwestern Georgia, where supplies remained abundant, rather than to impress it from farmers who had little or where the threat if impressment kept the grain from market.[69]

Farmer and planter complaints about the impressment process forced the Confederate Congress to clarify the circumstances that permitted the seizure of farm commodities. In March Congress attempted to rationalize or at least regulate the impressments of agricultural goods by approving "An Act to Regulate Impressments." This legislation allowed impressment officers to seize food and fodder. If the farmer and the impressing officer could not agree on the price or value of the commodity taken, two individuals, one selected by the farmer and the other by the impressing officer, would decide the payment. If they could not agree on the price they were to select a third person who would take an oath to appraise the property fairly, and his judgment would be final. The impressing officer also had to provide a document that specified the battalion, regiment, brigade, division, or corps to which he belonged and to certify that the commodities impressed were essential for the army, that it could not be otherwise procured, and that he had taken it only because of absolute necessity. And he had to record the time, place, and amount of provisions taken and the amount of compensation due, which theoretically would be paid quickly.[70]

This impressment legislation provided an alternative procedure. It authorized the president and the governor of each state to appoint two appraisers who would determine the prices for all agricultural commodities. These prices would be published bimonthly. If the board commissioners could not agree on a price for the schedule, they were to choose a third commissioner to decide the issue. Farmers could now look at the published price schedule and know precisely what the impressment officer had to pay. This pricing policy gave system and order to the process of acquiring agricultural products from farmers and planters by providing a recommended guide for all purchasing or impressments, and it indicated a reluctant but important realization that the war effort mandated Confederate regulation and control over the agricultural economy. Still, farmers complained that the schedule prices were too low and did not account for local conditions, and that they could make more money on the private, that is, commercial, market. In February government agents, for example, offered 35 cents per pound for pork but farmers in Florida demanded more than a dollar.[71]

By July the impressment price of corn averaged 70 percent less than the market price. The legislation authorizing the government price schedule had the potential to solve impressment and pricing problems because it provided for arbitration at the local level, or for published prices adjusted every two months. Nevertheless, army foraging parties operated on the premise that need superseded the formalities of law. As a result, some southerners close to Union lines preferred to sell their grain and livestock to Federal forces to avoid impressment at low prices paid in worthless Confederate currency.[72]

In May farmers in Jefferson County, Georgia, remained so unhappy with the low prices paid by impressment officers that they met in Louisville to set the prices that they would accept from the army. With more hope than certainty, they set their prices at 50 cents per pound for bacon, $1.50 per bushel for corn, $3 per bushel for wheat, $8 per bushel per hundred pounds of flour, $1 per bushel of oats, and $1.50 per gallon for sorghum molasses. The quartermaster at Augusta apparently ignored their price demands, because those commodities were not in his jurisdiction. In August, the impressment price per barrel of flour reached $20, but the market price ranged between $27 and $45 depending on the area. The Confederate agricultural price schedule for impressment of farm commodities was a form of price control that did not function smoothly and only with considerable farmer and planter complaint.[73]

As food prices escalated, the public continued to blame farmers for hoarding produce to drive food prices still higher. One South Carolinian confided in his diary, "Shame on farmers who are now asking four and five dollars per bushel of corn & seven and eight dollars for wheat!"

Agriculturists argued that their costs had risen exorbitantly and that they charged fair prices, but this contention fell on deaf ears unless they blamed speculators for hoarding food and charging high prices, or the Commissary Department for its impressment policy. In reality, high food prices resulted from an inflated currency, inadequate transportation, and insufficient agricultural production in some areas.[74]

By the end of 1863, the editor of the *Southern Cultivator* noted, the impressments of provisions by Commissary Department officers seemed to have become "settled policy, if not for the government itself, at least, for its minor officials." The requisition of food and forage proved easier and cheaper than the purchase of those commodities from farmers on the open market. As a result, one contemporary observed that "the farmers near the army lines find themselves without horses, neat stock, or provisions to nourish their hands and their little ones." Yet with the Confederate currency "worthless," farmers were reluctant to accept it. Consequently, commissary agents either took the provisions and provided a receipt or paid about half the value of the agricultural commodities taken. Either way, southern farmers essentially conceded their crops, animals, meat, and forage to the army without adequate remuneration. In December, a Florida farmer complained that "the abuse of the act of impressment is causing the people to regard their own government as its enemy." Legalities aside, the army had to be fed, and only farmers and planters could provide food and forage. Essentially, the law further legitimized impressment while attempting to make it fair and systematic. Although it failed to meet the needs of the army for food, farmers and planters generally abided by the law, even while they complained bitterly about it.[75]

By the spring southern farmers and planters could not ignore impressment of their crops and livestock, but they also could not ignore that considerable agricultural land had been lost and its production no longer available for the Confederacy. Moreover, where the Confederate and Union armies had gone, their farms and plantations had been decimated and would remain unproductive for the remainder of the war. "Here is to be found the weakest point in our defenses," wrote one southerner. In April, a foraging expedition led by a contingent of Joseph Hooker's army entered Virginia's Northern Neck and took 300 pounds of bacon, 1,000 pounds of pork, 230 bushels of wheat, 3,000 bushels of corn, a substantial quantity of oats, and a large number of horses and mules from area farmers. A Confederate soldier near Fredericksburg, Virginia, noted similar damage to farmers when he wrote, "It be gins [sic] to look like Spring, but I dont think the Farmers can do much on their farms here for their fenses are all burnt and the timber is all burnt til they can get nothing to fense their farms with[.] You have no idea how the Army weads out things where they go." For him, the agricultural power of the South was slipping away. One Georgian believed that the only difference between Confederate and Union soldiers who plundered farms was that the Yankees burnt their houses after they took what they wanted.[76]

In the spring one Union officer reported that during a three-week raid in northern Alabama, his men had destroyed or carried off 1.5 million bushels of corn, 500,000 pounds of bacon, and large quantities of wheat, oats, rye, and fodder and confiscated all of the horses, mules, hogs, sheep, cattle, and slaves possible. In July a Confederate soldier reported that in northern Virginia, "nearly all the farms are deserted and the country a perfect waste." Another observed that in Culpeper County, "plantation after plantation lay as bare of cultivation as a wilderness." Near Orange County Court House a Virginian noted that "the farmers find it impossible to cultivate with our army trampling over their fields and fences, in every direction, not to speak of the Yankees coming upon them." This latter fear was well-founded. As a Union officer commented, "We left the country in such a devastated condition that no crop can be raised during the year." Little wonder, then, that many Confederate soldiers appealed for furloughs to return home and help their wives plant and harvest crops. When these appeals were rejected, desertion became an increasing problem, particularly as conscriptions took men away from their farms. One southern girl urged her brother not just to desert but to flee to Union lines "whear you can get plenty and not stay in this one horse barefoot naked and famine stricken Southern Confederacy." By 1863, then, the Union strategy of exhaustion had begun to wear away at Confederate farmers and planters.[77]

SLAVES CONTINUED TO FLEE to Union lines if they had the opportunity, particularly in Virginia. By late April so many had departed that a Yankee traveler reported that plantations remained unfenced and unplanted and that desolation characterized a large portion of the state for want of agricultural labor. Despite the urgings of Governor John Letcher, he reported that "a large crop cannot be raised the present season, even in the part of Virginia now in possession of the Rebels, because thousands of her negroes have left to become free, and their other thousands have been sent farther south to prevent their running away." In the Shenandoah Valley one Virginian speculated that farmers and planters would not provide much food during the year for want of labor. The reporter believed that "the recent proclamations of Davis and several Rebel governors, urging the people to raise food, cannot save the rebellion from starvation for another year." Even if this report suffered from overstatement of Virginia's agricultural labor problem, it contained sufficient truth to indicate the severity of the situation, and other reports made much the same assessment of agriculture in the state. Portions of North and South Carolina and Florida suffered the same agricultural labor problem.[78]

By the end of the year, slave owners in northern Georgia began fleeing south *en masse*. The exodus from the region became so great that farmers and planters in southwestern Georgia could not hire all of these bondsmen. As a result, the plantations in northern Georgia essentially ended agricultural operations, while farmers and planters elsewhere in the state had to provide for their slaves, thereby increasing the food shortage in the Eastern Confederacy. Many slave owners now worried about their investments, and one Virginian wrote, "Am afraid to buy negroes . . . in view of the uncertainty of such property in the present condition of the country to say nothing of their high price."[79]

Despite the flight of many bondsmen, slave prices remained high. In January slaves brought more than acceptable prices at an estate sale in Christiansburg, Virginia, when a man sold for $3,150 and a girl for $2,540. These prices were the highest received, which some believed made the town the leader in slave sales. In Charleston, South Carolina, where Robertson Blacklock and Company conducted a steady slave-selling business, a twenty-eight-year-old woman with three children – a ten-year-old girl and boys ages eight and three – a single twenty-five-year-old woman, and two boys ages twenty and seventeen brought $6,870 for an average of $980, which observers considered fair. Even recalcitrant slaves brought good prices, as did one from a rice plantation, whom his owner judged unproductive. Upon the slave's sale for $1,700, the planter received $1,648 after deduction of the commission fee. In Richmond, prime male field hands brought from $2,200 to $2,500, "best girls" between $1,500 to $1,700, and "fancy girls" from $2,000 to $2,500, "according to appearance and qualification." Boys and girls from ten to twelve years of age brought $1,200 to $1,400. One "very likely fancy girl," a mulatto, brought the astonishing price of $2,900, while another female slave who was "entirely white" brought $3,080. In June a Southampton, Virginia, planter paid $2,480 for

TABLE 1. Land and Slave Valuations, by Owner, for Sandy Creek District, North Carolina, 1863

Land (in acres)	Valuation (in dollars)	Number of Slaves	Valuation (in dollars)
662.5	7,950	24	17,150
765	11,375	12	7,950
169.5	1,525.50	7	5,650
1,073	10,730	33	24,800
310	3,100	29	23,950
245	1,784	9	6,300
200	1,800	7	5,150
1,073	16,095	33	21,550
35	280	4	2,300
355	3,550	10	8,800
174	1,392	8	6,550
380	5,700	20	15,850
16	2,500	3	2,900
24.5	1,900	7	4,800
506.75	6,081	13	8,900
287	2,256	3	1,750
82	820	1	750
67	536	2	800
395	3,160	3	2,150
1,472	22,080	20	16,800
369	4,428	22	15,850
274	2,192	11	9,250
461.5	4,622.50	14	9,350
		4	3,250
195	2,340	6	3,400
645.5	6,450	35	28,550
92	920	3	1,150
211	1,688	4	2,800
9,512	1,146	7	5,900
165	1,320	3	3,000
		3	1,900
		3	2,500
		2	1,700
832.75	8,327.50	22	16,600
918.75	1,016.25	27	17,625
965	9,650	20	14,300
		10	8,525
		13	8,850
		3	2,800
211	1,688	13	7,950

Land (in acres)	Valuation (in dollars)	Number of Slaves	Valuation (in dollars)
1,478	21,088	68	55,300
927	9,270	15	9,900
104.5	836	3	2,500
		16	13,775
713	5,704	19	13,650
3,500	49,500	58	42,237
530	7,950	21	22,250
		1	350
100	1,000	1	750
236	2,360	2	1,700
204.75	2,047.50	5	4,550
1,300	15,600	23	18,800
366.5	4,031.50	6	5,400
		1	1,400
100	600	2	1,500
2,400	28,800	47	32,500
672	9,408	22	18,250
350	4,200	17	12,800
396	3,960	13	11,700
350	4,200	18	13,275
1,000	20,000	73	54,252
		12	9,350
745	8,940	19	10,550
161	1,288	3	2,950
		6	4,900
473	4,730	13	7,450
291	2,439	2	1,700
121	1,210	2	1,150
266	5,320	6	5,600
315	4,725	3	3,000
325	3,250	5	3,800
		4	1,400
83	830	11	9,550
		5	3,500
500	4,000	15	10,150
350	2,800	7	7,350
546.75	8,193.75	18	15,400

Source: 1863 tax valuation list showing owners, lands, slaves, and valuations for the Sandy Creek District in Warren County, North Carolina, Steed and Phipps Family Papers, Southern Historical Collection, University of North Carolina at Chapel Hill.

Note: Here slave valuations for tax purposes do not indicate individual values or market prices. Tax valuations were lower than market prices. Tax valuations are given in Confederate dollars. This tax valuation is suggestive of slave property values in this North Carolina locality.

a boy, age unknown. An observer of the "Negro Market" wrote, "The offerings are large, and the demand equally heavy." These brisk slave sales indicated that local slaveholders were, if not selling out, at least disposing of the surplus labor as the Union army continued to threaten their plantations and farms.[80]

In Richmond most of the slaves offered for sale came from counties threatened by the enemy, and their owners often offered them for sale at prices lower than customary to gain some remuneration if Union forces overran their farms and plantations. By mid-October, however, the value of slaves on the Richmond market increased, which observers attributed "to the strong faith in the perpetuity of the institution of slavery as to the depreciation of the currency." The recent sale of a woman for $5,000 cash, the most ever paid at public auction, brought considerable attention. At the same time, such sales required buyers from areas farther south, where they believed their property would be safe and where slave labor remained profitable for agricultural production and investment purposes.[81]

On the Atlanta market, slaves remained scarce and in great demand, and they sold at "stiff" prices as late as mid-May. Prices held firm or advanced on the Macon slave market, where in November a black woman with three children sold for $2,950 and similar sales brought comparable prices. On South Carolina rice plantations, male slaves could bring $1,700, and in Anson County, North Carolina, they hired out at rates as high as $165 for nine months. Investments in slave labor proved costly across the Confederacy. John Jarnell, a Georgia planter, for example, owned forty-two slaves valued at $37,800. These bondsmen and -women needed to be kept busy to occupy their time and to return a profit on the owner's investment. Consequently, farmers and planters who did not have sufficient work to keep their slaves busy, but who did not want to or could not sell them, continued to hire them out to gain some income.[82]

Early in 1863 Confederate departments, particularly the Engineering Bureau, began pressing slaveholders to hire out their bondsmen to government agencies, and they threatened to impress the slaves and put them to work building fortifications and performing other tasks. In January planters and farmers in Rockingham County sent a letter of protest to the Virginia General Assembly complaining about the call from the central government for slave labor. The hiring or impressment of their slaves would diminish the labor supply and "impair" their ability to cultivate and increase agricultural production. The petitioners argued that "we cannot believe that it is less important to prepare an ample supply of food for our armies, and we are painfully impressed with the apprehension that the great danger lies on the side of a scarcity of provisions." As Richmond imposed impressment quotas on the counties, farmers and planters complied with the state governments, and the governors could not easily override these allocations. The depletion of slave labor from government impressment soon affected harvesting and other tasks: threshing wheat, hauling grains to the mills, slaughtering hogs, and performing other seasonal activities, which kept bondsmen and -women busy throughout the year.[83]

In April one farmer in Chatham County, North Carolina, objected to an impressment call and informed Governor Vance that "it is my honest opinion we need something to eat worse than we do breast works and fortifications, if our negros are taken from us, our corn cannot be tended, and our wheat, and oats will rot in the field, with the force left behind the grain cannot be saved." The army, however, took slaves as needed, but with most white men of fighting age in the ranks, the impressment of slaves hindered agricultural production.[84]

Although the army impressed slaves, the War Department promised to return them for critical work, such as harvesting grain, or when their military work had been completed. Frequently, this did not happen, at least in a timely manner. In June a Caswell County, North Carolina, farmer requested the return of his slaves from Wilmington, where the army had taken them to build fortifications. In his appeal to Governor Vance he wrote, "I am in need of them to save my crops of grain and to make some corn which I shall not be able to do without my hands." Secretary of War James A. Seddon tried to accommodate farmers whose slaves he needed by delaying impressments until after the harvest of the major crops. However, farmers and planters never accepted the impressment of their slaves as fair and equitable.[85]

In October the editor of the Staunton *Spectator* warned that slave impressment discouraged production. "The practice of withdrawing every now and then hundreds of our stoutest and most athletic negroes from farming operations, to work on the fortifications near Richmond," he noted, "is an enormous evil. These negroes are our best farm hands." Moreover, he continued, "for everyone withdrawn the production of grain is diminished several hundred bushels." Some slaveholders also argued that the impressment of their bondsmen, plus the tax-in-kind, had depleted their own food supply. One North Carolina farmer thought that "the loss of a hand is embarrassing in this situation." The periodic impressment of slaves would continue to plague farmers and planters who complained loudly about it. As the conflict wore on, however, military needs superseded any claims to the agricultural labor. When the Confederate government assumed responsibility for the enforcement of slave impressments from the states after 1863, slaveholders continued to complain about government intrusion on their property rights and to demand recognition of their mandate to increase agricultural production, all to no avail. At best by spring, when Congress passed impressment legislation relating to slaves, the act provided that bondsmen could not be seized if the government could hire them or obtain them by consent of their owners. In addition, Congress provided that before December 1, "no slave laboring on a farm or plantation exclusively devoted to the production of grain and provisions shall be taken except in cases of urgent necessity without consent."[86]

On May 1, Congress amended the "Twenty Slave Law" of 1862. The modifications excluded only the plantations of dependents, minors, *femme soles*, and men in the field from conscription. On plantations with twenty or more slaves, one white man remained exempt from conscription, provided he had served as an overseer before April 16, 1862, and the law required the owner to pay $500 to the Treasury. The law also did not become effective until autumn, so the plantations would have sufficient overseers to produce large grain crops. In addition, the president could exempt agricultural workers when necessary. These revisions did little to ease the labor shortage or mollify small-scale farmers, but it comforted whites who worried about slave rebellions emanating from the plantations.[87]

While slave owners grappled with their agricultural labor problems, white women and their children necessarily went into the fields in numbers that became noticeable to anyone traveling in the countryside. One Georgian wrote, "God bless the girls, they wear homespun, and *plow* and *hoe* and make *corn*." In June, South Carolina farm women followed the few remaining male cradlers who cut the wheat crop, and they bound and shocked the sheaves. Across the Eastern Confederacy, white women on the small-scale farms worked in the fields and tended livestock while planter women continued to supervise their slave labor force despite the increasing insubordination and flight of their bondsmen and -women. Farm women with only a few slaves directed the needed work, often with the advice of their soldier husbands to have their hands sow wheat, gather corn, feed cattle, and kill hogs. In December one soldier in Lee's army told his wife not to shy away from butchering hogs. "Pitch in like a man and attend to it, and every thing of that sort." She managed the farm and slaves with little need for assistance, but the loss of men decreased agricultural productivity and lowered food supplies in the towns and cities.[88]

In April, Governor Brown told the Georgia legislature that the poor pay of soldiers of $11 per month in depreciated currency and high food prices had forced women into the fields, where "thousands of them are now obligated to work daily . . . to make bread. . . . Many are living upon bread alone." He considered this disgraceful: "A large portion of the wealthy class . . . have avoided the fevers of the camp and the danger of the battlefield." This was not the first criticism, nor would it be the last, that the conflict had become a rich man's war and a poor man's fight – complaints that were usually most vocal in areas of food scarcity. The conscription of men to age forty-five after the battle of Gettysburg took even more labor from the fields and necessitated more fieldwork for women. The government's plans to draft all men over forty-five years of age, however, brought considerable criticism. The editor of the *Macon Telegraph* called the plan "suicidal," because these men would be "thrifty planters and farmers whose place could not be supplied." The *Charleston Courier* also attributed the scarcity of food "solely to the rude and wholesale conscription acts of the Confederate Government, which have not left labor in the country sufficient to till the fields and gather the crops." Agricultural production would further fall, he contended, and "with inadequate supplies of food, our cause is certainly ruined, although you should double her armies."[89]

The lack of mechanized or horse-drawn implements contributed to the agricultural labor shortage. Primarily harvesting the grain crops were workers with a cradle scythes. They were followed by binders, who gathered and tied the gavels into sheaves with twine and set the sheaves in shocks. Some Virginia farmers used threshing machines, but by 1863 few had these implements because the equipment had either broken or worn out, and replacement parts or new implements could not be purchased. In Georgia reapers who used a cradle scythe or sickle received a bushel of wheat per day in pay. Some farmers used a two-bottom plow and steers or oxen for plowing, and they hoped that Confederate and Union soldiers would not take them. Union soldiers made fun of southern farming implements, which they considered a half century behind the North's. They noted that the plows did not turn a furrow and only stirred the soil three or four inches deep. Many of those implements probably were shovel plows, which farmers and planters used as an implement of choice to prepare the soil and to cultivate between the rows of corn and cotton. These plows were common because they cost little and could be easily made by plantation or local blacksmiths.[90]

Farmers whose lands had been confiscated had additional labor problems. Until spring the U.S. War Department controlled abandoned lands, while the U.S. Treasury collected cotton and taxes for the Federal government. This overlapping authority caused friction and led the Treasury to request total jurisdiction over the abandoned and confiscated plantations. On March 12, 1863, Congress granted that authority. This legislation authorized the secretary of the Treasury to appoint agents, locate abandoned property, appraise it, and appropriate it for public use, or to sell it at auction to the highest bidder on behalf of the Federal government.[91]

In South Carolina Union authorities, building on previous policy, continued a system for employing freedpeople. On the captured plantations, each field hand received one acre and work assignments. The freedmen were paid 25 cents a day for fieldwork, ginning, and other tasks. In exchange for the use of government land, animals, and plowmen, the freedpeople would plant and cultivate as much corn as possible for themselves and one acre for the superintendent of the plantation. When the cotton harvest had been completed, the black workers received 2½ cents per pound of cotton picked. The government also collected a tax from them in corn to feed the livestock and draft animals provided by the government and private owners. The workers received partial, small payments each month for their work, with their remaining earnings paid after the harvest, similar to the previous year.[92]

In March, Edmund Ruffin reported that the Federal government had provided seed and land to freedpeople who remained on their plantations—that is, on land "stolen from their owners." He did not believe this agricultural experiment would be any more successful than the one tried in South Carolina the previous year, where it allegedly had cost the Federal government $20 for every pound of cotton produced. In Georgia slave owners considered this scheme nothing less than a plot by Yankee overseers on the newly confiscated or purchased plantations to defraud "Sambo and Dinah" of the "small pittance" promised to them: the overseers would fine the former slaves for poor performance or behavior and thus take all of the money paid to them. As one contemporary observed, "The whole management is a scheme to put money in Yankee pockets, and is a miserable farce so far as it makes any pretense to benefit the negro." Southerners could recognize servitude, if not slavery, no matter what northerners pretended to call it.[93]

On the plantations where this military agricultural policy applied, black women and children and old men conducted most of the work because the Union army had taken the younger men for service. They planted 814 acres of cotton and harvested 72,000 pounds of the fiber (88.4 pounds per acre), or about two-thirds of the former average per acre. Knowledgeable observers estimated that the cost of production averaged 31½ cents per pound, including interest on the investment, but they believed that improved manuring and cultivation practices could boost production. By March, Sea Island cotton averaged about $1.50 per pound, or four times the cost of production, and the new northern planters believed they could make a substantial profit by producing this long-staple cotton with black labor. If this labor system could be transferred to the uplands for the production of short-staple cotton at a cost of about 8 cents per pound (or 10 percent of its market value), they believed that a profitable form of agricultural labor could be wedded to the production of cotton. This agricultural system continued until the Federal government sold its 60,000 acres on March 16, 1864, of which only 16,000 acres were reserved for purchase by the freedpeople.[94]

By 1863, the Federal government faced increasing pressure to sell confiscated plantations in the Port Royal District of the Sea Islands. General Rufus Saxton, military governor of South Carolina, who supervised the plantations, believed that the freedpeople should receive parcels of land for subsistence agriculture before any land sales were made to whites. In March, New England planter-missionaries became the first purchasers of the confiscated plantations, and they eagerly continued the agricultural labor experiment. The missionaries were certain that the freedpeople could raise more cotton, more cheaply, and more efficiently than slave labor while also providing for their own subsistence.[95]

In March a joint stock company of six Boston investors purchased eleven plantations at auction. Each plantation cultivated cotton with paid black labor, and employed families received approximately one and a half acres for adults and lesser amounts for children to raise crops. Each family was also given land to cultivate long-staple cotton. These new owners paid their workers monthly for planting and hoeing at a "small rate," reserving the principal payment for completing the harvest. Freedpeople earned additional money as piecework for plowing, collecting, manuring, ginning, cleaning, and packing cotton. Each family prepared the cotton for market. Overall, these laborers made about 55 cents per day for working in the cotton fields. They also received free housing. The freedpeople could not afford the nominal price of $1.25 per acre for Confederate land sold by Federal tax commissioners, but the former slaves clearly understood the importance of landownership to ensure their economic independence and freedom.[96]

The government proved reluctant to lease or sell plantation acreage to freedpeople; instead, it favored white owners and operators. Although a few black farmers ultimately purchased and leased acreage from both government and private owners, their landholdings remained minuscule compared with those of northern whites, who increasingly took control of the plantations, in part, because government officials believed that the new white plantation owners would be able to provide employment for landless blacks and those with only a few subsistence acres. By so doing, they would employ a large black workforce, prevent land redistribution based on race, and keep freedmen and -women sufficiently engaged in agriculture to discourage their migration to the North. Northerners believed the workers on the Sea Island plantations needed "new masters" who would teach them to survive in a free-market economy, particularly for the production of cotton. With cotton selling at record, albeit wartime, prices, northerners saw great opportunity in buying and renting plantations at prewar prices and to use a nearly captive black labor force for their own gain. For the freedpeople in the Eastern Confederacy, the perils of freedom loomed ominously across the plantation South as the year ended.[97]

Even so, General Saxton issued a circular authorizing the freedpeople to locate on lands that the Federal government was about to sell for tax purposes. Each head of a household could claim 20 to 40 acres, provided those lands were not reserved for military or educational purposes. The government offered these lands for $1.25 per acre, with 40 percent of the price due upon preemption and the remainder upon receipt of a deed. Any loyal person of twenty-one years of age could claim preempted government land, provided they had lived on it at least six months since Federal occupation, or if they were in residence on December 31. Here, then, was the genesis of freedpeople's expectation across the Confederacy that they would receive 40 acres when the war ended.[98]

BY AUTUMN VIRGINIA farmers who risked the loss of their produce to soldiers or impressment agents sold their provisions in Richmond for the highest prices possible. Peaches that once brought 5 cents apiece now sold for $6 a dozen, watermelons brought from $5 to $10 each, and apples $35 per barrel. Butter was scarce at $2.50 per pound. On September 4, a crowd of women in Mobile "rendered desperate by their sufferings" assembled with banners that read "Bread or Blood" or "Bread and Peace." Armed with knives and hatchets, they marched down Dauphine Street, breaking open stores and stealing food and clothing. "It was," some northern sympathizers reported, "a most formidable riot by a long-suffering and desperate population." When the Seventeenth Alabama refused orders to put down the riot with force of arms, the Mobile Cadets broke it up, and the women returned peaceably to their homes.[99]

By late September many Richmond residents wanted the government to fix prices for every article of food and seize agricultural produce if farmers withheld provisions from sale. Food and agricultural prices remained high in South Carolina, where rice brought $135 per hundredweight and cattle $150 per head, corn brought $3 per bushel, and bacon $2 per pound. In October a rumor spread in Richmond that corn that now sold for $8 per bushel and cornmeal for $10 per bushel might soon be in short supply, because the harvest in the counties above Richmond and east of Albemarle had been less abundant than predicted. By the end of the month, corn sold for $11 per bushel. The hogs that fattened on the short crop already brought $2.50 per pound in blocks, or $3 per pound for sliced bacon. Corn whiskey commanded a good price of $35 or more per gallon despite public admonishments to farmers to feed corn to hogs and cattle to produce meat. Eggs, meanwhile, brought $2.50 per dozen, up a dollar since April, and butter $4.50 per pound, an increase from $1.25 per pound in January. Turkeys brought $4.00 each, chickens as much as $7.00 per pair, and beef by the quarter from 75 cents to 85 cents per pound, with the buyer responsible for cutting it. All of these prices were substantially higher than when the year began. Moreover, farmers had stopped bringing hay to Richmond because they seemingly lost most of it to impressment before they arrived. With farmers still withholding their wheat from market, the Richmond mills could not meet consumer demands for flour. Wheat farmers refused to accept the fixed government price of $5 per bushel. Critics attributed this decision to "obstinacy," greed, and insufficient patriotism. Some millers, however, purchased wheat at a higher price on the black market to remain in business. High agricultural prices and an inflated currency caused the editor of the *Richmond Dispatch* to blame farmers for "weighing down the people."[100]

In October Richmond grocers stopped purchasing even limited quantities of produce from farmers because they waited for news about a

"Maximum" or "Extortion" bill pending before the legislature that authorized price fixing on various commodities. Until they knew what their expenses might be, they let their shelves become bare. Farmers in northern Virginia, however, contended that they could not haul wheat to Richmond for the millers because they were too busy seeding next year's acreage and cutting hay. Skeptics responded that farmers had their wheat ground into flour at local mills and stored it. As a result, the Richmond market was nearly bare of wheat and flour, a situation that farmers seemed to accept with "frigid indifference." Grocers in Richmond, Lynchburg, and Petersburg adamantly opposed fixing a maximum price, arguing that they should be free to charge the highest possible price. Otherwise, they might pay more for farm produce than they could recover by law. Moreover, the state legislators considering the bill would soon go home, and if they passed it, they would leave Richmond in a state of starvation while they enjoyed adequate, if not ample, food supplies in their hometowns and counties. Yet others accused the commissary general of creating the problem. If the government stopped impressing wheat, farmers would bring it to market, prices would decline, and consumers would have enough flour and bread to meet their needs. By late October, Richmond commission merchants charged $60 per barrel for flour, and near Asheville, North Carolina, $7 per bushel for corn and $10 per bushel for wheat. Animosity against farmers festered.[101]

The coming winter brought the threat of widespread hunger to the Eastern Confederacy. By early November flour reached $75 per barrel in Richmond. The price spike was caused not by the scarcity of wheat in the countryside but by the commissary officers who seized so much of it for the army. The problem was, some argued, due to "beardless and senseless boys, who do not know how many bushels of wheat it requires to make a barrel of flour . . . and, without knowing what is needed, they serve written notices upon the farmers that their whole crops are impressed, and that they must not send one bushel of grain to market." Secretary of War James Seddon attempted to alleviate this problem by ordering his commissary officers to support a resolution of the Petersburg City Council, which requested exemption for its agents to purchase food for the needy rather than compete with impressment officers for limited farm produce. To prevent a serious food shortage in Richmond during the winter, Seddon halted all impressment of grain and food from farmers except "one-third, or such other proportion thereof, as may be required for the use of the army." Yet Seddon's exception worried farmers and planters – it could reopen the door to excessive seizures. Before the month ended, however, the War Department ordered commissary officers to halt the impressment of farm produce in transit to the Richmond market to ease the food shortage. Still, prices there remained high, with wheat at $20 and corn at $11 per bushel, respectively. Soon butter reached $5.50 per pound, flour $110 per barrel, cornmeal $16 per bushel, bacon $3.25 per pound, beef $1 per pound, onions $35 per bushel, Irish potatoes $10 per bushel, sweet potatoes $15 per bushel, and eggs $3 per dozen. Sorghum molasses brought $14 per gallon, rice 32 cents per pound, and whiskey as much as $75 per gallon. Food could be obtained in Richmond, but only at high prices.[102]

In Georgia and North Carolina the impressment system, which included published scheduled prices, no longer functioned. Georgia governor Brown complained to Seddon that unauthorized people posing as impressment agents preyed upon farmers and planters, while legitimate agents often stripped them of nearly all their provisions and livestock – all in violation of the congressional act that mandated proper procedures, particularly the right of arbitration, for impressing farm commodities. Indeed, across the Confederacy, some southerners had seen opportunity born of destitution and, posing as government officials, began impressing hogs and selling them on local markets. A Richmond editor urged the public to give a severe beating to these thieves. Other swindlers spread the rumor that the government would soon increase its impressment of hogs and pay only 20 cents per pound, but would offer hog raisers a few cents more in an attempt to frighten farmers into selling. Government officials worked quickly to put down the rumor, but not before some hog producers had been duped.[103]

Governor Brown also complained that the price schedules remained too low. By denying farmers and planters market value for their produce, the impressment prices essentially served as another tax on the farm population that others did not share. Farmers responded to this policy, he said, by withholding supplies from the market and by concealing provisions from government agents. "The result," he contended, "has inaugurated the system of supplying the army by impressment instead of by purchase, which is contrary to the true policy of Congress which forbids impressments until after there is a refusal to sell." Most important, disregard of the law has led to "open disloyalty." Impressment agents should pay market prices and treat all farmers and planters equally, and Brown asked Seddon to get the law changed to require agents to pay market prices to farmers and planters.[104]

Governor Vance of North Carolina agreed. He, too, complained to Seddon in the waning days of 1863 that food supplies remained limited in the state and that impressment officers were making matters worse. "Impressing agents," he wrote, "in many instances act in such a manner as to create great dissatisfaction among our people." These agents often judged the quantity of produce that a farm family needed for the year and impressed the remainder as the surplus. Usually, those estimates proved incorrect and the family was left without adequate provisions. "This crying evil and injustice shall be corrected without delay," Vance told Seddon. Moreover, he charged, "many military officers also, in violation of the law of Congress, assume the right of impressment. This evil cannot longer be tolerated, and I invoke your aid in its suppression."[105]

By November the tax-in-kind had broken down, because the government did not provide for adequate storage and distribution. As result, thousands of bushels of potatoes rotted in warehouses and became unfit even for hog feed. Wet and bruised potatoes rotted quickly and became inedible if not quickly and efficiently transported to the army. The government, however, never developed a tax-in-kind policy for perishable commodities that met soldiers' needs. In addition, planters could pay the tax-in-kind easier than small-scale farmers because they produced more hogs, cattle, corn, and other crops. A 10 percent loss affected them far less than it did farm families. Farmers and planters also complained that if they fed their corn to their hogs, they were taxed twice, because they had to tithe the remaining corn and pork to the government. Congress responded on December 28, 1863, by commuting the tithe on sweet potatoes to a monetary payment and exempted farmers who produced less than 250 pounds of bacon. This action did little to ease the hostility of farmers and planters against the government because they believed that low impressment prices, worthless Confederate money, and overzealous impressment officers placed the burdens of war on them alone. Many resisted by hiding and hoarding produce and refusing to accept payment in Confederate paper money for their commodities; they instead demanded gold — that is, specie.[106]

Efforts by the Richmond City Council to improve the food supply largely failed because nearby farmers had little or nothing to sell and the army used the railroads for other purposes. In the capital the food shortage had reached a critical state, causing the editor of the *Richmond Whig* to lament that "we see every day evidences of an approaching bread famine in this city, while within the limits of the State, it is believed there is food enough for all the people for twelve months. The population of Richmond cannot live upon air." But he worried that bread supplies would remain inadequate during the coming winter. Provisioning the towns and cities came as a last resort. The new year did not bode well for farmers, planters, and consumers. Inflation made matters worse, even if farmers brought agricultural provisions to market.[107]

Increasingly, the public branded farmers and planters as unpatriotic, greedy speculators and believed that avarice was trumping patriotism in the countryside. In November Richmond residents continued to complain that farmers seldom brought flour to town for sale or would accept Confederate Treasury notes for payment. Others charged that while a "great abundance" of cattle grazed in the Piedmont and the Upper Valley, beef sold for 35 to 50 cents per pound on the hoof. These prices merited droving to city markets in Richmond and elsewhere, if only the impressment officers would stop seizing the cattle to feed Confederate soldiers and Union prisoners. Richmond residents worried that the arrival of more Yankee prisoners would further tax their food supply. The result would be an imposition "worse than that which the locusts inflicted on Egypt." Area farmers cared not at all.[108]

By the end of 1863, then, many southern farmers knew that the war could not be won by patriotism and sheer force of will. Many southerners in the towns and cities now went hungry. A report from Charleston indicated a food shortage and that "all kinds of eatables" were "scarce and enormously high." A Virginian also wrote that "the whole question now turns on food. If we can get meat enough, or our own Soldiers will do on less than enough, we can weather all the other blunders of Mr. Davis & the Generals." But he was not optimistic: "I hope yes; I fear no." Systematic, dependable agricultural production based on the traditional rhythm of the seasons had broken down. Georgia farmers planted 1 million more acres of corn, wheat, and potatoes than they had in 1862; North and South Carolina followed with 500,000 more acres each, and Florida produced 50,000 more acres in these crops. Collectively, farmers contributed 50 million more bushels of corn, 20 million more bushels of wheat, and 20 million bushels of potatoes to the food supply than they had the previous year. Even so, southern farmers and planters had failed to produce enough food due to Federal occupation of Confederate lands, transportation problems, insufficient agricultural labor, and inadequate time for converting from cotton and tobacco to food crops and livestock. Farmers and planters preferred to plant cotton because soldiers could not eat it, and because their food crops might be impressed by Confederate forces or seized by Union soldiers. Moreover, if cotton growers lived close to Union lines they preferred to trade it for greenbacks rather than worthless Confederate currency, or they wanted to raise cotton and store it until the war ended when they anticipated reaping high domestic and international prices. The tax-in-kind had failed to provide the necessary provisions for the army, and, on December 28, Congress in desperation authorized farmers to pay this tax in money based on impressment rates.[109]

On December 31, John M. Daniel, editor of the *Richmond Daily Examiner*, wrote, "Today closes the gloomiest year of our struggle." Union raiders continued to harass Confederate farmers and planters. The general price index for the Eastern Confederacy had increased from 762 in January to 2,464 in December (January–April 1861 = 100). Federal forces had gained control of the Mississippi River and physically divided the Confederacy. "The cry of scarcity resounds through the land," he wrote, "raised by producers in their greed for gain, re-echoed by the consumers in their premature dread of starvation and nakedness." Farmers, planters, and speculators who had withheld "any necessary of life" had done their worst to ruin the country. A North Carolina planter's wife concurred. As a heavy rain fell during the last day of the year, she could only write, "So died 1863! – a year of calamity & distress the like of which may never fall to our lot either as individuals or members of the community to see again."[110]

CHAPTER FIVE

Western Losses

On January 8, 1863, Federal troops camped in front of Robert H. Cantrell's house near Nashville. As a southern farmer and slave owner he felt aggrieved. They had taken his corn, fodder, and horses and used his fence rails for firewood. Cantrell confided in his diary a belief, no doubt expressed openly by many farmers like him, that "the man who takes the oath of allegiance in good faith and ardently desires a restoration of the Union and peace once more, suffers equally with one who is an out and out Rebel." By the time the war ended he believed that only the land would remain. John Houston Bills, a nearby planter, complained after the Fifth Ohio Cavalry passed through his farm that "it seems the last vestige of property & food for man and beast will be taken & no prospect of relief." His sense of loss, however, was assuaged, no doubt, because he sold 3,014 pounds of cotton, at 50 cents per pound, to the Union army at Middlebury for $1,501 in U.S. Treasury notes. He also hedged his bets on the outcome of the war by purchasing $2,800 in South Carolina, Georgia, and Alabama currency at the rate of 80 cents on the dollar in U.S. Treasury notes. He preferred to trade greenbacks that he received from cotton sales for gold, which he exchanged at the rate of $1.90 in greenbacks for $1 in gold. With cotton selling for 85 to 90 cents per pound in Memphis, he did not believe he could lose no matter who won the war. In the meantime, farmers and planters went about their business, shucking and shelling corn, building fences, repairing equipment, and plowing fields for corn, potatoes, and cotton, as well as marking newborn hogs, branding yearling cows, and hauling manure.¹

Southern farmers near Union-controlled Nashville gained safer access to the city's markets by late January, when the army provided passes that permitted them to haul their produce free from fear of impressment by Union soldiers. In the city they sold hogs for $8 per hundredweight, eggs for 25 to 30 cents per dozen, and butter for 40 cents per pound, while beef brought as much as 15 cents per pound and chickens 75 cents each. With improved safety farmers in the Nashville vicinity could make money, given the great needs of the occupying army and hungry citizenry – provided the war left them alone.[2]

It did not leave them alone in Mississippi, at least not the small-scale farmers. By February some people were going hungry. "The public mind is just now so occupied with conscription and impressment," one Lawrence County resident complained, "that one who talks about old men and women and children and bread and meat for them, stands a sorry chance of being heard." The state legislature had recently passed a law creating a state militia that would take more farmers from the fields, particularly in southern Mississippi, where farms and not plantations prevailed. Moreover, the Lawrence resident charged that the planters were not meeting their responsibility to provide food for the public. The planters represented about one-quarter of the population, and they had "several hundred thousand negroes," but they "show no disposition to divide; and we have no security that they will produce corn and meat more than sufficient to supply themselves." As a result, many Mississippians went to bed supper-less and rose without breakfast. He overstated his case, but many Mississippians now believed more than ever that the planters did not contribute their fair share to the war effort and that small-scale farmers could not meet the population's food needs partly because of the conscription and state militia laws.[3]

Another Mississippian wrote, "If all the men are to be called out and put into the militia, who are to make the crops and raise bread? How is the army to be fed? Who is to make corn for the women and children of the poorer counties, where there are no slaves?" Poignantly he noted, "It requires something more than a grand army to carry on war." The Confederacy needed a strong agricultural sector in the form of people who would remain on their farms to plow, plant, and reap. Others argued, however, that Mississippi farmers and planters produced enough food for the army and civilians; the problem was that planters and merchants withheld it from sale in hopes of gaining still higher prices. Yet another Mississippian charged that "those producers who held their breadstuffs at high prices, and their bacon at seventy cents per pound, embarrassing the government in its effort to create supplies are simply men whose love of country has been eaten out of the most sordid of all human passions." Greedy farmers, planters, and merchants were endangering the Western Confederacy. Military impressment with reasonable compensation seemed justified. The solutions seemed clear – the confiscation of their property by the state to ensure ample food supplies at reasonable prices. Seizing property in the name of public safety indicated a profound ideological shift from prewar beliefs.[4]

Lieutenant General Pemberton, commanding the Department of Mississippi and East Louisiana, responded with Special Orders No. 63, which mandated the acquisition of all corn from farmers and planters that exceeded their personal needs. Quartermaster agents would canvass the area and pay $1.50 per bushel for corn; those who refused this price would have their grain impressed. The corn would go for the relief of Confederate troops at Vicksburg and Port Hudson. Some people worried that the army would take too much corn and leave the public destitute of food. This order was not executed, however, because the army's chief quartermaster found an adequate supply of corn in the northern Mississippi counties. Still, one editor warned that "it is plain that not only patriotism, but interest, require that the agricultural power of the country should be devoted to the production of grain." Although cotton and tobacco would have speculative value for years to come, corn and oats brought $5 per bushel – a price high enough to make every farmer who planted these crops well off while also enabling them to feed soldiers and civilians alike because of higher yields. One Mississippian expressed confidence in the state's agriculturists because they had planted a large wheat and cotton crop. But he noted that some planters had "overstepped the bounds of reason and patriotism" by planting too much cotton, and he hoped that a "blight" would fall upon their fields. Then, with a passing nod to the beatitudes, he wrote, "Blessed are the corn raisers for they shall not want for bread or buyers."[5]

Gentle rains and warm spring temperatures also made farmers in the Western Confederacy optimistic and created great anticipation that the wheat crop would be bountiful. Near Chattanooga a middle Tennessee farmer reported that the land promised "a rich crop of wheat from every seam and furrow," and it grew "fresh and lively." By autumn barns would overflow with grain; only the harvest awaited to vindicate his prediction. But he recognized that the harvest required labor and farmland free from Yankee control. To ensure each he advised, "We must possess the country – Let the soldiers fight for their territory, and the women and children will gather the tillage. We will not starve." The problem was that Union forces occupied large portions of Arkansas, Louisiana, Mississippi, and Tennessee. With the Federal army controlling a considerable amount of the most fertile land in the Western Confederacy, farmers would produce a "short crop" at best for civilians still in areas under Confederate control. Planters also would have increasing difficulty getting their slaves to work, which would further reduce agricultural production. Northerners who professed knowledge about agriculture in the Western Confederacy believed that farmers and planters in the region could not "save the rebellion from starvation for another year."[6]

Clearly, the spring did not begin with unbounded promise for better agricultural days. By mid-March some Natchez butchers had closed their shops, and residents were almost entirely without beef. They appealed to cattle dealers in Mississippi, Louisiana, and Texas to supply them, "if in their power." The Natchez mayor also sought 5,000 bushels of corn to meet public needs, and he offered to pay a "liberal price." In the Louisiana sugar parishes, many planters had set out little seed cane in 1862 because of wartime destruction and inadequate labor and financing. Now they could only let their cane grow from ratoons – cane that sprouted from roots that remained in the ground from the previous year. Other sugar planters switched to cotton and rice.[7]

A Union soldier in the Bayou Teche region of Louisiana observed, "There is not a single planter in this department who has not personally suffered through this war. Their crops of sugar cane, yielding from five hundred to a thousand hogsheads of sugar, are still standing in February.... I have ridden through miles of plantations which only a few hogsheads of sugar had been made. Cane is standing now in March, thousands and thousands of acres of it. Thus the crop of the past year is nothing, and that of the coming year will be the same." Federal troops had destroyed sugarhouses and mills and seized horses and mules needed for cultivation and pulling cane wagons to the mills. Sugarcane fields had become battlefields, and many planters had fled to Texas and taken their slaves with them. Some sugar plantations became Union encampments or civilian refugee camps, and the cypress rail fences made excellent campfires. As a result, in 1863 sugar production totaled less than 3 percent of the 1861 crop.[8]

In spring, the Seventy-Fifth New York Volunteers maneuvered through the sugar-plantation country near Franklin, New Iberia, and Opelousas, Louisiana. "The plantations are planted mostly to corn, only now and then we saw a cane field," one soldier reported. He saw a "great deal of cotton stored in buildings but little growing in the fields." Yet, with cotton selling for 82 cents per pound on the New Orleans market and with northern demand high, many planters seeded cotton instead of corn, and they saw no reason not to return to production as usual. Still, the efforts of western farmers to substitute corn for cotton had achieved considerable success by the early summer of 1863. One New York soldier remarked that the farms near Opelousas "seem[ed] to have been planted and tilled as though no fear of devastation had been entertained . . . though the effect of the war has been to cover the fields with corn instead of King Cotton and sugar cane, the usual crop of the section." In Mississippi, however, the planters, whose number some counted as "Legion," still preferred to seed cotton, which one observer warned would "culminate in the establishment of Yankee despotism over these lands."[9]

DESPITE THE COMMITMENT BY FARMERS and planters to raise corn, in late February a resident of Jackson, Mississippi, noted the declining availability of food: "We have more to fear from a dearth of food than from all the Federal armies in existence." Poignantly he asked, "Who can fight starvation with hope of success?" An ample supply of food existed, he contended, but at enormous prices. A month later eggs sold for $2 per dozen, turkeys $5 to $7 apiece, and chickens $1.50 each. Butter and bacon brought $2 per pound. Flour sold for $75 to $100 per barrel, pork 25 cents a pound, whiskey $10 to $20 a gallon, and corn $1.50 to $2.50 per bushel depending on local needs. In March cornmeal ranged from $4 to $5 per bushel, and pork brought $1 per pound in Jackson. By mid-March Mississippi planters sold corn for $3.80 per bushel and sheep, including lambs, for $14 per head. These high prices resulted from hoarding by farmers and planters as well as merchants who held out for the highest prices possible. The public also blamed Confederate agents for high food prices – they allegedly paid high prices to farmers because "the government was rich," a charge that reflected the growing desperation of consumers.[10]

By February the growing animosity between those who had much or at least adequate food and those who had little or none became increasingly strident. When news about people starving in Mobile reached New Orleans, not all residents sympathized. One proclaimed, "It is their own fault; but perhaps the remark is incharitable, for we should endeavor to cover all faults with the mantle of charity, and feel for the unfortunate everywhere; and perhaps those who are suffering . . . for most had least to do with bringing about the rebellion." Food supplies in the New Orleans Garden District were more than adequate and merchants had ample food supplies, one boasting the "finest assortments," and starvation posed no threat to the city. But, then, New Orleans had been forcibly returned to the Union nearly a year earlier, and these observations probably came from northern partisans. Planters were now more concerned with securing their runaway slaves than raising food crops because they wanted to return to producing cotton now that northern buyers were offering high prices at newly opened markets. In the meantime, the editor of the *Houston Telegraph* admonished planters that to ward off hunger, corn "must be grown on plantations. Negroes must plant and cultivate and gather it." In contrast, some Texans urged farmers to raise their own tobacco because they could sell it for a high price since Virginia tobacco was unavailable.[11]

Planters who raised cotton in 1863 still consigned some of their crops to the Confederate government under the produce loan program and received the value of their cotton in 8 percent bonds. One Mississippi farmer consigned cotton valued at more than $3,000 for the produce loan. Yet the produce loan program did not put a reliable currency in the pockets of farmers and planters. As a result, they had problems paying their bills because merchants and other creditors refused to accept Confederate currency. During the battle of Vicksburg farmers had difficulty supplying city markets. When they did, fresh pork brought $2 per pound and cornmeal $35 to $41 per bushel, which caused one contemporary to conclude that "such prices denote almost starvation" for consumers. Although Mississippi planters sold wheat, corn, and fodder to government agents, they often received receipts for promises of payment later. They also sold cotton to the state of Mississippi — more than 100,000 bales by late January — and negotiated for additional sales, particularly if they could reach Union lines. Cotton planters operated on the premise that they had a better chance of earning a profit if they transferred the crop to the government, which would pay for it, unlike Union or Confederate forces, which would likely burn it.[12]

IN TEXAS CATTLEMEN DID NOT want to accept Confederate currency for their beeves, and the government soon resorted to impressing cattle. It paid $25 per head if the livestock raisers rounded them up or $22 per head if impressment agents collected the cattle themselves, but the government paid in Confederate money. The Texans considered this price too low and Confederate currency worthless. As a result, cattlemen resisted sales to the government by either contract or impressment, and the price of beef cattle escalated. Some Texas cattle producers drove their cattle across the Rio Grande for sale to Mexican buyers. In August, one Confederate officer wrote, "The export of beef-cattle to Mexico . . . is now being carried on to such an extent that the supply of fresh beef to the troops will be in a short time very difficult." Another officer reported that cattle-droving across the Rio Grande to Mexican buyers was "being carried on from every portion of the state with the energy of avarice and appetite long held in abeyance." The lack of the required crossing permits and bills of sale did not hinder the movement of cattle across the border.[13]

By March, the beef shortage in the West had become critical, particularly for the army. Commissary agents had taken almost all of the cattle from farmers between Murfreesboro and Chattanooga. After Vicksburg fell to Union forces on July 4, the beef supply became worse. Union patrols ranged up and down the Mississippi River and prevented drovers from swimming most cattle across from the west side. Confederate soldiers needed meat to maintain sufficient calories and nutrition for living and fighting in the field, and farmers in Tennessee could not make up for the loss of Texas cattle. Florida livestock raisers could not help, either, because their beeves supplied the Eastern Confederacy, particularly the Army of Northern Virginia and General P. G. T. Beauregard's men in South Carolina. One officer reflecting on the beef supply for the Army of Tennessee near Chattanooga said, "Starvation stares us in the face; the handwriting is on the wall." The beef supply for soldiers and citizens remained grim in the West, and impressment agents could not find the cattle to meet army needs, while farmers did not have many cattle to market in the towns.[14]

Occasionally, the horses of Union cavalry spread disease, which debilitated and often killed the horses and mules of the farmers and planters. When the 11th Illinois Cavalry camped on Robert Cantrell's farm, some of the horses suffered from distemper and glanders. Cantrell's mules and horses soon contracted the diseases, compounding his losses from Federal seizures. Scarcity drove the price of horses and mules upward. In March, Tennessee mules brought as much as $150 each. Before the year ended some Tennessee farmers sold their horses for greenbacks because they believed Union soldiers would soon take them or they would lose them to disease. Yet desperate sales of draft animals to protect their investment further hindered agricultural production in the Western Confederacy. One Louisiana planter put the cultivation problem for corn and sugarcane succinctly, writing, "*Mules* are what we want."[15]

In Mississippi planters hid their remaining horses and mules in the woods to keep them from seizure by both the Yankees and Confederates. With mules bringing $100 to $230 and horses $175 each, they could not afford to lose more draft animals. The violence of war also killed livestock and further decreased their numbers. During the battle of Vicksburg one observer noted that "there has been a great number of horses killed by shells and small balls and cattle grazing on the hillsides are killed and wounded by scores." A Union soldier referring to Mississippi in general wrote, "Our armies are devastating the land and it is sad to see the destruction that attends our progress — we cannot help it. Farms disappear, houses are burned and plundered, and every living animal is killed and eaten."[16]

IN FEBRUARY JOHN HOUSTON BILLS, the planter near Nashville who had already been pillaged by the Fifth Ohio Cavalry, complained that the 10th Michigan Cavalry had killed or taken most of his corn, hogs, horses, and mules. He confided in his diary that "I consider it useless to make any effort for reclamation." His neighborhood had been so thoroughly stripped by foragers that he believed few people would have enough to eat during the year. His horses and mules were weak from lack of grain and fodder. "Hungry soldiers," he noted, "without distinction regard all as enemies to forage upon." He lamented, "I shall have no stock left anywhere." Bills had little prospect of making a crop because his fences had been burned and most of his slave labor force had fled. Two months later he reflected, "It is 10 months today since we have lived in the midst of a Federal camp. Have we not suffered enough to atone for all our political sins?" He had reached the point of great despair: "We are in the midst of trouble no one knows what to do. Whether to try to plant. If we do not *Want* will be upon us. . . . No protection from the soldiery & no prospect of an end to this desolating war." Near Vicksburg, Union soldiers turned plantations into a "sea of fire." One reported that "coton gin after coton gin was laid in ashes." He reflected, "Large crops of corn shared the same fate, and thus the flames did their work faithfully." The soldiers also took hundreds of mules and horses, sheep and cattle, chickens and geese, wagonloads of hams from smokehouses and inflicted millions of dollars' worth of damage to agricultural property. The year began with loss for farmers and planters in the Western Confederacy, and their situation only got worse.[17]

In areas such as northern Mississippi, Union incursions left the land desolate. By late July a Delta planter in Washington County reported that Yankees had ransacked his plantation; they were left with "no corn, very little meat, in fact little or nothing [was] left on the place." Another planter lamented that "everything looks gloomy! The Yankees are said to be destroying all the crops in Adrian County." Confederate armies also had driven off livestock and impressed horses for the cavalry. One correspondent wrote that "you hear none of the usual sounds of country life; no lowing of cattle, or neighing of neither horses, nor braying of mules, nor bleating of sheep, nor shout or song of laborers in their fields." Most of the plantations had been abandoned, and the countryside was dangerous because Confederate guerrillas preyed on southern farmers and planters by burning cotton "under the delusion that the whole North [was] about to tumble into anarchy for want of cotton." They also settled old grudges and family feuds and made every farmer as "apprehensive of his neighbors" as he was of Federal troops. Planters and farmers in the Western Confederacy became increasingly vulnerable. One Mississippian wrote, "We never feel safe as there is nothing to keep the Yankees from us." A DeSoto County planter petitioned Governor John J. Pettus asking for aid and protection: "It is utterly impossible for us to plant and cultivate a crop this spring unless we have some guarantee of being protected."[18]

On March 31, General Henry Halleck notified General Grant that it was government policy "to withdraw from the enemy as much productive labor as possible to cripple the agricultural labor force." The Union would now make war on southern agriculture as much as on Confederate armies. With southern agriculture destroyed, the Confederacy could not endure. Grant understood the power of southern agriculture to sustain the Confederacy, and he ordered his generals to destroy corn and wheat crops, and everything agricultural that the enemy could use to prolong the war. Troops should take mules and horses to meet their own needs as well as destroy agricultural implements if such destruction did not cause too much delay.[19]

Blackened chimneys and burned houses marked the path of war in western Arkansas. Driven out by war and hunger, pro-Union families departed for Kansas, Missouri, and other points north. One reporter noted that "the wealthiest planters are as destitute as the poorest squatters." So great was the destruction to farms and plantations that one observer contended "a generation cannot repair the ravages of two years." In northwest Arkansas, "jayhawkers and banditti" also caused grave difficulties for farmers. Moreover Federal forces had robbed "friend, foe and neutral alike," taking horses, slaves, wagons, and large quantities of corn and forage. Soldiers with "the avowed determination to starve the people into submission" cut down fruit trees, destroyed agricultural implements, and prevented farmers from planting crops. Union officers also denied farmers access to mills for the grinding of their corn unless they took an oath of allegiance.[20]

In the White River country, Union soldiers shot cattle and hogs and left the livestock lying unbutchered. Although locals attributed most of the stealing of chickens, killing of livestock, and tearing down of fences to Federal soldiers, they also complained that blacks, who had been liberated or had fled their masters, engaged in a "little private stealing of provisions" from farmers. Many farmers and planters in the Arkansas River Valley removed their slaves and mules to the Red River Country in hopes of protecting their property from the invading Union army. Some observers, however, called them alarmists and saw no great threat to property as long as Vicksburg held. These planters needed to return with their slaves and plant their now idle fields, they advised, because "the farming interest must not be neglected anywhere." As long as farmers remained within Confederate lines, they should stay and produce food for the army and the civilian population.[21]

By early April 1863, Union forging parties had largely devastated middle Tennessee. A cavalryman wrote home that "it is really sad to see this beautiful country so ruined. There are no fences left at all. There is no corn and hay for the cattle and horses, but there are no horses left anyhow and the planters have no food for themselves." A Confederate soldier confirmed the destruction: "The country wears the most desolate appearance that I have ever seen anywhere. There is not a stalk of corn or blade of wheat growing." At the same time, a planter complained that "the Federal soldiers have taken every horse mare and mule that I have. They have broken into my smoke house repeatedly and have taken all my hams. They have taken a good deal of my corn and all of my hay and near all of my fodder." Middle Tennessee had become not the breadbasket of the Confederacy but the food basket of the Union army.[22]

As a result, middle Tennessee farmers hesitated to plant crops in the spring of 1863. One planter complained that the Yankees had taken his best mules and that his plowing lagged "owning to a poor weak team" that they left behind. But he considered Confederate soldiers no better than Yankees: "Southern and Northern soldiers take our property each pretending to fear it may fall into the hands of the other & be turned against them." One Confederate soldier reported, "The farmers in this section are not planting much. They are in a bad fix—they do not know whether to plant or not, for if we do not hold the country the enemy will destroy the whole crop." When General Ambrose E. Burnside's forces moved into northern Tennessee, Confederate farmers paid a high price, as his men destroyed flour and meal and other stores near Knoxville. Soon planters complained that the Confederate Commissary Department had caused them considerable grief as the army retreated. One wrote, "We have had hard work to keep them from taking everything they can get their hands on, horses, mules, cattle, etc." From Texas a Tennessee soldier wrote home that "I went out in the country foraging, but could not find anything. Starvation seems to stare them in the face."[23]

In the spring, General Nathaniel Banks planned to sweep through southern Louisiana and ruin the agricultural productivity of that area by taking at least 20,000 cattle, mules, and horses. His incursion into the Bayou Teche country proved successful because his men, in the eyes of one observer, left "scenes of spoliation and devastation unparalleled in civilized warfare" throughout the countryside. One plantation woman likened the arrival of Federal soldiers to a swarm of bees. In one place, "excited troopers were firing into a flock of sheep," she reported. "In another, officers and men were in pursuit of the boys' ponies; in another crowd were the excited chase of the work animals." Another woman reflected, "I can only say . . . it was bedlam let loose."[24]

A Union soldier confirmed the destruction on these farms and plantations: "We were turned loose . . . [and] were suffered to kill cattle, pigs, and poultry. All this marauding went on ruthlessly and wastefully. We left the road behind us foul with the odor of decaying carcasses." One observer claimed that near Vermilion, Louisiana, Union soldiers killed 1,700 cattle, more than the soldiers could themselves eat, residents noted, but which now deprived them of beef. At the same time, Confederate and Union soldiers raced to seize cotton in storage, the former intent on burning it, the latter to confiscate it for later sale by the government. In May, Federal troops in Louisiana continued to seize horses, mules, and beef cattle along with bacon and other provisions, and farmers and planters had no hope of replacing livestock or provisions. By June, a report from Mississippi indicated that Union forces had left a sixty-mile stretch between Milliken's Bend and Hard Pines an "abomination of desolation," as soldiers burned farmhouses and barns. John Perkins's plantation was ransacked and 5,000 bales of cotton and his granaries were burned; the flames could be seen in the dark for seven miles. In Mississippi Federal soldiers also destroyed farm implements and carried off all the slaves from the plantation of Jefferson Davis as well as the plantation of his brother.[25]

By July 1863, Union soldiers had confiscated 3,000 horses and mules from the sugar parishes. One Union observer wrote, "The planters' horses have all been stolen, their mules and teams have all been confiscated. They stand in the midst of their great plantations, with the interest on a heavy mortgage staring them in the face, perfectly powerless. . . . Uncle Sam with more than his usual foresight and severity, has pressed into the service of his soldiers the whole mule-force of the department." They took more than horses and mules, of course, and weathered verbal abuse from the rebel women whose plantations they pillaged as they brushed aside the women's pleadings for mercy. Without mules and horses, planters and their slaves could neither prepare the fields for planting sugarcane nor haul it to the sugarhouses for processing, and the oxen that they sometimes attempted to substitute proved poor replacements. In mid-July, the Union army also attempted to destroy the agricultural sector in the Jackson vicinity. William Tecumseh Sherman laid down his hard hand of war on these Mississippi farmers and planters, and informed General Grant that "we are absolutely stripping the country of corn, hogs, sheep, poultry, everything, and the new-growing corn is being thrown open as pasture fields or hauled for use of our animals." No longer did Union soldiers leave enough food for farm families. But Confederate troops had already done much the same.[26]

At the same time Grant secured a hard-fought victory at Vicksburg in July. He had laid siege to the Confederate entrenchments during May and June. Food ran short in the city with merchants selling flour for $1,000 per barrel and meat at $250 per pound. On July 4, when Lieutenant General Pemberton surrendered "the Gibraltar of the West," the Union gained control of the Mississippi River and divided the Western Confederacy. Farmers and livestock raisers would now have considerable difficulty getting food and forage from the west side of the river to soldiers and civilians on the east bank. The agricultural power of the Confederacy continued to slip away.[27]

During the siege of Vicksburg, Confederate forces burned a large quantity of cotton in the vicinity and Union forces also captured the staple. Planters lost an estimated 10 percent to 20 percent of the cotton that they had consigned to the government but stored on their property. They also lost a similar quantity of their own cotton. In July the Confederate government began hauling government cotton south of Alexandria, Louisiana, to the Sabine River for shipment to Texas and eventual sale in Mexico. In August, Confederate general Edmund Kirby Smith, commanding the

Trans-Mississippi Department – which included Louisiana west of the Mississippi River, Texas, and parts of Arkansas – organized a Cotton Bureau. Soon bureau wagons hauled produce loan cotton to Waco, San Antonio, and Laredo or Eagle Pass, Texas, for sale across the Rio Grande. If cotton planters were not able to send their cotton across the enemy's lines or gain permission to sell it to northern factors through local Union commanders, they confronted seizure of the crop as contraband. Slowly, contraband cotton made its way north.[28]

WHILE SOUTHERN FARMERS STRUGGLED IN the east, the free-market principles of capitalism worked better in the West, particularly in New Orleans where planters and farmers, now firmly under Union control, sold 2,000 bales of cotton in late March and another 1,200 bales reached brokers in Baton Rouge. Some 840 cotton bales also reached Cincinnati by way of Memphis, the product of army confiscation and planter sales. July brought a report that a "great amount of Government cotton" – as much as 12,000 bales below Memphis – would soon be shipped to St. Louis for auction. Much of this fiber had been concealed for months, as farmers and planters waited for the opportunity to reach northern buyers offering high prices. They saw no reason to sell to the Confederacy or wait for a military victory and the return of the British trade when Union forces seemed poised to occupy their countryside and reopen their trade with profitable northern markets. If planters burned their cotton to deny Yankee troops that pleasure, or suffered seizure without compensation, they did so under duress from Confederates agents, the army, and self-styled officials. Indeed, by spring, Louisiana cotton planters were more interested in northern than Confederate currency; more interested in profits than loyalty or patriotism. In Mississippi, farmers would not take Confederate money for their cotton, preferring credit instead. And this meant they were hoping they would eventually be paid with Federal dollars. Some contemporaries reported "immense" quantities of cotton carefully concealed by owners, who hoped for some way to ship it to New Orleans for sale to northern factors. An observer in New Orleans offered a unique perspective by calling southern planters "patriots" if they sold their cotton to northern buyers in occupied territory or across Union lines rather than burning it to keep it from Union hands.[29]

Although the cotton trade further depreciated Confederate currency and compromised any sense of national self-sufficiency, it did not indicate disloyalty in the minds of many planters, particularly if they traded to support their families. Moreover, these planters seldom expressed loyalty to the Union—they just wanted and needed sound Federal dollars and various necessities. Unlike in the Eastern Confederacy, Union forces occupied considerable territory in the West, which eventually enabled the Federal government to reestablish Memphis, Vicksburg, New Orleans, and Natchez as trade centers for farmers, planters, and speculators. Moreover, Union trade goods that passed south into Confederate territory strengthened those trading families and thereby the Confederacy. One Mississippian contended, "The proceeds of the cotton will surely do us more good than cotton will do them."[30]

Still, agricultural trade with the Union meant subjugation. Some of the cotton reached Great Britain, thereby helping to keep that nation out of the war. Trade also strengthened northern manufacturing. Nevertheless, in the minds of some, these exchanges aided the Confederacy and were thus patriotic. In the end, by 1863, justification for the cotton trade with the enemy depended on complicated rationalizations, if not self-justification. Mississippi and Louisiana farmers and planters could have things both ways. Trade enabled them to meet their families' needs while they were patriotically and loyally helping the Confederacy. In addition, they wanted to maintain their traditional trade with the North, but as citizens of an independent and vibrant new nation. Yet trade with the enemy indicated a flagging loyalty to the Confederacy by some farmers and planters, because the government and military could neither meet their needs nor protect them.[31]

In contrast, Union officials believed they were using the cotton trade to bribe southerners into giving up their loyalty to the Confederacy. Earlier, Senator Orville Browning of Illinois expressed this belief, saying that "every Treasury note we put in the pocket of a rebel makes him, to that extent, interested in the government and its friend, and will become one of the means of destroying the Confederacy." General Lorenzo Thomas agreed while he was in the lower Mississippi Valley in late April: "The prospect of a sale of two or three hundred bales of cotton, at the present high prices, is a powerful weight in the scale of loyalties." From this perspective, the self-interest of Confederate farmers and planters would harm their political loyalty to the Confederacy in favor of the Union.[32]

In May a report from Jackson, Mississippi, charged that many cotton producers now sold their fiber to Yankee traders at Memphis. Steamboats carrying planters arrived at Memphis, where the planters took the oath of allegiance and sold their cotton for greenbacks. Then, they often exchanged those greenbacks for Confederate money at a discount of 60 cents on the dollar and used it to purchase more cotton in areas not yet overrun by Federal troops. The planters' hope was that they could get the cotton north to the Memphis market. The newly opened railroads running from Memphis to the interior also brought tons of cotton into the city for sale. "So much," one Mississippian remarked, "for the high patriotism of a large number of cotton producers within Federal lines." As Union forces captured more areas, the cotton trade across Federal lines increased. Produce loan agents also frequently diverted cotton to northern buyers, thereby aiding themselves rather than the Confederate war effort.[33]

The growing cotton trade across Union lines caused Senator James Phelan of Mississippi to introduce a bill in the Confederate Congress in late January that required the appropriation of all cotton in the Confederacy not necessary for domestic use. If a planter or farmer tried to hide his surplus cotton, he forfeited payment for it. Planters and farmers trading cotton to the enemy would be executed for treason. The planters would deliver their cotton where government officials instructed or suffer fine and imprisonment. Upon delivery of their cotton to government storage facilities, they would receive Confederate bonds at the rate of 15 cents per pound with interest from the date of delivery. All cotton in danger of seizure by the enemy would be destroyed upon the order of army officers above the rank of colonel, with compensation at the same rate as if it had been delivered to the government. Anyone exporting cotton would "suffer death." This bill did not pass, but Senator Phelan's attempt to bring rigorous government supervision and order to cotton farming indicated waning support for the Confederacy by some farmers and planters.[34]

One Mississippian considered Phelan's bill a movement "towards centralism." Neither agriculture nor the Confederacy needed more control by the government in Richmond. Phelan's plan would enable the government to gain a monopoly of the cotton trade, control the price abroad, and earn a great profit that would create a "monster" because it would enable the government to take private property for trade and speculation. If the government could take cotton, it could also take tobacco, sugar, corn, and other provisions. Moreover, if the government paid only 15 cents per pound for cotton, it could also arbitrarily decide to pay only 5 cents per pound. Moreover, to the planter's loss, payment in bonds was not payment in circulating, sound currency. Only free markets should determine agricultural prices, not a government arbitrarily fixing prices. Many planters wanted the Confederate government to acquire all of their cotton but at free-market prices. Phelan's bill, however, was, to its critics, despotic. Agricultural policy of any kind meant too much governmental regulation for most southern farmers and planters.[35]

In October Grant issued General Orders No. 141 from Memphis, which made it easier for southerners to sell their cotton, provided they were less than honest about their Confederate sympathies. The order authorized residents in the Department of Tennessee to haul their cotton to any military post or station along the Mississippi River; upon receipt of a permit they could ship it to dealers in Memphis or New Orleans. To receive a permit to sell cotton, farmers and planters had to affirm that they were "well disposed to the Government of the United States" and the owner of the cotton, because all fiber belonging to the Confederate States of America or by anyone bearing arms against the United States would be seized and sold. They also had to affirm that the cotton had never belonged to the Confederacy, thereby giving previous secessionists a reprieve – provided they lied about their past agricultural activities. Military commanders had orders to privilege the sale of cotton by producers rather than speculators, especially if the owners had only small quantities of cotton and appeared to be "in poor circumstances." The orders thereby aided small-scale farmers. Soon the levy at New Orleans became laden with cotton and other agricultural produce.[36]

Both northern and southern speculators and southern planters and farmers benefited from trading across lines. Union policy permitted southern planters to sell cotton to government agents, who paid 25 percent of the purchase price immediately with the remaining balance due after the war. Confederate farmers, planters, and cotton dealers profited, and this policy helped keep the fiber from reaching Europe. The Union also needed cotton for manufacturing and for diplomatic purposes, and Confederate farmers and planters needed the money. Profit trumped politics on the western farm front throughout the Civil War. While cotton went up and provisions down the Mississippi River, this trade eventually aided the Confederate army, but President Lincoln believed that it also benefited northern manufacturers and helped weaken the loyalty of Confederate farmers to their cause.[37]

IN 1863 FARM WOMEN IN the Western Confederacy now commonly worked in the fields. During the early spring, soldiers foraging for the Thirteenth Tennessee Regiment reported that near Shelbyville, Tennessee, "the women was plowing in almost every field." By July southerners in Lincoln County observed that on the small farms, "many a woman who never before held a plow is now seen in the corn field—many a young girl who would have blushed at the thought before of handling a plow-line, now naturally and unconsciously cries 'gee up' to Dobbin." One observer noted that "Many a Ruth, as of old, is seen today, binding and gleaning in the wheat fields but, alas! no Boaz is there to console or to comfort." In Mississippi white women in hoop-less skirts and broad sunbonnets plowed fields. In Tennessee farm women also cut wheat during the harvest, but it is unclear whether they used grain cradles or the lighter scythes to harvest because the men who remained on the farms used scythes to mow hay. Slave women also continued to work in the fields. In Mississippi they used hoes and knives to chop down cornstalks, and they planted corn. Near Memphis black women went about the business of cultivating cotton and corn with their hoes, and they appeared to be the "sole workers on the land."[38]

In May a Confederate soldier reported that in middle Tennessee, Federal troops had taken all of the male and female slaves as well as horses and mules. The white men of fighting age had gone to either the Confederate or Union armies, and only women remained to operate the farms. Primarily these farm women milked a few cows and sold or bartered their milk to the Union army at "enormous prices." When these country women marketed their butter and eggs in nearby towns, they too refused Confederate money. Instead, they wanted to barter for rice, salt, and molasses, contending they could not eat money and their families were hungry. When one farm woman traded her butter for molasses, an observer reported that "her delighted urchins gathered round and stuck their fingers in the molasses for a taste. Such are the pictures of life around us." In the meantime, other white women along with their children and old men planted and cultivated the corn. They, too, refused Confederate money, which they considered "useless" because they could not buy anything with it. Farmwives in the Western Confederacy, like their counterparts in the East, also received advice about planting, harvesting, and raising livestock from their husbands in the army, who also confided plans for the farm when they returned. Often, however, the letters stopped coming.[39]

SLAVEHOLDERS NEEDED MORE THAN WIVES and daughters to provide sufficient labor to produce crops of any kind. In January a planter near Nashville complained that his slaves worked only as they saw fit, and generally did "little" or "no good." They seemed restless, and "I think the value of them is about out." He hired a manager for his plantation and paid him $25 per month, but he did not expect his workers to improve. Still, they produced at least six bales of cotton, which he sold for 50 cents a pound to the Union army with payment in U.S. Treasury notes. But he complained that Federal troops had taken more than 900 slaves from the area. He considered this nothing less than theft and caustically noted that the seizure of slaves was "a nice way [to] win friends by robbing the people of more than *half* a million dollars worth of property in one day." In mid-May only a few slaves remained on his plantation, but"I think my people [are still] pretty faithful so far & I give them credit for fidelity." By midsummer a Claiborne County, Mississippi, farmer reported that "all Negroes on the large places in the county have left for the land of promise or a great many of them were forced away." Another planter reported, "All the negroes [were] doing nothing" and departures for Union lines were increasing. But a planter's wife near Natchez wistfully and optimistically wrote, "I hope they will all prove faithful to the end."[40]

Despite these problems inflation caused slave prices to increase. In Mississippi, male field hands brought from $1,700 to $1,800 and as much as $2,500 during March, while "common field hands" brought as much as $3,020 for an eighteen-year-old male and $2,025 for a twenty-five-year-old woman, while a thirteen-year-old boy brought $2,415, a twenty-five-year-old man $1,750, and a fifty-five-year-old man $1,150, all in Confederate money. In April a Houston slave dealer sold sixty slaves, "mostly field negros [sic]" in lots or families, which brought $105,000, for an average of about $1,750 per slave. Buyers expected to pay about $2,250 apiece for males if they were "good field hands." By the end of the month buyers paid $4,000 to $4,500 for women ages eighteen to twenty years old, while "ordinary negro men" brought more than $4,000. Observers considered these prices "unusually high."[41]

After the fall of Vicksburg, however, the slave market essentially collapsed. By autumn one Tennessee planter had lost at least $16,300 in slaves, with prime male and female field hands valued at $1,250 each. Such a price led him to conclude that "slavery under the influence of our Yankee invaders is of no value." At the same time the exodus of planters and their slaves from Louisiana to Texas became "immense." No one knew how they intended to live, but some owners hired out their slaves at whatever task could be found, such as driving wagons or doing construction for railroads. One Louisiana planter lent twenty slaves to a Texas planter for $25 per month for men and $20 per month for women (boys and girls went for $15 per month), with payment in cotton ready for market based on the rate of 8 cents per pound. One slave owner received $225 per month for the hire of six slaves. But with milk selling at $1 per quart and other foods comparatively expensive, most Texans could not afford slave labor, even if they paid with Confederate dollars.[42]

Although slavery still appeared to be flourishing, at least to some observers in the East, problems developed when Union forces captured sugar plantations in Louisiana. Sugar planters protested to Federal troops that they had not been responsible for the rebellion and that they were victims of politicians and young radicals whose actions oppressed and ruined them. Although the cotton planters on the Sea Islands of South Carolina had lost their plantations, they often had abandoned their lands before Union forces arrived. As a result, Yankee soldiers occupied nonworking plantations. In Louisiana, however, General Banks occupied functioning sugar plantations. The problem was not an absence of plantation management but rather a lack of labor. Lincoln's Emancipation Proclamation did not apply to the portions of Louisiana occupied by Federal troops. The slaves were exempt from the proclamation, and Banks could not free them or return runaway slaves to their masters. At best he could only encourage the slaves to remain on the sugar plantations and work for their masters, and to hope their owners would treat them kindly and fairly and pay them a small wage. The alternative was to let the sugar plantations deteriorate and production languish. Agriculture on the sugar plantations meant placating the planters, which meant ensuring a labor supply.[43]

General Butler's agricultural labor policy instituted in late 1862 at first applied only to a limited area where federal authority prevailed — basically the sugar plantation region along the Mississippi River — but other Louisiana parishes soon fell to Federal forces, which brought more slaves into Union lines. Lincoln's Emancipation Proclamation took effect on January 1, 1863, further demonstrating that a new labor system for the planters would necessarily replace the old. Spring planting seemed like an unprofitable exercise for most sugar planters, because a consistent and reliable labor force could not be guaranteed. However, General Banks (who had replaced Butler in December) understood the planters' need for labor, the freedmen's need for self-supporting work, and the planters' need for control of their workers, as well as the army's need for peace and order. But the planters were unhappy that Banks continued Butler's contract labor policy because it prevented them from using force to compel work and mandated them to pay their hired laborers, who theoretically remained slaves. Overall, the planters accepted the concept of "free labor" as a mere technicality, and they did their best to treat their workers as slaves, to the disgust of the freedmen. As a result, Federal labor policy for the sugar plantations experienced a troubled year.[44]

In mid-January, a group of planters in Terrebonne Parish, Louisiana, told Banks that their former slaves would not work. "The time has come," they reported, "when preparations [sic] for planting & cultivating the crops of 1863 should be made. But without teams & the ability to command the labor of our negroes, nothing can be done." Banks ignored their belief that their former black workers still belonged to them, but he asked a group of planters and the Sequestration Commission to develop a labor system that would provide "food, clothes, and proper treatment and just compensation for negroes." In early February, upon their advice, Banks issued General Orders No. 12, which authorized the Sequestration Commission to establish new guidelines for operating the plantations behind Union lines. The Sequestration Commission, with Banks's support, ended the seizure of plantations and attempted to appease planters by agreeing to "induce the slaves to return to the plantations where they belong," and by requiring them "to work diligently and faithfully . . . for one year [and] to maintain respectful deportment to their employers, and perfect subordination to their duties." The planters, in turn, would agree to feed, clothe, and treat their workers humanely. Banks also ordered that the former slaves could not be taken from the plantations without his approval.[45]

Essentially, Banks met the agricultural needs of the planters by ordering the slaves to labor in "perfect subordination" for less generous terms than Butler had authorized. Black plantation workers now would collectively receive one-twentieth of the crop proceeds at the end of the year for division among themselves. They also would receive monthly wages of $2 for men and $1 for women. Banks, like Butler, did not consult the freed black men and women, but the planters were assured a labor force that would enable them to resume sugar production. The planters still considered their workforce slave labor because, in addition to long-standing social and cultural norms, the Emancipation Proclamation did not apply to slaveholders in Union-controlled areas. Technically they were correct because the Emancipation Proclamation freed slaves only in areas under rebellion. Slaves in Union-controlled territories were still slaves under the law if not in reality. Black workers, however, refused "perfect subordination" and to work like slaves, clear evidence that they understood as the planters did not that a revolution had occurred in southern agricultural labor. Even so, the planters often shorted their wages, failed to provide adequate clothing, and used force to ensure compliance with their directives. Yet the freedmen and -women worked on the sugar plantations as long as the planters did not treat them entirely like slaves, thereby melding together free labor and sugar production for the first time.[46]

The Sequestration Commission administered the labor contracts between the black workers and native white plantation owners, while the Quartermaster Department created the Plantation Bureau to lease abandoned plantations, usually to northerners for $1,000 annually. The commission also established a Bureau of Negro Labor to recruit African Americans for plantation work. Black workers assigned to government-supervised plantations accepted the new labor system better than those workers sent to plantations operated by native whites, who invariably treated them like slaves and who considered them "their negroes."[47]

Confrontation occurred, not surprisingly. Freedpeople in Louisiana told military authorities that they desired to work on government-occupied plantations and were reluctant to return to their old masters. In the end, most returned to their old plantations anyway, because the government told them that they must work for the planters or labor upon the levees and roads for the army with pay only in rations. Confronted with this stark choice, the former slaves opted to work for wages on the plantations. This Federal policy helped remove refugees living behind Union lines where they had to be fed and sheltered. So successful was Banks's labor program, many Louisiana planters thought by mid-April that they now suffered more from a lack of mules than from insufficient black labor. Federal officials also advocated the return of the freedmen and -women to their plantations to prevent disease in overcrowded refugee camps. This policy, supporters believed, would help the former slaves learn the value of money and elevate them to the position of white labor on the social scale, as well as gain planter support for political reconstruction. Confronted with returning to their former plantations and working for wages or laboring for food on Federal projects, freedmen and -women "cheerfully" returned to their plantations where they "actually performed the average work of slaves," according to some observers. This system, of course, was free labor in name only.[48]

The new labor regime required all workers to sign a yearlong contract. Task work would be assigned when possible and "lazy work" would cause a deduction in wages. The workday would run from daylight to dark.

Anyone reporting to work ten minutes late would be fined 10 cents, with the money going to the hospital fund. All hands would be in their cabins by the "last tap of the bell," or pay a 10 cent fine. They could not leave their cabins until the bell rang again in the morning. Damage of farm implements and tools and abuse of mules brought fines, as did the failure to wear clean clothes on Sundays. Workers who treated the mules well could receive a bonus at the end of the year, and they also could receive a bonus for producing more than the required amount of sugar allotted per hand. Each family would receive a half acre for a garden. No worker could leave the plantation without written permission from the manager or owner. Good behavior would be rewarded with a monetary prize. The manager ran the daily affairs of the plantation with absolute authority.[49]

One Louisiana planter, who said he spoke for many, thought that Banks's plantation labor policy made sense and that, in fact, he had been practicing it for a long time. Arguing that the planters had been misunderstood and were poorly represented by "young, ignorant men" in Richmond, he contended that the planters supported the Union and added that "wealth and agriculture never breed revolution." Secessionists had forced war and independence upon Louisiana's planters. As a result, the value of his property had depreciated by 50 percent, and he had lost seven good men, although he had never whipped a slave in his life. For many years, the planter contended, he had paid his slaves not less than $75 per year, "except those who were too lazy to work." Anticipating the sharecropping system that would soon replace slavery, he had allocated seventy-five acres to his slaves for cultivating cotton, and they gave him half of the proceeds. Sensible people should recognize that successful agriculture and slavery went hand in hand, he maintained. The secessionists had ruined a good agricultural system, but his form of sharecropping could save it.[50]

By July Banks's contract labor system had reinvented agriculture on many Louisiana plantations. Overseers and the proximity of the plantations to Confederate lines continued to cause problems, but Banks had succeeded in creating a new agricultural labor system. Agricultural slavery in the Western Confederacy behind Union lines had ended. Although native planters considered Banks's contract labor system a radical policy, the black workers considered it little better than slavery. Until the end of the year, some planters tried to hire white workers and talked about importing workers, but they ultimately resigned themselves to competing for black agricultural labor.[51]

Additional free-labor systems developed in other parts of the Western Confederacy. In March, General Grant, Secretary of the Treasury Salmon P. Chase, and President Lincoln, drawing on Banks's contract labor policy in Louisiana, authorized Adjutant General Lorenzo Thomas to take control of the plantations from Columbus, Kentucky, to Grand Gulf, Mississippi, in the Department of the West. Thomas's responsibility was to develop an agricultural labor plan for the freedpeople or contrabands in the Mississippi Valley. He intended to locate a "loyal population" along the Mississippi River that could lease the abandoned plantations and rejuvenate agriculture. To accomplish his plan, Thomas appointed three commissioners who were to supervise the renting of plantations to "persons of proper character and qualifications," and to ensure that the "mutual obligations" between black workers and employers were "faithfully performed." The commissioners also had authority to safeguard the moral and intellectual needs of the black labor force, and to "carry out the policy of the Government regarding the negroes that [were] to be put to agricultural pursuits." This Federal policy would make the employment and subsistence of the free black men and women the matter of private enterprise, and the plantation lessees would not pay rent but rather a tax on the products of the plantation to the U.S. Treasury Department.[52]

The Federal superintendents would provide as many negroes of "average quality" that the lessee requested. The lessee would sign a contract to employ the workers until February 1, 1864, and was responsible for feeding and clothing them and treating them humanely. The cost of their clothing would be deducted from their wages but furnished at cost. If the superintendents could not find lessees to manage the captured plantations, the government could employ blacks under the terms that it deemed in the best interests of the workers – provided that they became self-sustaining and not a burden on the Federal government. Thomas set the wage rate for black workers on government-operated plantations at $7 per month for able-bodied men over fifteen years of age and at $5 per month for women in that same category. Children between the ages of twelve and fifteen would be paid half that wage, while children under twelve years of age were prohibited from conducting fieldwork. Families had to be kept together. The tax on the produce of the land in lieu of rent was calculated at the rate of $2 per 400-pound bale of cotton and 5 cents for every bushel of corn and potatoes produced. Thomas expected black soldiers to provide the necessary security for the workers on the plantations. The commissioners were to report their activities to the secretary of war every two weeks.[53]

In August Grant also issued General Orders No. 57, which authorized the provost marshal at every military post in the Department of Tennessee to ensure that all freedpeople within their jurisdiction were "employed by some white person" or sent to camps for the African Americans. Planters could contract with their former slaves for their labor and pay a monthly wage, or they could support them with food and clothing, plus provide one-twentieth of the crop for plantation work on a yearly basis. Anyone hiring a former slave had to post bond and promise kind treatment and proper care. White adjustment to the new system proved difficult for most planters, however. During the sugarcane grinding season in the autumn, one Louisiana planter complained that "a man had as well be in purgatory, as attempt to work a sugar plantation under existing circumstances." Another sugarcane planter contended that planters needed a "thorough control of ample and continuous labor" and that "without coercion, & without fear of punishment which is essential to stimulate the idle and correct the vicious," sugarcane production would not return to Louisiana.[54]

Speculators quickly sought the abandoned or seized plantations behind Union lines, because they could produce a cotton crop for 3 to 8 cents per pound and sell it for 50 cents or more per pound, and the Federal government eagerly welcomed northerners who wanted to lease plantations. General Thomas also permitted superintendents to manage some plantations exclusively for the Federal government and to hire black workers to produce a cotton crop. Even so, the plantations, no matter whether supervised by northerners or southerners or the army, produced only a half crop in 1863, and reports emerged that "very few secured even this return." The planting season was delayed because many leases were not contracted until late, because planters did not have adequate horses and mules, and because of Confederate raids.[55]

By December, northerners who leased plantations and hired freedpeople to work the land had, in the words of one observer, "no motives either of loyalty or humanity. The desire of gain alone prompts them; and they care little whether they make it out of blood of those they employ or from the soil." Another contemporary noted, "The majority of the lessees . . . were unprincipled men, who undertook the enterprise solely as a speculation. . . . Very few of them paid the negroes for their labor, except in furnishing them small quantities of goods for which they charged five times the value." In Natchez the superintendent of the freedmen also denounced the lessees, charging that their "highest thought is a greenback, whose God is a cotton bale, and whose devil is a guerrilla." Freedpeople paid a high price for the renewal of agriculture in the Union-controlled areas of the Western Confederacy.[56]

IN THE EARLY AUTUMN UNION forces had pursued Confederate forces under General Braxton Bragg into the mountains near Chattanooga. The armies clashed in mid-month near Chickamauga Creek. Several days of fighting resulted in terrible losses on both sides, but Union general George Thomas held the high ground, and the Confederates retreated. It was another loss for southern military power and another loss for southern agriculture: more dead soldier-farmers and more farmland land now under Federal control. Although Bragg maintained a fortified position near Chattanooga, Grant's forces led by Sheridan, Hooker, Thomas, and Sherman forced him to retreat into Georgia. With Chattanooga in Union control, the "Gateway to the South" lay open. Independence was proving elusive, and the Confederate army and civilian population needed flour, cornmeal, bacon, pork, and beef. Southern farmers and planters had an enormous task before them as they awaited a new planting season.[57]

In September the Mississippi River opened to unrestricted trade. Beef cattle brought $23 to $25 and hogs $10 to $20 per head, respectively, in Jefferson City, Louisiana. In New Orleans, the wholesale price of cornmeal brought $4 to $5 per bushel – high prices that indicated scarcity, consumer demand, and profits for livestock men and farmers. Much of the wheat and rye crop, however, remained unharvested for want of labor, although a few black workers could be seen with cradle scythes in the fields. Cotton factors now began shipping great quantities of cotton upriver. During one week in October alone, buyers shipped 1,013 bales of cotton from New Orleans to New York. Farmers and planters hoped these sales indicated a return to normalcy, as did sugar planters, who sent 2,500 hogsheads up the Mississippi River to markets in the Northwest and by ship to Boston. The highest-quality sugar now brought 12 cents per pound. Sugar planters also sent hogsheads of molasses to northern markets at prices ranging from 32 to 35 cents per gallon depending on quality.[58]

Still, food supplies remained depleted in New Orleans where, by late October, little flour remained. Common flour sold for $12.50, and extra fine brought $15 per barrel, respectively, up from $9.50 to $11 in February. Beef and pork supplies were nearly exhausted, and salt pork sold at $22 per barrel and bacon no longer remained in stock. Farmers who sold potatoes and onions on the landing received as much as $5.50 per bushel, while apples brought $6 per barrel. Chickens sold for $5 to $7 per dozen — prices that would be considered cheap by a Richmond resident.[59]

Feed and forage remained in short supply, with Louisiana hay bringing $15 per ton, compared with $11 per hundred pounds in Richmond. Although a few steamboats now arrived at New Orleans with food and forage from northern farmers, prices remained exorbitant. Northern hay brought from $75 to $85 per ton. Small shipments of cheese and butter and salt pork began arriving from the North via the Mississippi River and sold quickly at high prices. In October cotton planters brought their first picking to market. Trade with New York became so great that the price declined from 1 to 3 cents per pound depending on the grades, but still brought as much as 73 cents per pound for the best fiber. Northern corn brought $1.67 and oats $1.60 per bushel, and flour from $7.50 to $7.60 per barrel at the landing.[60]

The opportunity to trade across Union lines for greenbacks proved too tempting for many planters. Consequently, in November, the Mississippi legislature sought to discourage planting of the spring cotton crop by imposing a tax on planters of 5 cents per pound if they produced more than one 500-pound bale of ginned cotton per worker. Although cotton production plummeted by 90 percent, the price rose, and many planters could not resist trading with the enemy. With cotton averaging about $1 per pound on the New York market by the end of the year, farmers and planters could make money on local and regional markets, such as Memphis, if they could get their crop to the factors or speculators who would buy it. Although the Federal government also purchased cotton from loyal southerners, including those who had taken the oath of allegiance, it continued to seize the cotton of disloyal planters and sell it. Some observers believed Union forces would capture or burn 250,000 bales of cotton in Texas, most of which rested along the levees of the Rio Grande at Brownsville, where the amount stored was "immense."[61]

By July in the far Western Confederacy, Confederate money was a rarity. In Laredo, Texas, where corn sold for $6 per bushel wholesale and $8 per bushel retail, U.S. and Mexican specie changed hands between farmers and merchants. By October farmers near Seguin, Texas, who had abundant produce would not sell for Confederate money. As Confederate currency depreciated, they charged higher prices for their grain and vegetables. They sought specie but reluctantly accepted Confederate money for beef and cornmeal at the ratio of 20 to 1. One resident reported, "People are now buying up and driving cattle to Mexico, because they get specie for them, and these very men have been exempted from conscription on account of their stock." Increasingly, town-dwelling Texans blamed their "country friends" for the cost of cornmeal, flour, and produce. Texas farmers also continued to raise cotton. They hauled the staple to border towns, where agents sold the cotton to Mexican buyers. Inadequate transportation had driven the price of corn on most markets to at least $3 per bushel, in part, because freighters privileged the hauling of government cotton.[62]

In early December several thousand bales of cotton sold in Memphis for 55 cents to 72 cents per pound. High cotton prices in the Western Confederacy prompted a Union army officer to write an open letter to northerners, pointing out that the Western Confederacy was an *"immense gold field"* of abandoned plantations stretching from Helena, Arkansas, to Natchitoches, Louisiana. Although northerners had worked some of the plantations with hired black labor, only a few operated with leases, and these would expire in February 1864. Such plantations now existed for the taking. If a northerner leased or bought 200 acres, he could expect to produce 200 bales of cotton, which, given the current price in New York, meant $40,000. With hired black labor he could produce cotton for five cents and earn a profit of forty-five cents per pound, respectively. Put another way, after paying $20 for labor, he could earn $180 per bale. The northerner believed that the people who cultivated the next cotton crop, blacks excluded, would receive preference for purchasing land, and he expected a land run into the Western Confederacy during the coming spring. In some respects, his estimation of profits from cotton production on the abandoned and now army-supervised plantations proved too modest, at least for the time.[63]

In late December, a Tennessee planter still complained about Federal troops who invariably took what they wanted without providing "pay or paper," or a document promising reimbursement. In Arkansas farmers confronted other problems. Brigadier General John McNeil, headquartered at Fort Smith, ordered the confiscation of all cotton in the District of the Frontier. The Federal government would then sell the cotton and pay "loyal owners" for damages due from seizure of their plantations. He also prohibited the sale of agricultural produce to middlemen and speculators. Farmers could sell wheat, corn, oats, hay, flour, meat, and livestock only to agents of the U.S. government or limited quantities for immediate public consumption. When northerners received reports of confiscated sugar plantations and burning cotton, they believed that Confederate planters and farmers got what they deserved. Perhaps so, but they could do little at the time to rectify the past and went about the tasks of threshing oats and rye and plowing land for small grains.[64]

At the end of December, farmers and planters looked back on a year of loss. Vicksburg had fallen and Bragg's army had been defeated at Chattanooga. Many sugar and cotton plantations had been abandoned or seized by Federal troops. Slave labor had been ended in fact if not by law. In Union-occupied areas, much of the land remained uncultivated and many farm and plantation homes stood vacant. Other farms and plantations suffered continued pillaging by Confederate and Union soldiers. Agriculture as known in the Western Confederacy when the war began had largely been relegated to the past, and much of it was never to return.

CHAPTER SIX

Eastern Hard Times

In the Eastern Confederacy farmers and planters greeted 1864 with a feeling of despondency. In this last full year of the war, Union forces pressed General Lee's army hard and made incremental territorial gains at great cost to both sides. Attrition wore away at Confederate armies. Farmers and planters now confronted even greater difficulty supplying soldiers and civilians with food due to disrupted production, impressment of provisions, worthless currency, and conscription. Feared by all, the year would bring the collapse of Confederate agricultural power. A Florida farmer wrote that "every body is tired and disgusted with the war." A Virginian agreed: "We have many privations to encounter.... You do *now* 'feel the war' most basically in the way of living necessities [that] are at most fabulous prices." Indeed, clear signs of distress could not be ignored. Lee did not have enough salted meat or fresh beef to feed his men beyond half rations, and the prospects for receiving cattle from the western counties in Virginia had become slim. His best prospects remained raiding enemy lines and stealing the needed livestock. Across the South many merchants accepted corn, wheat, fodder, and other agricultural products as payment for shoes, cloth, and newspaper subscriptions among other goods. With Confederate currency nearly worthless, a barter economy emerged among farmers and merchants. At the same time, planters held 3 million bales of cotton, of which the government's Produce Loan Office owned about 10 percent of that amount. These planters reserved the right to raise cotton and sell it to whomever they pleased, or to hold it until peace – and high prices – returned.[1]

Confederate commissary agents and army officers continued to impress farm produce, paying with paper currency or, more likely, a piece of paper promising to pay, but always at lower prices than the farmers wanted. Georgia planters had become so distressed over conditions that they urged the governor to call a convention to determine a uniform and fair price for corn, pork, bacon, fodder, and other farm provisions for the duration of the war. Planters in Monroe County also met to establish reasonable prices for their produce. They agreed to sell corn for $2.50 per bushel, wheat for $5 per bushel, bacon for $1, and beef for 40 cents per pound, respectively. They considered these prices cheap and affordable for both government commissary agents and consumers. With land in the county averaging $10 per acre (little changed since 1860), with slave values averaging $1,000 per person, and with mules valued at $200 each, the agricultural situation remained sound, they believed, with one exception: government officials acquiring their produce for less than the price they deemed fair.[2]

Residents in Albany saw the situation differently. As one commented about food prices, "Our people have found out that a war is going on, and that they have regulated their prices accordingly." By late February Georgia farmers sold corn for $3 per bushel, bacon for $2 per pound, and whiskey for $5 per gallon. In Houston County, South Carolina, farmers and planters acted in their own best interests, setting prices for the army at $3 per bushel for corn, $5 per bushel for wheat, and $1.25 per pound for bacon. They agreed to sell uncut pork for 60 cents per pound and stall-fed beef at 50 cents per pound. They also urged farmers in other states to take similar action, arguing that "the planter who does this is equally a patriot with the man who shoulders a musket." The Confederate government, however, continued to set its price schedules based on its own needs and "want of money" – not on the wishes of farmers for higher prices.[3]

Hungry Richmond residents still blamed farmers for their plight, contending they withheld their produce in a search for higher prices. Often they were correct because farmers did not want to sell their produce for Confederate currency, so they hoarded their provisions. In the meantime, many people in the Eastern Confederacy went hungry. Most families could not afford butter at $6 per pound, up a dollar since December, or beef at $1 or pork at $2.50 per pound, respectively, or bacon at $3.50 or more per pound, if available. Corn brought $12 per bushel and flour as much as $120 per barrel, an increase of $10 per barrel from January to February. Reports from the Shenandoah Valley and southwestern Virginia indicated that supplying cattle for eastern markets would soon become more difficult, if not impossible, which further increased the public fear of hunger.[4]

The food shortages that accompanied the beginning of the new year brought more criticism of the government and finger pointing across the South. In South Carolina farmers held back from taking their provisions to market, in part because they distrusted the currency and "partly from real scarcity." Complaints came from Georgia that farmers charged too much for their produce during these "troublous times." The public had food security; it would not starve, but consumers assumed that farmers had few operating costs, especially if they worked their fields and tended their livestock with their own labor. Farmers countered that they barely made enough to survive from the sale of their produce, but most Georgians in the towns and cities had little sympathy for such arguments. One Virginian noted, "Rations scarce as hen's teeth."[5]

Along with these complaints came the call for farmers to "dispense liberally of their products" to the army when it was in danger of being overrun by the enemy. Northern Virginians who made this call believed that Lee's forces would fall back as General George Meade's Army of the Potomac advanced, exposing good farmland and its produce to the Yankees. Would it not be best to give everything away to help feed the army rather than have it captured by the enemy? The rationale given was that "if the farmers of Virginia prefer the condition of the people of Culpeper, Norfolk, and New Orleans, to their present state, they have only to keep fast their grip on their corn and wheat, and their desires can be gratified." This view, of course, hardly expressed optimism about ultimate victory, but it held a kernel of truth that invading Union forces should not find food and livestock for their own use on farms that Lee's army could not protect.[6]

In January another southerner wrote, "There is no doubt that national character and national progress depend a good deal more upon food than is generally acknowledged." Slaves and white workers in the fields – as well as the army and the civilian population – particularly needed meat, the supply of which had become dangerously uncertain. Others, trying to be helpful, suggested that southerners ate too much meat and needed to practice restraint. A sound public policy and common sense would lessen the crisis. If Congress did not swell the army beyond the ability of the government to feed it, if the "capricious impressments of lazy beef-agents" did not sweep the markets bare, and if legislators provided a sound currency that people could trust, then farmers and planters would bring their ample produce and livestock to market, and all would be well.[7]

As the scarcity of grain for millers in Richmond continued, the best grades of flour brought $125 per barrel. Even if shoppers had money, they confronted "prices almost fabulous" and could expect to pay prices that had doubled since the end of 1863. Farmers liked getting $30 per bushel for wheat and $18 per bushel for cornmeal, but the high cost of food had become daily problems for many southerners. When superfine flour reached $235 per barrel in Confederate currency, the equivalent of $10 in gold, one resident sarcastically remarked, "We are a great people."[8]

Most residents could not afford such a high price and resigned themselves to doing without, particularly beef. Empty market stalls for cattle brought complaints that while the country was "full of beef" outside the city limits, lazy government impressment agents waited for butchers to prepare the meat and seized it once the carcasses had been cut. These "government vultures" not only decreased the meat supply intended for the public but also paid only half the market price. Some whites believed the meat shortage could be alleviated by feeding less beef to their slaves. In South Carolina consumers suffered from a lack of meat, which increasingly lowered morale. One planter reflected that "if the *Food question* can be satisfactorily disposed of . . . we have nothing else to fear." At the same time, food prices for city dwellers were two to three times higher than in small towns, and both the quantity and nutritional value of food declined. Meals became monotonous. In the coastal lowlands, many people lived on rice and bread. Cornbread, field peas (or regular peas), bacon, and milk constituted the diets of many uplanders. Two meals a day became the standard in many areas. Although hunger did not know class lines or social distinctions, one astute South Carolina woman noted that "I have never heard of genteel people starving so I suppose something will turn up." Yet, day-to-day living became a challenge, particularly when children needed food.[9]

In January Governor Joseph E. Brown of Georgia told James A. Seddon, secretary of war, that "many of our fields now lie uncultivated, and if large additional levies of troops are to be made . . . many more must be neglected. How, then, are we to make a support for another year?" He had traveled through his state's most productive portions and found a country drained of agricultural produce. "I do not see how it is possible to supply the people and the army with bread till another crop is made, while the supply of meat is entirely inadequate," he wrote. Moreover, "the cattle have been so generally taken for the army as to leave a still less encouraging prospect of meat for another year, and if heavy calls are to be made for troops to be taken from the agricultural pursuits the prospect for bread will indeed be gloomy." To help meet the food needs of Georgians, Brown prohibited the export of corn and salt from the state.[10]

In late January Seddon authorized the Chatham Railroad to exchange tobacco through Union lines for bacon. Some argued that such trading would deprive Confederate soldiers of their tobacco and increase prices, but the need for meat drove this decision. Destroyed railroad tracks, insufficient rolling stock, poor logistical coordination, military priority, northern raids, and bad weather deepened the food crisis in the Eastern Confederacy, particularly in Richmond. Food supplies ready for shipment from outlying towns and neighboring states often remained in warehouses. The condition of agriculture remained grim. By February scarcity and speculation drove food prices upward. In Richmond flour brought at least $225 per barrel, up more than $100 since January, and cornmeal went as high as $30 per bushel, an increase of $5 in a month. Bacon cost as much as $6.50 per pound – double the price from thirty days earlier – pork went for $4 per pound, and beef for $3.50 per pound, while rice proved scarce at 45 cents per pound. In March prices rose even higher, with bacon at $7.50 per pound, pork at $5.50 per pound, and beef at $4.50 per pound. Turkeys cost $6 each and chickens $6 per pair; butter was $10 per pound, up from $4 in February, and eggs were $5.50 per dozen, an increase from $2.50 in January. Only the forethought of the Supply Committee of the Richmond City Council had led to the stockpiling of several thousand bushels of corn for distribution to needy families facing starvation.[11]

Yet northern Virginia farmers still withheld their commodities from the Richmond market. The government had announced in February that a new currency would replace the old, effective July 1, and farmers hoped that the combination of high prices and sound money would allow them to reap good profits. They believed that even if prices declined, they would make as much from later sales of their produce under the new currency as they would from sales under the old paper money. Either way, they reasoned, they could not lose. In the meantime, many people in Richmond went hungry. One cynic contended that the "country people" would not bring their produce to the bare markets of Richmond until April 1, which, he observed wryly, was "All Fools' Day."[12]

This strategy worked. By late March the price of white beans had increased during the month from $60 to $75 per bushel on the Richmond market. Corn, which sold for $1.25 per bushel in Georgia and Alabama, was $40 per bushel in Richmond – up from $20 in February. As agricultural and food prices increased, newspaper editors once again urged farmers and planters to make the proverbial two blades of grass grow where only one grew before. It was said, "Every plow driven through the fertile soil of the South helps drive back the ruthless destroying invaders of it." With whiskey selling for $100 per gallon in Richmond, however, some farmers could see the value of selling their corn in liquid form.[13]

By late winter the price of food in Athens, Georgia, had reached "exorbitant rates," caused, in part, by wholesalers and merchants buying and selling among themselves and raising the price each time before food reached grocers' shelves. Some residents suggested forming a joint stock company to buy provisions and sell at cost, thereby circumventing middlemen. But consumers also accused farmers, particularly in Virginia and North Carolina, of being "utterly devoid of humanity and patriotism, holding their surplus back, in order that they may filch the last dime out of their suffering and needy fellows, and boastingly assert that their corn is not for sale until a fabulous price is attained." When a Georgia farmer sold thirteen bushels of wheat for $15 per bushel in Rome, their fears seemed confirmed. In Asheville, North Carolina, bacon brought $2.25 and beef 90 cents per pound, respectively, which one farm woman said, "'Tis a fair price I think.'"[14]

IN JANUARY THE DISTRICT COMMISSARY agent for the army in Montgomery, Alabama, needed 200,000 pounds of bacon, 1,500 cattle, 10,000 bushels of wheat, and 12,000 hogs, but he did not have the currency or credit to acquire those provisions from area farmers and planters, who balked at accepting Confederate money anyway. Others across the Eastern Confederacy felt the same. A North Carolinian contended that farmers and planters should not be so "ignorant" to accept Confederate money as a loan or payment, which he considered nothing more than "trash." As a result, on February 17, Congress passed a currency reform act to resolve this problem, provide a stable currency, and end rapid inflation. This legislation required the conversion of all existing Confederate currency except $1, $2, and $5 bills into bonds bearing 4 percent interest by April 1, 1864. One South Carolina farmer thought those bonds to fund the new currency would be worth "devilish little." Thereafter any currency still outstanding could be exchanged for new money at the rate of $3 for $2 until July 1, after which it would be subject to a 5 percent discount when used to help withdraw the old currency from circulation. On January 1, 1865, all old currency would become worthless. By that time, however, many southern farmers refused to accept any Confederate currency—they demanded specie or Union dollars if they could get them. Unsupported paper money, then, continued to finance the war. Despite the reduction of Confederate currency by one-third, prices declined only slightly.[15]

Still, consumers hoped the new money would encourage farmers to bring their produce to market because they could sell it under the old paper money, which would be worth a third more in face value than the forthcoming currency. One cynic scoffed at such reasoning, noting that the difference between the old and new currency was that of "tweedledum" and "tweedledee." Many others agreed, calling the new money "little better" than the old currency. Yet the congressional plan to reduce the currency in circulation caused some farmers to argue that they should sell their produce at high inflated prices, even though the old currency was not worth much, because less new money would soon circulate and prices would decline. As a result, the money that they made now would total more dollars for later exchange. If farmers sold their produce at the current "*enormous*" prices and put their earnings into Confederate bonds at 4 percent interest – and if they then sold their remaining produce after April 1 to earn sound dollars, albeit at prices reduced by 100 percent to 200 percent – they could profit from both approaches. War could still pay for farmers without too much financial risk.[16]

In mid-April a South Carolina planter confided in his diary that he "went to Augusta to sell something having no money. Found that there was no *current money* there & everything down & utter want of confidence in Govt. finances. We are literally without money in the whole Confederacy. The old issues depreciated one third, & not wanted by any, & of the new none of consequence, & not esteemed more highly. It is a serious state of things & no prospect of much relief." By spring, then, many southerners had already lost confidence in the new Confederate monetary policy. But not all. In Montgomery, grocers and other merchants refused the old Treasury notes and waited for the new money. One resident observed, "If you ask a man now if he has corn, or meat, or anything for sale, the answer almost invariably will be that he has, but prefers new money." After a brief decline, however, food and farm prices climbed steadily. In April flour brought $235 to $240 per barrel in Richmond, and consumers paid $7 per dozen for eggs, up from $5.50 in March, and $7 per pound for salted meats. By June horses sold for $3,000, and the army paid as much as $1,200 in some areas of Alabama.[17]

On February 17, Congress renewed the tax-in-kind, but it approved more exemptions for small-scale farmers. The new law permitted farmers to pay their corn tithe in money when they did not have sufficient grain to supply their families. Congress also exempted garden vegetables intended for family use and "crops destroyed by fire or any other accidental cause or by the enemy." Each farmer and planter could now reserve for his own use fifty bushels of Irish and sweet potatoes, and one hundred bushels of corn, and fifty bushels of wheat produced during the calendar year. Then, they would pay and deliver to a government agent 10 percent of all wheat, corn, rice, oats, rye, buckwheat, beans, sweet and Irish potatoes, and cured hay and fodder. They also had to deliver sugar and molasses made from cane and sorghum if the farm produced more than 30 gallons of these syrups. Ginned cotton, wrapped or baled, had to be delivered by March 1 and stripped tobacco packed in boxes transported to an agent by July 1. The tithe included 60 pounds of bacon for every 100 pounds produced. Farmers with estates valued at less than $500 could not be taxed, and farmers who did not produce the minimal amount before the tax could be levied were also exempt, as well as those farmers who did not produce more than ten pounds of wool or fifteen pounds of cotton for each family member. If a farmer disagreed with the tax assessor's levy, he could ask two disinterested people to determine the quantity of produce owed. The farmer then had thirty days to deliver this "tithe in kind," except for cotton and tobacco, from the date of notice to a depot not more than twelve miles from the place of production. If the farmer or planter did not deliver the produce, the government would assess a fine of five times the portion of the crops in default.[18]

Before this agricultural legislation could become fully operational, the war ended. Nevertheless, its passage not only indicated that the Confederate government wanted to establish a better system and bring order to the tax process, but also showed that the government recognized the continued need, if not desperation, of the army for food and fodder. Overall, farmers and planters evaded paying the tax-in-kind if possible. North Carolina, Georgia, and Alabama farmers provided approximately two-thirds of the tax-in-kind valued at $62 million by the end of the year. Produce and forage from the tax-in-kind primarily sustained the armies in Virginia during the autumn, but complaints continued about the inefficiency of collection and the distribution of farm commodities as well as waste. Farmers and planters also charged that Treasury agents ignored the law: instead of arbitrating disagreements with the producers, they often took what they wanted under the auspices of "collecting the tithe."[19]

THE HINT OF SPRING BROUGHT more editorial pleading for farmers and planters to seed a bountiful vegetable crop for their slaves because the meat supply was not sufficient to feed the army and the white population. The editor for the *Columbus Times* in Georgia contended, "The meat rations of the negro must be reduced to at least two pounds per week.

With plenty of vegetables, this is sufficient, or will do very well." He urged planters to seed at least a half acre in collards for every ten hands so that more meat could be sent to the army and to whites. Other editors advised farmers and town people to produce vegetables to help prevent scurvy in the army and to aid civilians who could not afford the "inordinate price of meat." They reminded farmers that vegetables produced a good profit because the government did not take perishable foods for the required tithe. Farmers paid only an income tax on the earnings from these sales.[20]

Food prices remained high. In Selma, Alabama, bacon brought $13.50 per pound by late March, while corn sold on the ear from the wagon got $13 per bushel. In Richmond cornmeal brought $40 per bushel, a $20 increase from February to March; bacon $8 per pound, up from $3.50 in January; molasses $41.50 per gallon; and rice as much as 95 cents per pound. Snap peas sold for $5 a half pint. When bacon reached $15 per pound and cornmeal $50 per bushel, one resident noted that "this is the famine month." He observed, "The market-houses are deserted, the meat stalls all closed, only here and there a cart, offering turnips, cabbages, parsnips, carrots, etc., at outrageous prices." The impressment of foodstuffs, poor transportation, reduced production in some areas, the tithing tax, a worthless currency, and a significant price gap between government and market prices kept provisions from reaching Richmond and other towns. This failure further convinced hungry people that farmers were extortionists and hoarders. Any slight price decline brought unwarranted optimism that the worst times had passed.[21]

In late April when flour prices reached $300 per barrel in Richmond, bakers stopped making bread. They said they could get only 275 loaves from a barrel of flour and warned they could not remain in business with a loaf fetching only $1. One resident purchased flour for $1.50 per pound and paid $40 per bushel for potatoes. In Richmond the Church and Union Hill Humane Association decreased its distribution of flour and cornmeal because of inadequate supplies. As a result, the poor suffered even greater hunger than more affluent citizens. Yet distribution and regional variations, as well as the presence of Union forces, remained essential problems: while the people of Richmond went hungry, Georgia granaries reportedly overflowed with wheat from the 1863 crop, and farmers expected this year's crop to substantially increase the surplus on hand.[22]

One Richmond resident now reported that "food is still advancing in price; and unless relief comes from some quarter soon, this city will be in a deplorable condition." Many people suffered from want of bread and meal, which could not be bought "owing to scarsety." In May, corn sold for $300 per barrel in Southampton County, Virginia. In Richmond, a cow with a calf brought $2,500, which caused one resident to reflect, "I fear a just retribution may entail ruin on the farmers, who seem to think more of their cattle than their sons in the field." He believed that "greed for gain was the worst feature in our people." The price of flour rose to $400 per barrel and cornmeal to $125 per bushel due to fighting near the city, which cut the roads so that farmers could not get their provisions to market. They hoped the summer's wheat crop then under the scythe in Georgia and Alabama and the ripening grain in the peaceful areas of Virginia would save them.[23]

Some argued that radicals bent on breaking the law – not hungry people – had instigated the Richmond riot a year earlier, but the growing food shortage in many parts of the Eastern Confederacy now made bread riots a real possibility. One editor reminded readers that hungry people "most assuredly help themselves by violent means to food, when to be found in the land, let it be in whose possession it may." The danger of a bread riot loomed, particularly if farmers continued to send their corn "clandestinely" to distilleries to "realize enormous profits." The corn crop of 1863 also had fallen short of expectations and need. Whiskey would not feed hungry people. Avarice and greed on the part of some farmers now indicated a growing danger within.[24]

These fears were not misplaced. In March a bread riot occurred in Raleigh, North Carolina, where a group of women who could not purchase corn, wheat, or flour with Confederate money raided a government tithing depot and seized flour and grain, then attempted to pillage a gristmill. Before the year ended other raids or disturbances, if not riots, that involved women as well as men plundering merchants and government commissary warehouses occurred in Savannah, Georgia, Barnwell, South Carolina, and Waco, Texas. Hunger drove people to desperation. For the want of food, the social order continued to crack. As food shortages persisted in some areas, women continued to take matters into their own hands. In April, five women received jail sentences for stealing seven sacks of grain from a warehouse in Blandenboro, North Carolina. In May a group of women in Randolph County, Alabama, also seized government wheat and corn to prevent the starvation of their children. They asked President Jefferson Davis for exemption from the impressment acts or at least a delay for payment until autumn when the crops had been harvested.[25]

Unless the food situation improved quickly in many southern cities and towns, some urban residents believed, they would soon find themselves in the "very jaws of famine." In May the food crisis became worse when many people in northern Georgia began arriving in Atlanta fleeing the advance of Sherman's army. Although Georgia had been the granary from which Lee's Army of Northern Virginia had been supplied, the surging refugee population caused serious food supply problems in the city, and the Relief Committee put out a call for the people of Georgia, Alabama, and South Carolina to send bacon, salted meats, meal, and corn.[26]

NATIONAL AND STATE GOVERNMENT OFFICIALS still begged farmers to plant as much corn and other food crops as possible, but editors admonished the government and the military to follow the letter of the impressment law because improper seizures would prevent farmers from pursuing maximum production. In January, Governor Thomas H. Watts of Alabama told Secretary of War Seddon that "it is a better policy of the Government to pay double price than to make impressments. . . . The impressment of property only aggravates the price and creates opposition to the Government and our cause. The practical operation of the impressment system has been disastrous." John Walker, a Virginia planter, agreed, particularly when an impressment agent paid him only $4 per bushel for 534 bushels of corn instead of the $40 per bushel that it would have brought on the Richmond market. He considered his monetary loss an "abominable and unjust act."[27]

In February, as farmers' complaints mounted, Congress restricted the impressment power of the War Department by repealing the act of 1863 that authorized boards of commissioners in each state to fix prices for impressed agricultural goods and livestock. Local appraisers now had to determine the value of farm commodities based on the "usual market price" in the locality at the time of impressment. If a farmer rejected the commissary agent's price, state commissioners still could hear appeals from farmers and impressment agents and determine the price. Because farmers never claimed a surplus that could be impressed, local appraisers would determine the amount available for any produce. The government hoped this new impressment policy, along with currency reform, would gain the support of farmers and planters. If not, the army would fail from the lack of food and forage.[28]

At the same time, Congress authorized the impressment of meat "from any suppliers that may exist in the country" whenever the president declared a public emergency. The impressment of meat would be made under the authority of the secretary of war, but the agents could not appropriate more than half of the meat that a farmer or planter needed to support his family for the year. If a farmer objected to the impressment or the price paid, the agent could seize the meat anyway if the need proved critical. Then, the impressing officer would appoint one "loyal and disinterested" citizen of the county, district, or parish and the farmer appoint another representative, and they would determine the quantity liable for impressment and the value of the meat for payment. Their decision would be final. The impressing officer would give the farmer a certificate indicating the quantity taken and the agreed-upon compensation and the circumstances for the appropriation. The disbursing officer was to "promptly" pay for the meat impressed. Under the new impressment act, Adjutant General Cooper also ordered that no milch cows on farms or plantations be impressed, but South Carolinians complained that impressment officers willfully ignored the order. By April, most of the milch cows had been taken for beef across the South, and few cattle and hogs remained for breeding stock. If the war continued for several more years, as many believed it would, meat would almost entirely disappear from southern tables. Some suggested substantially increasing the production of poultry of every kind.[29]

In April Alabama governor Thomas A. Watts criticized commissary agents for taking 10 million pounds of bacon from the state for the collection of the tax-in-kind and impressment. He considered the impressment, if not the tax itself, "utterly illegal." The disparity between government and open market prices further encouraged farmers and planters to hoard produce from the commissary officers or sell it on the open market. When Confederate agents impressed the horses of farmers now valued between $400 and $1,000, they could seldom be replaced – and that made plowing, cultivating, and hauling far more difficult, if not impossible. In May impressment agents paid $22 to $40 per barrel for flour, which increased to about $130 per barrel after a good wheat harvest (the market price, however, reached $400). When government price schedules increased, consumers complained; farmers and planters, of course, approved, but they demanded still higher agricultural prices. Many farmers and planters expressed their outrage when impressment officials took their horses and mules after passage of the new currency act but paid with the old money, which had depreciated by one-third.[30]

Yet the impressment problem remained serious, because military seizures of food and fodder were made, in the words of one editor, "as a general rule, by men wholly unsuitable to their duty—chiefly by noncommissioned officers, sent out with wagons, attended by a dozen or two privates, whose rule has been to take what they saw, and enjoy whatever they found in their irresponsible rovings." Impressment agents broke into corncribs, demanded meals from farmers' wives, and stole chickens and honey. As a result, they ruined the morale of the very people needed to ensure the provisioning of the troops.[31]

While contending that they would meet the food and forage needs of the army, southern farmers said they had to protect their farms from their own impressment agents, who had been "let loose upon the people." If farmers stopped producing in the areas with a large concentration of soldiers, the army would necessarily need agricultural products from other regions—and that would further diminish the food supplies for the civilian population. Some observers called the impressment policy nothing less than "imbecility." Others urged farmers to expand their production of root crops, noting that potatoes and turnips were too heavy and bulky for the impressment agents of the Commissary Department. This suggestion was hardly what the government wanted to hear, because farmers and planters considered impressment of their surplus as nothing less than theft.[32]

As a result, on June 14, 1864, Congress provided for the payment of claims for property impressed for the army's use. It authorized the secretary of war to appoint a civilian agent in each congressional district, who would receive claims from farmers and planters regarding impressment of forage, provisions, cattle, sheep, hogs, horses, mules, and wagons by the army without payment. All claims made west of the Mississippi River would be reported to an accounting officer of the Treasury Department in the Trans-Mississippi Department. These agents would take testimony and investigate claims. The act remained in force until January 1, 1865, east of the Mississippi River and until May 1, 1865, west of the river, after which time all claims not presented by then would be rejected. Farmers and planters had to state when, where, and by whom their property had been impressed and the price, if any, paid for the seizure. The agents also would take testimony from the army officers involved with the impressments. Eventually the agents would determine a fair price for the appropriated provisions, livestock, and wagons and authorize payment.[33]

Confederate and Union soldiers also continued to take provisions from farmers. One Georgia soldier wrote to his wife, "I have but little or no fears that the Yanks will ever get down to where you are but I think you will be pestere[d] by our own soldiers . . . strowling about . . and stealing your chickens, etc. I had almost as leave have the Yankees around my hous as our own men, except they will not insult ladies." In March, Lee attempted to aid local farmers by prohibiting soldiers from trampling through fields, burning fences, and burying their dead in cultivated fields. If Confederate soldiers did not stop these practices, he warned, farmers would not have any reason to plant crops. Union pressure on northern Virginia also continued to affect Richmond's food supply. One Virginian spoke for many city residents and farmers in a letter to Governor William Smith when he wrote, "Many of us . . . will actually starve for Bread unless we can get some help. . . . The Yankees took from us our stock, corn . . . and we could not make more than one third enough [crops] to last us, and now are suffering."[34]

The war, however, did not physically touch Georgia farmers and planters until early May, when nearly 100,000 Union soldiers under Sherman swept into the state. This moving and pulsing wave of dark blue came southward from Chattanooga and swept across agricultural lands, forcing farmers and townspeople alike to flee. In the chaos that followed, Union and Confederate soldiers plundered the farms of the small-scale, nonslaveholding agriculturists. Sherman soon required farmers to bring their surplus commodities to collection points, where the Georgians would be given vouchers for their produce with prices based on a Federal schedule and paid in greenbacks. Sherman wrote that his men feasted on the bounty of a land so great that "our poor mules laugh at the fine corn-fields and our soldiers riot on chestnuts, sweet-potatoes, pigs and chickens."[35]

Sherman's drive through Georgia and the Carolinas killing cattle, burning cotton, and seizing grain proved that, if there remained any doubt, Confederate forces could not protect southern agriculture. One Union soldier reflected that Sherman's men had "burned all cotton, took all provisions, forage, wagons, mules, horses, cattle, hogs and poultry and the many other things which a country furnishes. . . . As we left the country I do not see how the people can live for the next two years." Another reported, "Our work has been the next thing to annihilation." A Confederate officer decried Sherman's 60-mile swath of agricultural destruction: "I found nothing, no hogs, cattle, sheep, chickens or anything else to eat. I saw a number of the very finest ladies in Georgia in the camps picking up grains of corn for the purpose of sustaining life, who a week before that did not know what it was to want for anything." Sherman used Federal military power to destroy southern agricultural power.[36]

While Sherman moved on Atlanta and beyond, Grant engaged Lee in Virginia near Spotsylvania Court House in the area known as the Wilderness. This exceptionally bloody battle led to an arguable draw, but Grant pressed on to the south as Lee withdrew toward North Anna in late May and to Cold Harbor in June. Grant's losses exceeded Lee's, but Confederate desertions increased as the soldier-farmers saw the cause as hopeless and went home to assist their destitute families. In early June Grant's drive stalled at Petersburg, where he would lay siege with nine months of trench warfare until March 25, 1865. With his supply lines cut and his men hungry, Lee had no choice but to abandon the city.[37]

Other food problems occurred in Hanover County, Virginia, where some two dozen women and children were destitute because the Yankees had "swept the neighborhood of corn, bacon, and cattle of every description, besides ruining the growing crops." In Prince Georges County, Virginia, Union troops "scoured" the countryside for food and forage. One observer reported, "The enemy's cavalry horses are turned into large fields of wheat, corn, and oats, and allowed to trample and graze the crops as they like." To the south, Union raids from Rome, Georgia, into Cherokee County plagued farmers and planters in June and October. Sarah Espys's farm lost 500 bushels of corn, 100 bushels of oats, 200 pounds of flour, 200 pounds of bacon, and most of the fencing and livestock. "There is not a living thing on the place," she wrote after an October raid, "except a few chickens. God help us, for we have almost nothing. . . . My beautiful farm is in ruins. . . . We had hogs enough for two years but they are gone and [our] corn too, and desolation all around."[38]

To the west, the Shenandoah Valley, along with Georgia, served as a breadbasket for Lee's army, and its farmers provided an abundance of wheat, corn, and barley as well as cattle and sheep. Shenandoah grain and livestock reached the Army of Northern Virginia on the Virginia and Central Railroad via Charlottesville, Lynchburg, and Richmond. A good road network in the valley also facilitated the shipment of agricultural commodities. Shenandoah Valley farmers led Virginia in the production of grain and cattle, and Confederate forces could rely on them for food and fodder. The *Richmond Whig* affirmed the value of the Shenandoah, reporting that "it is important that [General Jubal Early] should hold this country, in order to save the luxuriant crops that burden every plantation." But the country surrounding Winchester would change hands a half-dozen times between late July and mid-September, and Confederate and Union armies ended any hope for a peaceful, unscarred harvest.

Southern soldiers reportedly cut ripening wheat and threshed it, using some twenty threshing machines in Frederick and Jefferson counties. Lee wanted the wheat for his army and Grant wanted to keep it from him. Valley farmers wanted it for themselves.[39]

On May 25, Grant ordered Major General David Hunter to enter the valley and destroy its agricultural power. By mid-June Hunter had burned granaries, barns, and fences and destroyed farm equipment. In July Grant informed General Henry Halleck that he wanted Hunter to so destroy the valley's agriculture that "crows flying over it for the balance of the season will have to carry their provender with them." Displeased with the slowness of Hunter's work, his defeat at Lynchburg, and his retreat from West Virginia, Grant created the Army of the Shenandoah and gave command to Major General Philip Sheridan. Sheridan believed that "it was time to bring the war home to a people engaged in raising crops from a prolific soil to feed the country's enemies." In August Grant ordered Sheridan to "do all damage to rail-roads and crops you can. Carry off stock of all descriptions and negroes so as to prevent further planting. If the War is to last another year we want the Shenandoah Valley to remain a barren waste." Sheridan, however, ordered his officers to avoid burning houses and that "the object is to make this Valley untenable for the raiding parties of the rebel army." One Union officer believed the "namby-pamby work of protecting the inhabitants during the growing season," which benefited Lee's army, was now over and war in earnest would soon descend on valley farmers.[40]

A month earlier Shenandoah farmers reported a wheat crop of "excellent quality and well filled." When the wheat fell to the scythe or reaper, the mills busily ground it into flour, and the corn crop looked promising. Sheridan reported that from Harrisonburg to Staunton, the country was "abundantly supplied with forage and grain." As Union forces moved into the valley toward Winchester, Sheridan's men took hogs, sheep, cattle, corn, apples, and peaches – virtually anything edible – and liberated slaves, and valley farmers suffered greatly for it. Confederate soldiers occupied Winchester until September 19 and contributed to the farmers' misery, but it was Union soldiers and not Confederates who burned barns and haystacks.[41]

And so "The Burning" that began with Hunter reached its peak with Sheridan. One Confederate soldier watched from a high vantage point and reported, "Immediately in my view were burnt not less than one hundred hay stacks and barns." He believed that "nearly every farm large or small has been visited by the torch." Another report claimed that "Union cavalry stretched a cordon across the Valley floor and systematically fired barns and herded away animals." A Union cavalryman counted 167 barns burning simultaneously. A Mennonite bishop in Rockingham County called the destruction of Confederate and loyalist farms a "holocaust of fire," which left "a sum of destruction that baffles the pen to describe." Union soldiers systematically shot cattle, hogs, and sheep, took the horses, and burned the wheat, corn, and hay. In late August a soldier from Iowa reported that the Shenandoah Valley "is splendid country, the best I ever saw," but that Union and Confederate foraging parties had "laid waste" to the farms as they seized fresh meat, green corn, and fruit and burned fences. He added that "the cavalry destroyed everything that would be of service to the enemy." Still, the beauty and fertility of the land captivated him, and he noted that "this is the only part of the 'Confederacy' that I have seen yet worth fighting for if that were the object." One Union officer wrote, "How the people of Virginia will live this winter I cannot imagine. Nothing is left where we have been but corn and not much of that. Barns and mills are all destroyed. Hay and grain has been given to the flames." The "rebel granary" had largely been destroyed.[42]

But not entirely. When Sheridan's men had completed their systematic destruction of agriculture in the Shenandoah Valley, he reported that "I have destroyed over 2,000 barns filled with wheat, hay, and farming implements, over seventy mills filled with flour and wheat; have driven in front of the army over 4,[000] head of stock and have killed and issued to the troops not less than 3,000 sheep." In all, Sheridan's men had killed or captured 3,772 horses, 545 mules, 10,918 beef cattle, 250 calves, 15,000 hogs, and 12,000 sheep as well as seized 20,397 tons of hay and fodder, 435,802 bushels of wheat, 77,176 bushels of corn, 71 flour mills, and 1,200 farms. The loss of grain and livestock indicated hard times ahead for Lee's Army of Northern Virginia and the valley people that winter. Nevertheless, Sheridan's forces were not large enough to wipe out the entire agricultural sector in the Shenandoah Valley and many farms and neighborhoods escaped. Overall, though, Shenandoah's farms could no longer support Confederate armies and many of its civilians. In October, valley farmers had returned to their fields to sow oats, but they would reap that crop as Unionists – not as Confederates – after the war ended.[43]

Because of the Union occupation of Winchester and extensive foraging, inflation rose as food became more scarce. If farmers had anything to sell, they wanted greenbacks and not Confederate money. By November bread brought $1 per loaf, while butter sold for 75 cents, cheese for 50 cents, ham for 30 cents, and sugar for 25 cents per pound, respectively, and potatoes cost $2.50 per bushel, all in Union money. Sales in Confederate money brought considerably more; butter, for example, went for $5 per pound in Confederate currency. For burned-out Shenandoah farmers and those who depended on them for food, difficult days lay ahead.[44]

BY EARLY JUNE, FARMERS WERE bringing the first of their summer vegetables to nearby Richmond markets, but prices remained high. Although a large supply of fresh butter also became available, farmers had few buyers because they charged "enormous" prices that ranged from $16 to $20 per pound. Confederate plans to expand conscription to boys of seventeen and to men between forty-five and fifty for home units that would respond to emergency defense also dampened the good news about the improved food supply coming from the newly and seasonally producing gardens and fields. Opponents of this plan urged Congress to leave the conscription law alone because the South needed "an army of producers quite as much as fighting men," and the Confederacy had more to fear from the "diminution of producers than from the army in our front." The Union could be defeated, provided the South created an "army of production" from the age group now in jeopardy of being consripted.[45]

Across the Eastern Confederacy, most observers remained convinced that the region's agricultural capacity could prevent the North from starving the South into surrender. Only Texas proved the exception to the bounty of the South, some argued, because drought damaged grain crops there and harmed livestock raising. Optimism, however, could not displace reality for long. In June, a Virginia woman wrote, "What is to become of us?" By July, the Army of Northern Virginia needed flour and bread so urgently that the government disregarded its scheduled prices and offered market rates for wheat if producers delivered it by July. The wheat crop had fallen short of expectations; that failure, along with the depreciation of the currency and the fact that farmers were busy harvesting oats and hay, forced the government to offer competitive prices to secure the needed grain. The government acted because it feared that wheat farmers would not sell their grain but would instead hide it from government procurement agents.[46]

To stimulate sales, the government increased the price that it would pay for wheat to $7.50 per bushel from $5 per bushel, to $6 per bushel for corn from $4, and to $6.30 per bushel for cornmeal from $4.20. Unbaled oats and hay would now bring $6 per hundred pounds, and baled feed and forage $7 per hundredweight, if delivered in August. The government still would pay $500 as the "average value" for first-class horses and mules. All prices were good east of the Blue Ridge Mountains. The government now hoped that all "impediments" for the sale of agricultural produce and livestock had been removed and that farmers would come forward as patriots and sell their foodstuffs and forage to sustain the army.[47]

By July Richmond residents, however, continued to suffer from an inadequate meat and vegetable supply. The farmers that provisioned the city market had suffered stunted crops from drought. Beef, butter, and milk had become scarce, and the prices of all farm products remained "as vigorous as ever." Tomatoes cost $20 a dozen, onions $1 each, and cucumbers as much as $8 per dozen, prices that few people could pay. On July 1, flour sold for $250 per barrel on the Atlanta market, and corn brought $20 per bushel and bacon $6 per pound. Butchers charged $5 per pound for beef, mutton, and pork. Whiskey brought $100 per gallon. In South Carolina many farmers had essentially stopped selling corn by August. One planter, however, who marketed it in Aiken received $14 per bushel and as much as $2.50 per pound for beef and $4 per pound for bacon. Drought had damaged his new crop, and he expected higher prices because of it. He also received $15 per bushel for potatoes, and he planned to seed more potatoes and less corn the next year. Increasingly, merchants and grocers accepted farm produce in exchange for their goods, and a barter economy emerged in many areas where farmers refused Confederate currency, either old or new. Farmers complained that goods that had cost 400 bushels of wheat in 1863 now cost 1,600 bushels, so great was the inflation and depreciation of the currency as well as the inadequate supply of consumer products. These high prices brought further acrimony and led to accusations of extortion against farmers. One housekeeper unhappy about the high price of vegetables suggested that farmers should be hanged.[48]

The decline of feed and forage in northern Virginia due to the Union occupation compelled farmers still behind Confederate lines to sell cattle at younger ages, which meant at lighter weights, to meet public needs for beef. Some consumers considered eating mutton, although most southerners, like northerners, had never become accustomed to the taste. Instead, they believed they needed meat – which meant beef or pork – each day to maintain good health. When cholera struck hog herds in Alabama, Florida, and North Carolina, the meat supply problem worsened. By spring many farmers and planters had also lost most of their draft power. The lack of horses and mules had become so serious in some areas that a contributor to the *Columbus Enquirer* (Georgia) urged farmers to use cows as a substitute for mules to cultivate their crops. He admitted that cattle were usually neglected on plantations. But if farmers would fatten them in a stall and treat them like a horse or a mule, the animals could provide more draft power than the farmer or planter otherwise had available. Although farmers understood the axiom that necessity knew no law, most were not yet ready to substitute cows for mules if they could in any way secure the latter.[49]

By November, with Texas cut off from the East, commissary officers looked to Florida cattle raisers as their last supply source for beef. However, inadequate railroad transportation prevented raisers there from selling beef cattle to the army. In addition, their beeves were in poor, even emaciated, condition, and the Floridians could drive only 300 to 400 cattle a week out of the state by late October. Citizens in Charleston complained about the lack of beef, while soldiers in South Carolina and Georgia received little, if any at all. By late November drovers collected an estimated 500 cattle from Florida livestock raisers per week. Some Confederate officials believed that 25,000 cattle, which would yield 10 million pounds of beef, remained in Florida pastures and on rangelands when the year ended. No one knew for certain whether livestock raisers had that many head, or how they could get them to civilian and military consumers.[50]

Farmers and planters had great difficulty procuring horses and mules by the spring of 1864. In late April the Richmond horse market offered a few "splendid roadsters, cavalry, and draught horses," at prices ranging from $1,000 to $3,000. Owners had reluctantly brought these horses to market after keeping them from seizure by impressment officers because the "enormous price" of feed and forage became too burdensome. Most of the horses, however, were merely nags, "slow of hoof, shaggy of coat, and attenuated to the last degree of fame." Auctioneers tried to sell them as good, serviceable animals, prompting one observer to label such acts as dishonest and nothing less than "a libel on the physical condition and appearance of the majority of the horses." In late May Edmund Ruffin worried because "our cavalry is almost worthless for fighting, because of the broken-down condition of a large portion of the horses, & the inability to replace them from any surplus stock in the country, & the impossibility of providing half enough provender." Union soldiers had taken "every serviceable horse left for agricultural & private uses," Ruffin continued. They also had provided themselves "abundantly with forage, even from the most destitute localities."[51]

By summer both farmers and the army desperately needed horses, but the prices paid by impressment officers in Virginia and North Carolina – despite being as high as $2,500 in Confederate currency – were far below market prices, and few farmers willingly gave up their animals. Payments of $1,500 to $2,500 violated the new impressment schedules that required compensation of $500 for "first class artillery and wagon horses and mules," with price reductions for those animals not deemed of that quality. Impressment officers had orders to leave sufficient horses and mules for farmwork, but they usually took what they needed. With the average life of artillery and wagon horses at seven and a half months and sometimes less for cavalry horses, and with Lee needing an estimated 7,000 horses and 14,000 mules every fifteen months, southern farmers could not meet the military's needs, nor could they provide the feed to sustain them. By winter many of the horses that remained had died by the thousands on farms now barren of grain and hay. Lee's horses also continued to suffer from want of grain and forage. By the end of the year, the general's horses were dying by the score from starvation.[52]

THE MANPOWER NEEDS OF THE Confederate armies had become acute by the spring of 1864. As a result, few young men remained at home to fill the increasingly decimated ranks of agricultural laborers. The men who still occupied the farms and plantations – and who until now had been able to provide substitutes, secure deferments from the draft, or by some means avoid conscription – now became vulnerable. Yet the further loss of men from the farm labor force threatened to decrease agricultural production. Still, the military's desperation trumped the farms', and in mid-February the House of Representatives passed a Senate bill that broadened the age groups for conscription. The Confederacy had now reached the bottom of the manpower pool, and it had little choice but to mandate conscription for all able-bodied men between the ages of eighteen to forty-five. The act also authorized the secretary of war to exempt farmers from service in the army, particularly those who produced grain for the army or those farmers and planters whom he deemed more essential for agricultural production. These exemptions could be revoked if the farmer failed to "engage exclusively in the production of grain and provisions," or if he failed to sell his surplus to the government or public at prices set by the appraisers under two laws – one that imposed a tax-in-kind, and one that regulated impressments. Put more starkly, if a farmer sold his surplus grain for a price greater than the government allowed, he could lose his draft deferment.[53]

Exemptions related to agriculture included deferments for one overseer for each farm or plantation that now held at least fifteen slaves, provided no adult white male ineligible for military duty lived on the premises. Overseers now had to post bond with good security to provide 100 pounds of bacon, pork, or beef for each able-bodied slave. The law also required them to sell provisions at reduced prices to soldiers' families, with impressment officers in each state fixing the prices. If planters could not provide the meat requirement, they could commute two-thirds of it with grain or other provisions upon approval of the secretary of war. This new regulation eliminated the $500 payment required by the conscription act of 1863, thereby changing the monetary responsibility of planters to a food supply obligation. Many planters ignored their obligations under the law and openly stated that they would not produce a marketable surplus. Small-scale farmers considered their attitude more proof that the conscription laws privileged the planter class.[54]

The new conscription order immediately caused many to wonder who would cultivate the crops and raise livestock. More than at any time during the war white women worked in the fields, tended livestock, and managed the farms. One southerner noted, "One no longer sees but women in the families and Negroes in the fields." For many agricultural observers, fewer men in the fields meant less food for the soldiers and public. The editor of the *Southern Cultivator* remarked that "we need every man in the field, it is true, but it is the 'corn field,' chiefly." Many southerners believed the new law would further diminish the food supply. Joseph Gorgas, chief of Confederate ordnance, put it simply: "Some must labor or all will starve."[55]

Edmund Ruffin agreed, contending that his slaves willfully skirted their work because plantation owners and overseers now taken by the army could not properly supervise their bondsmen and -women. Ruffin made his grievance clear: "When farms are this deprived of all their labor, or all superintendence & direction, & control of laborers, all the products which might be thence derived from proper direction & labor are reduced to the lowest degree, & the public loss is tenfold greater than the value of the military service of the proprietor." For Ruffin and other planters, conscription policy significantly restricted agricultural production and harmed the war effort.[56]

By 1864, the young and the old in the draft pool increasingly considered army service a death sentence. Farmers sought deferments, but most could not easily get them because only the planter class retained that privileged protection. In Georgia the governor favored deferments of planters with "age and experience" and contended that many young men hid behind the "paper entrenchments" of the law by claiming they were planters. The state of Georgia agreed and rejected their claim. Instead, it declared that farmers were now more useful in the ranks than in the fields until the enemy could be driven from the land. By mid-August, however, Georgia's governor called the state's "detailed" planters to arms. If they did not report for conscription, they would be forced into the army. As a result, by late 1864, desertions increased, and these desertions were often encouraged by letters from home reporting on the dire need for help, as wives struggled to feed their children and operate their farms.[57]

Before winter ebbed into spring other agricultural labor problems worsened. The *Charlestown Mercury* reported, "The great mass of [negroes] are still engaged in cultivating the soil, and still loyal to their masters and the Southern cause." But elsewhere, the institution of slavery had nearly crumbled, which caused social, economic, and cultural stress. Where slaves remained, owners conducted their seasonal agricultural tasks of plowing, planting, and cultivating as well as harvesting wheat and picking cotton. On January 1, 1864, hiring day for slaves came as usual. In Richmond an observer said that "Negroes of any colour, black, brown, gingerbread and molasses, of both sexes and of all ages, congregated around the doors of the hiring agents, like the lepers at the pool, waiting for their turn to step in and be hired." The practice of hiring out surplus slave labor seemed routine, except for the observation that "servant-seekers were numerous, too, but not as numerous as servants seeking masters and mistresses." While the rates of hiring varied as usual according to the age, sex, and abilities of the "servants," more masters offered their slaves for hire than the market could absorb. In Petersburg, field hands hired at rates ranging from $100 to $275 per year, plow boys from $75 to $110 per year, and house servants from $60 to $90 annually. By the end of 1864 slaves in Southampton, Virginia, hired out for as much as $1,000 per year. Although hiring was a common practice for slave owners to gain some monetary return on their investments, their inability to hire out all of their extra labor served as an indicator that the institution of slavery was in danger.[58]

During the summer slave prices escalated due to rampant inflation. An eight-year-old girl sold for $2,650 and a young woman aged eighteen brought $4,250, while a man of unstated age sold for $3,980 on the Augusta slave market. By late September slave prices still held firm and high.

In Augusta a man with his wife and three children brought $16,000 on the auction block while a woman with two children sold for $6,450, a twenty-three-year-old man for $3,100, a thirty-year-old man for $3,600, a seventeen-year-old boy for $3,900, and a woman of forty-five for $1,000. All buyers remained optimistic that the Confederacy would achieve independence and that their investments in slave labor would be profitable for years to come. Besides, as one small-scale planter in Southampton County, Virginia, argued, "Owning slaves is [not a] Crime."[59]

Late in the year, slave sales in Charlotte, North Carolina, still returned deceptively high prices. An eleven-year-old and a sixteen-year-old girl brought $4,700, and a forty-year-old woman $3,600, a twenty-five-year-old man $5,700, a twenty-four-year-old man $6,200, and a forty-year-old man $3,800. Observers considered only the eleven-year-old girl to be "likely," while they found the others "very inferior looking." These high prices, however, no longer reflected optimism that slavery would continue to furnish the needed agricultural workers or that the war would soon end. The problems were many, and one was the collapse of the Confederate currency, which directly influenced slave prices. In Georgia, a bill came before the state legislature authorizing the state treasurer to pay the legislators at the rate of "six dollars in gold equal to one hundred and fifty in currency." This bill then set the exchange rate. As a result, the twenty-four-year-old slave who sold for $6,200 in Charlotte would have returned only $248 in hard money. When the war began this slave would readily have brought $1,500 in specie.[60]

When Governor Brown of Georgia received an order from Richmond in late October telling him to authorize the impressment of slaves to work on the fortifications at Rome, he refused because this action would damage the state's agriculture. With the harvest season for corn and cotton fast approaching, he believed the order would "create much dissatisfaction among farmers and planters," and that it would be "productive of serious injury in the cultivation of this year's crops." Instead, he recommended that impressed slaves be taken from the cities and towns or from among the refugees who had arrived with their masters from other states, because their impressment would not damage the labor needs of Georgia's farmers and planters.[61]

Slave owners, including Brown, continued to move slaves into safer areas where the threat of Union attack seemed less likely and their bondsmen would be discouraged from fleeing to Federal lines. Yet the slaves' attempts to reach freedom became only worse. As Sherman's army moved toward Savannah, an estimated 19,000 black refugees followed, leaving the plantations and farms desolate of the labor necessary for spring planting. As the war dragged on, slaves continued to flee to Union lines. A resident of Charles County, Virginia, reported that more than half of the slaves – including most of the male field hands – had fled. By late 1864, fewer than seventy-five slaves between the ages of eighteen and fifty remained from a prewar population of 6,000 in Culpeper County, Virginia.[62]

Many slaves who remained on the farms and plantations refused to work, and their masters considered them "ungrateful." One mistress on a Virginia plantation lamented the loss of her slaves and recognized that she now faced "a life of labour & servitude. . . . I felt that my time of ease was over, & I must labor for my daily bread. . . . I put my hands to work – & actually fed the horses myself." A Georgia plantation woman also recognized the changing times. She had fled from Marietta to Atlanta, but by July that city no longer provided safety, and she needed to sell some slaves to raise the cash to flee again. With the cotton economy in shambles, slaves did not give an adequate return on their investment, and the woman complained that her brother would have to go into debt to support his bondsmen and -women for another year.[63]

Other agricultural labor problems developed. In February, Secretary of the Treasury Salmon P. Chase withdrew his December authorization to permit the preemption of government-owned lands in the Sea Islands and opened those plantations for sale. Although only a few thousand acres were reserved for "charitable" purposes and purchase by the freedpeople, a large amount of plantation land remained under government control. In April, General Rufus Saxton ordered all planters and superintendents to make written contracts with the black workers on their plantations. The Department of the Treasury, however, did not publish its rules concerning the management of abandoned lands until July, and the military districts operated under their own responsibility and rules while the Treasury tried to exert its own authority. Essentially, government officials and philanthropists believed that white management of abandoned plantations remained necessary to ensure the agricultural productivity of the freedpeople.[64]

On July 2, Congress gave the Treasury Department full responsibility for the freedmen and -women and the abandoned lands. By the end of the month, Secretary of the Treasury William Pitt Fessenden, who had succeeded Chase on July 1, established rules for leasing the abandoned plantations and provided for the management of those lands. Treasury agents now had the responsibility to take control of abandoned lands under the Confiscation Act of July 17, 1862, and rent it to loyal planters. This plantation and labor management plan went into effect across the occupied Eastern Confederacy during the fall of 1864. A plot on each plantation would be set aside as a "Home Farm" for the freedpeople until the district superintendent could find work for them on plantations. Most of the freed blacks could contract for wage work on the plantations at rates ranging from $10 to $25 per month. No one could be compelled to work more than ten hours per day, and housing, food, and garden plots would be provided. This policy to encourage agriculture and landownership, with the exceptions for adjustments to meet local conditions, remained in effect until organization of the Freedmen's Bureau in March 1865. By the end of 1864, the Federal government proved more interested in leasing and selling abandoned or confiscated lands to northern whites than to the former slaves. The freedpeople considered this labor organization, if not yet the system itself, little different from slavery, given the restrictions concerning movement, subservience, and planter treatment. For the freedmen and -women who worked the fields dark days were ahead.[65]

IN LATE SUMMER AN ABUNDANCE of vegetables reached the Richmond market and prices fell for a time. Even the cost of eggs at $5 to $6 per dozen and meat at $3 to $4 per pound now seemed reasonable. Yet Confederate soldiers near Richmond and Lynchburg continued to raid farmers' gardens and steal their produce as they transported it to market – despite military officers reminding them that the 52nd Article of War provided for the execution of any soldier who "quit his post to plunder and pillage" if convicted in a court-martial. With flour selling at $350 per barrel and cantaloupes bringing 50 cents apiece, up from 2 or 3 cents before the war, most hungry residents believed that punishment fit the crime. In mid-September one Richmond resident complained that the price of peaches and apples would "make pippins blush for themselves." Moderate-sized apples brought 50 cents apiece and peaches sold for $1 each. Consumers attributed the abundance of fruit to good farmers, but blamed high prices in the markets on "negro vendors" and "itinerant hucksters."[66]

Others attributed the Richmond food shortage to government officials. One resident noted that "it will be wonderful indeed if we can survive the efforts of the Confederate Secretary of War." No one begrudged sacrifice for the benefit of the soldiers, but they objected to food shortages arising from "an enormous system of bribery and corruption." Commissary agents still took agricultural provisions not only from farmers but also from railroad loading docks after wholesalers and grocers had purchased those commodities. These impressments further raised the prices of provisions at city markets. Some merchants used bribery to ensure they had a freight car waiting for them at a railroad station to transport agricultural provisions. They also passed the cost of their bribes on to consumers – a practice that made food even more expensive. Yet bribery ensured that at least some foods made it onto merchants' shelves. The great cost, of course, was that the price of food increased, more people went hungry, and some corrupt government officials got rich. One Virginian reflected on this situation by noting that "with this sort of administration of publick affairs, our Confederate candle is burning at both ends."[67]

In the autumn, the chief commissary agents for the various states met in Montgomery to reach an agreement about new, lower rates that would save the government money while continuing the impressment policy for food and forage. They agreed to pay not more than $1.31 per pound for bacon, $15 per hundred pounds for flour, $2.25 per bushel for corn, $750 for first-class horses, and $600 for first-class mules. Impressment agents would pay these prices uniformly in Alabama, Florida, Georgia, Louisiana, Mississippi, South Carolina, and Tennessee. Southern farmers still considered the government prices too low, but those who had surplus commodities and livestock for sale were comparatively fortunate.[68]

At the same time, General James L. Kemper's orders that no military official in Virginia interfere with the transport of agricultural produce and other farm commodities enabled farmers to bring their meat, vegetables, and fruits to market by early October. Compared with previous days, Richmond residents believed that the markets were well supplied and prices reasonable. Once farmers were assured that the commodities would not be seized by military or commissary agents, they eagerly brought an "abundance" of provisions to Richmond because it was in danger of rotting, and they considered any waste of their food and forage a moral, logistical, and governmental failure.[69]

In October the Subsistence Department issued a circular to rice planters in South Carolina informing them that the government required them to contribute half of the year's crop to the army. The government would pay a fixed price of at $4 per bushel for rice, but planters refusing to sell would have their allocation impressed. At that time, middling rice sold for $5 per hundred pounds on the commercial market. This government policy encouraged the planters to sell their rice, even at government prices, rather than risk losing it without compensation. Some planters who had removed their slaves early in the war to upland areas had not produced a lowland rice crop since 1861, and their financial resources for supporting their hands had been exhausted. The Subsistence Department requested that each planter inform it about the size of his anticipated rice crop when it neared harvest and the amount he expected to deliver to a government warehouse. Despite the war and Sherman's incursion into the rice-planting area of South Carolina's tidal coastal plain, planters continued to produce thousands of bushels of rice. At this time, rice sold for 20 cents per pound in Charleston, and planters and millers often bartered the staple for other needed goods. The rice crop was still abundant, but corn remained scarce and the price "exorbitant."[70]

On November 5, when Sherman moved out of Atlanta and headed to Savannah and the coast, the Confederate army impressed every horse, ox, mule, and wagon from the farms near Macon and Milledgeville, unless the farmers and planters could hide them or use them to help move government provisions and military supplies to safer areas. Union foraging parties followed, scouring the countryside for bacon, cornmeal, poultry, and forage so the Union army could live off the land. Burning fence rails and cotton bales lit the night sky. Dolly Sumner Blut, who lived on a plantation near Covington, reported the arrival of Yankee soldiers: "Like demons they rush in! My yards are full. To my smoke-house, my dairy, pantry, kitchen, and cellar, like famished wolves they come, breaking locks and whatever is in their way. The thousand pounds of meat in my smoke-house is gone in a twinkling, my flour, my meat, my lard, butter, eggs, pickles ... wine, jars, and jugs all gone. My eighteen fat turkeys, my hens, my chickens, and fowls, my young pigs are shot down in my yard and hunted as if they were rebels themselves." David Dickson, a planter near Sparta, also wrote that "for two days the invaders marched by." He grieved that "by the second evening there was nothing left to eat, even for supper." Soon Sherman's men drove some 10,000 cattle and more than 15,000 horses and mules; left in their wake were farmers and planters destitute of draft power, a hungry civilian population, and more than 154,000 freedpeople. Dead horses, mules, and cattle lay strewn about the countryside, the stench of which caused travelers to hold their noses along the roads. Burned-out homes, barns, and gin houses dotted the land. Soldiers and civilians alike now experienced a hunger they had thought impossible in the South. By Christmas Day, Sherman's men occupied Savannah and captured 500,000 bushels of rice, as well as warehouses filled with cotton. For Georgia farmers and planters, the war had essentially ended. The agricultural power of the Confederacy had been destroyed.[71]

Five days after Sherman left Atlanta, the Produce Loan Bureau issued its last annual report. Farmers and planters had subscribed provisions worth $28,078,905, but the bureau had collected only $16,897,000 worth by November 10, for an unpaid balance of $11,173,095. Under the Production Loan Act of April 21, 1862, Congress had emphasized the purchase of cotton and tobacco. The Treasury Department, however, had purchased only $1,462,558.93 worth of tobacco but had acquired 430,724 bales of cotton for $34,525,219.40. After deductions for captured and destroyed cotton, government sales, and army usage, only 191,049 bales remained, of which 15,000 bales of tithed cotton brought the total on hand to 206,049 bales. Authorities did not believe the various losses of cotton would cause a financial loss to the government, because the price had increased substantially since the war began. The bureau estimated the value of its 191,049 bales at 50 cents per pound for a total of $38 million.[72]

In mid-November the Senate Committee on the Judiciary considered a bill to require that all food prices established by the commissioners who appraised and set prices for acquisition by the army be extended to everyone in the Confederacy. The senators argued that the arbitrarily low prices set by the government for the acquisition of agricultural commodities, while keeping food costs down for the military and government, encouraged producers to charge higher prices for noncombatants. The bill provided that "the prices fixed from time to time by the Appraising Commissioners shall during the same periods be the maximum prices which can be charged to private consumers, under heavy penalties." Supporters argued that the bill's passage would end speculation in food by making it unprofitable. The bill also would increase the value of Treasury notes by making them exchangeable for commodities that had a real or legitimate value. They contended that the bill was necessary as a "war measure," but opponents countered that it would only cause farmers to reduce production even more if they could not earn all the market would bear. Yet with corn at $55 per bushel, beef and pork at $4 and $5 per pound, butter at $10 to $12 per pound, and eggs as much as $8 per dozen, many residents in Richmond and elsewhere in northern Virginia believed that some form of food and agriculture price controls were necessary. By the end of the year the general price index for farmers, planters, and consumers in the Eastern Confederacy reached 4,285, up from 2,801 in January (the first four months of 1861 = 100).[73]

Others suggested even more radical government control of agriculture to ensure an adequate food supply. One Virginian proposed that the Confederate Congress authorize the government to purchase or rent land for farming. These farms could be worked by disabled soldiers and by slaves who had been impressed, purchased, or hired. Government shops would furnish implements. The quartermaster would oversee these "*publick lands*" and provide horses and mules that were no longer fit for army service. Government farmers would be paid "salaries commensurate to their services." The Confederacy, these advocates believed, had sufficient lands beyond the reach of the enemy to furnish enough grain, pork, and vegetables to meet all national food needs; the government thus had the capacity to ensure the cultivation of every acre within Confederate lines. Such a policy, the argument went, would end any possibility that the North could starve the South into submission.[74]

Suggestions for the government control and operation of southern agriculture seem extreme, even fanciful, from the perspective of a different age. But southerners—who did not have access to adequate food due to government policy that reserved the railroads for military use; commissary officers who impressed provisions destined for city and town markets; and inflated prices charged by farmers and merchants—believed the government needed to do something to aid its people. When Henrico farmers and merchants asked $100 apiece for small hen turkeys on the Richmond market on Christmas Eve, few if any civilians could purchase them. Observers attributed this high price to an army plan to provide the soldiers with a major dinner on New Year's Day. As a result, farmers held back their supply and sought high prices from civilians because they expected commissary officers to pay those "enormous prices" to ensure the soldiers had their feast. For many southerners in the Eastern Confederacy, the government needed to regulate agriculture in many ways for the national good.[75]

Not all areas of the South, however, suffered from want of food due to a disrupted agriculture. In eastern Georgia, planters and farmers raised enough food to provide for themselves, their slaves, and the soldiers and civilians. Sherman's soldiers ate well when they foraged in this region. Southerners suffered not because planters and farmers produced too little food in this area but because the Union army took it before it could be distributed to Confederate soldiers and civilians. Even so, in North Carolina cornmeal brought $60 per bushel and fruit brandy $45 per gallon. Consumers paid $10 to $12 per pound for bacon and butter, which they considered a "good deal." On Christmas Day, well-watered milk sold for $10 per quart in Richmond. Still, Commissary General Lucius B. Northrop contended that many parts of the Confederacy did not suffer food shortages, but he acknowledged that "the idea that there is *plenty for all* in the country is absurd. The efforts of the enemy have been too successful."[76]

On the last day of the year, an Alabama planter recorded that "food is scarce and if the war continues we may look for scenes among our own people to equal the Spanish and French troubles." Much of southern agriculture lay in shambles. Farmhouses, barns, and fences had been burned in many areas; cotton gins and rice and grist mills were destroyed. Horses, mules, cattle, and hogs had been taken or killed, farm implements worn out or destroyed, slaves captured or escaped; currency had become worthless, and credit was nonexistent, while Union forces occupied large areas of farmland. The future did not bode well for southern farmers and planters.[77]

And so the year ended.

CHAPTER SEVEN

Western Collapse

Cold, rainy weather accompanied the new year in the Western Confederacy. Union forces had regained Arkansas, Tennessee, and most of Mississippi to the panhandle, and only Texas and western Louisiana remained in Confederate hands. Many Mississippi cotton and Louisiana sugar planters had taken the oath of allegiance, and they had peace and northern markets on their minds. The cotton trade up the Mississippi River to northern markets boomed. Farmers and planters in both occupied and unoccupied territory wanted to sell their fiber for Federal greenbacks. Confederate currency proved an imposition. These farmers might be loyal in their hearts and minds, but they were economic realists. As Union forces occupied more and more territory in 1864, farmers and planters could see that the end was near. Isolated Confederate forces and partisans still disrupted agriculture in some areas, but for most farmers and planters in the region the war had ended. As they turned their attention to cotton, sugar, and daily subsistence, they continued to adjust to a new system of free labor that had been instituted in 1863. Bad weather hampered the provisioning trade in New Orleans, but 700 hogsheads of new sugar and 1,200 barrels of molasses awaited export. Sugar and molasses prices held steady, and ranged from 9 to 12½ cents per pound and from 50 to 54½ cents per gallon, respectively. Flour remained in relatively short supply, although prices had fallen by $5 to $6 per barrel to $8.50 to $9.75 per barrel, largely due to trade with the North. Louisiana corn sold for $1.62 per bushel, down from $1.70 in December. The cotton market remained slow because of haggling between buyers and sellers in New York, with the price ranging from a low of 51 cents to a high of 68 cents per pound and soon to rise higher. Steamship rates for carrying cotton to New York were 2½ cents per pound, while sailing vessels bound for northern ports charged $1.25 per bale for cotton, $1.25 per hogshead for sugar, and 40 cents per barrel for molasses. Cattle brought $30 to $75 per head based on quality in Confederate-controlled Jefferson City, Texas. In February salted pork transported down the Mississippi River and destined for plantation use brought $26 per barrel.¹

Union forces had not yet succeed in preventing cotton growers in Texas from marketing their crop to Mexican buyers. Although Union soldiers occupied Brownsville, a major trading city for Texas cotton, some 12,000 bales awaited shipment from San Antonio, Goliad, Refugio, and Gonzales to Matamoros, Mexico. The trade continued to a "considerable extent," despite the Union capture of wagon trains laden with cotton, and it would not end until the army had sufficient soldiers in Texas to block all routes and confiscate the cotton destined for Mexico. Optimists hoped that by spring Texas and Louisiana would succumb to Union control.²

While the supply of agricultural commodities improved in the river towns from New Orleans north to Memphis where Federal soldiers controlled the river valley, many Confederate towns in Louisiana suffered severe food shortages, much like those experienced in Richmond. By mid-February in Alexandria, the shortage had become "alarming," and the *Louisiana Democrat* reported, "No beef in the market; not a pound to be had for love, prayer or money; and no better prospect ahead." One butcher had traveled to Point Meagre and purchased a few cattle and some hogs, but Confederate troops impressed them before he could drive them to Alexandria for slaughter. The editor complained that "our Texas friends won't sell any under any considerations." He attributed their unwillingness to market their cattle to the fact that they had "as much Confederate money as they care to be bothered with." He was angry that "the boast of Texas has been that she could furnish beef to the whole Confederacy, now she refuses, or her people refuses, to sell one to a neighboring parish." Essentially the cattle trade in Louisiana by land west of the Mississippi River had become impossible. The editor also was unhappy that local farmers had not brought cornmeal to town for ten days, even though it was fetching $8 per bushel, while a few "mean" potatoes sold for $5 per bushel and flour $1 per pound. The people of Alexandria went hungry, and no one seemed to know what to do about it.³

In February the Confederate quartermaster general A. R. Lawton wanted to authorize agents to use produce loan cotton to purchase horses at the rate of 600 pounds per horse in Mississippi, with the goal of buying 3,000 first-class horses. This suggestion failed to materialize because Mississippi farmers and planters could not provide that many horses and because the Treasury Department did not cooperate. Mules also cost more than $200 each, and the price did not decline even though Kentucky and Missouri mules began arriving overland in Union-controlled areas during the spring. In Tennessee, the Confederate army paid $250 for Class 1 horses and $150 for Class 2 horses, but farmers could not meet the demand, and they considered that payment too low anyway. In Jackson, Mississippi, one contemporary reported that "the largest plantations are thinning out, grown up in weeds & pastured upon by a few scattering cattle; fences are pulled down & destroyed; houses burned; negroes run off. A general gloom pervades everything and the people appear to be in a listless spirit . . . and utterly devoid of any disposition to continue longer the struggle for Independence."[4]

IN JANUARY, THE EDITOR OF the *New Orleans Times* believed "the era of war on a great scale to be nearly gone." For him, the "great question" of the time was agricultural labor. The Western Confederacy and, indeed, the South in general, he contended, would remain an agricultural country for a long time. Cotton would be in great demand, production limited, and the price high. The crop could now be raised by "white men or freed negroes," and farmers and planters needed to concern themselves with the "urgent present" and the "swift coming future." Reality dictated, however, the need to pay wages to their workers, although southerners greeted this changed relationship with a "frown of displeasure" and "contemptuous disgust." Cotton planters still lacked the cash and credit to make those payments. As a result, within the next year they would commit to a new agricultural labor system that permitted the freedpeople to rent plantation lands and pay the owner half the crop or more for the privilege of residing on and working the land. By so doing planters and farmers overcame the absence of credit to produce cotton using a hired labor force.[5]

In the meantime, they struggled to meet their labor needs and maintain production. By February a Tennessee planter complained that Union soldiers made "terrible drafts" for cornmeal, fodder, hay, oats, mules, and wagons "from almost all directions." His slaves had "little disposition" to work, and if he did not raise a corn crop he would have to "beg the Yankees to take and feed all my negroes." The planter lacked seed corn and mules to plant a crop. "Negro slavery," he lamented, was "about played out." Still, he owned forty-nine slaves and sowed a wheat crop large enough to merit threshing (the planter, however, did not have a threshing machine; instead, he relied on horses to tread out the grain). He likened himself to a modern-day Job. "My people work slowly," he wrote, "indeed they are very lazy." They would not work without the threat of the lash, and they were "not earning their bacon." In the past he had raised 100 bales of cotton. Now it was thirteen bales, which he would sell in Memphis. He would plant one more crop, but he planned to give it up if he could not return to cotton production on the scale he enjoyed before the war.[6]

One Tennessee farmer hired freed black workers to split rails to rebuild his destroyed fences and paid "Old Ben" $30 for making 3,340 rails. Another Tennessee planter reported that "negroes go or stay now as suits them. We have been so accustomed to them we cannot do without them not withstanding that they are of little value now." In this section of the Western Confederacy, the war had so disrupted agriculture that masters could not keep their slaves sufficiently employed on their farms or plantations. In occupied Louisiana, the Union-controlled Constitutional Convention soon provided for the prohibition of slavery by a vote of 70 – 16, recognizing an already admitted fact that "the slave had ceased to be recognized as of any value to his owner."[7]

White women continued to work in the fields and were becoming a common sight. They spun their own yarn and thread from the cotton that they raised in small patches or bought at the local market. Nearly all women wore homespun rather than store-bought calico clothing, and they lived a "primitive life." In late October white women were hired out to pick cotton on plantations near Memphis, earning wages apparently higher than they could obtain in the city (an absence of urban jobs may have been a motivating factor).[8]

Union general Nathaniel Banks, commanding the Department of the Gulf, continued to develop an agricultural labor system that would bring the freedpeople and planters together, often on the same plantation. On February 3, he issued General Orders No. 23 – known as the "Free Labor" order – to coincide with the signing of labor contracts for the coming year. It required that all plantations had to be worked, and it essentially continued the labor system established in 1863. The Federal government had not decided what should be done with the thousands of freedmen and -women behind Union lines. It also had not made any decision on the status of the former slaves, other than decreeing that they had to be paid for plantation work and that they needed to remain on the plantations to continue agricultural production. Federal authorities wanted the freedpeople to provide for their own subsistence, thus reducing, if not eliminating, the need to support them.[9]

Banks's agricultural labor policy ensured freedom in little more than name. Although the institution of slavery was essentially dead in occupied Louisiana, the vestiges of slavery could not be eliminated immediately because of custom, if not law. Plantation "hands," for example, remained the term used to describe agricultural workers, just as it had been used to describe slaves. Moreover, in Louisiana freedmen and -women were not permitted to pass from one plantation to another without the permission of the parish's provost marshal. Blacks were required to work ten hours per day between daylight and dark in the summer and nine hours a day in the winter. During that time they were to provide "respectful, honest, faithful labor" for which they would be provided rations, clothing, and shelter. Plantation owners or leaseholders also would care for sick and disabled blacks "upon the plantations to which they belong." And they would pay a monthly wage, half of which the government would keep in escrow until the end of the year. Those wage rates ranged from $8 per month for "first class hands" to $3 per month for "fourth class hands." If planters and their black workers agreed, the freedmen and -women could be paid one-fourteenth of the net proceeds of the crop, to be determined at the end of the year.[10]

In addition, Sunday work would be "avoided when practicable," but laborers were to be paid extra "when necessary." Black workers could choose their employers, but once they agreed to work for a particular plantation owner or manager they entered into a contract that bound them to the plantation for a year. If they failed to perform satisfactorily, the plantation owner could turn them over to the provost marshal, who would assign them to public works projects without pay for the remainder of their contracted time. Planters, however, could not use physical punishment if the former slaves did not work to their satisfaction. Freed plantation workers had the right to cultivate land based on ability and need. First- and second-class hands with families could cultivate one acre or if single a half acre. Second- and third-class hands with families were allocated a half acre or one-quarter acre if they did not have a family. Women were paid $3 to $5 per month; single women also received one-quarter of an acre for their use, plus cornmeal and a house. Children from twelve to seventeen years of age would receive $3 per month for their labor on the sugar and cotton plantations, as well as pork and cornmeal, and they would live with their parents. Freedom did not mean that African Americans did not need to work. These army regulations considered agricultural labor a "public duty."[11]

The planters could dock the wages of their black workers for disobedience and for work absences. Freedpeople could not use horses or mules without permission, and they could not drink or swear. If their employer required task work — that is, a specific amount of work per day — they were to comply. They also were to pay for damaged farm equipment. Workers would receive one-half of their monthly wages the first Saturday of each month, a practice that left some workers after deduction for advances on provisions with no income at the end of the year. At the end of the year the payout usually ranged from $10 to $20 per hand. By garnishing half of their wages, the planters had a strong means to control their workers. These provisions became basic to the sharecropping system, and after the war were soon institutionalized across the South. The new system kept workers in an economic and social condition not far removed from bondage or peonage. In addition, the planters agreed among themselves not to employ the former slaves of others. One Louisiana planter contended that only unity of action would head off further changes to the agricultural labor system. "If planters don't standby each other," he wrote, the freedpeople "will become more and more exacting every year until in a short time we will be slaves and they the masters."[12]

Banks's General Orders No. 23 declared that "labor is a public duty, and idleness and vagrancy a crime." In southern Louisiana the Treasury Department's superintendent of plantations established a curfew and prohibited the freedmen and -women from raising livestock and cultivating cotton and sugarcane on their allocated quarter-acre plots. They were agricultural workers for the benefit of plantation agriculture — nothing more. Here was the great paradox on the plantations. The freedpeople would be pushed to labor in the fields, or at least given the opportunity to make the land productive. But they would not be permitted to own or rent sufficient acreage; nor could they cultivate cash crops and raise livestock that would enable them to be free and independent farmers. Instead, black labor would remain coerced labor under white supervision for the purpose of producing profits from cotton and sugarcane for their new white masters. Clearly, this labor system was neither slavery nor free labor. At best it represented an agricultural labor system in transition. No one knew where it would lead, and neither white planters nor the freedmen and -women were happy with it, but the Federal government compelled adoption, if not acceptance, as long as the war lasted.[13]

Yet plantation owners and managers also had an obligation to cultivate the soil. If they failed to make their plantations productive, they risked forfeiture of their lands to someone else who promised to make it profitable. This obligation also required planters to submit a roster of their black hands to the local provost marshal, who had orders to keep families together if at all possible when determining the labor needs of a plantation owner. General Orders No. 23, then, guaranteed the planters and leaseholders in the sugar country an adequate and relatively dependable labor force despite its unpopularity. Native planters reportedly treated their workers more equitably than northern leaseholders, who often came south only to gain quick profits before returning home. And that meant exploiting the land and the black labor force.[14]

Overall, these new army regulations seemed a sensible and necessary way to use black labor to revitalize southern cotton plantations during a time when a single crop selling at inflated prices could be worth more than the plantation. When the year ended, however, the planters still did not believe that wages were sufficient motivation for black laborers. Plantation owners and leaseholders often refused to pay their workers until forced to, or they sold the crops and disappeared, leaving their workers without compensation. Some planters charged their workers for rations and medical care in violation of their contracts. Although the planters and leaseholders had no choice but to accept Banks's labor system if they wanted agricultural workers, they did so only reluctantly. General Orders No. 23 worked best in areas where labor contracts had been implemented in 1863 and where Union forces were the strongest; it worked less well where the contracts were signed for the first time in 1864.[15]

Abolitionists considered this plantation labor system the "re-enactment of slavery." Wendell Phillips complained that Banks's labor policy ensured "serfdom" for the freedpeople. In truth, it was little removed from that institution. Although planters did not particularly like this labor system either, Banks demanded full compliance and said that if the planters did not follow the regulations he would remove their laborers and strip their plantations "as bare as the palm of my hand."[16]

Still, in the Department of the Gulf, the planters and ex-slaveholders were "universally hostile" to General Banks's plan, knowing that if paid labor succeeded, slavery would be destroyed. Planters still clung to the hope that, somehow, the institution would survive the war and that they could return to cotton and sugar production as usual. Even so, the planters reemployed their workers for the 1864 crop year. Others enjoyed self-deception. Colonel George H. Hanks, superintendent of negro labor for the Department of the Gulf, believed that Banks's Orders No. 23 had proven so successful that the transition of black labor from slavery to freedom had been a "perfect success." Soon, however, planters, freedpeople, and government officials would realize that this transition would be long and difficult—more than the adjustment of an agricultural labor system was involved in reconstructing the Union in the Western Confederacy.[17]

In September, Assistant Adjutant General George B. Drake issued another order for the planters in the Department of the Gulf. It required owners, lessees, and plantation managers to reserve one-fourth of their sugarcane for seed cane. If the plantation changed ownership, the owner would receive the market value of this portion of the crop after the sale. In addition, the products of the plantations would be held on the land and under Federal control until the workers had been paid. The provost marshal general and the superintendent of the Bureau of Free Labor had the authority to ensure the execution of these directives.[18]

Complaints, if not clear resistance to Banks's free-labor order, caused the Department of the Gulf to issue Circular No. 13 on October 6, which reminded the planters of their obligations to their agricultural workers. This circular reiterated that planters could not transfer their workers to another plantation unless they had paid all wages due in the presence of an authorized agent, who would issue a certificate that payment had been made. If a planter could not pay his laborers, the Federal government would place a lien on his crop to the extent necessary so that when sold the proceeds would be sufficient to pay the workers. In addition, no planter could sell his property without first settling his account with his workers. Failure to do so would ensure seizure of his property. If a planter sold his land, the crops belonging to his workers would be disposed or retained as they pleased. Plantation owners who paid their workers with one-fourteenth of the crop had to provide a statement that certified the size of the crop, and it could not be sold until they had paid their workers. These regulations would be "rigidly enforced." Put differently, the sugar and cotton planters could employ black labor for agricultural work, but they could not treat them as slaves, even though they were not yet technically free everywhere. The planters knew they depended on "negro labor" and would continue to do so, but they preferred to maintain their old relationship with their field hands, absent the technical recognition of their freedom or even with it.[19]

In late December Thomas W. Conway, superintendent of the Bureau of Free Labor in the Department of the Gulf, notified Louisiana's planters that the agricultural and labor year would end on February 1, 1865. At that time all workers had to be paid according to the existing regulations – which meant at least one-half of their wages earned during the previous year. Each planter would receive a roll prepared by the bureau and issued through the parish provost marshal that told the planter whom he had to pay in the presence of the provost marshal or his agent. When the work year ended, the superintendent of the Bureau of Free Labor informed both the planters and the black field hands that the laborers would be "allowed to select their places of employment for the coming year, subject to such regulations as may be promulgated by the proper authority."[20]

In the Department of West Tennessee, District of Arkansas, and District of Vicksburg – a region stretching from Cairo to Milliken's Bend, Louisiana – the Union army followed a similar contract labor system established by John Eaton, who supervised the work of the freedpeople in Mississippi, Tennessee, and Arkansas in 1863. Feuding between the Treasury and War departments over the control of the black labor force, however, continued through the year, and it did not end until the establishment of the Freedmen's Bureau in 1865.[21]

BY EARLY SPRING PLANTERS HAD their field hands seeding corn and cotton. In Mississippi the war dragged on, often around them, as planters and their laborers went about their work and listened to guns firing in the distance. Agricultural commodities from the Old Northwest began reaching New Orleans in quantity as the Mississippi River increased its flow from the melting snows to the far north. Flour, lard, butter, and cheese reached the commission men at the landing, but pork and bacon from the North remained scarce with demand and prices high. Even so, agricultural trade at New Orleans improved slowly but steadily toward prewar conditions, as ships laden with cotton cleared the port for New York or steamed upriver to markets in Memphis and Cincinnati. Midwestern corn arrived for export to Matamoros at $1.75 per bushel. Moreover, the food supply for New Orleans seemed plentiful: one resident compared it to "gaunt, half-starved, God-forsaken Richmond."[22]

In contrast to the food shortages and the high prices in the Eastern Confederacy, particularly in Richmond, northern butter and cheese brought 35 cents and 16 cents per pound, respectively. Western whiskey remained in demand, with prices ranging from $1.10 to $1.20 per gallon. So much winter-milled flour from the Northwest had arrived that purchasers had the luxury of not buying; they hoped that the price would decline still further from the asking price of $9 to $12.75 per barrel. When hunger did not drive the decision-making of purchasers, more normal business transactions could occur. By April food prices in New Orleans were a sign that agricultural production was recovering locally. Farmers sold eggs on the landing for 27 to 30 cents per dozen, prices that declined a nickel in May. Chickens brought $12 and turkeys $48 per dozen, respectively. Farmers had a good supply of potatoes, which they sold for $3.50 to $3.75 per bushel. Apples and onions remained scarce and brought $7 to $8 per bushel. In Natchez, flour brought $14 per barrel and shelled corn $1.25 per bushel. Soon more provisions arrived from the Northwest at relatively cheap agricultural prices, compared to the Eastern Confederacy.[23]

Louisianans anticipated a good year for cotton, despite the inadequacy of the climate. Some hoped that at least 100,000 bales could be raised from the fertile fields that lined the Mississippi River and its tributaries, lands that in better times could produce at least 300,000 bales of cotton. Given the current price of cotton, 100,000 bales would earn approximately $30 million. Resumption of the sugarcane crop still seemed unlikely because of the lack of labor, mules, seed cane, and equipment. This assumption proved correct. Although demand for sugar and molasses continued to improve, few sugar planters attempted to raise a crop in 1864. By the end of the year, only 175 sugarhouses in sixteen parishes produced 10,000 hogsheads of sugar; in 1861, 1,090 sugarhouses in those parishes produced 400,000 hogsheads. Eight parishes with 201 sugarhouses, which produced 60,000 hogsheads during the first year of the war, produced no sugar.[24]

Although sugar planters could normally compete with the cotton planters from the region of Bayou Sara to Memphis, these times were "extraordinary" and the high price of cotton overcame all other considerations. By May, one planter reported a "tolerable stand of cotton." Although a "full" cotton crop could not be raised for want of labor, enough black field hands remained to do the necessary work. One observer believed that — based on consumption, the cost of labor, and the exchange rate — the price of cotton would soon fall to about 30 cents per pound in specie and 50 cents per pound in currency, but it would remain in great demand at home and abroad. Moreover, despite a railroad system that would not be able to meet the transportation needs of planters for many months, Louisianans suspected that "there will still be a wide margin of profit for the prudent and skillful planter" during the 1864 crop year — provided, of course, that the weather cooperated and they could obtain adequate labor.[25]

Still, many agricultural problems remained. In Claiborne County, Mississippi, one planter confided in his diary that, even though he had just sold four bushels of potatoes for $4 per bushel, he doubted he would accept Confederate currency because he could not buy anything with it. Mules cost $100 to $150 in greenbacks. Near Shreveport, planters acquired black workers through the free-labor plan and began planting cotton in April, but the army had taken all of the mules in the vicinity, and they struggled to get the land plowed for seeding. Most planters did not believe they would make much of a cotton crop in 1864. In Mississippi, many farm women and the men who remained could no longer maintain their farms beyond a subsistence level, and raiding armies from both sides made even these efforts difficult. As a result, townspeople suffered along with small-scale farmers from a lack of food. In early May a report from Greensboro, Mississippi, informed residents that "corn can scarcely be bought at any price – and as for meat we do not know of a pound for sale."[26]

By early June, while some Mississippi planters had their hands cultivating corn, threshing wheat, and harvesting oats, so much northern pork had arrived in New Orleans at $28 per barrel that buyers considered the market "well supplied." At the landing, local farmers sold potatoes and onions for as much as $5.50 per bushel and whiskey for $1.35 per gallon. Dealers easily met the food needs of New Orleans from shipments that arrived from the Northwest. Northern hay brought $50 per ton in bales. By July, Baton Rouge cotton factors had a large quantity to sell northward for greenbacks; two-thirds of the cotton supposedly belonged to the Confederate government, but it was listed as the property of individual farmers and planters. About 37 percent of the 225,000 bales of cotton delivered to New York City after September 1, 1863, had been shipped by sea from New Orleans, and the demand sent the price by late July to as high as $1.64 per pound, depending on the grade. These prices made the planters optimistic about the future. And, by early August, the cotton crop looked promising in the regions of Louisiana, Mississippi, and Arkansas that were under Federal control. High demand and prices had encouraged planters to seed as much cotton as possible; nevertheless, given the scarcity of labor and the continuing danger of Confederate raids, much of the crop would be lost. Reports of a bountiful wheat crop in the Northwest brought hope to residents in New Orleans that the price of flour and bread would decline still further.[27]

IN EARLY JANUARY A MISSISSIPPI planter reported that Union soldiers had taken almost all of his corn and fodder and burned his rail fences. He saved his horses by hiding them in the woods. Louisiana farmers and planters suffered the same fate. One resident in Landry Parish wrote, "Our country I fear is destined to starve. The Yankees took all the corn.... All the cattle, nearly all the hogs and sheep have been destroyed.... All the fencing is gone." A Union officer also reported after a two-week cavalry expedition into northeast Louisiana and southeast Arkansas that in his path, "the people have neither seed, corn, nor bread, or mill to grind the corn ... as I burned them wherever found.... I have taken from these people the mules with which to raise a crop the coming year, and burned every surplus grain of corn." In Rapides Parish, Louisiana, a planter complained that even "if the Yankees could be kept off, we cannot live here for our own men, and they will not let us live, but destroy everything we can make." In March a St. Mary Parish planter also complained in his diary that "our beautiful Parish is laid waste & likely to become a desert — Plantations abandoned fences & buildings destroyed, mules, horses & cattle driven off by the federals.... There can be no crop made in this country and of course starvation will be the dreadful consequence.... The Lord help us — such is war, civil war." In the Western Confederacy the new year, then, began with both Confederate and Union forces taking cattle, hogs, horses, and sometimes slaves from the farmers and planters in Tennessee and Mississippi. One farmer reported near Columbia, Tennessee, "Some alarm amongst our negroes for fear of being impressed" by Confederate soldiers. Planters and farmers in areas of Confederate control continued to face the problems of the past — impressment of their grain, meat, and forage. In eastern Tennessee, both armies had "stripped" the region of draft animals, and the Confederate commissary officer in charge could not get the minimal surplus grain from a disappointing wheat crop to government storage facilities.[28]

In east Tennessee Confederate soldiers had wreaked havoc on farmers loyal to the Union. One contemporary, appealing for Federal protection, wrote that "our farms are wantonly laid waste, all our horses and cattle are taken unnecessarily, all the hogs killed that will do to eat, and the stock hogs shot down to prevent us from raising more. Our best farmers will not be able to start a single plow when spring comes, and if they had the horses they have nothing to feed them on." He could not see how a population of 150,000 women and children could long survive. In his opinion the Union army also "robbed and plundered" its supporters, and the officers did not provide vouchers for compensation when they took food and forage from farmers. The food situation was particularly grim because the Confederates had plundered the countryside before the arrival of Union troops.[29]

Much the same could be said of the agricultural situation in Fort Smith, Arkansas, but in this area many secessionist farmers had fled and abandoned their lands. Bushwhackers robbed the farmers who remained when Federal troops left a neighborhood. Few farmers had made plans for spring planting, and only a few patches of wheat grew where thousands of acres had been raised. Piles of ashes now marked rough field boundaries after Union forces, particularly the 14th Kansas Cavalry, burned thousands of rails used for fencing. Although Union brigadier general John M. Thayer, commanding the Department of the District of the Frontier and the Department of Arkansas at Fort Smith, ordered the pillaging and burning to stop, Arkansas farmers did not believe their plight would soon improve. In Louisiana Confederate impressment agents ranged so efficiently that farmers threatened to stop raising corn and to let their fodder rot in the fields rather than sell at government prices.[30]

Although Confederate soldiers had orders to burn all cotton destined for northern markets, in March, a farmer taking two wagonloads of cotton to Natchez was overtaken by a contingent of Confederate cavalrymen, who required payment of $125 in greenbacks before they permitted the driver to proceed. The editor of the *New Orleans Times* noted that this action "looks more like a private speculation on the part of the cavalry force than obeying anything like Confederate orders." Actions such as this further indicated the collapse of the Western Confederacy. At the same time, hungry Confederate soldiers continued to take what they liked from farmers and planters. In June 1864, a Mississippi farmer wrote home to his wife from a camp in the northern part of the state: "Our soldiers act outrageously . . . in reference to . . . private property. . . . [They] have not left a fat hog, chicken, turkey, goose, duck, or eggs, or onions behind."[31]

In Indianola, Texas, occupying Union soldiers subsisted on fresh meat and cornbread. One soldier reported, "Flour or wheat bread is not to be thought of," and they paid 25 cents for a cake of cornbread that measured six inches by ten inches and three-fourths of an inch thick. It was, he said, "made up with the bran in it somewhat after the manner of chicken feed, a little salt being added to give it a taste." The civilian population, many of whom were loyal to the Union, had reached "desperate circumstances" and appealed to the Union provost marshal's office for rations, which the government provided to prevent starvation. The gratitude of the residents and farmers, however, soon began to wane. One Iowa soldier noted that "we promised them protection and they were glad; we fed the destitute, both friends and foes, and they thought the Government gracious and forgiving; we took their horses, killed their cattle, burned their fences & buildings, appropriated their property whenever it was wanted, but at this they began to complain a little; we quieted their fears, pleading 'military necessity' and assuring them that they would be fully remunerated for every loss and they were satisfied."[32]

Union raiders continued to plague Mississippi farmers and planters. In late July near New Albany in Union County, one farmer wrote that Yankee soldiers had "thronged" her property and taken corn, fodder, chickens, and vegetables: "They took *every thing* they could *find* that we have to eat." They had killed her husband's hogs, but she had managed to save some cows, although "they killed every bodys cows and calves around here." She described how she saved her calves: "They started to shoot [the calves] but I ran after them and begged them not to kill them. . . . If they would leave the calves . . . we could live on bread and milk." When the soldiers left, there was a "general stampede with the negroes," who set off to accompany them.[33]

Cotton continued to play a role in the strategic and tactical maneuverings of the Confederate and Union armies. In June, Confederate general Kirby Smith told planters in the Trans-Mississippi Department that he intended to purchase or impress half of the cotton in the department and use it to acquire guns, ammunition, clothing, and medicine. Writing from Shreveport, Louisiana, he said, "Cotton is the sole means of purchase. . . . The impressment of Cotton will be avoided if possible. But, supplies for the army *must be had*. It is left with you to determine whether, for the preservation of your homes you will force the Government to resort to impressment." The army needed supplies and if the planters would not furnish the required provisions, he intended to take their cotton, by force if necessary, and sell it.[34]

At the same time, Sherman preferred to burn all cotton seized by Federal soldiers as a matter of convenience, but he agreed to let "sutlers and army followers" purchase it, provided they made their own arrangements for transport and sale. He did not have the railroad cars to ship it north or the clerical support in the Quartermasters Department to deal with accounting and sale of the seized cotton. "If people have cotton," he wrote, "let them haul it to market." This policy benefited the planters now behind Union lines, as well as northern entrepreneurs and thieves who could make money by seizing or stealing abandoned or stored cotton that had been left unprotected. Overall, cotton farmers and planters lost more than they gained economically from both Confederate and Union military policies.[35]

THE CONFEDERACY HAD OTHER PROBLEMS in Tennessee and northern Mississippi, where cotton farmers now readily traded through Yankee lines for greenbacks. So much Union money circulated in Tennessee that Confederate currency had greatly depreciated. By late January one observer reported that in the country near Memphis, little could be bought with Confederate money. Major W. Damron, chief commissary of subsistence in Mississippi, also reported that "there is a growing indisposition among the people residing on the borders to sell for our currency." The money problem did not improve with the new currency and, by early May, Texans reportedly refused to accept it for the sale of their cattle; they instead demanded specie — that is, gold. From New Orleans, the editor of *The Era* reminded southerners that "outside Union lines famine reigns; inside are peace, plenty, and prosperity." Although he overstated his case about famine, many citizens behind Confederate lines did feel the deficiency of an adequate food supply, and those in Union territory began experiencing the return of traditional, if not yet normal, agricultural trade. "Politics may be won," he wrote, "but commerce is peace." In the Western Confederacy cotton farmers and planters had also come to that conclusion.[36]

As the cotton trade resumed behind Union lines, planters near Memphis eagerly sought greenbacks for their fiber. Staunch Confederates complained that greenbacks had so depreciated their currency that it damaged their cause more than Union soldiers. In this and other areas of the Western Confederacy, farmers and planters refused Confederate currency; they accepted it for the sale of their provision only under duress, when Confederate troops or partisans struck an area for supplies and paid with Confederate money. Farmers, planters, and merchants in the Union-occupied Western Confederacy now readjusted their lives based on the premise that "trade waits for no man." The editor of the *New Orleans Times* told his readers that peace would enable farmers and planters to provide for their families while a continuation of the war meant hunger and want. "The contrast is marked," he wrote, "and will and should remain so."[37]

In late 1864 a Confederate captain in Jackson wrote to General Braxton Bragg that because "there are few persons along our military frontier who have not sold cotton to the enemy... the disgraceful fact of subjugation is almost complete." Some Mississippians, however, could abide trading cotton for basic necessities — but not for luxuries. Others thought this excuse was merely a ruse for the opportunity to speculate and make money. For traders, loyalty could be conditional and dependent on the price of cotton.

A Confederate quartermaster reported that women, apparently from the planter class, "residing in this region, eminent for wealth, respectability, intelligence and beauty, make nothing of taking government cotton without authority and traveling in the night to the enemy's lines." They bribed Confederate pickets and sold their stolen cotton for goods, which they resold behind Confederate lines for a profit. But, here again, this issue is complex, and they may have seen themselves as patriots loyally aiding the Confederacy. They also may have been renewing their traditional prewar trading activities out of loyalty to their families. Many Confederates, however, viewed them as traitors. In the Western Confederacy, then, the loyalty of farmers and planters depended on circumstance, the past, and present. In contrast, Unionists saw things in black and white – the cotton trade was a weapon to destroy the Confederacy. The government in Richmond was far from the fields of the Western Confederacy. Its currency was worthless, its protection nearly nonexistent, and loyalty to it was fading rapidly. For many farmers and planters, self-interest rather than patriotism or nationalism ruled.[38]

Between December 11, 1863, and February 19, 1864, cotton planters sold 23,620 bales in New Orleans, a huge increase from the 3,868 bales sold during the corresponding period for 1862–63. During January and February Confederate cotton planters sold several hundred bales through enemy lines in St. Landry Parish, Pointe Coupée Parish along the Ouachita River, and areas along the Atchafalaya River, although the sales probably were not as large as trade sanctioned by permit. Confederate officials authorized the cotton trade across Union lines for needed supplies. In addition, in January, General Banks learned that planters had stored large quantities of cotton in the Red River Country and southern Arkansas, and he developed a plan to seize it and sell it for the benefit of the Federal Treasury. With cotton selling for $1.90 per pound in Boston, speculators eagerly sought the fiber, acquired legally or otherwise, through trade across Union lines. Banks's spring expedition into the Red River area succeeded in seizing much of that cotton, usually in connivance with planters and speculators. After Banks's arrival, reports from the Red River Country indicated that almost every farmer and planter took the oath of allegiance and began to plant cotton with free labor. After the Union army secured their neighborhoods, they became "intensely loyal" and eager to sell their cotton. Most of the cotton in that region, however, had been burned by either the planters or Confederate soldiers to keep it from confiscation by Union forces. Nevertheless, planters sold much of their remaining cotton to speculators – unless Union soldiers confiscated it and turned it over to speculators. Speculators believed that if Federal forces could occupy and hold the landings on the Red River between Alexandria and Natchitoches, cotton planters would be willing to market their crop to buyers with greenbacks. Otherwise, any substantial increase in the cotton trade depended on planting a new crop in the spring for harvest in the autumn.[39]

The editor of the *Richmond Daily Examiner* castigated those western planters who sold their cotton to northern buyers. "When it is remembered that the secession movement," he wrote, "was inaugurated by the cotton population of the South, that the Confederate Government is conducted almost exclusively under the auspices of cotton states men . . . these shameful transactions of mercenary cotton planters on the flats of the Mississippi appear still more strange and reprehinsible [sic]. If the secession Government is to be used as a private tart of cotton men, the infamy of the treachery of these cotton planters becomes the more black."[40]

Farmers and planters who had not burned or hidden their cotton when Union forces approached now often had their cotton stolen from isolated barns, with the thieves selling it at various landings, including New Orleans. The editor of the *New Orleans Times* urged buyers to avoid acquiring cotton by the bale or in small lots because of the possibility it had been stolen. With cotton selling for 70 to 73 cents per pound and soon to rise higher, Louisiana and other planters had to fear the loss of their cotton to thieves once Confederate forces no longer threatened to burn it. Some northerners contended that the more cotton Confederate growers burned, the higher the price would be when their plantations were taken over by northerners.[41]

By September so many planters and farmers had transported their cotton through Federal lines in Mississippi that Confederate major general Nathan Bedford Forrest prohibited that trade. He reminded the cotton producers that they were duty-bound to plant little, if any, cotton and instead should emphasize food crops for both the military and civilian populations. Effective September 15, anyone attempting to transport cotton from Confederate territory through Federal lines, Forrest ordered, would be arrested and their cotton confiscated. In Memphis the editor of the *Bulletin* noted that Forrest's order would be countered with a Federal policy that permitted the free trade of Confederate cotton in an attempt to further weaken the Confederacy.[42]

Planters in Union-occupied areas had to secure permits from U.S. Treasury Department officials before they could sell and ship cotton and sugar from their storage facilities. These permits verified that the planter had paid his rent on the confiscated plantation and that the crop had been grown on the plantation during the preceding season. At Natchez, Treasury agents gained a notorious reputation for charging a host of fees, which they often pocketed, before they permitted shipments to New Orleans. To gain control of the cotton trade, the U.S. Treasury Department on September 24 directed that only government agents should purchase cotton. They could not pay more than one-third of its value in supplies—which ultimately could aid Confederate forces—and they had to pay the remaining two-thirds of the cost in greenbacks. The establishment of a government monopoly in the cotton trade effectively prevented Confederate officers, such as Kirby Smith, John B. McGruder, and Nathan Bedford Forrest, from impressing or buying cotton from secessionist planters and farmers and selling it to middlemen who would transport it through Union lines.[43]

BY AUTUMN THE REVOLUTION IN labor became the most pressing concern for the planters, while the absence of mules and horses for plowing, clearing and draining land, and powering the sugar mills that pressed the cane posed another serious problem. Shortages of seed cane further slowed recovery, although Banks issued General Orders No. 138 on September 22, which required all owners, lessees, and managers of sugar plantations to reserve one-fourth of their cane yield for replanting. Not until February 1865 did the sugar plantations show any signs of recovery, and these hopes proved to be false. Conscription caused other problems, when Confederate general Joseph Johnston issued a proclamation in September that ordered the drafting of white and black males between the ages of eighteen and fifty. It created "very considerable excitement" in Tennessee among both races. Johnston's conscription edict also encouraged more slave men to seek protection behind Union lines.[44]

At the same time, the cotton crop did not meet expectations in the Mississippi River Valley because of damages resulting from the boll or army worm, unusually heavy autumn rains, and the inability of the field hands to keep the weeds down for the lack of mules. All of this reduced the cotton crop in the Vicksburg area from an anticipated 40,000 bales to an estimated 8,000 bales. The planters then concluded that the free-labor order had failed, as they knew it would, because black men and women would not work in their fields without compulsion. Wages would not and did not encourage them to complete the necessary work in their cotton fields, the planters contended. Yet slavery was dead whether official or not, and they had no remedy to offer for this new labor system. The only alternative to free, paid labor for black men and women would have been to distribute land to the freedpeople so they could cultivate their own crops for both subsistence and profit. However, no cotton or sugarcane planter supported this alternative. As a result, the planters could do little more than complain that free black field hands did not work as hard or as productively as during slavery and that Banks's free-labor order was a failure.[45]

By November some Tennessee farmers gleaned their cornfields to gather any ears lost between the rows when the crop was cut and shocked. Although gleaning provided little grain, one farmer believed the work was worth his time because it was "better saved than lost for we are doing nothing else." If a farmer had shelled corn to sell, however, it brought $6 per bushel if he could haul it safely to market. In Tennessee corn remained "Scarce and high" through the autumn. To the far west in Texas, Confederate currency exchanged at the rate of twenty-eight to one for gold, but little specie existed for such monetary trades. In northeastern Mississippi farmers refused to accept it for the sale of their corn, and they used the corn as well as cotton seed to make necessary purchases. The new Confederate currency act had done little more than create great confusion among farmers, planters, and wholesalers, among others. Although the essential premise of exchanging three old Confederate dollars for two new ones seemed clear, government officers – whether from the Commissary, Quartermasters, or Subsistence departments – quickly found that farmers distrusted the new money as much as the old currency, and no one seemed able to explain the conversion rate as it related to agricultural commodities. In Texas, cotton planters avoided the tax-in-kind and impressment officers, if possible, because speculators paid higher prices in greenbacks.[46]

In late November General John Bell Hood, having escaped Sherman's attack on Atlanta, skirted Union forces in eastern Tennessee and approached Nashville to try to recapture the city. Union forces under General Henry Thomas defeated him on the outskirts of the city in mid-December, effectively destroying the Army of Tennessee as a military force. The war in the Western Confederacy had ended.[47]

Reports of the failure of the corn crop in northwest Mississippi accompanied news of Hood's defeat and signaled that shortages of meat and meal were coming, and with it hunger during the winter. One correspondent wrote, "The corn isn't here. It hasn't been made. The people haven't got it, and bread is something they cannot do well without." Virtually no corn could be obtained in Panola, De Soto, Marshall, Lafayette, Tunica, and Coahoma. He noted that if both armies conducted operations, particularly cavalry, in northwestern Mississippi during the next year they would need to transport their own food supplies, because they would not be able to live off the country. Farmers and planters in that region had no food to steal, impress, or buy. Hunger was unavoidable, and it would gnaw on the soldiers, blue and gray, and civilians alike.[48]

By the end of the year farmers and planters commonly shipped cotton from Memphis, Nashville, Vicksburg, and New Orleans to northern buyers. Confederate officials could not prevent the trade and northern agents encouraged it. For their part, cotton planters and farmers needed the money and no longer cared about prohibitive Confederate policy. Northern middlemen sold the cotton and purchased plows, axes, shovels, axes, rope, and twine and other agricultural tools and goods, as well as bacon, pork, and other foods in the North; they then traded or sold these items to southern farmers and planters. At the same time, cotton brought as much as $1.22 per pound in New Orleans and offered security in these unsettled times. A planter near Confederate-controlled Vienna, Louisiana, who owned nineteen slaves, urged fellow planters to "prepare the minds of your negroes to stay with you. Hide your gold if you have any; sell your horses and surplus stock of cotton, and hold on to the end." Cotton would maintain sufficient value to provide an economic safety net in the uncertain days ahead.[49]

By December, Jefferson City, Texas, remained the great beef supply center for the Western Confederacy – or at least the part of it not occupied by Union forces. There, the meatpacking firm of J. B. Dunn had a contract with the government to slaughter and pack 150 beef cattle per day with the meat smoked, salted, and pickled for the army. Texas cattlemen maintained at least reduced sales in the West now that they could no longer reach markets east of the Mississippi River. Soon Texas cattle could not reach the Jefferson City market, either, but local livestock raisers profited if they had cattle to sell, because buyers paid from $80 to $100 per head for first-quality beeves while the lowest quality brought prices of at least $40 per head.[50]

During the year Mississippi had provided most of the provisions for the Confederate army in the West through sales and impressment, as well as from provisions collected from the tax-in-kind. Mississippi farmers paid

595,000 bushels of corn as a tax-in-kind, compared with only 6,000 bushels in Tennessee, but Union forces held most of that state. Mississippi farmers and planters also contributed 14,400 bushels of potatoes and 11,000 bushels of wheat through the tax-in-kind. Tennessee contributed no potatoes and only 4,000 bushels of wheat. Agricultural production had declined significantly due to Union attacks, occupation, and plundering, particularly in the Jackson and Meridian areas, where marching armies from both sides trampled fields and killed livestock.[51]

The collective loss of agricultural production from labor shortages, Yankee movements through the countryside, and foraging by both armies caused considerable suffering for want of food. The destruction of agriculture in northern Mississippi had been severe, and the citizens of Tishomingo County petitioned the Confederate Congress for tax relief. Union raids and Confederate impressments had left farmers and planters so destitute that not more than one family in twenty had the means of subsistence. "Unless some relief can be had," they appealed, "*starvation* and *ruin* must ensue." Agricultural production had come to a halt in many Union-occupied Delta counties. The power of southern agriculture to sustain the army and civilian population in the Western Confederacy had essentially collapsed when the year ended.[52]

By the end of 1864, then, the hard times born of war were behind for many farmers and planters in the Western Confederacy, but peace would bring more difficult days for them, no matter whether they lived in Union-occupied areas or in neighborhoods still untouched by Federal soldiers. The future looked bleak. A Mississippi planter wrote, "The year goes out cold windy and blustering the ground frozen." On the last day of the year, one Tennessee farmer spoke for many when he said, "What a terrible year this has been."[53]

CHAPTER EIGHT

Last Things

The winter of 1864–65 brought despair and the realization that the military and agricultural power of the Confederate States of America had reached the end. Hunger wore at body and soul. Resentment festered against the government for the impressment of agricultural provisions, mandated low prices for army purchases, and the tax-in-kind, as well as for the impressment of slaves and conscription policies. In January southern farmers faced a bleak future. A Tennessee planter wrote, "The year 1865 was ushered in with poor prospects for the Confederacy." A cold rain kept Alabama farmers from plowing. Many soldiers and civilians suffered from want of food. Virginia's farmers could not supply the food and forage that Robert E. Lee's Army of Northern Virginia needed. Lee had put the Army of Northern Virginia on one-quarter rations. Josiah Gorgas, chief of ordnance, wrote in his diary that Lee's army was "almost without bread & quite without meat." Farmers could not help. Lee noted that "there is nothing within reach of the army to be impressed; the country is swept clear.... We have only two days rations." He asked the citizens of Richmond for food. Few responded.[1]

Atlanta had fallen; John Bell Hood's army had been destroyed in Tennessee. William Tecumseh Sherman had laid waste to a corridor from Atlanta to the sea and prepared to march with similar destructive force into the Carolinas. Ulysses S. Grant had nearly drawn a cordon around Lee's army in Virginia. Southern sympathizers felt the "greatest despondency everywhere." Farmers and planters in unoccupied areas feared that they, too, would soon see blue coats sweeping across their fields. One Alabama planter reported that "food and ra[i]ment are very scarce and should it [the war] continue much longer the result will be awful." Cornelia Phillip Spencer, who operated a plantation near Raleigh, North Carolina, wrote that "there was very little room left for 'belief' of any sort in the ultimate success of the Confederacy. All the necessaries of life were scarce, and were held at fabulous and still increasing prices." Farmers with produce to sell, however, received good prices in Confederate money if they could get it to market without impressment by Confederate agents or seizure by Union forces. But they preferred northern markets, even local markets across Union lines, if they could reach them and sell their provisions for greenbacks.[2]

In Richmond, food prices had escalated beyond the means of most residents. Flour brought $1,000 per barrel, cornmeal $80 per bushel, and beef $6 per pound in Confederate money. Prices such as these necessitated the continuation of a barter economy across many areas, as merchants willingly exchanged goods for agricultural provisions. Two bushels of corn or four gallons of "good syrup" would pay one year's subscription for the Augusta *Southern Banner*, where in that city flour now brought $300 to $400 per barrel, wheat $25 to $30 per bushel, and corn $22 per bushel in the ear and sold from farmers' wagons. Beef brought $1.50 and pork $3 per pound, respectively, while bacon brought $6.50 per pound, cornmeal $25 per bushel, and fodder $25 per hundredweight; chickens sold for $10 to $12 and turkeys for $30 to $40 per pair, respectively. Butter brought $10 per pound, eggs $6.50 per dozen, and cotton $1.25 to $1.40 per pound – all high prices for farmers and consumers and comparable to Richmond prices. Potatoes, however, had disappeared from city markets. In Albany, Georgia, farmers sold corn in the streets for $10.30 per bushel, but some commission men refused to sell at that price because they judged it too low. Butter brought $5 and bacon $3.50 per pound, respectively. The editor of the *Albany Patriot* asked, "In God's name, what will poor people do?" In northern Mississippi, farmers sold corn for $2 per bushel in greenbacks. No farmer wanted to accept Confederate paper money, and few residents in the towns and cities had specie. In San Antonio, Confederate money exchanged at the rate of $25 in paper to $1 of gold. Mexican traders conducted a "bustling" business for cotton, and merchants apparently grew wealthy from the amount of specie that circulated in the city. In the Eastern Confederacy, the price index reached 5,824 in January and rose to 9,211 in April – or ninety-two times the prewar base. (First four months of 1861 = 100.) By April the discount rate of Confederate currency for gold reached 100 to 1.[3]

As winter thawed, the agricultural situation looked grim across the South. In Georgia the best wheat lands lay behind enemy lines. Few slaves remained to work the plantations and farmlands. In February, the editor of the *Southern Cultivator* believed that Georgia farmers would not be able to produce more than half of the food crops harvested in 1864 and probably less than one-third of their production in 1863, even if the enemy left the state, which no one expected. Agricultural details — that is, deferments from military service for farm and plantation supervision and work — had been canceled. Men from forty-five to sixty years of age were now called to the army, further reducing the agricultural workforce. An Atlanta editor expected the labor shortage to result in an "alarming deficiency in the next crop of wheat." So great had the manpower need become for the Confederate armies that farm women and children confronted a heavy burden as they looked ahead to a new planting season. With the unshackling of slave labor from the land, white women on small-scale farms continued working in the fields because labor costs remained prohibitive. When General William N. Pendleton, chief of artillery for the Army of Northern Virginia, returned to his Virginia plantation, he reported that his "daughters, accomplished ladies as they were, went into the fields and planted the corn and potatoes."[4]

Many farmers and planters who remained on the land had sown less wheat than previously, because they had become too discouraged to plant a full crop. Confederate agents had impressed so much of their grain at below-market prices and with a "constantly depreciating currency" that they saw no reason to continue raising grain. An Atlanta editor reported that "none but the very sanguine and very patriotic, have sown much more than they will require for home consumption, and even that was sown generally too late." In March, Nimrod Porter, a Maury County planter in middle Tennessee, reported that "verry [sic] few of the citizens are trying to raise a crop in this county." Generally, the farmers who planted wheat for the 1865 crop year only seeded enough to meet household needs. One critic of Confederate agricultural policy contended that the impressment system now ensured that the army would lack food and that the civilian population would face "imminent" starvation. The meat supply also had been greatly reduced. Fewer than half the cattle slaughtered in Georgia during the previous year would be available for the army and civilian population. Cholera had further decimated hogs across the region. Some southerners believed that they would necessarily live on corn, more so than ever before, during the coming year. They also lamented that "the negroes, left to themselves, will not make their own subsistence for the year." The immediate future looked desperate for lack of food for the army, and starvation loomed for all.[5]

In late April one correspondent traveling with Sherman's army in North Carolina reported near Fayetteville that farmers had averaged only five to eight bushels of corn and wheat per acre, respectively, the previous year and that little increase in production would occur in 1865. Oats had provided the best return on "good lands in favorable seasons," yielding twelve to fifteen bushels per acre, but many farmers and planters had returned their focus to cotton and expected to produce 400 to 500 pounds per acre. They did not raise hay. The correspondent believed, however, that only slavery could provide the necessary labor for cotton production, contending, as would most southerners, that "now in taking the negro, we take the very life out of the confederacy." At the same time, Georgia planters complained they had reaped no benefit from their exemption from military service and that they had "undergone as hard service and discharged their duties as faithfully as any soldiers in the army." They also had been compelled to leave their plantations entirely to the mercy of slaves, Yankees, and Confederates. Planters in the militia believed they had been deprived of their rights by their illegal induction into Confederate military service, and they wanted financial restitution. The revival of southern agriculture seemed problematic.[6]

To make matters worse, on January 9, the government halted the collection of cattle in Florida for droving north. Sherman's army had made the movement of cattle into Georgia too dangerous, and northern Florida and southern Georgia did not have sufficient feed, forage, or pasture to sustain passing cattle herds. Still, Commissary General Lucius B. Northrop remained optimistic. In early February he reported to Secretary of War J. C. Breckinridge that "some thousands of beeves have been obtained within the past few months by swimming the Mississippi, and when the river is again in a suitable state and the season admits of it, the proceeding shall continue." He also optimistically and incorrectly expected some 20,000 head of cattle to arrive from Florida. But one Alabaman reported that "our stock of neat cattle is getting greatly reduced and not more than half the quantity of beef can be furnished in 1865 that was killed in 1864." By April, drovers had managed to take a few cattle north, but neither Florida nor Texas cattlemen could make a significant contribution to the war effort. Even if a sufficient number of cattle could have been collected, the government did not have the money – that is, specie – to pay for them, and cattle raisers would take nothing less. Civilian thieves were also seizing Confederate army cattle that grazed on rented pastures. One farmer reported that the people who took them "say they have as much right to the cattle as anyone, now there is no government here in Virginia."[7]

In Virginia impressment agents could not meet Lee's need for horses. General Pendleton noted that "the question of our horse supply is hardly second to that of supplying men for the army, or food for the men." Moreover, Virginia farmers needed their remaining horses for plowing. The only effective way Confederate forces could acquire the necessary horses and mules was to raid behind enemy lines or purchase them from Mexico. Raiding Union lines might yield 3,000 horses and mules in Mississippi, and 2,000 could be acquired from Virginia and North Carolina farmers. Although southern farmers behind Union lines might sell, Confederate raiders would need specie, and buyers could expect to pay $60 in gold for first-class horses and mules and $40 for second-class ones. In Confederate areas of Mississippi, purchasing agents would need to exchange 600 pounds of government cotton for first-class horses. Any purchases from Mexico would require gold coin.[8]

In Georgia, Sherman's army had taken most of the horses and mules needed for plowing and cultivation. By mid-February Lee estimated that he needed 3,270 horses and 2,409 mules for service in Virginia and North Carolina, and another 2,650 horses for the soldiers gathering to oppose Sherman's move northward into the Carolinas from Georgia. Archibald H. Cole, inspector general of field transportation, reported to Quartermaster General Alexander R. Lawton that the army needed 10,000 horses from the trans-Mississippi Confederacy, but he did not have the gold to buy them or the railroad cars to ship them east. Impressment seemed the only alternative, yet farmers balked and the necessary procurement of horses and mules failed with the coming spring, in part, because the government could not afford to feed them. Philip Sheridan's men riding strong, well-fed horses from northern farms easily outmatched Lee's cavalry. The horse and mule supply for Lee had failed. Southern agricultural power had collapsed. The end was near.[9]

While southern farmers struggled to supply horses, cattle, and hogs for the Confederate armies and civilian population, they also confronted disastrous livestock diseases, particularly in Virginia. By 1865 equine glanders, cattle fever, and hog cholera, the latter of which had been negligible, now became devastating problems for livestock producers. Although both sides blamed the other for introducing glanders, Union horses carried many diseases to the livestock of Virginia farmers. When Lee surrendered at Appomattox, Grant let his men keep their horses, many of which suffered from glanders and which now spread the disease throughout the South as their owners returned home. Grant's kindness ironically left a "legacy of the war" on southern agriculture that would last into the twentieth century.[10]

At the same time, when Confederate forces disintegrated and Union armies departed various areas never to return, local farmers appropriated for their own use the cattle and horses left behind by both forces. The Union armies also began selling horses and mules soon after the war ended, which benefited farmers and planters. In Columbia, Tennessee, the army sold horses shortly after the war ended, but at the "most extravagant prices," and few farmers and planters could afford them. In August the sale of a large number of cavalry horses and mules at Lynchburg, Virginia, prompted one reporter to write, "Some of the animals are nearly worthless, but many of them are valuable, and all are cheap; and these sales will doubtless enable the farmers much more easily to get this year's produce to market, and to prepare a much greater breadth of land for the new wheat crop than they otherwise could."[11]

EARLY IN THE YEAR THE failure of the Subsistence Department to acquire the necessary provisions for General Lee's Army of Northern Virginia led, in part, to a revision of impressment regulations. On February 8, Lee wrote to Secretary of War Seddon that his commissary officers reported the general had "not a pound of meat at his disposal." Lee complained that "if some change is not made and the commissary department reorganized, I apprehend dire results. The physical strength of the men, if their courage survives, must fail under this treatment." Although Lee, Jefferson Davis, and others blamed Commissary General Lucius B. Northrop for incompetency — which ultimately led to his replacement by I. M. St. John on February 16 — farmers had contributed to the food and forage shortage in Lee's army because many withheld or hid their provisions to avoid impressment at low prices. Some critics urged the immediate end of the impressment of produce at below-market prices. As a result, Davis made a final effort to change procurement practices: "Let supplies be had by purchasing, or borrowing, or other possible move."[12]

Although impressments continued unabated and even increased in areas where the commissary officers could secure agricultural commodities and transportation, agents now paid higher prices. In Virginia agents paid fixed impressment prices of $25 per 60-pound bushel of wheat, $123 to $128 per 196-pound barrel of flour, $21 per 50-pound bushel of cornmeal, and $15 per 32-pound bushel of oats. They also paid $4 per pound for bacon, $8.25 per pound for salted pork, and $2.75 per pound for fresh

TABLE 2. Agricultural Prices, Athens, Georgia, and Confederate Government, March 1, 1865

Commodity	Market Price	Impression Price
Bacon, pound	$5.00	$2.25
Beef, pound	2.00	0.70
Corn, bushel	25.00	3.50
Cornmeal, bushel	25.00	3.50
Flour, barrel	200.00	65.00
Irish potatoes, bushel	25.00	7.00
Lard, pound	6.00	2.25
Sweet potatoes, bushel	15.00	2.75
Wheat, bushel	30.00	12.50

Source: Coulter, *The Confederate States of America*, 226.

pork, as well as $1,200 for first-class artillery horses and mules. Agents paid $7 per hundredweight for baled, and $6 per hundredweight for unbaled, hay. They paid farmers from $5 to $10 per month to use their pastures for army horses and mules. Even so, major discrepancies existed across the Confederacy for market and impressment prices.[13]

Impressment officers necessarily paid with Confederate currency that continued to depreciate in value. Farmers naturally objected, and the Virginia Board of State Commissioners urged impressment officers to pay an average price of $600 in new currency for artillery and wagon horses impressed since the Confederate Congress passed the currency reform act. The board urged officers to visit all farmers and planters from whom they had appropriated horses and mules at the scheduled prices and pay any additional compensation; these add-ons were to be based on the judgment of county appraisers or, in their absence, the agents' own evaluation – provided they did not pay less than $400 or more than $800 in the new currency. The commissioners hoped that "this plan would perhaps be most satisfactory to the people." If not, dissatisfied farmers could appeal to the board for reconsideration.[14]

The problem, though not new, had become so serious that it necessitated mandatory change, and it came in March when Congress repealed the impressment law of 1864. It now authorized the abandonment of the price schedule payment plan and required the payment of "just compensation" – which meant the "usual market price" at the time of impressment, subject to appeal to the Board of Commissioners in the Confederate states. Congress also prohibited impressment of milch cows, broodmares, stallions, bulls, breeding hogs, sheep, and jacks. Desperate times had forced Congress to take dramatic action, albeit too late to appease farmers and gain access to needed food and forage for the army. This change in the payment policy proved futile because—absent the setting of agricultural prices by schedule and the lack of arbitration or amending—it forced impressment agents to pay exorbitant free-market prices, which they could not afford. Many agents chose instead to simply seize the needed provisions with verbal promises to pay later or to pay in paper. In late February, Confederate soldiers took "turkies corn & potatoes" from a planter near Aiken, South Carolina. They also burned his cotton. The disintegration of the Confederacy and southern agriculture seemed at hand: "We are almost now in a state of anarchy & lawlessness. The future looks dark & uncertain." When Federal troops occupied his farm a few days later, they took his horses and "killed all the turkeys & fowls & cleaned out the potatoe celer." Essentially, the procurement problems for securing food and forage remained, but time had run out.[15]

Indeed, farmers and planters could not ignore impressment officers. On April 10 Catherine Ann Devereux, a North Carolina planter's wife, reported that impressment agents sent by General Joseph Johnston with orders "to *take all the best of our team*, to leave us only the worthless and inferior to deprive the enemy." The army used her plantation as a temporary depot for the impressment of horses and mules for the area. Angrily, she wrote that since "the Government [is] confessedly too weak to protect us. . . at least it ought not thus deprive us of a means of making a support." She doubted the army could feed the impressed horses and mules for a month and feared they would soon be dead. Then, she wrote, "upon the heels of the horse impressers is to come another gang with direction to take all our meat save three months supply! The Yankees themselves could hardly do worse." Although she would "cheerfully and willingly" live on vegetables for "the sake of *the Cause*," she resented "forced patriotism." She lamented, "What is to become of our eighty five negroes thus deprived of food & employment? The Government says make them work with *hoes*, but suppose we have no hoes & no ability to get them, what then?" For Devereux and others like her, the collapse of the old agricultural system brought bewilderment and resentment.[16]

Confederate guerrillas continued to steal horses near Nashville. Where Union soldiers roamed, farmers and planters also lost corn, hay, bacon, and other provisions as well as horses and mules. One Tennessee planter remarked that "breaking into smoke houses [by Federal soldiers] seems to be the order of the day." In Virginia, Union forces continued to raid farms for provisions, horses, and mules and destroyed agricultural equipment in the process. Occupying Union soldiers burned Confederate warehouses storing cotton, sugar, tobacco, and other agricultural commodities that could have been used, with the exception of tobacco, to provide food relief for hungry people. Southerners learned that the war did not end for them with Lee's surrender. Federal confiscations and pillaging of food stores, farms, and plantations would continue for weeks. When Sherman took possession of the Raleigh area in April, a female planter complained that his troops let their horses and mules trample her garden and orchard; destroyed a field of corn, potatoes, and peas; took her horses and mules; and killed her poultry and more than thirty hogs. In May a North Carolina woman farmer wrote that on one plantation, "ten miles of fencing were burned up, from one end to the other; not an ear of corn, not a sheaf of wheat, not a bundle of fodder was left; the army wagons were driven into the cultivated fields and orchards and meadows, and fires were made under the fruit trees; the sheep and hogs were shot down and left to rot on the ground, and several thousand horses and cattle were turned in on the wheat crops, then just heading. All the horses, seventeen in number, were carried off and all stock." Until the very end and beyond, farmers and planters paid a high price for secession.[17]

In the Western Confederacy, Federal troops continued confiscating cotton. In March a Union expedition up the Yazoo River seized 1,728 bales, which the Federal government sold to compensate Union loyalists for their property damages and losses to Confederate guerrillas. The hunt for "C.S.A." branded cotton continued until searches for it terminated in September. Cotton that the Confederacy had impressed, purchased, or received as a tithe and which Union forces had not seized now melted away into the possession of the farmers and planters who had originally possessed it, or to thieves.[18]

The Confederate Congress also dealt with continued farmer and planter opposition to the tax-in-kind. On March 13, it authorized government officials who estimated the value of crops and livestock for payment of the tax to use the "fair market value in the neighborhood" as the standard of valuation. If the assessor and farmer could not agree on that valuation, the disagreement would be resolved by a disinterested person as provided by Section 10 of the tax-in-kind law of February 17, 1864.

Farmers and planters could also pay this tax with money at the assessed value of their crops. Farm families with a disabled head of the household resulting from military service — and "composed entirely of white members" and whose farms were now cultivated by their families — were excused from paying the tax. Congress set the penalty for failure to pay the tax-in-kind for cotton and tobacco at five times the estimated value of the tax. By mid-March, however, farmers and planters ignored the law.[19]

BY FEBRUARY COTTON HAD FALLEN from 75 cents per pound to 40 cents per pound in Memphis, as buyers anticipated gaining access to large quantities of fiber stored on plantations when the war ended. By late March, cotton had fallen to 30 cents per pound in Nashville. In Wilmington, North Carolina, speculators held some 15,000 cotton bales as they awaited the arrival of Federal troops. They expected to make a great profit from its sale to northern buyers as soon as Union forces occupied the city and freed them from Confederate prohibitions against trading with the enemy. Grant, however, denied the shipment of sugar, coffee, and other foodstuffs across Union lines for trade in Virginia and in North Carolina for cotton. This trade, he believed, would feed the enemy and prolong the war while enriching speculators who only wanted to make money from desperate planters, farmers, and townspeople. He also ordered the stoppage of all supplies heading south between Charleston, South Carolina, and the James River. "Cotton only comes out on private accounts," he ordered, "except in payment for absolute necessities for the support of the war." In mid-March, though, the Confederate Congress authorized farmers, planters, and merchants to transport cotton and tobacco across Union lines "free from any molestation on the part of the authorities of the Confederate States" to raise specie for the army to purchase supplies. Desperation prevailed for most southerners.[20]

But not for all. In April, during the last days of the Confederacy, the editor of the *Weekly Intelligencer* in Atlanta solemnly reminded his readers that cotton, and, by implication southern agriculture, "is yet a great element of power," even though the long-held belief that "our cotton is King" had been "particularly exploded." He called on the cotton states to trade across enemy lines, particularly for salt for the curing of meat during the next winter. He also called on these states to export cotton by running the blockade — an impossible dream that he could not forsake. Confederate trade across enemy lines now increased, and so much cotton reached the Memphis market that the price fell to 20 cents per pound, which one Tennessee planter considered "greatly depressed."[21]

When the war ended, the Federal government attempted to restore the cotton trade and injected much needed cash into the occupied South to boost the economy now that both Confederate and state-issued currency had become worthless. On May 9, just days after Johnston surrendered in North Carolina and a day before Union cavalry captured the fleeing Jefferson Davis at Irwinville, Georgia, President Andrew Johnson approved a new policy that permitted the secretary of the Treasury to appoint agents who would purchase cotton from southern planters and farmers at designated locations, provided the fiber had not been captured or abandoned. Legitimate owners could sell their fiber free from any export taxes or fees. In Savannah, U.S. Purchasing Agent T. P. Robb announced that "cotton owners may rest assured that it is now perfectly safe (so far at least as any interference on the part of the Government is concerned) for them to bring in and dispose of their cotton." He urged all farmers in the interior to transport their cotton by whatever means to Savannah for sale. Later, the Treasury Department announced, "The war is virtually closed, and ... to reap the benefits of peace, it is desirable that the old and regular channels of trade be re established [sic], new ones opened and the occupations of the people both in city and country be resumed." Cotton planters welcomed the termination of trade restrictions, and they assumed that they could safely transport their cotton to market.[22]

When the war ended, tens of thousands of cotton bales labeled "C.S.A." remained scattered among the plantations. This cotton, as well as tobacco, now came under the jurisdiction of the Treasury Department with special agents sent to collect it for sale on behalf of the Federal government. Although most of the cotton and tobacco came under government control, an apparently large, but unknown, quantity disappeared and enriched Confederate produce loan officers who secreted it way. In Mississippi many people confiscated abandoned C.S.A. cotton because the Federal government considered it "common property," free for the taking. In Louisiana some 200,000 bales of Confederate cotton remained stored in warehouses or on plantations. Only the army could adequately protect it from theft for sale by the Federal government or northern factors. From Virginia, Grant ordered Major General Edward Canby in New Orleans to "Ship North all captured cotton as rapidly as possible," and he encouraged planters, farmers, and speculators to bring private holdings of cotton to military depots for their sale. Grant made his policy for the sale of cotton clear by writing, "Let there be no military interference whatever to the sale and shipment of cotton, nor no search made for Confederate cotton. It is in the interest of finances to get all the cotton to market possible and without delay." This policy benefited northern factors first and cotton planters and farmers to a lesser degree. By late June the arrival of some 20,000 bales of confiscated cotton kept the price at 40 cents per pound in New York City.[23]

IN APRIL, A SAVANNAH RESIDENT reflected that "eating is a most expensive amusement, and few do it that can possibly do without it." In Augusta a barrel of flour brought $700, eggs $12 per dozen, and a drink of corn whiskey $5. A restaurant meal consisting of tainted bacon, hard bread, and rice or sometimes fried potatoes cost $10; so did a meal of ham and eggs. Customers had to pay in advance because Confederate soldiers often "devoured" their food and left without paying. Food shortages and high prices caused another riot in Richmond. The situation soon became worse. In late March Lee abandoned Petersburg and withdrew from Richmond in early April, as he fled with his army to make a last stand near Danville or Lynchburg. But his Army of Northern Virginia had been shattered, and Sheridan blocked his retreat. On Sunday morning, April 2, Jefferson Davis learned that Lee's army faced encirclement, and he was marching west to try to link up with Joe Johnston's army in the mountains to continue the fight. His withdrawal made the seat of the Confederate government untenable, and Davis and other government officials fled the capital by train for Danville. With the Confederate government and army gone, civil authority collapsed. Quickly a riot ensued as hungry people broke into the government commissary for food and fought with Virginia militiamen who stayed behind to destroy anything that the Federals might use – including whiskey, which many residents tried to prevent from being dumped into the streets. The end came on April 9 at Appomattox Court House. The war was largely over. Attention now turned to reconstructing the South politically and economically, and agriculture became a major part of that mission.[24]

Several days later, Charles Baker Fields, a soldier in Lee's Army of Northern Virginia, recorded in his diary having no rations while encamped near Appomattox. Eleven days later he wrote that he had returned home and was burning brush for his grandmother's farm. In the days ahead he planted and plowed corn, oats, and grain sorghum for molasses. Like Fields, many Confederate soldiers returned to their farms to often find their barns and fences burned, their livestock gone, their slaves departed, and their fields growing weeds instead of cotton, tobacco, and grain. They accepted emancipation but nothing more regarding the former slaves.[25]

As white farmers and planters struggled to adjust to a new order for agricultural labor, they slowly began to reenter their past lives. Despite the ruin that war brought to southern agriculture, by mid-May a sense of normality began to return to some areas. A Natchez editor reported, "We noticed hundreds of familiar faces from the country in town yesterday and day previous. It looked a little like old times again, when our country friends made daily visits to the city to sell products and secure supplies. Harmony, concession, and kind feeling will soon bring all things right again." Concession proved difficult, however, particularly concerning race and labor. Still, by the summer, most southern farmers had returned to the rhythms of the season, plowing, planting, and harvesting. Soon new split rail fences enclosed fields of tobacco and wheat; and cattle, horses, and mules grazed on green pastures. In Virginia, a Confederate soldier's experience proved typical. He returned to his parents' farm in King William County and turned his attention "to getting the farm out of the confusion in which it had remained since the great Yankee army had passed over it." Confederate soldiers became farmers once again, often with the attitude that it was time to move on.[26]

When many soldiers returned home they planted cotton because it provided the highest return per acre than any other crop, particularly in the Lower South. They needed an income, and cotton sold for high prices on regional markets. Farmers and planters anxiously sought a return to the agricultural work they had known before the war, albeit without slave labor. One northern observer noted that a South Carolinian insisted "with much vehemence that cotton is king, and that a resolution on the part of the South not to sell any for a year would bring the North upon its knees." Another remarked that he was "very confident that the North depends entirely upon the cotton trade for a living, and that a failure to get at least one million bales before spring [would] bring a tremendous financial crash." Given these views, one can only wonder where they had been since 1861. Reality again eluded them.[27]

Peace made plowing and planting safe for the returning soldiers, although a shortage of plows often necessitated sharing implements or exchanging work with a neighbor. Some farmers and planters used young horses and cattle for draft power, but plowing proved difficult for these animals. Many fields, which had not been plowed for several years, remained uncultivated due to a lack of labor, horses, mules, implements, and capital. Other lands that had been overused and under-fertilized had begun to wear out. In Virginia one traveler observed that from Alexandria to Manassas, he saw "no sign of human industry save here and there a sickly half cultivated corn field.... The country for the most part consisted of fenceless fields abandoned to weeds, stump lots and undergrowth." Many southern farmers and planters had lost everything except their land. Some could begin anew, but the road to subsistence and profitability would be long and difficult, and it would entail a return to cotton production at the expense of diversified farming. A revolution in agricultural labor, insufficient technology, and a one-crop cotton economy soon defined farm life across the old Confederacy. So did a new poverty for whites and blacks as they worked to restore their farms and establish new lives on the land, features of southern agriculture that remained well into the twentieth century.[28]

IN JANUARY 1865, QUARTERMASTER Alexander R. Lawton wrote that "nearly everyone succumbs to the notion that *slavery* is a doomed institution in any event, though they differ much as to its slow or rapid death." With the institution of slavery virtually destroyed in Virginia, Tennessee, and Arkansas — and on its knees in Mississippi, Louisiana, Alabama, Georgia, Florida, South Carolina, North Carolina, and Texas — the revolution in agricultural labor neared completion. A Tennessee planter reported, "Negro slavery of no value, but much expense." While farmers and planters in Confederate-controlled areas worried about the collapse of slave prices and their ability to keep their slaves, southerners behind Union lines grappled with the agricultural labor problem created by the freeing of 4 million bondsmen and -women. Everyone understood that black men, women, and children were technically free, because the Federal government so proclaimed this by force of arms and the ratification of the Thirteenth Amendment on December 18, 1865. Yet freedom for blacks meant different things to whites, North and South. To most southerners the "freedom bestowed upon him [blacks] is not to be wasted in idleness . . . he is *free*, but free only to labor." Yet plantation owners and farmers who raised staple crops, such as cotton and sugarcane, that required extensive human labor did not have the capital to hire agricultural workers. At the same time, the largely unskilled black men and women did not have the capacity, whether through government policy or credit, to acquire land or rent it for agricultural purposes.[29]

TABLE 3. Tax Valuations of Slaves in Georgia, by Age, 1865

Age (in years)	Valuation
2	$370
2–6	733
12–16	2,394
Males, 16–25	3,600
Females, 16–25	2,187
Males, 25–35	3,443
Females, 25–35	2,850
Males, 35–45	2,768
Females, 35–45	2,057
Males, 45–55	1,652
Females, 45–55	1,134
Males, 55–65	663
Females, 55–65	410

Source: *Atlanta Weekly Intelligencer*, April 19, 1865.
Note: The valuation was increased by 50 percent for slaves who were mechanics, body (personal) servants, coachmen, or seamstresses.

In the first month of the new year, the price of prime male field hands brought $5,000 in Georgia, but this was in Confederate money. In San Antonio and Houston, slave prices had collapsed. A large quantity of stout, able-bodied field hands of both sexes could be purchased at prices ranging from $400 to $500. Slave prices were lower than anyone could remember. In Austin, slaveholders attempted to sell a "large quantity of negros" at "very low prices," and the slave market soon became overstocked. By April slave prices in Atlanta had tumbled. Perhaps the printer had already set the type for the issue which listed slave valuations (see Table 3) before he learned of Lee's surrender. Because the valuation of slaves varied widely across Georgia, the last Confederate state legislature authorized the comptroller general to provide a uniform rate of valuation based on reports from the justices of the Inferior Courts, who forwarded the slave prices from estate sales. In mid-April those valuations ranged from $370 for slaves under two years of age to a high of $3,600 for males slaves from sixteen to twenty-five years of age, and $2,850 for females aged twenty-five to thirty-five. An additional 50 percent of the assessed value would be added to the valuation of any slave, such as a mechanic or seamstress, who practiced a trade. Even at this late date some slave owners remained optimistic that they could still sell their bondsmen and -women, if only to get some return on their investments before a dictated peace financially ruined them.[30]

As the Confederacy collapsed, on February 3, the Louisiana legislature legalized the removal of mortgaged slaves from the state when they were in danger of being captured by Union troops. Slave owners had to apply to the district judge for permission to move them to another state – which essentially meant Texas – and they also had to post a bond. The legislature authorized the governor to appoint "syndics" with fixed salaries, funded by the sale of agricultural provisions, to operate abandoned plantations. Any surplus production would be sold and the proceeds held in escrow until the plantation owners returned. These measures proved too little too late to protect both slaves and property.[31]

On February 20, the House of Representatives authorized the use of slaves in the army, and the Senate approved the legislation on March 8. As a result, one Alabama planter reported that he could plant only a small corn crop because "congress has put the negroes in the army. I fear the present great distress for food will be increased by a deficiency in the next crop," due to insufficient labor. In early April he reported that "food is scarce." In South Carolina Union officers gave the freedpeople on the rice plantations license to raid their old masters' barns for grain and meat and to take hogs, poultry, and sheep and to ransack their houses. Little corn and potatoes and no rice had been planted because the freedmen and -women chose not to work.[32]

As the end of the war neared, the agricultural slave labor system continued to disintegrate. In Virginia, many freedpeople left the farms and plantations, and their former owners worried about harvesting their summer wheat and autumn corn crops. Some farmers would not hire blacks who had left their former masters, but some helped their "servants" plant corn. By early June farmers in Fluvanna and Albemarle counties in Virginia had hired freedpeople for $5 per month in specie for a "first class" man and $3 per month for a similarly rated woman. Federal government regulations provided that those who remained on the plantations could raise a garden and keep poultry as during slavery, and they could be fed but not provided clothes. Some planters fixed November 15 as the end of the year for contract labor. One Virginia resident observed, "The negroes must get prompt employment or starve. There is little to eat in this country and less currency. Hence wages are low and subsistence dear." As a result, he reported in July, the farmwork by the hired freedpeople "progressed pretty well." In Florida, many freedmen and -women chose to remain on their plantations because they did not have any place to go, and the planters who had lost some $21.6 million in their slave investments compensated them with money or a share of the crop for their labor.[33]

General Sherman attempted to solve the black refugee problem in the Eastern Confederacy with Special Field Orders No. 15, issued on January 16. It established a thirty-mile-wide strip along the Georgia coast, including the Sea Islands, for agricultural settlement by the freedpeople. Sherman's order gave heads of households "possessory title" to "not more than forty acres of tillable land" for subsistence and limited commercial agriculture. Sherman did not have government authorization to issue this order, but it reaffirmed the belief of the freedpeople that they would receive forty acres and a mule when peace came. Only time would tell whether the freedpeople would develop their lands for market agriculture in a postwar world where white planters and farmers ultimately maintained control of the land and developed a new labor system to meet their own agricultural needs. Until then, black and white farmers continued to draw upon their experience with slavery, where conciliation, accommodation, and supervision had shaped race relations and agricultural labor.[34]

In April some rice planters worried that the freedmen and -women would be given their land. One adamantly contended that "the land is mine[;] you [his former slaves] can either leave it or pay ⅓ crop as rent." Racial adjustments, even in terminology, came hard or not at all. A South Carolina planter argued that "the negro must remain in this country & that his condition although a freed-man, must be to labour on the soil. Nothing but necessity will compel him to labour." In Alabama on June 2, 1865, Josiah Gorgas, former chief of Confederate ordinance, reported that at Demopolis, "the slaves are of course in great commotion. Their freedom has been announced to them, & they are in a state of excitement & jubilee not yet knowing what responsibilities their new condition brings with it."[35]

By summer many freedmen and -women in Alabama had fled their plantations, and their former owners believed the corn crop would nearly fail for lack of labor. One planter complained that the freedmen and -women who remained on his plantation demanded more money for their labor than they were worth. He believed they would return to his fields when they got hungry and, with the threat of force, work. In Nelson County, Virginia, a group of farmers met in Lynchburg and adopted a resolution whereby they agreed to pay "number one field hands" $5 per month and "number one women" and plowboys $2.50 per month. They would provide housing, fuel, and rations as before, and the hands would agree to submit to the orders of their employers. These Virginia planters, like those across the South, would agree to labor contracts, but they demanded "complete deference." Although they were willing to be kind masters, they would not become merely employers. They expected the labor tradition of slavery to remain even though they accepted the formal and legal demise of the institution.[36]

In late July the typical freedman's contract in South Carolina provided that workers would agree to remain on the plantation for a year. They would conform to "reasonable and necessary plantation rules and regulations," and they would not keep guns or leave the plantation without permission of their employers. They would remain orderly, avoid drunkenness, and abstain from "other gross vices." They promised not to misuse plantation tools and equipment, or they would be charged the value of the broken implement. The replacement cost would be deducted from their portion of the crop at the end of the year. For each work animal, the plantation owner would also deduct seventy-five bushels of corn from the crop divided at the end of the year, and the freedmen and -women would pay him half of the remaining corn, peas, and potatoes raised during the season for rent. In addition, the planter agreed to furnish the usual rations during the year, the value of which would be deducted from the wage payment made at the end of the crop year. Any worker dismissed from the plantation forfeited his portion of the crop. This adjustment to slavery's demise and the need for agricultural labor seemed fair to the planters.[37]

In the Western Confederacy the transition from slave to wage labor had essentially been achieved. On some Louisiana plantations the freedpeople had received monthly wages and on others a share of the crop. Contracts established the wages to be paid and the working conditions. These contracts differed only in the details: some paid $12 in monthly wages, others $10, while the amount of land allocated for subsistence crops and the food provided varied. The operation of plantations based on shares did not emerge in the sugar country because of the high cost of machinery for the mills, a fact that later kept the plantations from being broken up into small-scale farms. Wage labor, and not sharecropping, would remain the common form of employment in the sugar parishes. As production declined, the sugar planters believed that only slavery would make their operations profitable, and they lamented that northerners could not understand the economics of sugar production and the importance of slave labor.[38]

In middle Tennessee some planters, such as Nimrod Porter, had begun paying their former slaves $10 per month for agricultural labor. In March as planting time approached, Porter also let two former slaves farm some of his land, and they paid him one-third of the crop. Porter reported, "All hands are preparing to go to work in a fine manner," with the men plowing, making a fence, and repairing plows and the women cutting stalks in the field — "all doing something." In May, however, another Tennessee planter revealed his longing for the past, complaining that his black workers "do as they please and eat their master's meat and bread."[39]

In Carroll County, Mississippi, a planter signed contracts with his former slaves in which they agreed to remain on his place until January 1, 1866, and to "do good work" and obey all instructions as well as "behave themselves as they heretofore have done." In return, he would provide "good and sufficient clothing & rations & medical attention." The contract did not mention wages. One planter in Claiborne County, Mississippi, solved part of his labor problem by indenturing a boy, age twelve, and a girl, age nine, to him until December 26, 1874, when they would be twenty-one and eighteen years old, respectively.[40]

Guerrilla attacks on government-operated plantations west of the Mississippi River continued to disrupt the transition from a slave- to a free-labor system. Moreover, considerable time would be required before the planters and Federal authorities could agree on agricultural labor regulations for black workers and how to enforce them. Cooperation and goodwill between white planters and black workers were understandably lacking. Even so, the planters and the army both wanted stability, and the agricultural labor system previously developed in the Department of the Gulf began to reorder and meet those mutual needs, with the objective of producing a cash crop as quickly as possible.[41]

Still, by early 1865, most contract agricultural workers had not received much, if any, monetary compensation for their first year of work as free men and women. After the planters had deducted expenses for food, clothing, and shelter, as well as any monthly advances, little remained for payment as wages. In March a Mississippi planter paid his forty-two "servants," including "Yellow Hariett," "Big Jim," and "Big Mandy," from $5 to $10 each for working during the previous year. Simply put, the free-labor system that had replaced slavery now kept black men and women in a position of dependency. And this dependent status would soon morph into a near peonage during the immediate postwar years. Equally alarming, the army played an instrumental role in the creation of this new degrading agricultural labor system.[42]

In March 1865 General Stephen A. Hurlbut, who replaced General Nathaniel Banks the previous September as commander of the Department of the Gulf, reaffirmed the application of General Orders No. 23 for Louisiana. Hurlbut reminded the planters that the superintendent of the freedmen had to approve all contracts made between them and their workers. He also authorized a pay scale ranging from $6 to $10 per month for male workers and $5 to $8 per month for females. Boys under fourteen years of age would be paid $3 and girls $2 per month. The workers could not own livestock, which pleased the plantation owners because that regulation freed up more land for sugar, cotton, or subsistence crops. Planters would pay their workers quarterly, thereby easing their need for cash on a monthly basis. One-half of the workers' wages would be held until the end of the year to protect the planters from early departures. Hurlbut's order also returned the management of the freedpeople to the army. This share-wage system created a nether world between planters and the freedpeople that would take time to standardize and end before southern agriculture changed again.[43]

The sugar planters, while grateful that the Federal government did not confiscate their lands, wanted an agricultural labor system that approximated slavery as closely as possible. They also complained that their newly hired black labor force did not work like slaves, and that they could not use force to motivate them. Sugar planters, in short, resented paying wages to agricultural laborers. In mid-April, one planter wrote, "I have agreed with the negroes to pay them monthly wages. It was very distasteful to me, but I could do no better. Everybody else in the neighborhood has agreed to pay the same and mine would listen to nothing else." Yet as late as July, some Louisiana planters still clung to the hope that slavery would survive, and they avoided signing contracts with their former bondsmen, or they did so only when financial necessity required it. Most expected the free-labor system to fail, particularly in the sugar parishes that had not experienced contract labor before 1865. Slavery might be dead, but these planters wanted to bury the free-labor system along with it.[44]

In general the contract labor system in the West at war's end enabled the freedmen and -women to choose their own employers. But once they signed a labor contract, they were bound to the plantation for a year, and they could not leave it without permission. If they left, all wages earned would be forfeited, and they would be "otherwise punished, as the nature of the case may require." The trappings of slavery died hard, even when administered by northern officials. At the same time, the government held the planters "to rigid accountability for their conduct toward the laborers, and any cruelty, inhumanity, or neglect of duty [would] be summarily punished." At least in theory. The black field hands would labor ten hours per day between daylight and dark in the summer and nine hours per day during the winter. They received Saturday afternoons and Sundays off, except on sugar plantations at grinding time, when the hands had to keep regular watches on the reduction pans to ensure proper granulation (but they would receive extra pay for overtime). The government would hold a lien on all plantation crops and property to ensure payment of wages before the planters paid their creditors. The field hands would receive a land allocation from the planters for private cultivation at the rate of one acre for each first- and second-class hand with a family or a half acre for individuals. They could not raise animals except poultry on these allocations. The provost marshals in the sugar parishes were responsible for ensuring contractual compliance by both planters and workers. All previous contracts would be amended to comply with these new provisions, effective and backdated to February 1, 1865. These contractual requirements essentially continued the Federal policies instituted before the war ended.[45]

While the army and the Department of the Treasury attempted to provide a system and order to the employment of the freedpeople, Congress entered the fray. On March 3, 1865, it created the Freedmen's Bureau, officially known as the Bureau of Refugees, Freedmen and Abandoned Lands. Congress used the Port Royal experience to help frame the legislation. It provided that "every male citizen, whether refugee or freedman," should receive forty acres for rent for three years. After that period, he could purchase the land from the government. The legislation did not provide for the free distribution of land, nor did it apply to the public domain in the southern states. Rather, it applied only to "abandoned and confiscated" lands.[46]

Soon, however, many planters on the Sea Islands began returning home and demanded the right to keep their property. But the freedpeople wanted their own land for farming, and one group informed their previous master that "we own this land now. Put it out of your head that it will ever be yours again." The planters' desire to return and resume farming as usual, less their slaves, could not be reconciled with the desires of the freedpeople for land of their own. The planters expected to get their abandoned lands back, and President Johnson befriended them. On May 29 he granted amnesty to all southerners who had participated in the rebellion, and "with restoration of all rights to property, except as to slaves." Individuals owning more than $20,000 in taxable property had to apply to the president for a pardon, but few expected difficulties. Johnson admitted that he planned to grant pardons to the planters in this class, but he wanted them to first grovel: "I intend they should sue for pardon, and so realize the enormity of their crime." Quickly, letters of remorse flowed into his office.[47]

During 1865, the Freedmen's Bureau gained control of all confiscated and captured property that the Treasury Department and the military had seized during the war. The bureau also continued to seize other abandoned lands whose owners presumably had been Confederate sympathizers. By late summer the bureau controlled approximately 800,000 acres, which it planned to reallocate to the freedpeople. Although the bureau attempted to divide its lands into forty-acre farms for lease or sale at a low price to help the freedpeople achieve economic independence, President Johnson in September barred the bureau from redistributing land. One observer on St. Helena Island, South Carolina, reported: "Nearly all the Secesh are back in Beaufort, confidently expecting that they will get their land back in season to plant next year."[48]

They had little reason to worry. Landowners whose property had been sold for the nonpayment of taxes could regain it if they paid the back taxes, took the oath of allegiance, and secured a presidential pardon. Quickly, more land returned to planter control. The Federal government would not confiscate southern lands and redistribute it to freedpeople. O. O. Howard, bureau director, could, at best, only advise the freedmen to make the best terms they could with their former masters or those who now held legal title to the land. Howard informed them that "squatter negroes" who had settled on abandoned plantations would necessarily be removed by congressional mandate. Until Congress told him otherwise, however, he planned to insist that the planters leave the crops that the freedpeople had planted and to let them remain on the land "so long as the responsible freedmen among them would contract or lease" the acreage. Many freedmen, however, vowed "never to make contracts with, or work for, their former owners." Agricultural reform based on the redistribution of land to the former slaves would not be a consequence of the Civil War. Early in 1866, the government forced all freedpeople to leave the coastal plantations if they had not signed contracts.[49]

While planters in the South Carolina and Georgia Low Country waited for the restoration of their lands, they reaffirmed their long-held belief that only they could inspire the freedpeople to work in the fields because only they had the patience to deal with them. One observer noted, "I am satisfied that if Northerners emigrate to the South and undertake agriculture . . . they will be compelled to import white laborers [because] . . . they will not have the patience to get along with the negroes, even if there were enough of these freedmen to do all the work." Southerners still believed that blacks would not work in the fields unless compelled. In mid-October, another observer noted, "The rabble and the young men are still clinging to the hope that they are going to have their own way about managing the nigger." Most northerners did not expect the freedpeople to contribute to the restoration of southern agriculture.[50]

Still, the Freedmen's Bureau was responsible for overseeing the contract labor system and managing "a strong desire, amounting almost to a passion [of the freedpeople,] . . . to obtain land of their own." Without land redistribution to blacks, however, the Freedmen's Bureau could only work to keep the freedpeople on their plantations under contracts that paid in shares of the crop. Samuel Thomas, bureau commissioner for Mississippi, could only advise the freedpeople that "a good master is likely to prove a good employer," and he should "be trusted with respect and affection." So much for any hopes of agricultural land reform for blacks at the end of the war; hunger and want, not freedom and land reform, kept them on the plantations.[51]

The transition from slavery to freedom moved slowly, ambivalently, and disappointingly as well as inevitably when the war ceased. Most southerners, regardless of whether they had been slave owners, still believed slavery morally and ethically just, economically necessary for producing cotton, rice, tobacco, and sugarcane, and the natural order of white and black relationships. The freedpeople first believed in, then hoped for, change but eventually accepted that their social and economic situations had not altered much in this supposed era of freedom. Although they were no longer slaves, they were denied the opportunity to gain economic independence as landowners.

One southern farmer asked, "The freed negro of the Southern States — what should be done with him?" Few knew the answer, but most understood the problem. This southerner noted that "four millions of a helpless, ignorant, deplorably ignorant, and dependent race, in the twinkling of an eye ... were turned loose to take care of themselves – to rival the white man to advance in the scale of civilization and thrive, or to retrograde and perish." Few southerners expressed optimism about the freedmen's future, contending that "if the negro be saved from receding into a savage state, it can only be by some well regulated system of labor, and that this system must be devised by the white man – he will devise none for himself." If not, the agricultural South would become another Haiti or Jamaica, where freedom had failed to elevate ex-slaves to productivity and prosperity.[52]

Indeed, in the emancipated South, freedom had its limitations. The freedpeople did not receive financial compensation and land; nor did they get the economic, social, and political benefits that developed from it. Instead, their freedom came under immediate and long-term attack. Other than receiving a form of freedom on which no price can be given, the lives of black southerners would not improve. Black and white sharecroppers and tenants had little reason for optimism. They were trapped in a world of poverty, degradation, and despair, and were bound together by servitude outside the institution of slavery. The opportunity to escape was minuscule.[53]

Many weeks and months would pass before planters and the freedpeople would work out the meaning of freedom in relation to agricultural labor. Unfortunately for the black men and women who had worked on the farms and plantations, their lives as freedpeople remained tangled with their lives as slaves. Early in 1865, those who had not fled their plantations in Union-occupied areas, as well as those behind Confederate lines, went about their seasonal agricultural activities: they slaughtered hogs, repaired fences, and plowed, in addition to planting corn, potatoes, sugarcane, and cotton. When peace came, a black Georgian recalled that the former slaves continued to work, not breaking the rhythm of the season or the expectations of the past. "All the people," he observed, "thought they were slaves." He might have added that their owners continued to treat them as such. In the netherworld between passage of the Thirteenth Amendment outlawing slavery and the relative protective assistance of the Freedmen's Bureau before its near collapse by the late 1860s, the freedpeople negotiated their labor terms with early optimism that soon turned to despair.[54]

The freedpeople often remained or returned to their plantations because they had nowhere else to go – no shelter, food, and security. By late summer, the Freedmen's Bureau found many of them "quietly working" on these lands in Florida, Georgia, and the Carolinas. One agent reported that "this is almost universally the case." They believed they owned the crops in the ground, and to collect it they had to stay put, even though their status was not clear to them or their former owners. The former slaveholders understood that they could no longer legally compel people to work by force; lacking currency and credit, they turned to contract labor. Consequently, they reverted to a payment system much like they used during slavery: a cabin, a garden plot, clothing, and a few supplies in return for the crop (or most of it), but with sound controls little different from slavery. The former owners intended to maintain the old working relationship between whites and blacks in the "spirit of slavery." This goal would soon change as the freedpeople formally and informally negotiated their working relationships with landowners and as the government ensured certain contractual protections developed during the war years. Ultimately, the sharecropping system gave the freedpeople some independence and distance from the planters. Both groups looked to the land for profit and independence. While few blacks would own land, and while the rumor of redistribution proved to be untrue, sharecropping gave them some autonomy in their lives.[55]

Northerners assumed that once the freedpeople signed contracts to work in the fields, they would then transform into free laborers. Wages would depend on the market economy rather than personal sovereignty, and this change would create a new relationship between landowners and workers, employers and employees. In truth, the freedpeople fell somewhere in between slavery and freedom, both as contract agricultural workers and as sharecroppers. Agricultural labor had more regulatory restrictions for employees than for the employer, with the latter attempting to keep their black workers subservient, obedient, and dependent.[56]

Federal authorities also believed that labor contracts would put and keep the freedpeople in the fields, where they would not become a burden on society for food and shelter and other forms of relief. With the creation of the Freedmen's Bureau, the contract labor process became more orderly and systematic to ensure, as General O. O. Howard, bureau commissioner, declared in May, that able-bodied freedpeople "should be encouraged and if necessary, compelled to labor for their own support." The details of freely choosing employers, compensation, and supervision among other concerns would be worked out later as necessity dictated. In the meantime, oral and informal labor contracts prevailed in areas controlled by the army or the Freedmen's Bureau during the first year of free labor for agricultural workers. No one considered the freedpeople equal parties in negotiations with planters. In the words of one North Carolina planter, "They should work as usual, and I should treat them as usual."[57]

With freedom, the planters also did not want to hire women for fieldwork, because they now contended that women were not men's equals, and they often refused to employ them. Sharecropping, however, gave them women's labor with few costs. At first black women associated cotton picking with slavery, and they refused to do it. But the transition from contract wage labor to sharecropping forced black women back into the fields, particularly at picking time, because family labor could generate more productivity and theoretically more income than only work by the male head of the household. Black women who had rejected the idea of returning to the fields now became bound to the cotton and tobacco crops to help produce as much as possible not only for the landowner but also for their families. The planters assumed that a labor contract signed with a male head of the household obligated all family members to work, as they had in slavery. Landowners justified paying low wages, in part because they provided housing, food, clothing, and medical care for their workers. In the end, neither the army nor the Freedmen's Bureau had a sufficient number of agents to supervise the writing of labor contracts, and the transition to sharecropping best met the planters' needs.[58]

The transition from slave labor to freedom, then, involved passage to paid wages for the freedpeople, but not landownership and not independence from white control. In Louisiana and the Mississippi Delta, it involved the army's imposition of a contract labor system where planter and worker relationships differed little from master and slave. Yearly labor contracts became the approach of the Freedmen's Bureau; ultimately, the contract labor system evolved into sharecropping.[59]

Planters preferred sharecropping because it eliminated battles over work absences, the length of the workday, and other contentious landowner-employee relationships, and it avoided the cash payment of wages. Once the planters no longer paid wages to their employees, they largely were freed from the burden of supervision. The responsibility for production was now placed on the sharecropping family. Essentially, the freedpeople had the freedom to work and the planters had the freedom to take their crop without much worry about how they produced it, although they did give advice. With cotton prices falling from $1.25 per pound to 20 cents per pound, the advantage of sharecropping now belonged to the planters. The sharecroppers could leave if they did not like their contractual arrangements, but their options were few.[60]

The Freedmen's Bureau began as the American Freedmen's Inquiry Commission, which was established by the War Department in 1863 to determine how to deal with emancipated slaves. In March 1865, Congress approved legislation creating the Bureau of Refugees, Freedmen, and Abandoned Lands that was funded and staffed by the War Department. The bureau was authorized to allocate forty-acre plots to the freedpeople from abandoned and confiscated lands, which General Sherman had initiated in the Sea Islands in September 1864 when he issued Special Orders No. 15. By June some 40,000 freedmen and -women had been settled on 400,000 acres, which they considered their own. They would soon be disappointed, because they would not become free, small-scale farmers but agricultural workers severely constrained by contractual regulations and prohibitions.[61]

Ultimately, the Freedmen's Bureau controlled 850,000 acres of abandoned land – hardly enough to ensure economic agricultural independence for the freedpeople. But the situation became worse when President Johnson ordered the return of those lands to their former owners. In December, the best the bureau could do was to urge the freedpeople to sign labor contracts with their planters. Black men and women could be agricultural workers and later sharecroppers, but they would seldom become landowners. In this sense, the Civil War changed nothing.[62]

BY SUMMER SOUTHERN FARMERS HAD begun their old lives anew, but the vestiges of war would not free them from the past. In South Carolina, the government had prohibited the distillation of whiskey, brandy, and other spirits, but by late May and early July farmers had an abundant peach crop that rotted for lack of market. One planter lamented that if he could get his peaches to New York City, he could earn $45,000. His only source of income was the local sale of his peaches and grapes. With flour at $12 per barrel, bacon at 25 cents per pound, and corn at $1 per bushel, he felt financially burdened. By late July most of the farmland between the Potomac in northern Virginia and the Dan River along the border with North Carolina remained fallow, and only a few fields had been plowed and planted in wheat, oats, and corn. Farmers in this area raised only subsistence crops. The tobacco fields remained in "unproductive idleness" for two years. One planter near Richmond, whose fields and property had not been overrun during the war, reflected that while the wheat and oat crops had been good, few farmers had planted tobacco in February 1865 because they saw the future as too uncertain. The corn crop would be only fair because it should have been planted about the time Lee evacuated Richmond, and black labor proved scarce for the farmers in northern Virginia and considerable delay occurred. Yet signs of hope could be found, with the fruit crop "most encouraging" in the middle and southern counties.[63]

Still, by summer, farmers increasingly returned to normal operations, free from the threat of marching armies, mandatory tithing in-kind, and impressment officers. Food and agricultural prices generally declined and stabilized. In Atlanta corn brought $1.25 per bushel and fodder $1.50 to $2 per hundredweight, while wheat sold for $2.50 per bushel and flour for $16 per barrel, eggs for 25 cents per dozen, butter for 45 cents per pound, and beef for 10 cents per pound. Bacon brought 22 cents per pound and hams 25 to 30 cents per pound. Cane sugar from Louisiana could now be purchased for 24 cents per pound, while sorghum molasses brought about 40 cents per gallon. In cities and towns across the South, grocers' shelves became increasingly well stocked, although prices fluctuated considerably based on supply due to transportation problems related to the rebuilding of the railroads and to demand. Still, farmers and planters gained from the sale of their produce for sound money.[64]

Yet as southern planters and farmers returned to their fields and the business of agriculture, the obstacles to a quick recovery were numerous: abandoned farms, the loss of slave labor, and the high cost of free workers, along with the "uncertain condition of public affairs," as well as new county, state, and Federal taxes. Nature also caused problems. The tobacco crop largely failed due to excessive rains followed by drought. Postwar recovery in the tobacco country would have to wait. One tobacco farmer reflected that at a time when the country had just emerged from one of the most destructive wars in history, and with high labor costs, crop failure became "a very great calamity." Southern farmers now waged battle with nature rather than war, although the destructive results could be much the same. They also confronted the ruin of war — burned barns and fence rails, destroyed farm equipment, weed-infested fields, and depleted livestock herds. Across much of the Confederacy, ashes, destruction, and desolation charted the direction and outcome of the war. Capital and labor had disappeared or changed dramatically in source and organization. Some farmers believed that only time and nature could restore southern agriculture.[65]

As the summer of 1865 waned, a *New York Times* reporter wrote, "There is, perhaps nothing of which the Southern States to-day are in greater want than an adequate supply of agricultural implements. The past labor system has been such as to forbid the introduction of those improvements which have become of universal use in the Northern States. Where labor is performed by slaves, labor-saving machines find but a sorry market." Cultivation with hoes prevailed, because the importation of agricultural equipment had ended when the war began, except for a limited amount of tools brought into southern ports by blockade-runners. Foundries had beaten the proverbial plowshares into swords and pruning hooks into spears, while raiders, foraging parties, and guerrillas had left few implements undamaged. The farm equipment available cost two to three times the price of implements on northern markets. One Virginian reflected, "The country is almost entirely destitute of tools. This is not merely through the seizure of such implements for the use of the armies, but in consequence of the wearing out of these tools during the last four years, in which no new supplies have been obtained." Across the South, farmers used scythes, probably cradle, to harvest the wheat crop, while northern farmers used horse-powered self-rake reapers.[66]

Other problems remained. In October a North Carolina farmer wrote that the Union had "broken the old bond of master and slave, and in that deprived them of our protecting care and us their loyalty." As a result, a "feeling of hostility" had developed between whites and blacks that had not existed before. On Edisto Island, South Carolina, a committee representing the freedpeople wrote to O. O. Howard, head of the Freedmen's Bureau, protesting the Federal government's decision to return the lands on which they had settled and now farmed to the former plantation owners. They argued that they needed land to earn a living to become independent and free from white social and economic oppression. They believed they had earned the right to claim the rich cotton and rice lands of the Sea Islands after generations of enslavement. In a letter to President Johnson, a committee on behalf of the freedpeople pleaded that without land, they would remain "subject to the will of these Large Landowners." A Virginia freedman also argued that "we has a right to the land where we are located. For why? I tell you. Our wives, our children, our husbands, has been sold over and over again to purchase the lands we now locates upon; for that reason we have a divine right to the land." Johnson was not persuaded by this sweat-equity argument. By autumn, the Johnson administration had begun the return of some 800,000 acres confiscated from the planters or abandoned by them as soon as they received a pardon. By so doing, the Federal government transformed the freedpeople into an agricultural proletariat without hope and gave them lives not of economic independence but of continued subservience, desperation, and despair.[67]

When Congress reassembled in December, few members really cared about southern land reform and enhancing the agricultural productivity and economic freedom of the former slaves. Yet, while the freedpeople were no longer bound to the plantation, northerners and southerners expected them to remain there, producing cotton, sugar, and subsistence crops. Northerners did not want them, but southern planters needed them. Late in 1865, journalist John T. Trowbridge identified the agricultural labor problem in the South: "The whites were as ignorant of the true nature of the [free-labor] system as the blacks." He added that "capitalists did not understand how they could secure labor without owning it, or how men could be induced to work without the whip." Many wanted paternalism and profitable agriculture, and to keep the old management techniques while accepting a new age only to the least degree. A cotton planter on Edisto Island, South Carolina, clearly expressed this sentiment when he said, "Labor must be commanded completely or the production of the cotton crop must be abandoned." Soon, the planters restored their political and economic power, and hopes for agricultural reform had died by the end of the year. There would be no "forty acres and a mule" for the freedpeople as a matter of government policy. But many freedpeople in the Natchez District still hoped for land when the year ended.[68]

As the planters regained control of their land, they favored sharecropping because it involved less risk for them: if the crops failed, they would still take a percentage of the crop as rent. They also favored sharecropping because it kept blacks subservient in the absence of slavery. Crop failure, violence, and politics, then, rather than prosperity lay ahead for the freedpeople. Increasingly, the standard contractual agricultural labor arrangement between a planter and a black worker became payment in a share of one-third to one-half of the crop at harvest.[69]

By late autumn and early winter, cattle brought as much as $50 per head and hogs 12 cents to 14 cents per pound in Jefferson City, Texas. In New Orleans, farmers sold chickens at the landing for $9 per dozen and turkeys for $27 per dozen respectively. Eggs shipped downriver from the Old Northwest sold for $40 to $45 per barrel. Shelled corn brought $1.15 per bushel, northern butter 45 cents to 50 cents per pound, and flour $7 to $11.50 per barrel. Most farmers, planters, and merchants considered these prices lucrative. A cotton factor reported that the market was rebounding from a "period of great Depression." Sugar planter A. F. Pugh, however, complained that his prospects were "very gloomy." He reflected, "It all looks as dark as midnight to me with hardly a gleam of light appearing." He spoke for many sugar planters because they shared the same problems.[70]

With the completion of the cotton harvest at the end of the year, farmers and planters had worked hard to revive agricultural production, particularly in the Deep South. They had produced only 299,000 bales of cotton in 1864, the lowest amount of the war and a clear indication that they had converted their cotton fields to corn and other food crops. In 1865, however, they produced 2,094,000 bales. Although production was half of the 4,491,000 bales produced in 1861, the cotton planters were well on their way to returning to their prewar levels. Cotton remained in demand, and farmers and planters easily received more than 50 cents per pound. When the year ended, cotton averaged 83 cents per pound for the year on the New York City market, down from a high of $1.01 for the 1863–64 crop year, but considerably higher than the 13 cents average for 1860–61. The reemergence of southern agriculture depended on perspective.[71]

Still, one South Carolinian estimated the corn crop returned only six bushels per acre in 1865, down from fifteen bushels per acre in 1861 – a clear indication that farm women had been unable to maintain production without equipment, horses, mules, and adequate labor. Across the Lower South, this estimate probably held true. In addition, with half of the white cotton farmers dead or suffering from crippling war injuries, and with essentially all of the black agricultural labor force still landless and working for impoverishing wages or a share of the crop, the agricultural future of the South seemed grim at best. Ruined farms and plantations greeted the returning farmer-soldiers. Land values had plummeted. In the Louisiana sugar parishes, land that sold for $100 per acre in 1860 now commanded only $5 per acre. In South Carolina and Louisiana, one-third of the land was no longer cultivated. Desolation in the form of uncultivated lands, burned barns, and destroyed fences, as well as pastures empty of cattle, horses, and mules, gave an eerie silence to much of the countryside. On August 20, 1866, when President Johnson proclaimed the end of the war, southern farmers and planters faced considerable challenges and decades of work to return agriculture to its prewar conditions. Even so, the Civil War had not changed the fundamental basics of southern society.[72]

WHEN THE WAR BEGAN, MOST farmers and planters believed the agricultural power of the Confederacy, along with a potent army, guaranteed victory and with it independence. One farmer had boasted, "If our people have enough to eat, they can defy the world in arms — forewarned is forearmed." After four years of war, the agricultural power of the Confederacy had been destroyed. On December 31, 1865, a North Carolina farmer who had lost a son at Kingston on March 19 during the final days of the war could only write, "The last day of the year, a year of sorrow for us." Catherine Ann Devereux agreed, writing from her North Carolina plantation: "So ends this terrible year of 1865! Thank God it is over!" She hoped for better days.[73]

On January 1, 1866, Nimrod Porter, a planter near Nashville, put the last year of the war and the first year of peace in perspective when he observed: "Faerwell [sic] to the year 1865. We are in some better condition now than we were the 1st day of Jany last year but realy We have nothing to brag of, hardly able to live." Only a few days earlier, Josiah Gorgas spoke for many farmers across the South when he wrote, "The future is still uncertain to us, & we must wait patiently, & take our lot as it comes trying to do the best all the time." The Confederacy had been an agricultural region when the war began, and the South remained an agricultural region when the fighting ended, but with far less productivity, wealth, and economic and political influence than before. Better days would not soon return. The problems of southern agriculture proved nearly overwhelming. Slavery had been destroyed and replaced by a new uncertain agricultural labor system imposed by the North. Cotton and sugar planters faced a long recovery. Livestock had been seriously depleted. Weeds choked many fields, and charred buildings marked the path of war. Much rebuilding and time would be required to reestablish the economic power of southern agriculture. But, as one Tennessee planter reflected, "The war is over. God be praised."[74]

Epilogue

In January 1866 a South Carolina planter's wife wrote, "At the plantation all is quiet. Most of my negroes have remained and have gone to work under the new contract with great zeal, and are to have one third of everything grown, and if they make five bales of cotton to the hand they take half of the cotton.... They enter themselves as full or half hands as they please and draw shares accordingly. They feed themselves we gave them a gallon of molasses each and a month's allowance of meat to start them for which they seem very grateful." A Virginia planter saw things a bit differently. He referred to his sharecroppers as "hands" and "hoes," took three-quarters of their cotton and corn crops as rent, and operated on the principle that "eating will keep the negrows [sic] poor & down."[1]

Few white farmers and planters or black agricultural workers could express much optimism. Rice production in the coastal country of South Carolina and Georgia had been ruined. Dikes and drainage ditches had been cut or needed major repairs, and the skilled black labor force that understood tidal-flow irrigation would not soon return to the rice fields of their former masters. One overseer had informed his employer and plantation owner that "the stillness of the Dead Sea overspreads the land. No sound of a mill in operation – nor of a flail on the threshing floor. All is painfully quiet and silent." A northerner traveling in the South Carolina Low Country reported "acres upon acres of abandoned rice swamps." Agriculture on the Sea Islands languished; no bright future rose on the horizon. To the west, planters already had begun seeding rice in the Mississippi Delta, where they soon used steam engines to pump water onto the fields to replace the tidal-flow techniques used in the coastal lowlands of South Carolina and Georgia.[2]

In many respects the Civil War marked the end of rice agriculture along the East Coast. It would not recover its former importance. At best recovery proved slow. By 1870 rice planters produced only 73.6 million pounds, down from the 187.2 million pounds cultivated on the eve of the war. Only Arkansas, Florida, Louisiana, and Texas produced more rice than in 1860. Although rice production had declined in Mississippi, the industry had clearly moved west by 1870, with Louisiana producing

15.8 million pounds, compared to 6.3 million pounds before the war. In contrast, South Carolina produced 119.1 million pounds of rice in 1860 but only 32.3 million pounds a decade later.[3]

Tobacco planters also struggled. They had produced tobacco during the war because the Confederate armies created a large demand for the staple, while the civilian domestic market provided some income. But the impact of the Civil War on tobacco farming was relatively slight. With slavery ended, both white farmers and the freedpeople in tobacco country knew that they had to reach some form of accommodation. White farmers needed black labor, and the freedpeople needed employment and an income. Sharecropping met the needs of both, at least temporarily for the latter. Essentially, both white farmers and black workers would continue to do what they had done before and during the war — raise a high-value, profitable crop. Tobacco required land and labor and few tools. High postwar tobacco prices compared favorably with high antebellum prices in the Piedmont. In 1866 one Virginia farmer — along with his wife, a hired freedman, and a horse — raised a tobacco crop that earned $1,800. The return was large enough that he continued growing tobacco until his land wore out fifteen years later. One-crop agriculture that often depleted the soil returned to the South with the peace, if it had ever left at all.[4]

Most planters and farmers, however, had significantly decreased their tobacco production during the war, patriotically answering the government's call to emphasize food crops. When the war ended, new lands to the west and south, particularly in Kentucky and North Carolina, produced larger crops, especially the "bright" tobacco for cigarettes rather than the dark leaf of the Virginia Piedmont used for smoking in pipes and cigars and for chewing. Virginia tobacco planters had not recovered their prewar productivity in acreage cultivated or in pounds harvested by 1870, when they produced only 37 million pounds, down from 123.9 million pounds in 1860. Across the old Confederacy in 1870, tobacco planters harvested 103.3 million pounds, compared with 203.6 million pounds a decade earlier. Tennessee planters did not reach prewar levels until 1889. Equally important, the value of tobacco lands decreased during the war, which, along with the loss of slaves as collateral for bank loans, meant that planters had little access to credit for operating expenses, and many could not afford hired labor. As a result, the crop lien system developed in the tobacco lands, as it did in the cotton belt — all a further legacy of secession for southern agriculture. When the war ended tobacco farming did not recover quickly, and it could not until the northern market was reestablished and a sharecropping labor system was instituted.[5]

The Civil War temporarily ruined the sugar planters. The record sugar crop of 459.4 million pounds in 1861 earned more than $25 million in federal dollars, but production declined substantially by 1863 when planters produced only 76.8 million pounds. With the crop bringing in a mere $8 million that year, the planters and their factors were left with a debt of about $20 million. In 1864, sugar production essentially ceased when planters produced only 10 million pounds valued at $2 million. The next year, the problems of inadequate labor and credit prevented most planters from planning a sugar crop for 1866, and when the war ended, the season was too late for a renewal of sugarcane production. Most planters could only sell their crop for seed cane. They did so, however, at high prices that averaged $150 per arpent, but anyone who wanted the seed cane had to cut it themselves. Others ground their meager crop and processed it into molasses, but they stopped short of refining it further into sugar to avoid paying the Federal excise tax of 3 cents per pound. As a result, only 188 sugarhouses produced 18,000 hogsheads of sugar valued at $3 million in 1865. With sugarcane lands depreciating by an estimated 70 percent from 1861 – or approximately $18 million, along with the loss of $105 million in slaves and $70 million in equipment and buildings – Louisiana planters lost some $193 million in investments during the war. Many sold their plantations for 6 percent to 10 percent of their prewar property valuations because they could not cover their mortgage indebtedness that remained when the war ended. The planters who stayed confronted fields of weeds and briars, silted and overgrown drainage ditches, broken levees, destroyed fences, missing livestock, damaged or burned-out buildings, and an absent or reorganized labor force. These planters reaped the bitterness of financial ruin rather than the sweetness of a sugar crop.[6]

The sugar planters would not recover for decades. Louisiana's 1,300 sugar mills in operation when the war began numbered fewer than 300 by 1870, and they produced only 80,706 hogsheads of sugar, or roughly 80.7 million pounds. Only after 1870 did structural reorganization, technological change, and improved credit enable the sugar planters to begin a slow recovery. Not until 1893 did their production exceed the bumper crop of 1861, and then only 449 sugarhouses were processing the cane crop. Still, some sugar planters gave thanks that their situation was not worse. In Louisiana, one observer said that in St. Mary Parish, the wealthiest sugar parish in the state, plantations were "ground to powder between contesting armies; corn, sugar, cattle, horses, mules and almost all moveable property were carried off, consumed or destroyed; overflows and cotton worms, rains and politicians have done their worse, still we live and breathe." Another reported from the Red River Country that deserted and destroyed plantations "tell a tale of which the beginning and the ending are very different from each other."[7]

Before the war, cotton had been an indispensable agricultural commodity based on slave labor. After the war, cotton remained an indispensable agricultural product based on subservient black labor. In 1861, cotton farmers and planters had produced 4.5 million bales. During the war, they raised approximately 6.8 million bales. The South used about 400,000 bales and shipped another 500,000 by blockade-runners to Great Britain and Europe, while they traded another 900,000 bales across enemy lines. Union and Confederate forces and planters destroyed an estimated 3.3 million bales to keep it from the enemy. When the war ended, planters and farmers sold approximately 1.8 million bales that were in storage. In other words, about one of every two bales of cotton produced during the war was either destroyed or became unmarketable after being stored improperly (often because it was being hidden). In the end, the farmers and planters who sold their remaining cotton after the war received high prices in sound money that helped restore their financial and economic security and power. Even so, they did not exceed their prewar cotton production until 1878.[8]

As a result of the war, however, the cotton economy and government policy created a near caste system that provided cheap agricultural labor for white planters. Southern farmers and planters kept their land, northerners regained a stable and profitable supply of cotton, and the former slaves gained their freedom and became nearly free agricultural labor. White farmers and planters and black workers returned to the security of cotton production, which alone served as the basis of the South's commercial agricultural economy. It also became an Achilles' heel that stifled diversification, partly because of credit constraints arising from the fact that farmers could not get credit unless they planted cotton.[9]

But the flip side of this situation was that cotton production and its steady, reliable – albeit low – income enabled farmers and planters to acquire credit if they accepted a lien on their crop. In South Carolina one traveler observed, "The war not only swept away their stock and material resources of their plantations but also all values – all money, stocks, and bonds – and generally left nothing that can be sold for money but cotton, and only a small portion of the landholders have any of that." He failed to note the considerable loss of capital invested in slaves across the South, which for planters far exceeded their other financial setbacks. Yet, he added, "there is for most of them nothing but the beginning anew of life, on the strictest personal economy and a small amount of money borrowed in the city." Without money to hire labor or rent land, planters resorted to sharecropping to bring land and labor together. Wherever possible, particularly in the Lower South, planters and farmers returned to cotton production as soon as possible. They knew how to raise cotton, and they had a national and international market. Even as the price continued to fall, planters and farmers could plant it and make money. Only cotton reliably brought cash or kind into the farm home. Cotton always could be sold or used to secure credit, and it could not be eaten or easily stolen. It also had a higher value than corn. The average price for cotton in 1865 was 83 cents per pound, down from $1.01 in 1864 but substantially higher than the 13 cents per pound average in 1861.[10]

In 1865 cotton production rebounded to 2.1 million bales, up from 300,000 bales in 1864, and nearly half of the 4.5 million bales produced in 1861. One-crop specialization, particularly cotton, rather than diversification beyond subsistence production, again marked the agriculture of the postwar South. Once more, the South became dependent on the North to meet many of its food needs. Yet, by 1870, no state in the old Confederacy had regained its prewar cotton production. Those states had produced 4.8 million bales in 1859 but only 3.1 million bales in 1869. Some southerners contended that the only way to significantly increase cotton production for the benefit of the nation would be to exclusively use "negro labor," both male and female, and that this labor force should be "compelled" to work. If southerners could "regulate the labor of the freedman," some argued, they could meet the needs of American and European cotton manufacturers. For many, the agricultural future of the South depended on cotton. They could not foresee dark days ahead with a return to prewar production and prices.[11]

In the war's aftermath, one southerner lamented that Alabama's farms had "no fences, no hogs, no cattle, no agriculture, no nothing." His generalization applied to much of the region. Although open-range cattle grazing in the piney woods of Alabama had begun to decline before the war, peace brought a rapid expansion of cotton planting into these grazing lands, and open-range cattle grazing essentially ended. Moreover, the war devastated many livestock raisers across the South. Recovery would not come soon. By 1870 the number of cattle had not expanded beyond prewar levels. In 1860 approximately 10.5 million cattle grazed on southern farms, but only 8.1 million fed on old Confederate pastures a decade later. Florida was the lone southern state to show a slight gain in its cattle herds, although the Texas count probably was too low.[12]

By 1866, the South remained short of its prewar number of horses by 32 percent, its mules by 30 percent, its cattle by 35 percent, its sheep by 20 percent, and its hogs by 42 percent. In 1870 former Confederate farmers possessed only 76 percent of their prewar horses and only 76 percent of their cattle. No Confederate state exceeded the value of livestock held when the war began: in 1860, the valuation was $380.8 million; in 1870, it was $269.2 million. With the exception of Arkansas, Florida, and Texas, no other state increased the value of livestock from 1860 to 1900, and none would until 1910. The increase of livestock from significantly reduced numbers would take time, and southern farmers did not have the capital or credit to purchase cattle from northern farmers. Moreover, the best-quality livestock had been used up, and only poor-quality animals remained for breeding purposes. Southern farmers still had a deficiency of 454,644 horses, 207,146 mules, 1,063,776 cattle, 1,354,380 sheep, and 6,330,696 hogs, according to the 1870 census. At that time South Carolina needed a 70 percent increase in horses, a 76 percent increase in cattle, a 91 percent increase in sheep, and a 145 percent increase in hogs to reach its 1860 livestock level. Alabama, Georgia, Louisiana, and Virginia still had livestock deficiencies ranging from 20 percent to 70 percent.[13]

Livestock disease left other wartime imprints on southern agriculture. Cattle fever — known as "Carolina distemper," "Georgia murrain," and "Spanish fever" — had plagued southern cattle producers for a long time, but the disease spread across the South with the movement of livestock during the war. As Texas became the leading cattle producer in the South, the disease became known as Texas fever. When the Civil War began, Texas, Georgia, and Virginia served as the leading cattle-producing states, and the Piedmont of Florida, Georgia, and South Carolina had been a cattle-raising region for a century. In 1861, Georgia farmers raised more cattle than Iowa and Indiana combined; South Carolina raised more cattle than Wisconsin; and Florida grazed more cattle than Michigan. During the war, however, southern cattle producers lost livestock to a disease that many believed was caused by ticks, but proof would not come until the late nineteenth century. In the meantime, North Carolina prohibited cattle droving from the south between April 1 and November 1 of each year. During the winter months, the cold weather killed the ticks and the disease did not spread as the livestock moved north to local and regional markets. During the war, however, the armies and civilian population throughout the Confederacy could not wait for cold weather to permit the droving of tick-free cattle to markets. Hungry people needed beef, and livestock losses from cattle fever further reduced the supply for the military and civilians.[14]

By 1866 many farmers believed that cattle fever and hog cholera would remain a permanent legacy of the war. In Virginia farmers had lost from 25 percent to 75 percent of their hogs to disease, depending on the county. Certainly, glanders so reduced the horse population that many southern farmers could not have used horse-drawn implements, such as reapers, had they been able to afford them. Consequently, as northern farmers increasingly adopted horse-powered implements to expand production and reduce labor needs and costs, southern farmers remained mired in an age of hand-powered tools. The lack of sufficient horsepower for agriculture slowed the South's agricultural recovery for plowing, planting, cultivating, and harvesting as well as hauling grain and cotton to market. Fewer animals also meant less fertilizer to help replenish worn-out fields, and families ate less meat long after the war. Their diets also remained poor, particularly those of tenant farmers and sharecroppers, as it consisted mostly of pork, cornmeal, and molasses, and this poor diet contributed to malnutrition and pellagra.[15]

During the war southerners could never depend on a reliable supply of food. While farmers in some places could feed the army and the population, in other areas they could neither meet those needs nor rely on the railroads to transport food and forage. Southerners had learned quickly that neither cotton bales nor slaves or food crops provided the agricultural security and power needed to fight a long war, particularly since the Confederacy was confronted by a superior military and economic power.[16]

Unusual conditions, of course, compel people to do uncustomary things. Southern farmers and planters willingly let the state governments place restrictions on their traditional right to plant cotton and tobacco. The states prohibited them from distilling corn into whiskey, which sold for a higher price than grain. The national government forced them into the army and took their slaves for military projects, often never to return. The central government authorized the army to pay below-market prices and to impress agricultural commodities if farmers and planters refused to sell. They responded by hoarding and hiding their provisions and, in some cases, trading with the enemy for Federal dollars rather than Confederate currency. Their desire for profits often trumped patriotism and loyalty as the war dragged on. Confederate farmers at the barricades often had more staying power than the farmers and planters behind their plow lines at home.[17]

Southern farmers voiced other grievances as well. The Confederate government required a tithe of 10 percent on all agricultural commodities produced in surplus of family food needs for the year. Beginning in 1863, farmers and planters paid this tax with varying degrees of honesty. It was not that they were unfamiliar with the concept of tithing; they assuredly had learned from Sunday sermons that it was a beneficent practice that dated to biblical times. They knew that Deuteronomy 14:28 and 26:12–14 commanded the Israelites to tithe 10 percent of their produce to assist the poor or the orphans and widows, and that Numbers 18:21–28 required a 10 percent tithe of food and livestock to support the government and priests in Jerusalem. Many no doubt tithed money to their congregations. But it was one thing to hear about the practice of tithing crops and livestock in the days of Moses and another to pay it themselves, particularly when impressment officials took more than 10 percent and Confederate soldiers seized what food and forage they wanted. Resentment festered, and farmers and planters often hid or underreported their production. They could not abide government regulations that they considered unfair, inequitable, and oppressive. Confederate farmers were cautious, distrustful, and independent-minded when the war began and remained so when it ended.

Although not all areas of the South suffered from the movements of Confederate and Union armies, every section felt the effects of the war, and all for the worse. Without question the war paralyzed cotton, sugar, rice, and tobacco production. In some areas, however, such as the eastern Georgia counties, planters and farmers raised enough food to provision their families and slaves and to contribute a surplus to soldiers and civilians. Sherman's soldiers ate well when they foraged in this country. Here, southerners suffered not because planters and farmers produced too little food, but because the Union army took too much of it. Cultivated areas of the Confederate States of America had fallen by 18 percent between 1861 and 1865. South Carolina had lost one-third of its cultivated land, and Louisiana and Georgia nearly as much. In 1870 the decline of cultivated acreage still remained at approximately 6 percent in Arkansas, 37 percent in Louisiana, 20 percent in Alabama, 16 percent in Mississippi, 16 percent in Georgia, 34 percent in South Carolina, 20 percent in North Carolina, and 28 percent in Virginia. States with gains in cultivated land were Tennessee with a 1 percent increase, Texas with an 11 percent gain, and Florida with a 12 percent gain.[18]

The war affected agriculture differently depending on whether it was in the Eastern or Western Confederacy or in the Upper or Lower South, or whether farmers lived where the armies fought and marched. Some farmers and planters escaped relatively unscathed with fields untrammeled, fences and barns unburned, and livestock, grain, and forage neither stolen nor impressed. These lucky southerners had provisions capable of meeting household needs, with a surplus available for local markets and the armies. Overall, however, the Civil War brought considerable hardship and ruin to many farmers and planters. While the number of farms increased to 692,000 in 1870 from 551,000 a decade earlier, the improved acreage remained about the same at 46.9 million acres, largely due to expansion in Texas, Tennessee, and Florida.[19]

Land values plummeted in the Confederate states during the Civil War. By the end of the conflict, land values had fallen by an estimated 70 percent in Louisiana; 65 percent in Mississippi; 60 percent in Alabama and South Carolina; 55 percent in Georgia, Florida, and Arkansas; 50 percent in North Carolina; 28 percent in Texas; 27 percent in Virginia; and 18 percent in Tennessee. Put differently, the cash value of Confederate farms declined from $1.4 billion in 1860 to $974 million a decade later.[20]

In 1866 a report indicated that land throughout the South sold at 16 percent to 25 percent of its assessed value. Land values depreciated due to the want of labor, lack of capital, the large amount of land offered for sale, stay laws, and farms in ruinous condition. The asking price for farmland also discouraged the renewal of southern agriculture. Yet even "ruinously low" land prices still exceeded the resources of black farmers. In Georgia, a 40-acre farm with a mule cost $250 to $300. At $2 to $8 per acre and $50 to $60 for a mule, with few implements, and with poultry and hogs costing another $30 to $40 to get started, few black farmers could afford the entry costs. As a result, the poverty of sharecropping became their life.[21]

The cash value of farm implements also declined, falling to $45.1 million in 1870 from $82.9 million in 1860. South Carolina's recovery was the slowest: its farm equipment was worth only 37 percent of its prewar valuation by 1870; Louisiana's was 38 percent and Alabama's 44 percent. Texas held only 54 percent; Arkansas, 53 percent; Mississippi, 50 percent;

Florida, 56 percent; and Virginia, 52 percent. Three states fared better: Tennessee with 96 percent of the prewar valuations, Georgia with 67 percent, and North Carolina with 69 percent. Not until 1900 did the value of all farm property recover to the 1860 level.[22]

Certainly, the war caused an enormous loss of agricultural wealth. Slaveholders lost their investments in bondsmen and -women. Where farmers did not own slaves and worked the land themselves, slavery's destruction did not affect them adversely. In these areas, farmers would recover when credit and sound money returned to enable them to purchase implements to help them plow, plant, harvest, and market a surplus. In slave areas, however, the destruction of the institution substantially affected the labor supply and made recovery slow and tenuous. The sharecropping system that emerged remained a footprint of the war that marked poverty and desperation in the countryside.

During the peace that followed, the plantation system remained, but planters cultivated several farms within their holdings by using sharecroppers and tenants. The planters, however, often were not the same individuals (especially in sugar country) who owned the land in 1861, and they used the crop lien credit system to keep their sharecroppers on the land, dependent, and obedient. Planters needed workers, but they did not need slaves, a revelation that became clearer as the postwar years passed. Plantations still brought social prestige to their owners, with black and white sharecroppers and tenants reliant on planters for credit and the privilege of raising cotton and subsistence crops in a culture that demanded subservience. In many respects postbellum agriculture had changed hardly at all. White planters had become landlords, but their paternalism over tenant farmers and sharecroppers – black and white – kept these workers subservient. One contemporary reported that the planters remained "still lords of acres, though not of slaves." In other words, they had become landlords, not labor-lords. The planters, freedpeople, and credit system, then, preserved the plantation system, but the freedpeople did not immediately reinstitute their productive efficiency on those lands. One Tennessee planter reflected on the revolution in southern agricultural labor by noting, "All the traditions and habits of both races had been suddenly overthrown, and neither knew just what to do or how to accommodate themselves to the new situation." Although he overstated his case about a new era of race relations, he was correct about the prevailing uncertainty of farmers, planters, and freedpeople.[23]

The loss of 3.5 million slaves in the Confederate states cost farmers and planters approximately $1.6 billion. Yet the contract labor system that resulted from the war ensured cheap, yearlong agricultural labor from blacks with stability provided by force of law and the promise of the planters to pay wages due on December 31. Twelve-month contracts also kept black workers near the cotton, rice, and sugar plantations during that portion of the year when the crops had been laid by and everyone waited for harvest time. The sharecropping system that replaced the contract labor system gave planters their desired command and control and kept freedmen and -women near peonage Moreover, with the end of slavery and the rise of sharecropping and tenancy, race rather than bondage defined the agricultural labor force and relations between white landowners and black workers, who often had the same prejudices and animosities.[24]

While freedmen entered into sharecropping arrangements with their former masters or new plantation owners, their wives had been increasingly withdrawing from fieldwork. This symbolic rejection of slave labor did not always last, as family needs mandated that all members work in their fields under this new labor relationship, particularly at cotton-picking time. Plantation owners also wanted black families to labor diligently and selflessly, and any separation of family labor appeared as a challenge to traditional antebellum standards for labor control and discipline. During the transition from wage labor to sharecropping, black women conducted fieldwork for wages, which the Federal government regulated using scales. Black women could freely contract to provide agricultural labor if they cared to do so. But when they rejected it, landowners accused them of being "as nearly idle as it is possible for them to be." If they worked for wages they could help support their families. Some planters wanted agents from the Freedmen's Bureau "to make these idle women go to work." They scarcely hid their self-serving motive to gain additional cheap labor.[25]

In April 1866, one Georgia planter expressed this sentiment: "You would do them & the country a service besides gaining favor & good opinion of the people generally." He and others like him considered the unwillingness of freedwomen to conduct fieldwork as "a very great evil & one that the Bureau ought to correct – if they wish the Freedmen & women to do well." If they did not, only trouble could result, because "these idle women are bad examples to those who work & they are often mischief makers – having no employment their brain becomes more or less the Devil's work shop as is always the case with idle people—black or white & quarrels & Musses among the colored people generally can be traced to these idle folks that are neither serving God—Man or their country." These black women were a "nuisance" and should be arrested for vagrancy. The labor relationships between landowners and freedmen and -women took time to resolve, until both planters and freedpeople settled on sharecropping as their best solution to bringing land and labor together.[26]

Lack of unified lines, efficiency, and track had doomed the railroads' efforts to move food, livestock, and forage from 1861 on. Farmers, planters, and consumers had been ill-served by the southern railroads and the War Department during the entire course of the conflict. Railroad transportation broke down due to poor construction, lack of cars, and narrow gages that prevented connections with wide-gauge lines. Poor management and President Jefferson Davis's refusal to nationalize the railroads also proved an insurmountable hardship for farmers and planters and ultimately consumers.[27]

Overall, however, the government had sufficient food supplies to feed the Confederate armies in some areas when the war ended. Meat rations totaled 300,000 in Richmond, 180,000 in Lynchburg, 2 million in Danville, and 1.5 million in Greensboro. Other supply depots had food stores, but these provisions would only molder given the inability of Confederate supply and the railroads to get it to the soldiers in the field. The Deep South had even more food reserves than did Virginia—it was a region where Confederate armies had not particularly suffered for want of food and where many soldiers had been sent north. On March 31, 1865, the Macon depot had 274,394 pounds of bacon, 491,199 pounds of corn, 87,529 pounds of peas, and 29,429 pounds of sugar. In Mississippi the Subsistence Department held 1.5 million pounds of meal and flour, 10,000 cattle, 5,000 hogs, and 2,000 sheep, all of which had been purchased or impressed from farmers and planters.[28]

In addition, northern grain shipments to Great Britain did not keep England from recognizing the Confederacy. In fact, the Union had limited leverage with London, as events of 1861–63 show, when the British government was able to avoid famine in the isles despite crop shortfalls because of multiple factors: cheaper grain prices, the ease of shipments from northern ports, and increased grain purchases from eastern Europe. Nevertheless, to say that northern grain sales did or did not keep Great Britain from recognizing the Confederacy overly simplifies the situation. Britain was mindful that the North increased grain sales in time of need, enabling the government to prevent hunger and social unrest, and London was aware of the multiple problems that it would have if it recognized the Confederacy merely to ensure its major cotton supply.

In retrospect, the Civil War dramatically, but temporarily, changed southern agriculture. In the Lower South, farmers and planters reduced cotton production as the government requested, and they raised more corn and other food crops. In the Upper South and Southwest they also planted more corn. Still, food shortages became increasingly common, particularly among those southerners who were close to marching, fighting, and occupying armies. Both Confederate and Union soldiers scavenged for food and fodder. As a result, some areas experienced near starvation conditions as the war ebbed away. Yet farmers and planters in other areas produced an abundance of corn and other provisions but could not get their produce to market.

When the war ended, southern farmers and planters suffered from a shortage of capital and credit, declining agricultural productivity, insufficient equipment, and depreciated land values. They had lost one-third of their horses and mules and about half of their agricultural equipment. The result was a continued reduction of agricultural productivity due to reduced tillage. Moreover, southern farmers and planters did not have the capital to hire agricultural workers. Black workers were no longer credit assets, and the productivity of the free black men and women became temporarily less than when they worked as slaves. Farmers and planters, however, did not have the agricultural machinery, horses, and mules to compensate for the loss of productivity. In addition, continuous cropping of corn and cotton had worn out many acres across the South and land values had collapsed. By 1900 southern agricultural capital and productivity barely exceeded that of 1860. A generation had passed, then, before the recovery of southern agriculture could be proclaimed.[29]

ALTHOUGH THE CONFEDERATE States of America had the potential to meet the food needs of the civilians and soldiers, the odds were against it. Farmers and planters in the seceded states could do so only if Union armies did not destroy their crops and livestock and prevent railroads, steamboats, and ocean vessels from delivering provisions where needed. When Union armies occupied Confederate territory, farmers and planters might continue to raise crops, but their farmland no longer provided food for the Confederacy, unless guerrilla forces took provisions. Confederate forces also impressed or destroyed agricultural provisions both legally and illegally, which encouraged farmers to plant less and to take a wait-and-see approach to determine the effects of the war.

Farmers and planters became divided by economic ideology and class. Some opposed all government regulations of agriculture on any level. Their libertarian solutions for agricultural problems primarily meant no government interference in the agricultural economy. If the wartime market increased agricultural prices, farmers would produce more grain, vegetables, and meat, which they would not hoard but sell willingly. Other farmers and planters advocated self-sacrifice for the nation. They supported centralized government control to regulate production and prices. Neither group saw the achievement of its economic position during the war. Instead, they argued against but eventually accepted half measures out of necessity. In 1864, for example, impressment commissioners in Virginia fixed prices for enumerated agricultural provisions to encourage farmers to market their produce. The commissioners multiplied the prevailing impressment prices by six to set the new prices. Wheat that sold for $5 per bushel was increased to $30 per bushel, and flour from $28 to $168 per barrel. But these impressment prices still lagged behind free-market prices by 50 percent. In Richmond, flour brought from $350 to $400 per barrel.[30]

Some citizens warned that the government price increases for military purchases would encourage farmers to demand even higher free-market prices and that the new currency policy would mean that less money would circulate – all of which would double the problems of the poor to secure food. The planters, in turn, argued that they needed still higher impressment prices, which would increase free-market prices because the Fifteen Negro Law of February 1864 required them to sell provisions at stipulated fixed prices to the army and the poor in their neighborhoods while they paid escalating prices for operating costs and daily living expenses. If the government was going to fix agricultural prices, it should also fix prices on everything else. Essentially, the public wanted cheap or cheaper food and a good supply of provisions The central government never enacted legislation to permit everyone to purchase food at impressment prices. By the end of the war, the public wanted increased regulation of agriculture, but farmers and planters wanted less. Before this disagreement could be resolved, the Confederacy collapsed. As long as the armies could protect farmers and planters, the Confederate States of America could win, difficult though that would be. The faltering agricultural power of the Confederacy, however, made the fight for independence problematic, if not impossible.[31]

Although the war had ended slavery, few southerners believed the freedpeople had a future other than to labor in planters' fields as subservient workers or sharecroppers. Farmers and planters could do without slavery, but they could not do without an abundance of agricultural labor, and in the postwar South that meant black workers needed to farm much of the land.[32]

Public outcry against the new price list and the planters who would profit caused the commissioners to rescind their new impressment price schedule less than two months after it was issued. For some, the solution to the agricultural problem was simple. If the Confederacy could have free-market agricultural prices, a sound currency, no government interference with slave labor, protection against unauthorized impressment of provisions, and the proper regulation of the railroads, farmers and planters would not only produce food crops but would also willingly market their provisions. Idealism, however, could not create an ideal agricultural world in the Confederate States of America.[33]

No one can say what might have happened if things had been different. Counterfactual history is not history. So to ask whether the Confederacy could have prevented its agricultural demise can bring only problematic answers. What can be said is, during the course of the war the Confederacy did not mobilize agriculture for either a short or long war. The government depended on voluntarism for the production of food and forage. In 1863, the central government's directives provided too little regulation too late, and they were poorly enforced. Confederate armies did not keep Union soldiers from destroying the farms and plantations across much of the South. To ask whether land redistribution was a necessity to ensure economic freedom for the former slaves is one thing, but to ask for specific acreage allocations is quite another matter. Might-have-beens and what-ifs contribute only to speculation, not history. What if farmers and planters had had a better currency and good farm implements? What if Confederate soldiers had not pillaged, too? What if railroad transportation had been adequate and well managed? These questions and more merit pondering, but there can be no answers based on historical fact. The agricultural power of the Confederacy was substantial. But like the armies, it too wore down and withered from Union attacks. Rather than ask whether things might have turned out differently, it is more important to ask how things had come to be as peace returned.

In the end, the Union's destruction of southern agriculture contributed to the collapse of the Confederacy. The army could not protect agriculture, and farmers could not sustain the army. The Union armies did not salt the earth or poison wells, but their destructive force left farms and plantations significantly diminished. Those farmers and planters who produced the most grain and meat were exposed to Union armies in Virginia and Tennessee, or they resided beyond the Mississippi River in isolated and nearly inaccessible Texas. In these areas they could not meet the food needs of Confederate civilians and the military. As a result, by April 1865, the agricultural power of the Confederate States of America had collapsed. The indelible footprint of the war on southern agriculture would remain for decades, long after the scars on the land had healed.[34]

Appendix

Agricultural Prices, 1860

Commodity	Jan.	Feb.
Bacon (Baltimore)	9¾¢ lb	NL
Bacon (Richmond)	11–11½¢ lb	11–11½¢ lb
Butter (Richmond)	15–25¢ lb	18–22¢ lb
Corn (New Orleans)	75–80¢ bu	72½–85¢ bu
Corn (Baltimore)	68–70¢ bu	70–72¢ bu
Corn (New York)	78–80¢ bu	80–82¢ bu
Corn (Richmond)	85–90¢ bu	80–85¢ bu
Cotton (New Orleans)	5–12¾¢ lb	5–12¾¢ lb
Cotton (New York)	11⅛–11⅓¢ lb	11⅛–11½¢ lb
Flour (New Orleans)	NL	$3.60–4.75 bbl
Flour (Baltimore)	$5.50 bbl	$5.37 bbl
Flour (New York)	$5.50–5.75 bbl	$5.40–5.70 bbl
Flour (Richmond)	$6.50 bbl	$6.00–6.75 bbl
Hay (Richmond)	$1.25 cwt	$1.25–1.30 cwt
Oats (Richmond)	46–50¢ bu	45–50¢ bu
Pork (New Orleans)	$17.50–18.00 bbl	$18.37 bbl
Pork (Baltimore)	$11.00–15.00 bbl	$17.50–18.00 bbl
Pork (New York)	$13.75–17.25 bbl	$14.50–18.37 bbl
Sugar (New Orleans)	NA	6¼–7½¢ lb
Wheat, red (Baltimore)	$1.25–1.30 bu	$1.30–1.45 bu
Wheat, red (New York)	$1.55 bu	$1.28 bu
Wheat, red (Richmond)	$1.15–1.25 bu	$1.30 bu
Whiskey (New Orleans)	NA	24¢ gal
Whiskey (Baltimore)	25¢ gal	25¢ gal
Whiskey (New York)	24¢ gal	23½¢ gal

Mar.	Apr.	May	June
NL	11–11½¢ lb	11½–12¢ lb	11–11¼¢ lb
11–11½¢ lb	11–11½¢ lb	10–10⅔¢ lb	10–11¢ lb
18–25¢ lb	15–20¢ lb	15–20¢ lb	15–20¢ lb
70–75¢ bu	70–80¢ bu	71–83¢ bu	65–70¢ bu
65–74¢ bu	72–76¢ bu	73–78¢ bu	70–75¢ bu
78–82¢ bu	74–76¢ bu	80–85¢ bu	60–79¢ bu
80–85¢ bu	80¢ bu	80¢ bu	75–85¢ bu
10¾–11¢ lb	6¾–12¾¢ lb	10¢ lb	10¢ lb
11⅛–11½¢ lb	11½¢ lb	11⅜–11½¢ lb	11⅜¢ lb
$6.50–6.60 bbl	$5.75–5.87 bbl	$5.85–6.00 bbl	$5.75–5.87 bbl
$5.50–5.62 bbl	$6.00 bbl	$6.25 bbl	$5.50–5.62 bbl
$5.50–6.00 bbl	$5.90–6.20 bbl	$6.30–6.60 bbl	$5.75–6.20 bbl
$6.00–6.75 bbl	$6.50–7.00 bbl	$6.50–7.25 bbl	$6.25–7.00 bbl
$1.00–1.10 cwt	$1.10–1.25 cwt	$1.30–1.40 cwt	$1.20–1.25 cwt
55–60¢ bu	50¢ bu	45–50¢ bu	45–50¢ bu
NA	$18.00–18.25 bbl	$18.00 bbl	NA
$15.00–18.00 bbl	$15.00–18.00 bbl	$18.00–18.15 bbl	$15.00–18.00 bbl
$13.70–18.50 bbl	$17.45–17.87 bbl	$12.75–14.12 bbl	$17.50–18.25 bbl
6½–7¢ lb	6½–7½¢ lb	6½–7¼¢ lb	7½–8¢ lb
$1.40–1.45 bu	$1.46–1.50 bu	$1.40–1.48 bu	$1.36–1.49 bu
$1.38–1.42 bu	$1.35 bu	$1.50 bu	$1.35–1.40 bu
$1.25–1.30 bu	$1.30–1.35 bu	$1.25–1.35 bu	$1.30 bu
21¼¢ gal	20–21¢ gal	19½¢ gal	19¢ gal
22–23¢ gal	22½¢ gal	22¢ gal	21–21¼¢ gal
24¢ gal	24¢ gal	22¢ gal	21.75¢ gal

Agricultural Prices, 1860 (continued)

Commodity	July	Aug.
Bacon (Baltimore)	11–11¼¢ lb	12¢ lb
Bacon (Richmond)	10–11¢ lb	12¢ lb
Butter (Richmond)	18–20¢ lb	20–25¢ lb
Corn (New Orleans)	70–80¢ bu	56–75¢ bu
Corn (Baltimore)	65–76¢ bu	70–82¢ bu
Corn (New York)	62–65¢ bu	62–63¢ bu
Corn (Richmond)	80–85¢ bu	75–80¢ bu
Cotton (New Orleans)	10–10¼¢ lb	10¼–10¾¢ lb
Cotton (New York)	11½¢ lb	10⅜–10¾¢ lb
Flour (New Orleans)	$5.87 bbl	$5.40–5.50 bbl
Flour (Baltimore)	$5.87 bbl	$5.62 bbl
Flour (New York)	$5.50–5.90 bbl	$5.00–5.55 bbl
Flour (Richmond)	$6.50–7.00 bbl	$6.75–7.25 bbl
Hay (Richmond)	$1.00–1.05 cwt	$1.05–1.10 cwt
Oats (Richmond)	45–50¢ bu	40–45¢ bu
Pork (New Orleans)	$20.50 bbl	$21.00 bbl
Pork (Baltimore)	$20.00 bbl	$14.50–20.00 bbl
Pork (New York)	$18.25–19.12½ bbl	$18.50–19.12 bbl
Sugar (New Orleans)	7½–8¢ lb	7¾–8½¢ lb
Wheat, red (Baltimore)	$1.30 bu	$1.20–1.35 bu
Wheat, red (New York)	$1.30–1.32 bu	$1.30 bu
Wheat, red (Richmond)	$1.30–1.40 bu	$1.30–1.40 bu
Whiskey (New Orleans)	19–19½¢ gal	17½–18¢ gal
Whiskey (Baltimore)	20½¢ gal	21¢ gal
Whiskey (New York)	20½¢ gal	21¢ gal

Sources: Memphis Daily Appeal, Richmond Daily Dispatch, and Staunton Spectator (Va.).
Note: Agricultural prices changed frequently and varied by grade and quality. The prices shown here were recorded on random days during the months listed.
Key: bbl = barrel; bu = bushel; cwt = hundredweight; gal = gallon; lb = pound; NA = not available; NL = not listed.

Sept.	Oct.	Nov.	Dec.
12¢ lb	11¾¢ lb	11¾¢ lb	11¾¢ lb
13¢ lb	13¢ lb	13¢ lb	13¢ lb
18–20¢ lb	18–20¢ lb	18–22¢ lb	20–22¢ lb
60–73¢ bu	60–70¢ bu	63–72¢ bu	53–60¢ bu
72–74¢ bu	64–70¢ bu	70–75¢ bu	50–55¢ bu
64–65¢ bu	70–71¢ bu	71–72¢ bu	61–63¢ bu
75–80¢ bu	70–75¢ bu	70–75¢ bu	65–70¢ bu
10½–10⅜¢ lb	10½–10¾¢ lb	7½–12¼¢ lb	9¼–9¾¢ lb
10⅜–10¾¢ lb	11⅛–11¼¢ lb	11⅜–11½¢ lb	10¢ lb
$5.65–5.75 bbl	$6.00–6.05 bbl	$5.00–5.57 bbl	NL
$5.87–6.00 bbl	$5.75 bbl	$5.50–5.62 bbl	$5.50–5.62 bbl
$5.95–6.25 bbl	$5.85–6.00 bbl	$5.80–6.00 bbl	$6.00 bbl
$6.75–7.25 bbl	$6.75–7.50 bbl	$6.75–7.50 bbl	$6.50–7.25 bbl
$1.10–1.15 cwt	$1.05–1.10 cwt	$1.10–1.15 cwt	$1.15 cwt
35–40¢ bu	40¢ bu	40–45¢ bu	40–45¢ bu
$22.00 bbl	$19.50 bbl	NA	NA
$14.25–19.75 bbl	$14.75–19.75 bbl	$19.50 bbl	$16.00 bbl
$13.25–19.50 bbl	$16.75–19.00 bbl	$13.00–19.12 bbl	$10.50–17.25 bbl
9¼–9½¢ lb	10¾¢ lb	6–7¢ lb	4½–5¢ lb
$1.40–1.45 bu	$1.28–1.35 bu	$1.25–1.33 bu	$1.05–1.16 bu
$1.40–1.45 bu	$1.33–1.34 bu	$1.30–1.31 bu	$1.30–1.31 bu
$1.45–1.60 bu	$1.40–1.60 bu	$1.50–1.65 bu	$1.20 1.35 bu
NA	21¾¢ gal	NA	NA
24½–25¢ gal	22½¢ gal	20¢ gal	18¢ gal
23–23½¢ gal	24.5¢ gal	21¾–22¢ gal	18–18½¢ gal

Notes

ABBREVIATIONS

GSAL   Georgia State Archives and Library
LV   Library of Virginia
MDAH   Mississippi Department of Archives and History
MML   Special Collections, Mitchell Memorial Library, Mississippi State University
OR   *Official Records of the Union and Confederate Armies of the War of the Rebellion*
ORN   *Official Records of the Union and Confederate Navies of the War of the Rebellion*
SHC   Southern Historical Collection, University of North Carolina
TSLA   Tennessee State Library and Archives
VHS   Virginia Historical Society Library and Manuscript Collection

INTRODUCTION

1. *Southern Confederacy*, June 4, 1861.
2. Black, *The Railroads of the Confederacy*, 6.
3. Ibid., 3–4, 8–9.
4. McPherson, *Battle Cry of Freedom*, 575–76.
5. *Agriculture of the United States in 1860*, 222; *Population of the United States in 1860*, iv.
6. Stampp, *The Peculiar Institution*, 30–33.

CHAPTER 1

1. John Henry Dent Farm Journals and Account Book, January 1, 1861, 2, microfilm 1619, roll 2, TSLA; Diary, 1861, folder 10, Solomon Hilary Helsabeck Papers, SHC; Louis M. DeSaussure Journal, January 1, 1861, SHC; Escott, ed., *North Carolina Yeoman*, 302–5; Crofts, ed., *Cobb's Ordeal*, 182–91; Watkins, *King Cotton*, 30; Schoen, *The Fragile Fabric of Union*, 122–23.
2. *Southern Cultivator*, January 1861.
3. *Daily Picayune*, January 23, 1861.
4. Ibid., February 2, 1861; Allen (James) Plantation Book, February 21, March 2, 7, and 28, 1861, MDAH; Diary, February 2 and April 22, 1861, Parker (Huston Huling) Papers, MDAH.
5. *Standard*, March 9, 1861.
6. *Southern Confederacy*, March 6, 1861; Watkins, *King Cotton*, 30; *Richmond Daily Examiner*, March 15, 1861.
7. Alexander (Robert B.) Diary and Account Book, April 14, 1861, MDAH; *Richmond Daily Examiner*, April 4, 19, 30, 1861; *Southern Confederacy*, April 4 and 30, 1861.
8. *Richmond Daily Examiner*, April 23, 1861; William Conrad to wife, April 26, 1861, Robert Young Conrad Papers, VHS.

9. *Southern Confederacy*, April 12 and 18, and May 9, 15, 21, and 25, and June 1, 1861; *Standard*, April 4, 1861; *Richmond Daily Examiner*, May 27 and June 1, 1861.

10. Richardson, *Messages and Papers of the Confederacy*, vol. 2, 81–82; *Moore's Rural New Yorker*, May 4, 1861.

11. *Southern Confederacy*, April 23, 27, and 28, 1861; *Daily Picayune*, May 2, 1861.

12. Jones, *A Rebel War Clerk's Diary*, vol. 1, 34–35; Diary, May 27 and June 29, 1861, folder 3, box 1, Robert H. Cantrell Papers, TSLA.

13. Pratt, *A Short History of the Civil War*, 23–25; *Richmond Daily Examiner*, May 23 and 29, and June 4, 1861; Escott, *North Carolina Yeoman*, 308; John R. Henderson to Dear Friend, May 30, 1861, folder 13, box 1, McArn (Duncan) and Family Papers, MDAH; R. (?) Taney to Dear Friend, June 28, 1861, folder 14, box 1, McArn (Duncan) and Family Papers, MDAH; John R. Henderson to D. McArn, July 30, 1861, folder 30, box 2, McArn (Duncan) and Family Papers, MDAH.

14. *Daily Picayune*, May 11, 1861; Diary, July 24, 1861, folder 3, box 1, Robert H. Cantrell Papers, TSLA; *Austin State Gazette*, September 21, 1861; *Bellville Countryman*, June 12, 1861.

15. Schoen, *The Fragile Fabric of Union*, 263–64; Jones, *Blue Gray Diplomacy*, 49. Lincoln imposed the blockade on April 19.

16. Beringer, Hattaway, Jones, and Still, Jr., *Why the South Lost the Civil War*, 53–63, 432–33.

17. Schoen, *The Fragile Fabric of Union*, 264; Jones, *Union in Peril*, 48.

18. Schoen, *The Fragile Fabric of Union*, 265–66; Jones, *Union in Peril*, 48–59.

19. *Southern Confederacy*, June 1 and 19, 1861; Lerner, "Monetary and Fiscal Programs of the Confederate Government," 506, 512–15; Todd, *Confederate Finance*, 31–35; Ball, *Financial Failure and Confederate Defeat*, 79–85; *Moore's Rural New Yorker*, September 28, 1861.

20. *Richmond Daily Examiner*, June 25 and July 3, 1861; Bettersworth, *Confederate Mississippi*, 97–99; *Southern Confederacy*, July 19 and 21, 1861; *Mobile Register and Advertiser*, June 15, 1861; Todd, *Confederate Finance*, 31–32, 34–39.

21. Bettersworth, *Confederate Mississippi*, 99.

22. *Daily Picayune*, July 1 and 13, 1861; Todd, *Confederate Finance*, 35; *Richmond Daily Examiner*, July 23, 1861; Coulter, *The Confederate States of America*, 164–66.

23. Range, *A Century of Georgia Agriculture*, 50–51; *Richmond Daily Examiner*, October 12 and 18, 1861; *Southern Confederacy*, November 30, 1861.

24. *Southern Confederacy*, July 2, 1861; *Daily Picayune*, July 23, 1861; *Weekly Mississippian*, August 14 and 21, 1861.

25. Richardson, *Messages and Papers of the Confederacy*, vol. 1, 123; *Southern Confederacy*, September 1, 1861. By 1864, cotton producers had subscribed only $34,476,000 in farm products of the $100 million authorized by the legislation.

26. *Weekly Mississippian*, August 21 and September 4, 1861.

27. Lerner, "Monetary and Fiscal Programs of the Confederate Government," 514–15, 520; Coulter, *The Confederate States of America*, 164–65; Yearns, *The Confederate Congress*, 189–90.

28. *Richmond Daily Examiner*, April 4 and July 7, 1861.

29. *Weekly Mississippian*, October 23 and 30, 1861; Todd, *Confederate Finance*, 37.

30. *Weekly Mississippian*, November 6, 1861.

31. Ibid., November 6, 1861.

32. Ibid., November 20, 1861.

33. *Richmond Daily Examiner*, October 4, 1861.

34. Swanson, "Land of the Bright Leaf," 13, 154–55, 169.

35. *Weekly Mississippian*, October 30, 1861; *Natchez Weekly Courier*, November 6, 1861.

36. Lerner, "Monetary and Fiscal Programs of the Confederate Government," 514, 518, 520; *Weekly Mississippian*, August 7 and October 23, 1861; Coulter, *The Confederate States of America*, 155–56; *Natchez Weekly Courier*, December 4, 1861.

37. *OR*, Series 4, vol. 1, 341–42, 529; Gentry, "White Gold," 231; Coulter, *The Confederate States of America*, 286–87; Parks, "A Confederate Trade Center Under Federal Occupation," 290, 294–95, 300; *OR*, Series 4, vol. 1, 341–42, 529, and vol. 17, pt. 2, 123, 861. See also Coulter, "Effects of Secession upon the Commerce of the Mississippi Valley," and Coulter, "Commercial Intercourse with the Confederacy in the Mississippi Valley."

38. Roberts, "The Federal Government and Confederate Cotton," 262–65; Schuckers, *Life and Public Service of Salmon Portland Chase*, 319. For the failure of the Confederate government to regulate trade, particularly cotton, across Union lines see Johnson, "Trading with the Union," 308–25.

39. Parks, "Confederate Trade Center Under Federal Occupation," 290, 294–95, 300; *OR*, Series 1, vol. 17, pt. 2, 123. There was one exception to this generalization: many farmers preferred payment in Tennessee notes because they could easily exchange them for needed goods in areas still held by Confederate forces.

40. O'Connor, "Lincoln and the Cotton Trade," 270, Johnson, "Contraband Trade during the Last Year of the Civil War," 638, 642.

41. Dattel, *Cotton and Race in the Making of America*, 81–83, 88–89, 99, 166–67.

42. Ibid., 103, 169–70, 172.

43. *Moore's Rural New Yorker*, August 10 and 30, 1861.

44. Allen (James) Plantation Book, February 21 and March 7, and October 12 to December 31, 1861, MDAH; Watkins, *King Cotton* 30; Connor, "Letters of Lieutenant Robert H. Miller to His Family," 66; *Richmond Daily Examiner*, July 3, 1861; *Charlestown Mercury*, July 4, 1861.

45. Duncan, *Beleaguered Winchester*, 25, 28.

46. McPherson, *Battle Cry of Freedom*, 339–47; Pratt, *A Short History of the Civil War*, 45–47; Jones, *Blue and Gray Diplomacy*, 61–68, 74.

47. Richardson, *Messages and Papers of the Confederacy*, vol. 1, 123; McWhiney, Moore, and Pace, eds., *"Fear God and Walk Humbly,"* 288; *Richmond Daily Examiner*, July 27 and August 1, 1861; Iobst, *Civil War Macon*, 254; B. H. Walker Diary, June 26, 1861, LV; Westover Plantation Journal of John A. Seldon, August 22, 1861, SHC.

48. John Augustine Washington to Louise (Clemson) Washington, August 31, 1861, Letter, VHS; Diary, October 21, 1861, J. S. Newman Personal Papers, 55, LV.

49. *Charleston Mercury*, June 19, 1861; *OR*, Series 1, vol. 5, 845–46.

50. John Henry Dent, Farm Journals and Account Book, 204, 257, 258, 263, microfilm 1619, roll 2, TSLA.

51. *Daily Chronicle & Sentinel*, October 10, 1861; *Richmond Daily Examiner*, April 12 and November 13, 1861; *Southern Confederacy*, November 13 and 20, 1861.

52. *Southern Confederacy*, March 30, April 2, October 15 and 31, and December 4, 1861; *Richmond Daily Examiner*, April 12 and November 2, 1861.

53. William Conrad to Wife, November 13, 1861, Robert Young Conrad Papers, VHS; *Richmond Daily Examiner*, April 12, May 23, and November 11 and 23, 1861; Gates, *Agriculture and the Civil War*, 41; B. H. Walker Diary, December 2, 1861, LV.

54. *Richmond Daily Enquirer*, November 18, 1861.

55. *OR*, 1861, Series 1, vol. 6, 201, 337–38.

56. Report of the Commissioner of Agriculture, 1867, 100; Roland, *Louisiana Sugar Plantations*, 2–4, 10; Sitterson, *Sugar Country*, 165.

57. Sitterson, *Sugar Country*, 205–7; Roland, "Difficulties of Civil War Sugar Planting in Louisiana," 40–41; Roland, *Louisiana Sugar Plantations*, 27–30; Prichard, "Effect of the Civil War on the Louisiana Sugar Industry," 318; *Moore's Rural New Yorker* (Rochester), September 7, 1861. Planters shipped sugar in hogsheads that weighed about 1,000 pounds and molasses in 45-gallon barrels.

58. Parker Diary, September 10 and 12, 1861, Huston Huling Papers, MDAH; John R. Henderson to Dear Friend, May 30, 1861, folder 13, box 1, McArn (Duncan) and Family Papers, MDAH; *Daily Picayune*, January 24, 1861; *Weekly Mississippian*, December 25, 1861; *Natchez Weekly Courier*, December 11, 1861; Diary and Accounts, 1861, July 13 and August 7 and 8, 1861, folder 10, James Clarence Harper Papers, SHC; Diary, July 31, 1861, folder 10, Solomon Hilary Helsabeck Papers, SHC; Alexander (Robert B.) Diary and Account Book, June 10, 24, and 25, 1861, MDAH; Allen (James) Plantation Book, October 8, 1861; Evans (Dr. Holden Garthur) Diary, April 15, 1861, MDAH.

59. Gates, *Agriculture and the Civil War*, 7; "Hog Cholera," Annual Report of the Commissioner of Patents on Agriculture, 1861, 147; Alexander (Robert B.) Diary and Account Book, October 25, 1861, MDAH; *Moore's Rural New Yorker* (Rochester), September 14, 1861; *Southern Confederacy*, November 2, 1861; *Genesee Farmer*, September 1861; *Natchez Weekly Courier*, September 11, 1861. For a study of the importance of salt see Lonn, *Salt as a Factor in the Confederacy*.

60. Gates, *Agriculture and the Civil War*, 7–8.

61. Ibid., 8; Blevins, *Cattle in the Cotton Fields*, 27–29.

62. Blevins, *Cattle in the Cotton Fields*, 27–29.

63. Price, "'Don't Fence Me In,'" 61–62; *Natchez Weekly Courier*, November 13, 1861; *Southern Confederacy*, March 4 and 15, 1861; *The Constitutional*, February 2, 1861.

64. *The Standard*, December 21, 1861; *Dallas Herald*, November 20, 1861; *Texas Republican*, August 10, 1861; *OR*, Series 1, vol. 4, 122–23.

65. Ramsdell, "General Robert E. Lee's Horse Supply," 756–59.

66. Glatthaar, *General Lee's Army*, 210.

67. Basford, "Federal Administration of Abandoned Plantations," 5–6.

68. *Moore's Rural New Yorker*, November 30 and December 7, 1861; *Natchez Weekly Courier*, December 11, 1861; Pace, "Overwhelmed by the Storm," 7–8.

69. Bleser, ed., *Secret and Sacred*, 281; Glatthaar, *General Lee's Army*, 18–20; Bryant, *How Curious a Land*, 79.

70. Louis M. DeSaussure Journal, January to September, 1861, SHC; Plantation Record Book, Bourbon, April 19, May 21, August 5, September 7, December 21, 1861, Metcalf Family Papers, MDAH; Allen (James) Plantation Book, October 4, 1861, MDAH; Parker Diary, July 25, 1861, Parker (Huston Huling) Papers, MDAH; Bettersworth, ed., *Mississippi in the Confederacy*, 222–23; Krug, "Women and War in the Confederacy," 429.

71. Alexander (Robert B.) Diary and Account Book, December 31, 1861, MDAH; E. H. Riggan Account Book, January 4, 1861, SHC; Diary and Account Book, April 30, 1861, folder 10, James Clarence Harper Papers, SHC; Crofts, *Cobb's Ordeal*, 195–96; Anderson, ed., *Brokenburn*, 43–44; *Southern Confederacy*, April 5 and 6 and July 18, 1861.

72. *Population of the United States – 1860; Eighth Census*, 505; *Richmond Daily Examiner*, March 12, 1861; *Southern Confederacy*, March 5, 1861. In 1860 South Carolina had approximately 290,000 slaves.

73. Sitterson, *Sugar Country*, 61; Roland, *Louisiana Sugar Plantations*, 14; Russell, *My Diary North and South*, 272–82; Hurt, *Agriculture and Slavery in Missouri's Little Dixie*, 225–29.

74. *Richmond Daily Examiner*, June 20, 1861; *Weekly Mississippian*, January 2, 1861; *Southern Confederacy*, August 7, 1861; *Moore's Rural New Yorker*, August 31, 1861; J. D. G. Brown to Joseph B. Brown, September 19, 1861, J. D. G. Brown Personal Papers, LV; Plantation Record Book, Bourbon, August 5, 1861, Metcalf Family Papers, MDAH.

75. Nimrod Porter Diary, July 22, 1861, TSLA; Diary, March 20, 1861, folder 3, box 1, Robert H. Cantrell Papers, TSLA.

76. *OR*, Series 4, vol. 1, 767; Goff, *Confederate Supply*, 41–42; Allen (James) Plantation Book, October 5, 1861, MDAH.

77. Coulter, *The Confederate States of America*, 223–26; *Natchez Weekly Courier*, March 26, 1862; Ramsdell, *Behind the Lines in the Southern Confederacy*, 20–21. For an overview of southern railroads see Black, *The Railroads of the Confederacy*.

78. *New York Times*, September 26, 1861; McWhiney, Moore, and Pace, eds., *"Fear God and Walk Humbly,"* 292; Diary, October 5, 1861, folder 3, box 1, Robert H. Cantrell Papers, TSLA; Gates, *Agriculture and the Civil War*, 100–101; *Southern Confederacy*, October 29, 1861.

79. *Natchez Weekly Courier*, October 23, November 6, and December 11, 1861; *Weekly Mississippian*, December 4, 1861.

80. *Southern Confederacy*, November 20 and December 4, 1861; *Richmond Daily Examiner*, November 22, 1861; *Moore's Rural New Yorker*, November 30, 1861; Iobst, *Civil War Macon*, 96.

81. F. Nims to J. F. White, November 23, 1861, folder 13a, Nims, Rankin, and Sproot Family Papers, SHC; Diary and Accounts, May 8 and December 5, 1861, folder 10, James Clarence Harper Papers, SHC; Daniel Huff to Bettie, ? 1861, folder 3, Steed and Phipps Family Papers, SHC; F. Nims to J. F. White, November 23, 1861, folder 13a, Nims, Rankin, and Sproot Family Papers, SHC; J. S. Espy to Brother, December 22, 1861, folder 1, Joseph Espy Papers, SHC.

82. Jeannie M. Sehon to Bettie, November 9, 1861, folder 36, Series 1, John Kimberly Papers, SHC; Cathey, "Impact of the Civil War on Agriculture in North Carolina," 98; Bragg, *Louisiana in the Confederacy*, 74.

83. Allen (James) Plantation Book, October 15, 1861, MDAH; Bragg, *Louisiana in the Confederacy*, 78–79; Woodward and Muhlenfeld, *The Private Mary Chesnut*, 206.

84. Bettersworth, ed., *Mississippi in the Confederacy*, 216–17.

85. Diary, December 26, 1861, folder 3, box 1, Robert H. Cantrell Papers, TSLA; Louise M. DeSaussure Journal, November ?, 1861, SHC; Bettersworth, ed., *Mississippi in the Confederacy*, 215–16.

86. Todd, *Confederate Finance*, 38; Bettersworth, ed., *Mississippi in the Confederacy*, 99–103.

87. *Southern Confederacy*, December 25, 1861; Diary, December 6, 1861, folder 3, box 1, Robert H. Cantrell Papers, TSLA; Gates, *Agriculture and the Civil War*, 104; Samuel Henderson Diary, September 9, November 26, and December 31, 1861, TSLA.

88. Range, *A Century of Georgia Agriculture*, 38, 40; *Richmond Daily Examiner*, December 2, 1861; *Southern Confederacy*, December 28, 1861.

89. Coulter, "Movement for Agricultural Reorganization in the Cotton South," 6; *Weekly Mississippian*, November 20 and December 4, 1861.

90. *Weekly Mississippian*, November 11, 1861; *Bellville Countryman*, June 12, 18–61.

91. *Southern Confederacy*, November 20, 1861; *Richmond Daily Examiner*, November 25, 1861.

92. Glatthaar, *General Lee's Army*, 66; Allen (James) Plantation Book, November 14, 1861, MDAH.

93. Ash, "White Virginians under Federal Occupation," 179; Glatthaar, *General Lee's Army*, 81; *OR*, Series 1, vol. 6, 290.

94. Goff, *Confederate Supply*, 4–5, 20–22, 28; *Southern Cultivator*, January 1861.

CHAPTER 2

1. *American Citizen*, February 22, 1862; *Southern Cultivator*, January and February 1862.

2. *Southern Confederacy*, January 14, 1862.

3. Ball, *Financial Failure and Confederate Defeat*, 85–86; Todd, *Confederate Finance*, 39–44.

4. Todd, *Confederate Finance*, 39–44.

5. *Southern Cultivator*, January and February 1862; *Southern Confederacy*, August 23, 1862.

6. *Southern Cultivator*, February 1862; *Southern Confederacy*, January 17, 1862.

7. *Southern Cultivator*, January 1862; *Southern Confederacy*, January 23, 1862.

8. *Southern Confederacy*, January 23, 1862; *Southern Cultivator*, February 1862; Perry Curry to Father, June 20, 1862, folder 16, box 1, Curry Records, GSAL.

9. Childs, ed., *The Private Journal of Henry William Ravenel*, 129; Crabtree and Patton, eds., "*Journal of a Secesh Lady*," 140; John R. Surley Diary, May 31, July 24 and 25, 1862, SHC; James, "Mississippi Agriculture," 133; Watkins, *King Cotton*, 30; Woodman, *King Cotton and His Retainers*, 227; Cathey, "Impact of the Civil War on Agriculture in North Carolina," 98, 100; *Historical Statistics of the United States, 1789–1945*, E 211–24.

10. Perry Curry to Father, June 20, 18, 1862, folder 16, box 1, Curry Records, GSAL; *Southern Confederacy*, June 17, 1862; Phillips, "Correspondence of Robert Toombs, Alexander H. Stephens, and Howell Cobb," American Historical Association, *Annual Report, 1911*, vol. 2, 595.

11. *Richmond Daily Examiner*, February 26, 1862; *Southern Confederacy*, February 27 and 28, and March 6, 1862,

12. Goff, *Confederate Supply*, 81; *OR*, Series 1, vol. 6, 885; *Richmond Daily Examiner*, March 7, April 1 and 4, 1862; McWhiney, Moore, and Pace, eds., *"Fear God and Walk Humbly,"* 305.

13. McPherson, *Battle Cry of Freedom*, 72–84, 424–27, 461–72, 488–89; Pratt, *A Short History of the Civil War*, 65–84.

14. Diary, January 1 to 30, 1863, Philip Henry Pitts Papers, SHC; Coulter, "Movement for Agricultural Reorganization in the Cotton South," 9.

15. Bryant, *How Curious a Land*, 76; *Daily Southern Crisis*, January 12, 1863; Coulter, *The Confederate States of America*, 240–42. A farmer or planter charged with exceeding his allocation of cotton or tobacco could request a court order authorizing the survey of his acreage in question to determine accuracy. Virginia restricted farmers and planters to 2,500 tobacco plants for each hand between sixteen and fifty-five years old, or 80,000 plants per plantation. Small-scale farmers could not exceed 10,000 tobacco plants.

16. *Southern Confederacy*, April 1, 1862; *Richmond Daily Examiner*, April 18 and 24, 1862.

17. *Richmond Daily Examiner*, February 2 and 6, 1862; Kerr-Ritchie, *Freedpeople in the Tobacco South*, 17; tobacco lugs are a bound collection of leaves of varying size, weight, and quality taken from the bottom of the stalk.

18. Gates, *Agriculture and the Civil War*, 97–98; *Southern Cultivator*, March–April 1862; McKinney, *Zeb Vance*, 124; Coulter, "Movement for Agricultural Reorganization in the Cotton South," 15; Coulter, *The Confederate States of America*, 248.

19. McKinney, *Zeb Vance*, 124; E. H. Riggan Account Book, May 11, 1862, SHC; C. D. Epps to Wife, October 25, 1862, folder 3, C. D. Epps Papers, SHC.

20. *OR*, Series 4, vol. 1, 872–78.

21. Iobst, *Civil War Macon*, 93; Hurt, *American Farm Tools*, 11–12; Coulter, "Planters' Wants in the Days of the Confederacy," 40; *Moore's Rural New Yorker* (Rochester), January 11, 1862.

22. Schlebecker, *Whereby We Thrive*, 156; Wiley, *The Plain People of the Confederacy*, 40; Rose, *Rehearsal for Reconstruction*, 126.

23. DeLeon, *Four Years in Rebel Capitals*, 375; Ramsdell, *Behind the Lines in the Southern Confederacy*, 23–24; Wiley, *The Plain People of the Confederacy*, 41.

24. *Richmond Daily Examiner*, July 25, 1862.

25. *Southern Confederacy*, August 7, 1862; *Richmond Daily Examiner*, August 7 and 12, 1862.

26. *Charleston Mercury*, August 1, 1862; *Richmond Daily Examiner*, August 29 and November 17, 1862.

27. Dattel, *Cotton and Race in the Making of America*, 201–2.

28. Childs, ed., *The Private Journal of Henry William Ravenel*, 116–17; *Richmond Daily Examiner*, March 10, 1862; *Southern Confederacy*, March 13, 1862.

29. *Southern Confederacy*, March 18, 20, and 25, 1862; Childs, ed., *The Private Journal of Henry William Ravenel*, 129.

30. *Southern Confederacy*, April 8, 1862.

31. *Richmond Daily Examiner*, April 9 and 22, 1862.

32. *Southern Confederacy*, April 10, 1862.

33. *Richmond Daily Examiner*, April 21, 1862; Westover Plantation Journal of John A. Seldon, April 17, 1862–62, SHC.

34. *Richmond Daily Examiner*, April 25, 1862; *Southern Watchman*, April 30, 1862; *Southern Confederacy*, March 28, 30, and April 2, 1861.

35. *Richmond Daily Examiner*, May 2 and 3, 1862; Clinard and Russell, eds., *Fear in North Carolina*, 81; McWhiney, Moore, and Pace, eds., *"Fear God and Walk Humbly,"* 304–5.

36. Bleser, *Secret and Sacred*, 285–87; Account Book, July 9, 1862, folder 23, Series 1.1, Civil War Correspondence, Graves Family Papers, SHC.

37. *Richmond Daily Examiner*, June 9, 1862; *Southern Confederacy*, June 13 and July 1, 8, 15, 22, 1862; Escott, ed., *North Carolina Yeomen*, 328.

38. *Richmond Daily Examiner*, June 9, 14, 16, 21, and 26, 1862.

39. Ibid., July 7 and 19, 1862; *Richmond Price Current*, published in the *New England Farmer*, November 1862.

40. Sally Lyons Taliaferro Diary, July 8, 1862, LV; *Southern Confederacy*, July 27, 1862; *Richmond Daily Examiner*, July 23, 24, and 28, 1862; *New England Farmer* (Boston), November 1862.

41. *Richmond Daily Examiner*, July 19 and August 1, 1862; *Weekly Columbus Enquirer*, July 22, 1862.

42. *Richmond Daily Examiner*, October 20 and 30, 1862; Iobst, *Civil War Macon*, 268; *Southern Confederacy*, October 21, 23, and 28 and November 11 and 18, 1862; Account Book, folder 23, Series 1.1, Civil War Correspondence, Graves Family Papers, SHC.

43. *Southern Confederacy*, June 24, 1862; *Richmond Daily Examiner*, July 23 and 24 and August 7, 1862.

44. *Memphis Daily Appeal*, February 6, 1862; Ash, "White Virginians under Federal Occupation," 179; Duncan *Beleaguered Winchester*, 69.

45. *OR*, Series 1, vol. 12, pt. 3, 60–61.

46. Ibid., Series 1, vol. 12, pt. 3, 61–62, 74–77; Duncan, *Beleaguered Winchester*, 69; Goff, *Confederate Supply*, 72; Perry L. Curry to Father, May 28, 1862, folder 16, box 1, Curry Records, GSAL.

47. Ramsdell, "General Robert E. Lee's Horse Supply," 759; Crofts, *Cobb's Ordeal*, 210.

48. Duncan, *Beleaguered Winchester*, 70–71; *Richmond Daily Examiner*, March 21, 1862.

49. *Memphis Daily Appeal*, February 6, 1862; *OR*, Series 1, vol. 11, pt. 3, 526; Wiley, *The Life of Johnny Reb*, 43–44; Wiley, *The Plain People of the Confederacy*, 27; Bushman, *In Old Virginia*, 218; Glatthaar, *General Lee's Army*, 177–79.

50. Glatthaar, *General Lee's Army*, 102, 118, 177–79; *Moore's Rural New Yorker*, May 31, 1862.

51. Bushman, *In Old Virginia*, 216–17; Lerner, "Monetary and Fiscal Programs of the Confederate Government," 507; Geoff, *Confederate Supply*, 97.

52. Geoff, *Confederate Supply*, 98–99.

53. Glatthaar, *General Lee's Army*, 214.

54. McPherson, *Battle Cry of Freedom*, 528–33; Pratt, *A Short History of the Civil War*, 136–47; Westover Plantation Journal of John A. Seldon, April 30, 1862, SHC; *Southern Cultivator*, July–August, 1862; Goff, *Confederate Supply*, 45–46; Todd, *Confederate Finance*, 36–39; *Richmond Daily Examiner*, August 15, 1862.

55. *Richmond Daily Examiner*, August 15, 1862.

56. Geoff, *Confederate Supply*, 98; *Moore's Rural New Yorker*, August 30, 1862.

57. McWhiney, Moore, and Pace, eds., *"Fear God and Walk Humbly,"* 309–10; Escott, ed., *North Carolina Yeoman*, 328.

58. Mobley, *"War Governor of the South,"* 52; Moore, *Conscription and Conflict in the Confederacy*, 140–45.

59. Krug, "Women and War in the Confederacy," 416, 429.

60. Mohr, *On the Threshold of Freedom*, 221–32; Faust, *Mothers of Invention*, 32–33; Krug, "Women and War in the Confederacy," 428; *Richmond Daily Examiner*, July 19, 1862.

61. Faust, *Mothers of Invention*, 32–33, 51–57.

62. *Southern Confederacy*, January 9 and February 7, 1862.

63. *Richmond Daily Examiner*, March 24, April 1, May 13, and September 9, 1862; E. Philips to My Dear Friend, January 26, 1862, folder 2, box 1, Series 1, James Jones Philips Papers, SHC.

64. *Southern Confederacy*, January 1 and July 9, 1862; *Richmond Daily Examiner*, August 1, 1862. For a comparative list of slave prices in Forsyth County, North Carolina, in the early 1850s see Tadman, *Speculators and Slaves*, 287.

65. *Southern Confederacy*, August 7, 1862; *Richmond Daily Examiner*, September 9, 1862.

66. *Southern Confederacy*, October 22, 1862; Westover Plantation Journal of John A. Seldon, October 8, 1862, SHC; E. H. Riggan Account Book, October 27, 1862, SHC; Mary L. Curry to Husband, April 8 and 10, 1862, folder 16, box 2, Curry Hill Plantation Records, GSAL; Perry L. Curry to Father, June 6, 1862, folder 16, box 1, Curry Hill Plantation Records, GSAL.

67. *Southern Confederacy*, October 22, 1862; *Richmond Daily Examiner*, October 25, 1862.

68. *Richmomd Daily Examiner*, November 6, 22, and 29, 1862; *Southern Confederacy*, December 18 and 30, 1862.

69. E. H. Riggan, Account Book, March 15, 1862, SHC; *Richmond Daily Examiner*, January 6, 1862; E. P. Philips to James Philips, November 18, 1862, folder 2, box 2, Series 1, James Jones Philips Papers, SHC; Diary, March 4, 1862, Philip Henry Pitts Papers, SHC; Mohr, *On the Threshold of Freedom*, 164–65.

70. *Southern Confederacy*, August 23, 1862; *New York Herald*, August 18, 1862.

71. *OR*, Series 3, vol. 2, 275–77; *Southern Confederacy*, August 7, 1862.

72. Pierce, "The Freedmen at Port Royal," 296; Rose, *Rehearsal for Reconstruction*, 11, 19–21; Wiley, *Southern Negroes*, 177–78.

73. Rose, *Rehearsal for Reconstruction*, 22–29; Wiley, *Southern Negroes*, 178; Powell, *New Masters*, 2; Pierce, "The Freedmen at Port Royal," 297.

74. Pearson, ed., *Letters from Port Royal*, 45, 48.

75. *OR*, Series 1, vol. 6, 249–50; *New York Times*, July 29, 1862; Pierce, "The Freedmen at Port Royal," 299; Basford, "Federal Administration of Abandoned Plantations," 16, 18.

76. Basford, "Federal Administration of Abandoned Plantations," 12; *New York Times*, February 5, 1862; Wiley, *Southern Negroes*, 201–3.

77. Mohr, *On the Threshold of Freedom*, 80; *OR*, Series 1, vol. 12, 634, 756, and vol. 13, 21; *New York Daily Tribune*, August 9, 1862; *ORN*, Series 1, vol. 13, 144–45.

78. *OR*, Series I, vol. 12, 12, 756; Mohr, *On the Threshold of Freedom*, 82; Barnes and Barnes, *Naval Surgeon*, vol. 1, 15, 189, 217; *ORN*, Series 1, vol. 13, 159; Pearson, ed., *Letters from Port Royal*, 33, 48.

79. *OR*, Series 3, vol. 2, 276; Circular for Superintendents in the 2d Division, November 5, 1862, folder 1, David Franklin Thorpe Papers, SHC; F. E. Barnhard to M. Sharpe, October 7, 1862, folder 1, David Franklin Thorpe Papers, SHC.

80. Pierce, "The Freedmen at Port Royal," 315; *Moore's Rural New Yorker* (Rochester), November 8 and 29, 1862.

81. Basford, "Federal Administration of Abandoned Plantations," 23–24; Pearson, ed., *Letters from Port Royal*, 66–98; Rose, *Rehearsal for Reconstruction*, 204–5.

82. E. Philips to My Dear Friend, January 26, 1862, folder 2, box 1, Series 1, James Jones Philips Papers, SHC; Louis M. DeSassure Journal, January and April 1862, SHC; Mohr, *On the Threshold of Freedom*, 102–3.

83. McKinney, *Zeb Vance*, 125; Mohr, *On the Threshold of Freedom*, 100, 103, 112–14, 116.

84. McPherson, *Battle Cry of Freedom*, 538–44; Pratt, *A Short History of the Civil War*, 150–60, 167.

85. *Richmond Daily Examiner*, September 12, 1862.

86. *Southern Confederacy*, September 12 and 23, 1862; Childs, ed., *The Private Journal of Henry William Ravenel*, 136, 165; *Richmond Daily Examiner*, September 12 and 26, 1862.

87. Duncan, *Beleaguered Winchester*, 127; Lee, ed., *Memoirs of William Nelson Pendleton*, 228.

88. *OR*, Series 1, vol. 19, pt. 2, 699–700; Duncan, *Beleaguered Winchester*, 127–28; Childs, ed., *The Private Journal of Henry William Ravenel*, 166.

89. Ayers, *In the Presence of Mine Enemies*, 334; Diary, September 15 and October 16, 1862, Philip Henry Pitts Papers, SHC.

90. Ramsdell, *Behind the Lines in the Southern Confederacy*, 43; Jones, *A Rebel War Clerk's Diary*, vol. 1, 182, 207–8; Childs, ed., *The Private Journal of Henry William Ravenel*, 159; Ayers, *In the Presence of Mine Enemies*, 333–34; John R. Shurley Diary, November 21, 1862, SHC.

91. *Richmond Daily Examiner*, November 25 and December 25, 1862; *Southern Confederacy*, December 6, 16, and 30, 1862; L. H. Briscoe to Postmaster, New Madrid, Monroe County, Georgia, October 14, 1862, no. 12, 201, Adjutant General's Letter Book, GSAL; H. C. Wayne to General I. W. B. Edwards, October 28, 1862, no. 12, 233, Adjutant General's Letter Book, GSAL; *Charleston Mercury*, December 5, 1862.

92. McPherson, *Battle Cry of Freedom*, 571–74; Pratt, *A Short History of the Civil War*, 160–65.

93. Goff, *Confederate Supply*, 94; *OR*, Series 4, vol. 2, 132.

94. Gates, *Agriculture and the Civil War*, 67, 74, 78, 86, 90, 104.

95. Ibid., 39, 87; Glatthaar, *General Lee's Army*, 211–12; Lerner, "Inflation in the Confederacy," 171. This price index involved the averaging of fifty-seven commodity prices in Richmond, Virginia, Wilmington and Fayetteville, North Carolina, and Augusta, Georgia. These commodities included wool, corn, cotton, flaxseed, hay, oats, rye, tobacco, wheat, bacon, beef, butter, chickens, flour, lard, molasses, peanuts, peas, pork, Irish and sweet potatoes, rice, sugar, live and butchered turkeys, fruit brandy, and whiskey. See also Lerner, "Money, Prices, and Wages in the Confederacy," 22–24.

96. Goff, *Confederate Supply*, 52, 54; Archibald Curry to Brother, July 6, 1862, folder 24, box 2, Curry Records, GSAL.

CHAPTER 3

1. *Memphis Daily Appeal*, February 9, 1862; Bettersworth, ed., *Mississippi in the Confederacy*, 301–2.

2. Diary, February 19, 1862, Parker (Huston Huling) Papers, MDAH; *Daily Picayune*, April 7, 1862; Bragg, *Louisiana in the Confederacy*, 77.

3. McPherson, *Battle Cry of Freedom*, 392–405; Pratt, *A Short History of the Civil War*, 52–64.

4. McPherson, *Battle Cry of Freedom*, 419–20; Pratt, *A Short History of the Civil War*, 98–102.

5. *Southern Confederacy*, April 29, 1862; *Richmond Daily Examiner*, April 30, 1862; Bourbon Plantation Record Book, 1862, January 12 and 29, 1862, Metcalf Family Papers, MDAH; Plantation and Account Book, January 1, 1862, folder 300, box 26, Rice (Nannie Herndon) Family Papers, MDAH; Diary, March 3 to 7, and 30, 1862, Parker (Huston Huling) Papers, MDAH; Allen (James) Plantation Book, April 5 and May 1, 1862, MDAH; *Natchez Weekly Courier*, March 5, 1862.

6. Alexander (Robert B.) Diary, February 11 and June 2, 1862, MDAH; *Arkansas True Democrat*, June 12, 1862; Account of Cotton Sales, March 11, 1862, Nutt Family Collection, MDAH; Allen (James) Plantation Book, April 26, 1862, MDAH; Bragg, *Louisiana in the Confederacy*, 126.

7. *Natchez Weekly Courier*, March 26, 1862; Anderson, ed., *Brokenburn*, 100–101.

8. Allen (James) Plantation Book, April 26, June 6, 9, 14, and 24, 1862, MDAH; Diary of Amanda Worthington of "Willoughby," Washington County, Mississippi, April 23 and May 12, 1862, Washington Family Letters, MDAH; Hamilton Smith to Dear Sir, May 2, 1862, Nutt Family Collection, MDAH; Alexander (Robert B.) Diary and Account Book, June 23, 1862, MDAH; J. E. Parker to Wilson Humphries, March 1, 1862, folder 3, box 1, Humphreys (George and Family) Papers, MDAH.

9. *Southern Confederacy*, May 10, 18, and 23, 1862; *OR*, Series 1, vol. 10, pt. 2, 451; Bettersworth, ed., *Mississippi in the Confederacy*, 218; Cotton Certificate No. 64, Madison

Parish, La., August 30, 1862, folder 10, box 1, Humphreys (George and Family) Papers, MDAH; Sutherland, *A Savage Conflict*, 73, 151.

10. Gates, *Agriculture and the Civil War*, 85; *Boston Herald*, July 1, 1862; *Southern Cultivator*, July–August 1862; *Richmond Daily Examiner*, May 19, 1862.

11. *Richmond Daily Examiner*, March 24 and June 11, 1862; *Southern Confederacy*, March 22 and 27, 1862.

12. Powell and Wayne, "Self-Interest and the Decline of Confederate Nationalism," 30.

13. Ruminski, "'Tradyville,'" 517; Powell and Wayne, "Self-Interest and the Decline of Confederate Nationalism," 34–35, 42.

14. Ruminski, "'Tradyville,'" 518, 523–24, 528–29; Sutherland, *A Savage Conflict*, 154.

15. *Weekly Mississippian*, February 26, 1862.

16. *Moore's Rural New Yorker*, May 17 and 31, 1862; Bragg, *Louisiana in the Confederacy*, 124, 150.

17. *Southern Confederacy*, July 18 and 19, 1862.

18. Ibid., July 18, 1862; *Moore's Rural New Yorker*, June 7 and 28 and August 2 and 16, 1862; Woodman, *King Cotton and His Retainers*, 219–20.

19. *Richmond Daily Examiner*, April 16, 1862; *Natchez Weekly Courier*, April 2, 1862; Bettersworth, *Confederate Mississippi*, 150.

20. Coulter, *The Confederate States of America*, 240; "Letters of Lieutenant Robert H. Miller to His Family," 66.

21. *Weekly Mississippian*, September 19, 1862.

22. *Southern Confederacy*, January 1, 1862; Allen (James) Plantation Book, March 25 and April 9, 1862, MDAH; *Natchez Weekly Courier*, March 26 and April 2, 1862.

23. *Natchez Weekly Courier*, April 2, 1862.

24. Ibid., March 5 and 26 and April 2, 1862; Diary of Amanda Washington of "Willoughby," Washington County, Mississippi, April 13, 1862, Washington Family Letters, MDAH.

25. Allen (James) Plantation Book, May 1, 1862, Nutt Family Collection, MDAH; Alexander (Robert B.) Diary and Account Book, July 13, 1862, MDAH; Evans (Dr. Holden Garthur) Diary, May 5, June 20, and November 20, 1862, MDAH; Anderson, ed., *Brokenburn*, 109; Gates, *Agriculture and the Civil War*, 120; Lang, "J. F. H. Claiborne at 'Laurel Wood' Plantation," 1–17.

26. *Moore's Rural New Yorker*, July 19 and August 16, 1862; Allen (James B.) Plantation Book, May 3, 10, and 11, 1862, MDAH; *New York Times*, August 16, 1862.

27. *Tri-Weekly Telegraph* (Houston), August 1 and 27, 1862.

28. *San Antonio Herald*, August 2, 1862; *Galveston Weekly News*, August 13, 1862; *Tri-Weekly Telegraph*, September 1, 1862; *Arkansas True Democrat*, October 8, 1862; *Austin State Gazette*, September 3, 1862.

29. Roland, "Difficulties of Civil War Sugar Planting in Louisiana," 40; Sitterson, *Sugar Country*, 207–8; Pace, "'It Was Bedlam Cut Lose,'" 396; Roland, *Louisiana Sugar Plantations*, 45–46.

30. Roland, "Difficulties of Civil War Sugar Planting in Louisiana," 49–58; Roland, *Louisiana Sugar Plantations*, 46–48, 63, 65; Pritchard, "Effect of the Civil War on the Louisiana Sugar Industry," 319; Sitterson, *Sugar Country*, 208.

31. Prichard, "Effects of the Civil War on the Louisiana Sugar Industry," 319; *New York Times*, May 23, 1862.

32. Price, "'Don't Fence Me In,'" 61–62; *Southern Confederacy*, April 1, 1862; *Richmond Daily Examiner*, April 18 and 24, 1862; Coulter, *The Confederate States of America*, 246.

33. Price, "'Don't Fence Me In,'" 62, 64–65; Surdam, "The Antebellum Texas Cattle Trade Across the Gulf of Mexico," 491.

34. *OR*, Series 1, vol. 16, pt. 1, 605, 358, 390 495; Blevins, *Cattle in the Cotton Fields*, 33; Pace, "'It Was Bedlam Let Loose,'" 392; H. W. Allen to C. D. Hamilton, November 27, 1862, Hamilton (Charles D. and Family) Papers, MDAH.

35. *Richmond Daily Examiner*, June 19, 1862; Diary of Amanda Washington of "Willoughby," Washington County, Mississippi, April 23 and 24 and July 25, 1862, Washington Family Letters, MDAH; *Memphis Daily Appeal*, July 9, 1862.

36. Diary, August 18, 1862, reel 1, folder 3, box 1, Robert H. Cantrell Papers, TSLA; B. Stevens to C. D. Hamilton, September 11, 1862, Hamilton (Charles D. and Family) Papers, MDAH; H. W. Allen to C. C. Hamilton, November 14, 1862, Hamilton (Charles D. and Family) Papers, MDAH.

37. Diary, October 1, 1862, reel 1, folder 4, box 1, Robert H. Cantrell Papers, TSLA; Diary, November 1862, no date given, reel 1, folder 3, box 1, Robert H. Cantrell Papers, TSLA; *Montgomery Weekly Advisor*, October 22, 1862.

38. *Memphis Daily Appeal*, September 27 and November 6, 1862; Gallagher, *The Confederate War*, 149.

39. *Weekly Mississippian*, January 14, 1862.

40. *Nashville Daily Union*, October 5 and 29, 1862; *Nashville Dispatch*, September 11 and October 5, 1862; Glatthaar, *General Lee's Army*, 178–79.

41. William Worthington to Samuel Worthington, February 8, 1862, Washington Family Papers, MDAH; Sallie B. McRae Diary, January 1, 1862, Special Collections, MML; Allen (James) Plantation Book, March 20 and July 10, 1862, MDAH; *Richmond Daily Examiner*, March 24, 1862; Diary, August 14, 1862, reel 1, folder 3, box 1, Robert H. Cantrell Papers, TSLA; Samuel Henderson Diary, November 13, 1862, TSLA.

42. Sitterson, *Sugar Country*, 215–18; Roland, *Louisiana Sugar Plantations*, 41, 50–55, 60–61, 89; Wade, *Sugar Dynasty*, 73; Allen (James) Plantation Book, November 10, 1862, MDAH.

43. Sitterson, *Sugar Country*, 208–9; Roland "Difficulties of Civil War Sugar Planting in Louisiana," 41; Wade, *Sugar Dynasty*, 67.

44. Rodrique, *Reconstruction in the Cane Fields*, 34; Wiley, *Southern Negroes*, 183–84.

45. Roland, *Louisiana Sugar Plantations*, 102; Rodrique, *Reconstruction in the Cane Fields*, 35; Sitterson, *Sugar Country*, 219.

46. Rodrique, *Reconstruction in the Cane Fields*, 37–38; Roland, *Louisiana Sugar Plantations*, 73–77, 103, 118.

47. McPherson, *The Negro's Civil War*, 128; Roland, *Louisiana Sugar Plantations*, 42–43.

48. *Southern Confederacy*, November 19, 1862.

49. Rainwater, ed., "Letters of James Lusk Alcorn," 198–201.

50. *OR*, Series 1, vol. 17, pt. 1, 532; Rainwater, ed., "Letters of James Lusk Alcorn," 198–201.

51. Farm Plantation Record and Account Book, December 4, 1862, folder 300, box 26, Rice (Nannie Herndon) Family Papers, MDAH; Ramsdell, *Behind the Lines in the Southern Confederacy*, 29–30, 39.

52. *Tri-Weekly Telegraph*, December 1 and 8, 1862; *The Ranchero*, December 11 and 25, 1862.

53. James, "Mississippi Agriculture," 135; Samuel Henderson Diary, November 21 and December 1, 1862, TSLA; *Natchez Daily Courier*, November 29, 1862.

54. Diary, December 1, 1862, reel 1, folder 4, box 1, Robert H. Cantrell Papers, TSLA; Wiley, *The Plain People of the Confederacy*, 65.

55. Recollections of My Life: An Autobiography by J. B. Killebrew, vol. 1, 1866, reel 1, folder 1, box 2, Joseph Buckner Killebrew Papers, TSLA; *Moore's Rural New Yorker*, December 27, 1862.

56. *Arkansas True Democrat*, December 17 and 24, 1862; Roland, *Louisiana Sugar Plantations*, 56.

57. McPherson, *Battle Cry of Freedom*, 579–82; Pratt, *A Short History of the Civil War*, 117–27.

58. Diary, December 1–2, 1862, reel 1, folder 3, box 1, Robert H. Cantrell Papers, TSLA.

CHAPTER 4

1. Crofts, ed., *Cobb's Ordeal*, 211; *Southern Confederacy*, January 14 and 18, 1863; *American Citizen*, February 14, 1863.

2. *Montgomery Weekly Advertiser*, February 11 and 18, 1863; *Moore's Rural New Yorker*, March 26, 1863.

3. *Richmond Daily Examiner*, January 22, 1863.

4. *Southern Confederacy*, January 3 and 18, February 1 and 3, 1863; Childs, ed., *The Private Journal of Henry William Ravenel*, 168; *Richmond Dispatch*, February 6, 1863; Thomas, *The Confederate State of Richmond*, 113.

5. *Richmond Daily Examiner*, January 9 and 11, 1863; *Richmond Dispatch*, February 12, 1863.

6. *Southern Cultivator*, May–June, 1863; Childs, ed., *The Private Journal of Henry William Ravenel*, 172, 176.

7. Jones, *A Rebel War Clerk's Diary*, vol. 1, 290, 294.

8. McPherson, *Battle Cry of Freedom*, 639–45; Pratt, *A Short History of the Civil War*, 175–85.

9. *New York Times*, May 1, 1863.

10. *Charleston Mercury*, March 5, 1863.

11. Yearns, *The Confederate Congress*, 131.

12. *Southern Confederacy*, April 4, 1863.

13. *Richmond Dispatch*, March 2, 1863; *Southern Confederacy*, April 4, 1863.

14. *Southern Cultivator*, May–June 1863.

15. Swanson, "Land of the Bright Leaf," 164, 173.

16. *Richmond Daily Examiner*, February 16 and 23, 1863; *Richmond Dispatch*, March 11, 1863; Crofts, ed., *Cobb's Ordeal*, 213; Scarborough, ed., *The Diary of Edmund Ruffin*, vol. 2, 594.

17. *Richmond Daily Examiner*, February 23, 1863; *Richmond Dispatch*, March 2, 1863; *Daily Southern Crisis*, March 21, 1863.

18. *Richmond Daily Examiner*, March 11, 1863; *Southern Daily Crisis*, March 21 and 30, 1863.

19. *Southern Confederacy*, February 17, 1863; Clinard and Russell, eds., *Fear in North Carolina*, 132.

20. *Richmond Daily Examiner*, March 2, 1863; Younger, ed., *Inside the Confederate Government*, 41; *Richmond Dispatch*, March 2, 1863; Crabtree and Patton, eds., *"Journal of a Secesh Lady,"* 368.

21. *Southern Confederacy*, April 9, 1863; Wiggins, ed., *The Journals of Josiah Gorgas*, 58; Younger, *Inside the Confederate Government*, 117; Childs, ed., *The Private Journal of Henry William Ravenel*, 174–75; Clinard and Russell, eds., *Fear in North Carolina*, 137, 141–42.

22. *Southern Cultivator*, January, February, March, and April 1863.

23. *Richmond Dispatch*, March 2, 1863; *Southern Confederacy*, March 8, 1863.

24. *Southern Confederacy*, March 10, 1863; *New York Times* March 19, 1863.

25. *Richmond Daily Examiner*, April 16, 1863.

26. *Natchez Daily Courier*, November 20, 1863.

27. *Southern Confederacy*, March 8 and April 11, 1863; *Richmond Daily Examiner*, April 17 and May 4, 1863.

28. Iobst, *Civil War Macon*, 277–78; *Weekly Columbus Enquirer*, April 7 and 21, 1863.

29. *Richmond Daily Examiner*, March 11, 1863; *Savannah Republican*, April 19, 1863.

30. *Southern Confederacy*, March 18, 1863.

31. *Richmond Daily Examiner*, April 4, 1863.

32. McCurry, *Confederate Reckoning*, 180; Brock, *Richmond during the War*, 209; Wiggins, *The Journals of Josiah Gorgas*, 59; Chesson, "Harlots or Heroines?," 134, 136; Thomas, *The Confederate State of Richmond*, 119.

33. Scarborough, ed., *The Diary of Edmund Ruffin*, vol. 2, 621, 625; *Richmond Daily Examiner*, April 4, 11 and 13, 1863; *Richmond Dispatch*, May 8, 1863; Blair, *Virginia's Private War*, 74.

34. *Richmond Daily Examiner*, April 14, 1863; *Richmond Dispatch*, April 13, 1863; *Southern Confederacy*, May 14, 1863; Thomas, *The Confederate State of Richmond*, 120–22; McCurry, *Confederate Reckoning*, 184.

35. McCurry, *Confederate Reckoning*, 214–17.

36. *Richmond Dispatch*, April 14 and May 8, 1863.

37. Thomas, *The Confederate State of Richmond*, 117–22; Chesson, "Harlots or Heroines?"; McCurry, *Confederate Reckoning*, 186–88, 190; Blair, *Virginia's Private War*, 75.

38. Chesson, "Harlots or Heroines?," 136. In January flour brought $20 to $25 per barrel, cornmeal $8.50 per bushel, butter $1.25 to $1.50 per pound, and sugar 25 to 75 cents per pound in Richmond.

39. McCurry, *Confederate Reckoning*, 175–79, 181, 189–91.

40. Aley, "'We are all good scavengers now,'" 89; Mobley, "War Governor of the South," 148–49; Escott, *Many Excellent People*, 65–66.

41. Mobley, "War Governor of the South," 148–49; Henry C. Wayne to Commander of the 33 Regiment, Georgia Militia, April 10, 1863, no. 15, 196–97, Adjutant General's Letter Book, GSLA.

42. *Clark County Journal*, April 9, 1863; *Richmond Dispatch*, April 20, 1863.

43. McCurry, *Confederate Reckoning*, 189–91.

44. *OR*, Series 1, vol. 2, 468, 476–77; McCurry, *Confederate Reckoning*, 192, 198–203, 205; Blair, *Virginia's Private War*, 76.

45. *Southern Confederacy*, May 14, 1863.

46. Goff, *Confederate Supply*, 85–87.

47. Todd, *Confederate Finance*, 141–42; Yearns, *The Confederate Congress*, 199.

48. Todd, *Confederate Finance*, 51–52, 141; Coulter, *The Confederate States of America*, 145–46, 179; Mohr, *On the Threshold of Freedom*, 142.

49. McCurry, *Confederate Reckoning*, 155, 167.

50. Todd, *Confederate Finance*, 142, 146; Yearns, *The Confederate Congress*, 199–200; Goff, *Confederate Supply*, 86; Ball, *Financial Failure and Confederate Defeat*, 232; Lerner, "Monetary and Fiscal Programs of the Confederate Government, 1861–65," 512–13; Gates, *Agriculture*

and the Civil War, 64, 70; Ambrose, "Yeoman Discontent in the Confederacy," 262. By June 1, 1864, incomplete records indicated that farmers in Georgia and Alabama tithed only 118,000 and 63,000 bushels of wheat, 972,000 and 1,059,000 bushels of corn, 56,150 and 40,600 bushels of potatoes, 232,000 and 150,000 pounds of bacon, and 3,000 and 19,000 pounds of pork, respectively.

51. *Southern Confederacy*, March 10, 1863; Younger, ed., *Inside the Confederate Government*, 41.

52. *Richmond Daily Examiner*, March 25, 1863; *Moore's Rural New Yorker*, May 2, 1863.

53. *Country Gentleman*, April 30, 1863; *New York Times*, March 18, 1863; *Indianapolis Daily Gazette*, May 20, 1863.

54. *Daily State Sentinel*, July 19, 1863; *Southern Confederacy*, May 22, 1863; *Richmond Daily Examiner*, June 4 and July 2, 7, and 21, 1863; *Richmond Dispatch*, June 10, 1863; Jones, *A Rebel War Clerk's Diary*, vol. 1, 358.

55. McPherson, *Battle Cry of Freedom*, 653–65; Pratt, *A Short History of the Civil War*, 190–208.

56. McWhiney, Moore, and Pace, eds., *"Fear God and Walk Humbly,"* 324; Clinard and Russell, eds., *Fear in North Carolina*, 144.

57. Jones, *A Rebel War Clerk's Diary*, vol. 2, 9–10, 35–36; Childs, ed., *The Private Journal of Henry William Ravenel*, 179; Account Book, October 24 and December 2, 1863, folder 23, Series 1.1, Civil War Correspondence, Graves Family Papers, SHC; *Natchez Weekly Courier*, November 3, 1863; *Richmond Daily Examiner*, September 4, 1863.

58. *Richmond Dispatch*, August 6 and 7; *Richmond Daily Examiner*, September 3 and 17, 1863.

59. *Richmond Daily Examiner*, August 11, 17, and 27, 1863.

60. *Richmond Dispatch*, September 24, 1863; *Richmond Daily Examiner*, October 3, 19, 21, and 29, 1863.

61. *OR*, Series 1, vol. 23, pt. 2, 674–75; *OR*, Series 1, vol. 30, pt. 4, 551–62; McWhiney, "The Revolution in Nineteenth-Century Alabama Agriculture," 22.

62. *OR*, Series 1, vol. 26, pt. 2, 163; Vandiver, "Texas and the Confederate Army's Meat Problem," 226–28; *OR*, Series 1, vol. 51, pt. 2, 738; Jones, *A Rebel War Clerk's Diary*, vol. 1, 385.

63. Ramsdell, "Robert E. Lee's Horse Supply," 761–63; Sharrer, *A Kind of Fate*, 14. By using the term "country" Lee meant Virginia.

64. For the relationship of disease and the environment to the health of soldiers see Meier, *Nature's Civil War*.

65. *OR*, Series 1, vol. 29, pt. 2, 664–65; Ramsdell, "Robert E. Lee's Horse Supply," 764–66; Sharrer, *A Kind of Fate*, 14, 16–17.

66. Glatthaar, *General Lee's Army*, 216–18; Ramsdell, "Robert E. Lee's Horse Supply," 10; Joseph A. Espey to Sister, July 8, 1863, folder 3, Joseph Espey Papers, SHC; Clinard and Russell, eds., *Fear in North Carolina*, 153.

67. *Natchez Daily Courier*, December 4, 1863; Levi Pitman Diary, December 4, 1863, LV; Sally Lyons Taliaferro Diary, September 1 and November 16, 1863, LV.

68. James Thomas Butler Diary, February 7, 1863, VHS; Jones, *A Rebel War Clerk's Diary*, vol. 1, 321; Younger, ed., *Inside the Confederate Government*, 41; *Richmond Daily Examiner*, March 14, 1863.

69. Governor Joseph Brown to Jefferson Davis, February 18, 1863, in Candler, ed., *Confederate Records of the State of Georgia*, vol. 3; *Official Correspondence of Governor Joseph E. Brown*, 328.

70. *Richmond Daily Examiner*, March 25, 1863.

71. Ibid.; E. Philips to Jane J. Philips, December 8, 1863, folder 2, box 1, Series 1, James Jones Philips Papers, SHC; Goff, *Confederate Supply*, 99.

72. Ramsdell, *Behind the Lines in the Southern Confederacy*, 76–78; Gates, *Agriculture and the Civil War*, 50–51; Hay, "Lucius B. Northrop," 13.

73. *Southern Cultivator*, July and August, 1863; Lebergott, "Why the South Lost," 70–71.

74. Gates, *Agriculture and the Civil War*, 42.

75. *Southern Cultivator*, November and December, 1863; E. Philips to Jane J. Philips, December 8, 1863, folder 2, box 1, Series 1, James Jones Philips Papers, SHC; Ayers, *In the Presence of Mine Enemies*, 374; Thomas, *The Confederate Nation*, 196.

76. *Moore's Rural New Yorker*, April 11, 1863; *Southern Cultivator*, May and June 1863; Monroe, ed., "The Road to Gettysburg," 504; Ambrose, "Yeomen Discontent in the Confederacy," 263.

77. Glatthaar, *General Lee's Army*, 179; Ambrose, "Yeoman Discontent in the Confederacy," 264, 267; Henry C. Wayne to William L. Ellison, June 1, 1863, no. 15, 551, Adjutant General Letter Book, GSAL; Henry C. Wayne to Colonel R. L. Storey, June 4, 1863, no. 15, 591, Adjutant General Letter Book, GSAL.

78. *Country Gentleman*, April 30 and May 7, 1863; Ayers, *In the Presence of Mine Enemies*, 373.

79. Mohr, *On the Threshold of Freedom*, 116; Greene, *Civil War Petersburg*, 119–20.

80. *Daily Southern Crisis*, February 6 and 26, 1863; Easterby, ed., *The South Carolina Rice Plantation*, 194, 426; *Indianapolis Daily Gazette*, June 17, 1863; Crofts, ed., *Cobb's Ordeal*, 216.

81. *Richmond Daily Examiner*, February 28, April 29, and October 17, 1863.

82. *Southern Confederacy*, March 15 and 22, and May 17, 1863; *Nashville Dispatch*, March 15, 1863; Easterby, ed., *The South Carolina Rice Plantation*, 194, 276, 426; Gunn, "Jarnell Plantation"; Samuel Henderson Diary, August 1, 1863, a32, TSLA; Iobst, *Civil War Macon*, 280.

83. Martinez, "For the Defense of the State," 103–4.

84. Ibid., 112–15.

85. Ibid., 116, 118–19.

86. Ibid., 125, 128, 131–33, 157; Henry C. Wayne to J. M. Hamilton, April 27, 1863, no. 15, 308–9, Adjutant General Letter Book, GSAL.

87. *OR*, Series 4, vol. 2, 553; Moore, *Conscription and Conflict in the Confederacy*, 73–75.

88. Gates, *Agriculture and the Civil War*, 75; Clinard and Russell, eds., *Fear in North Carolina*, 167, 173, 180; Glatthaar, *General Lee's Army* 297.

89. Range, *A Century of Georgia Agriculture*, 59; Gates, *Agriculture and the Civil War*, 35–36; *Weekly Columbus Enquirer*, March 3, 1863; *Southern Confederacy*, May 5, 1863; *New York Times*, March 18, 1863; *Southern Cultivator*, November and December, 1863.

90. *Southern Confederacy*, May 15, 1863; T. G. Trimmer to Mary L. Trimmer, May 12, 1863, Theodore G. Trimmer Papers, TSLA; Cornelius Danby Diary, January 1–31, 1863, SHC; B. H. Walker Diary, December 31, 1863, LV; Sally Lyons Taliaferro Diary, November 16, 1863, LV; *Moore's Rural New Yorker*, September 5, 1863; Hurt, *American Farm Tools*, 11–12.

91. Wiley, *Southern Negroes*, 208.

92. System of Labor to Be Pursued on the Plantation for the Year 1863, folder 2, David Franklin Thorpe Papers, SHC; Rose, *Rehearsal for Reconstruction*, 225; *New Orleans Times*, April 21, 1863.

93. Scarborough, ed., *The Diary of Edmund Ruffin*, vol. 2, 598; *Southern Confederacy*, April 29, 1863.

94. *New Orleans Times*, April 21, 1863; Rose, *Rehearsal for Reconstruction*, 272, 275. For a detailed discussion of land acquisition during Reconstruction see Rose.

95. Rose, *Rehearsal for Reconstruction*, 208–16, 272–75; Pearson, ed., *Letters from Port Royal*, 177–78.

96. Powell, *New Masters*, 1–7; *New Orleans Times*, March 21, 1864.

97. Powell, *New Masters*, 1–7.

98. *Natchez Daily Courier*, December 18, 1863; Rose, *Rehearsal for Reconstruction*, 285; Pearson, ed., *Letters from Port Royal*, 229–30. In January, 1865, General Sherman's Special Orders No. 15 cemented the idea that a free forty acres would be distributed to the families of the freedpeople upon the conclusion of the war.

99. *Richmond Daily Examiner*, September 1 and April 4, 1863; *Richmond Dispatch*, September 1, 1863; *New Orleans Times*, September 11, 1863.

100. *Richmond Dispatch*, September 24 and October 2 and 31, 1863; Childs, ed., *The Private Journal of Henry William Ravenel*, 185; *Richmond Daily Examiner*, October 1 and 17, 1863; *New York Times*, October, 17, 1863.

101. *Richmond Daily Examiner*, October 12, 19, 21, and 22, 1863; Chinard and Russell, eds., *Fear in North Carolina*, 163.

102. *Richmond Dispatch*, October 23 and November 6, 1863; *Richmond Daily Examiner*, November 19 and December 21, 1863; Jones, *A Rebel War Clerk's Diary*, vol. 2, 113–14. For comparative purposes Richmond prices in January were the following: butter was $1.25 per pound, flour $20 per 100-pound barrel, rice 10 cents per pound, cornmeal $3.50 per bushel, bacon 70 cents per pound, Irish potatoes $3.50 per bushel, and molasses $7 per gallon.

103. *Richmond Daily Examiner*, November 9, 10, and 12, 1863.

104. *OR*, Series 4, vol. 2, 943–44.

105. Ibid., 1066.

106. *Richmond Daily Examiner*, November 14, 1863; Yearns, *The Confederate Congress*, 200–201.

107. *Indianapolis Daily Evening Gazette*, December 1, 1863; *OR*, Series 1, vol. 31, pt. 3, 834; *OR*, Series 4, vol. 3, 414; Ambrose, "Yeoman Discontent in the Confederacy," 268.

108. Blair, *Virginia's Private War*, 107; Todd, *Confederate Finance*, 147; Range, *A Century of Georgia Agriculture*, 555; Gates, *Agriculture and the Civil War*, 47; Younger, ed., *Inside the Confederate Government*, 41; *Natchez Daily Courier*, November 3 and 20, 1863.

109. *Moore's Rural New Yorker*, December 12, 1863; Gates, *Agriculture and the Civil War*, 104; Thomas, *The Confederate Nation*, 200–201; Schlebecker, *Whereby We Thrive*, 155; Yearns, *The Confederate Congress*, 201.

110. Lerner, "Inflation in the Confederacy, 1861–65," 171; *Richmond Daily Examiner*, December 31, 1863; Crabtree and Patton, eds., *"Journal of a Secesh Lady,"* 513.

CHAPTER 5

1. Diary, January 8 and March 28, 1863, reel 1, folder 3, box 1, Robert H. Cantrell Papers, TSLA; Diary, January 14, 20, 28, 29, 30, and February 6 and 7, 1863, John Houston Bills Papers, SHC; Fonsylvania Plantation Diary, January 25 and 27, and February 3, 23, and 24, 1863, Parker (Huston Huling) Papers, MDAH; *Daily Southern Crisis*, February 5, 1863; Forbes

(Alden Spooner) Diary, March 20 and 21, 1863, MDAH; Alexander (Robert B.) Diary and Account Book, March 30 and April 6, 1863, MSDA; Allen (James) Plantation Book, March 3, 1863, MDAH.

2. *Nashville Dispatch*, January 21, February 1, and March 28, 1863.

3. *Weekly Mississippian*, February 11, 1863.

4. Ibid., March 11, 1863; *Daily Southern Crisis*, February 27 and March 3, 1863.

5. *Daily Southern Crisis*, March 12, 13, 14, 17, and 28, 1863.

6. *Southern Cultivator*, April 11, 1863; *Southern Confederacy*, April 2, 1863; *Country Gentleman*, April 30, 1863.

7. *Natchez Daily Courier*, March 17 and 18, 1863; Prichard, "Effects of the Civil War on the Louisiana Sugar Industry," 319–20.

8. Hepworth, *The Whip, Hoe, and Sword*, 92; Wade, *Sugar Dynasty*, 73, 76; Roland, *Louisiana Sugar Plantations*, 55, 58, 63, 66.

9. Root, ed., "Private Journal of William H. Root," 644, 651–52; *Southern Confederacy*, April 11, 1863; Pace, "Abandoning Self-Sufficiency," 279; Bettersworth, *Confederate Mississippi*, 152.

10. *Daily Southern Crisis*, February 21 and March 11, 1863; Bettersworth, ed., *Mississippi in the Confederacy*, 259; Fonsylvania Plantation Diary, February 1 and March 19 and 27, 1863, MDAH; Evans (Dr. Holden Garthur) Diary, March 14, 1863, MDAH; Bettersworth, *Confederate Mississippi*, 112.

11. *The Era*, February 15, 1863; *Southern Cultivator*, March and April 1863; *Texas Republican*, February 12, 1863.

12. Certificate, April 20, 1863, Office of the CSA, folder 10, box 1, Humphreys (George and Family) Papers, MDAH; *Daily Southern Crisis*, January 30, 1863; Alexander (Robert B.) Diary and Account Book, July 25 and 28, 1863, MDAH; Drennen (William Augustus) Dairy, Kept May 30 to July 4, 1863, pages 39 and 44, MDAH; Plantation Record and Account Book, August 1, 3, 1863, folder 300, box 26; Rice (Ronnie Herndon) Family Papers, MDAH; *Southern Confederacy*, February 23, 1863.

13. Price, "'Don't Fence Me In,'" 70; Surdam, "The Antebellum Texas Cattle Trade Across the Gulf of Mexico" 491.

14. Taylor, "Rebel Beef" 18, 22–23.

15. Diary, March 8, 1863, reel 1, folder 3, box 1, Robert H. Cantrell Papers, TSLA; Samuel Henderson Diary, February 10 and 13 and March 31, 1863, TSLA; Diary, March 13, 1863, John Houston Bills Papers, SHC; Nimrod Porter Diary and Note Book, November 7, 1863, TSLA; Whittington, ed., "Letters from John H. Ramsdell to Governor Thomas O. Moore," 497.

16. Alexander (Robert B.) Diary and Account Book, April 23 and 25, May 17, June 26 and 27, and December 5, 1863, MDAH; Diary and Account Book, February 12, 1863, Parker (Huston Huling) Papers, MDAH; Diary, Kept May 30 to July 4, 1863, 19, Drenner (William Augustus) Papers, MDAH; Sherman, ed., *The Sherman Letters*, 185.

17. Diary, January 14, February 10, 14, 17, March 14, and April 4 and 6, 1863, John Houston Bills Papers, SHC; Sutherland, *A Savage Conflict*, 178–79.

18. Diary, July 31, 1863, Downs (Lettie) Collection, MDAH; Fonsylvania Plantation Dairy, May 9, 24, 27, and 31, 1863, MDAH; W. W. Allen to C. D. Hamilton, March 11, 1863, Hamilton (Charles D. and Family) Papers, MDAH; Forbes (Alden Spooner) Diary, July 18, 1863, MDAH; W. M. Worthington to Sister, June 29, 1863, Worthington Family Papers, MDAH; *Nashville Daily Union*, February 11, 1863; Ash, *When the Yankees Came*, 93. See also Sutherland, *A Savage Conflict*.

19. Brady, *War upon the Land*, 56, 69–70; *OR*, Series 1, vol. 24, pt. 3, 156–57, 187, 437.

20. *Nashville Daily Union*, February 15, 1863; *Arkansas True Democrat*, February 18 and April 22, 1863.

21. *Arkansas True Democrat*, March 18 and April 4, 1863.

22. *Moore's Rural New Yorker*, April 18, 1863; Gallagher, *The Confederate War*, 161–62; Diary, May 7, 1863, John Houston Bills Papers, SHC.

23. Diary, May 7 and October 19, 1863, John Houston Bills Papers, SHC; Ash, *Middle Tennessee Society Transformed*, 85–89; Watson, ed., "Letters Home," 32–33; Gemant and Anderson, eds., "Documents: The Shelby Papers," 187, 189–90, 193; Nimrod Porter Diary and Notebook, June 28, 1863, TSLA; William. J. Rogers Diary, April 10, 1863, Roy Waterson Black Collection, SHC.

24. *OR*, Series 1, vol. 15, 1118; Pace, "'It Was Bedlam Let Loose,'" 393.

25. Pace, "'It Was Bedlam Let Loose,'" 393–94; *Moore's Rural New Yorker*, May 2, 1863; *Country Gentleman*, June 18, 1863; *Natchez Weekly Courier*, June 10, 1863.

26. Roland, *Louisiana Sugar Plantations*, 67, 68, 70; Grimsley, *The Hard Hand of War*, 158–59; Forbes (Alden Spooner) Diary, May 7, 1863, MDAH.

27. McPherson, *Battle Cry of Freedom*, 626–38; Pratt, *A Short History of the Civil War*, 208–17.

28. Gentry, "White Gold," 232–33; *OR*, Series 1, vol. 52, pt. 1, 331; *The Era*, March 23, 1863.

29. *Moore's Rural New Yorker*, March 21 and July 4, 1863; *The Era*, March 22 and April 24, 1863.

30. Ruminski, "'Tradyville,'" 512, 515–16, 529–30.

31. Ibid., 531; Powell and Wayne, "Self-Interest and the Decline of Confederate Nationalism," 33.

32. Powell and Wayne, "Self-Interest and the Decline of Confederate Nationalism," 34–35.

33. *Southern Confederacy*, May 2, 1863; Bettersworth, *Confederate Mississippi*, 185; O'Connor, "Lincoln and the Cotton Trade," 30.

34. *Daily Southern Crisis*, February 13, 1863.

35. Ibid.

36. *Weekly Mississippian*, October 23, 1863; *Natchez Daily Courier*, October 16, 1863.

37. Dattel, *Cotton and Race in the Making of America*, 203–5; Johnson, "Contraband Trade during the Last Year of the Civil War," 638, 642.

38. William J. Rogers Diary, April 10, 1863, Roy Waterson Black Collection, SHC; *Richmond Daily Examiner*, July 15, 1863; Potter and Robbins, eds., *Marching with the First Nebraska*, 149; Fonsylvania Plantation Diary, February 6 and March 9, 1863, MDAH; Forbes (Alden Spooner), Diary, March 27, 1863, MDAH; Cotton Plantation Account Book and Record, April 18, 1863, Parker (Huston Huling) Papers, MDAH; Diary, September 21, 1863, John Houston Bills Papers, SHC; *Memphis Daily Appeal*, June 24, 1863.

39. *Mobile Register and Advertiser*, May 10 and October 10, 1863; Theodore G. Trimmer to Mary L. Trimmer, May 12, 1863, Theodore G. Trimmer Papers, TSLA.

40. Diary, January 1, 10, 24, March 14, and May 18, 1863, John Houston Bills Papers, SHC; Forbes (Alden Spooner) Diary, July 10, 1863, MDAH; Fonsylvania Plantation Diary, May 30 and June 2, 1863, MDAH; Catherine Olivia Foster Diary, June 16, 1863, MDAH.

41. Bettersworth, *Confederate Mississippi*, 168; *Tri-Weekly Telegraph*, April 15 and 29, 1863.

42. Wiley, *Southern Negroes*, 87–89; Diary, October 8, 1863, John Houston Bills Papers, SHC; *Tri-Weekly Telegraph*, October 21 and November 7, 1863; Sitterson, *Sugar Country*, 215.

43. *The Era*, April 2, 1863.

44. Rodrique, *Reconstruction in the Cane Fields*, 39–43.

45. *OR*, Series 1, vol. 15, 667–68; Eiss, "A Share in the Land," 52–53; Sitterson, *Sugar Country*, 220; *The Era*, February 20, 1863; *Natchez Daily Courier*, May 20, 1863; Ripley, *Slaves and Freedmen in Civil War Louisiana*, 48–49; Wiley, *Southern Negroes*, 21–12; Gerteis, *From Contraband to Freedman*, 75–76.

46. *Natchez Weekly Courier*, May 20, 1863; Rodrique, *Reconstruction in the Cane Fields*, 40–41; Sitterson, *Sugar Country*, 221; Wiley, *Southern Negroes*, 212–13; Gerteis, *From Contraband to Freedman*, 79–80, 85.

47. Ripley, *Slaves and Freedmen in Civil War Louisiana*, 48–49; Gerteis, *From Contraband to Freedman*, 83–84.

48. *The Era*, April 5, 1863; *Moore's Rural New Yorker*, May 2, 18–63.

49. *Savannah Republican*, April 29, 1863; *The Era*, April 5 and 11, 1863.

50. *Louisville Daily Journal*, April 28, 1863.

51. Ripley, *Slaves and Freedmen in Civil War Louisiana*, 52–53, 71–72.

52. *Southern Confederacy*, May 15, 1863; Gerteis, *From Contraband to Freedman*, 122–23; Basford, "Federal Administration of Abandoned Plantations," 53–54.

53. *Southern Confederacy*, May 15, 1863; Wiley, *Southern Negroes*, 231.

54. *Natchez Weekly Courier*, September 22 and 29, 1863; Sitterson, *Sugar Country*, 221–22.

55. Basford, "Federal Administration of Abandoned Lands," 55, 57; Wiley, *Southern Negroes*, 241–42; Gates, *Agriculture and the Civil War*, 371.

56. Wiley, "Vicissitudes of Early Reconstruction Farming in the Lower Mississippi Valley," 442; Knox, *Camp-fire and Cotton-field*, 316.

57. McPherson, *Battle Cry of Freedom*, 676–81; Pratt, *A Short History of the Civil War*, 226–49.

58. Coulter, "Commercial Intercourse with the Confederacy in the Mississippi Valley," 384; *New Orleans Times*, September 27, October 10 and 16, and November 5, 1863; *New York Times*, October 10, 1863; *Moore's Rural New Yorker*, September 5, 1863.

59. *New Orleans Times*, October 22 and 31, 1863; *Richmond Daily Examiner*, November 9, 1863.

60. *Richmond Daily Examiner*, November 9, 1863; *New Orleans Times*, October 31, November 28, and December 10, 1863.

61. Bettersworth, *Confederate Mississippi*, 152; James, "Mississippi Agriculture," 130; Smith, *Mississippi in the Civil War*, 93; Woodman, *King Cotton and His Retainers*, 227; Watkins, *King Cotton*, 30; *Moore's Rural New Yorker*, November 28, 1863.

62. *Austin State Gazette*, July 27, 1863; *Galveston Weekly News*, October 7, 1863; *Semi-Weekly News*, June 7, 1863.

63. *New York Times*, December 9, 1863; *Country Gentleman*, September 9 and December 3, 1863.

64. Diary, December 24, 1863, John Houston Bills Papers, SHC; *Fort Smith New Era*, December 12, 1863; *Indianapolis Daily Gazette*, November 2, 1863; Diary, November 24 and December 31, 1863, Parker (Huston Huling) Papers, MDAH.

CHAPTER 6

1. E. Philips to James J. Philips, January 14, 1864, folder 2, box 1, Series 1, James Jones Philips Papers, SHC; M. J. Fulton to Pena ?, January 23, 1864, Thom Family Papers, VHS;

OR, Series 1, vol. 34, pt. 1, 1065–66; *Southern Banner*, January 5, 1864; Lebergott, "Why the Confederacy Lost," 69.

2. *Albany Patriot*, February 4, 1864.

3. Ibid., and June 3, 1864; Account Book, folder 23, Series 1.1 Civil War Correspondence, Graves Family Papers, SHC; Rogers, *Confederate Home Front*, 127; *Richmond Dispatch*, January 28, 1864; *Richmond Daily Examiner*, January 28, 1864; *Charleston Mercury*, February 2, 1864; Jones, *A Rebel War Clerk's Diary*, vol. 2, 259.

4. *Richmond Daily Examiner*, January 11 and 18, 1864; Childs, ed., *The Private Journal of Henry William Ravenel*, 191.

5. Childs, ed., *The Private Journal of Henry William Ravenel*, 193; *Southern Cultivator*, January 1864; Glatthaar, *General Lee's Army*, 355.

6. *Richmond Dispatch*, January 11, 1864.

7. *Southern Cultivator*, January 1864; *Richmond Daily Examiner*, January 19, 1864.

8. B. H. Walker Diaries, January 20, 1864, 55; *Richmond Daily Examiner*, January 4, 1864; *Richmond Dispatch*, January 8, 1864; *Richmond Whig*, January 8 and 16, 1864; Westover Plantation Journal of John A. Seldon, January 4 and 20, 1864, SHC.

9. *Richmond Whig*, January 1 and February 20, 1864; *Richmond Daily Examiner*, January 8, 1864; Childs, ed., *The Private Journal of Henry William Ravenel*, 193; Rable, *Civil War Years*, 96–97.

10. Candler, *The Confederate Records of the State of Georgia*, vol. 3, 60–61.

11. Jones, *A Rebel War Clerk's Diary*, vol. 2, 126, 133; Childs, ed., *The Private Journal of Henry William Ravenel*, 196; Wineman, "Trains, Canals, and Railroads," 73–74; *Richmond Daily Examiner*, February 11 and 25 and March 7, 1864; *Richmond Dispatch*, March 3, 1864. In January Richmond prices were $110 per barrel for flour, $11 to $12 per bushel for corn, $15 per bushel for cornmeal, $4.50 to $5.00 per pound for butter, and $2.50 per dozen for eggs.

12. *Southern Cultivator*, March 1864.

13. Jones, *A Rebel War Clerk's Diary*, vol. 2, 178, 188; *Richmond Daily Examiner*, March 14 and 31, 1864; *Southern Cultivator*, March 1864.

14. *Southern Banner*, February 4, 1864; Margaret Espy to Joseph Espy, March 10, 1864, folder 3, Joseph Espy Papers, SHC; Clinard and Russell, eds., *Fear in North Carolina*, 200.

15. E. Philips to James H. Philips, February 23, 1864, folder 2, box 1, Series 1, James Jones Philips Papers, SHC; F. Nins to Horace, February 21, 1864, folder 13a, Nims, Rankin, and Sprott Family Papers, SHC; Todd, *Confederate Finance*, 112–14; Lerner, "Monetary and Fiscal Programs of the Confederate Government," 521–22; McKinney, *Zeb Vance*, 207; Lerner, "Money, Prices, and Wages in the Confederacy," 24. West of the Mississippi River the new exchange rate did not begin until July 1.

16. *Richmond Whig*, March 15, 1864; *Richmond Daily Examiner*, February 29, 1864.

17. Bleser, ed., *Secret and Sacred*, 293; Rogers, Jr., *Confederate Home Front*, 72; Younger, ed., *Inside the Confederate Government*, 142; E. Philips to James H. Philips, February 23, 1864, folder 2, box 1, Series 1, James Jones Philips Papers, SHC.

18. *Southern Cultivator*, September 1864.

19. Coulter, *The Confederate States of America*, 180; Todd, *Confederate Finance*, 147–48; Yearns, *The Confederate Congress*, 212–13.

20. *Richmond Dispatch*, March 3, 1864; *Charleston Mercury*, April 7, 1864.

21. Aley, "'We are all good scavengers now,'" 92–93; Jones, *A Rebel War Clerk's Diary*, vol. 2, 164, 168–70, 189; *Southern Confederacy*, April 25, 1864.

22. *Richmond Daily Examiner*, April 29, 1864; Jones, *A Rebel War Clerk's Diary*, vol. 2, 170; Wiggins, ed., *The Journals of Josiah Gorgas*, 97; *Richmond Dispatch*, April 29, 1864; *Southern Confederacy*, April 30, 1864.

23. Jones, *A Rebel War Clerk's Diary*, vol. 2, 193, 203, 209, 217; Crofts, ed., *Cobb's Ordeal*, 230.

24. *Southern Cultivator*, January 1864.

25. Gates, *Agriculture and the Civil War*, 40; Mohr, *On the Threshold of Freedom*, 95; OR, Series 1, vol. 53, pt. 2, 667.

26. *Richmond Daily Examiner*, May 11, 1864; *The Era*, June 12, 1864.

27. OR, Series 4, vol. 3, 37; Bushman, *In Old Virginia*, 225.

28. OR, Series 4, vol. 3, 249–50, 1169–70; Goff, *Confederate Supply*, 173–75.

29. OR, Series 4, vol. 3, 249–50; *Southern Cultivator*, May and April 1864.

30. Gates, *Agriculture and the Civil War*, 49; Crofts, *Cobb's Ordeal*, 225; Jones, *A Rebel War Clerk's Diary*, vol. 2, 217, 247, 259; OR, Series 4, vol. 3, 1172.

31. *Richmond Daily Examiner*, April 15, 1864.

32. Ibid.

33. OR, Series 4, vol. 3, 501–2.

34. Wiley, *The Plain People of the Confederacy*, 22–23; Glatthaar, *General Lee's Army*, 356–57; Ash, "White Virginians under Federal Occupation," 180–81.

35. Range, *A Century of Georgia Agriculture*, 61–62; Gray, Jr., "March to the Sea," 113.

36. Brady, *War upon the Land*, 97–98, 101–3, 107, 124–25; Harwell and Racine, eds., *The Fiery Trial*, 47; Nichols, The Story of the Great March, 81.

37. McPherson, *Battle Cry of Freedom*, 724–33; Pratt, *A Short History of the Civil War*, 328–34.

38. *Richmond Dispatch*, June 15 and 24, 1864; Ash, *When the Yankees Came*, 92.

39. Duncan, *Lee's Endangered Left*, 10, 188, 218; Gallagher, "Shenandoah Valley in 1864," 1–18; Duncan, *Beleaguered Winchester*, 196–97, 199–200.

40. OR, Series 1, vol. 37, pt. 2, 301; Duncan, *Beleaguered Winchester*, 209–10; Thomas "'Nothing Ought to Astonish Us,'" 237–38, 240; Brady, *War upon the Land*, 78–80, 82, 85.

41. OR, Series 1, vol. 43, pt. 1, 37; Duncan, *Beleaguered Winchester*, 212–16; Thomas, "'Nothing Ought to Astonish Us,'" 249, Brady, *War upon the Land*, 85–86, 88, 91–92.

42. OR, Series 1, vol. 43, pt. 1, 43, 816, 818; Duncan, *Beleaguered Winchester*, 209–10; Thomas, "'Nothing Ought to Astonish Us,'" 237–38, 240; Lehman and Nolt, *Mennonites, Amish, and the American Civil War*, 203, 207; Holcomb, ed., *Southern Sons, Northern Soldiers*, 153; Wittenberg, ed., *Custer's Wolverines*, 120–21.

43. OR, Series 1, vol. 43, pt. 1, 30, 37; Sharrer, *A Kind of Fate*, 200; Brady, *War upon the Land*, 85–86, 88, 91–92.

44. Duncan, *Beleaguered Winchester*, 201–2, 244.

45. *Richmond Dispatch*, June 7, 1864; *Southern Cultivator*, June 1864; Blair, *Virginia's Private War*, 104.

46. *Richmond Daily Examiner*, June 29, 1864; Sally Lyons Taliaferro Diary, June 18, 1864, LV.

47. OR, Series 1, vol. 42, pt. 2, 1151–53.

48. *Richmond Daily Examiner*, July 5, 1864; *Richmond Dispatch*, July 6, 1864; *Memphis Daily Appeal*, July 1, 1864; *Albany Patriot*, July 28, 1864; Gates, *Agriculture and the Civil War*, 43; *Richmond Whig*, July 22, 1864.

49. *Richmond Whig*, January 1, 1864; Gates, *Agriculture and the Civil War*, 91; Hamilton, ed., *The Papers of Thomas Ruffin*, vol. 3, 350, 401, 427; *Southern Cultivator*, March, 1864.

50. Taylor, "Rebel Beef," 25–30.

51. *Richmond Daily Examiner*, April 26, 1864; Ramsdell, "General Robert E. Lee's Horse Supply," 768.

52. *Richmond Whig*, August 6, 1864; Ramsdell, "General Lee's Horse Supply," 771–73; Glatthaar, *General Lee's Army*, 445–46.

53. Moore, *Conscription and Conflict in the Confederacy*, 83–89; *Laws of Congress in Regard to Taxes, Currency and Conscription, Passed February 1864*, 29–34, http://docsouth.unc.edu/imls/lawsofcong.html (September 2, 2012); *OR*, Series 4, vol. 3, 250–51; Blair, *Virginia's Private War*, 104.

54. *OR*, Series 4, vol. 3, 250–51; Blair, *Virginia's Private War*, 104.

55. Gates, *Agriculture and the Civil War*, 75; Gallagher, *The Confederate War*, 54; *Southern Cultivator*, March 1864; Aley, "'We are all good scavengers now,'" 88; Wiggins, *The Journals of Josiah Gorgas*, 92.

56. Scarborough, ed., *The Diary of Edmund Ruffin*, vol. 3, 306–7.

57. L. H. Briscoe to Lt. A. B. Pittman, August 16, 1864, no. 25, 355, Adjutant General's Letter Book, GSAL; L. H. Briscoe to Maj. John H. Jones, October 22, 1864, no. 27, 112, Adjutant General's Letter Book, GSAL; Ambrose, "Yeoman Discontent in the Confederacy," 267.

58. *Charlestown Mercury*, February 9, 1864; Crofts, *Cobb's Ordeal*, 245, 278; *Richmond Whig*, January 5, 1864; *Richmond Daily Examiner*, January 2, 1864.

59. Coulter, *The Confederate States of America*, 222; *Richmond Daily Examiner*, September 24, 1864; Crofts, *Cobb's Ordeal*, 234.

60. *The Era*, December 7, 1864.

61. Henry C. Wayne to Gen. Joseph E. Johnston, January 29, 1864, no. 21, 341, Adjutant General's Letter Book, GSAL.

62. Gates, *Agriculture and the Civil War*, 25; Mohr, *On the Threshold of Freedom*, 95; Ash, "White Virginians under Federal Occupation," 185.

63. Ash, "White Virginians under Federal Occupation," 187; Sarah to William, July 3, 1864, folder 1, William Smith King Papers, SHC; Bushman, *In Old Virginia*, 228.

64. Rose, *Rehearsal for Reconstruction*, 290, 296, 298; Wiley, *Southern Negroes*, 200, 208–10; *OR*, Series 3, vol. 4, 721–23.

65. McPherson, *The Negro's Civil War*, 128; Gerteis, *From Contraband to Freedman*, 48, 58.

66. *Richmond Daily Examiner*, August 3, 1864; *Richmond Dispatch*, August 2 and 27 and September 9 and 12, 1864.

67. *Richmond Daily Examiner*, September 19, 1864.

68. *Southern Cultivator*, November 10, 1864; Levi Pitman Diaries, October 8, 1864, LV.

69. *Richmond Daily Examiner*, October 5, 1864.

70. Easterby, ed., *The South Carolina Rice Plantation*, 200–201, 203–4, 310; Dethloff, *A History of the American Rice Industry*, 56–57.

71. Lunt, *A Woman's War-Time Journal*, 34–41; Range, *A Century of Georgia Agriculture*, 63, 65–66.

72. Todd, *Confederate Finance*, 60–61.

73. *Richmond Daily Examiner*, November 12 and 14, 1864; Lerner, "Inflation in the Confederacy," 171.

74. *Richmond Daily Examiner*, December 3, 1864.

75. Ibid., December 24, 1864.

76. Bryant, *How Curious a Land*, 12–63; Crofts, ed., *Cobb's Ordeal*, 276, 278; L. W. to Brother, December 2, 1864, folder 13a, Nims, Rankin, and Sprott Family Papers, SHC; Gates, *Agriculture and the Civil War*, 40; Wight, "Some Letters of Lucius Bellinger Northrop," 73.

77. McWhiney, Moore, and Pace, eds., *"Fear God and Walk Humbly,"* 344.

CHAPTER 7

1. Evans (Dr. Holden Garthur) Diary, January 1, 1864, MDAH; *The Era*, January 3, 13 and 28 and February 6, 1864; *New Orleans Times*, January 5, 1864.

2. *New Orleans Times*, January 10, 1864; *The Era*, February 6, 1864.

3. *New Orleans Times*, February 17 and 22, 1864.

4. Ramsdell, "General Robert E. Lee's Horse Supply," 776; Roland, *Louisiana Sugar Plantations*, 77–78; Nichols, *The Confederate Quartermaster in the Trans-Mississippi West*, 87–88; Bettersworth, ed., *Mississippi in the Confederacy*, 213.

5. *New Orleans Times*, January 20, 1864.

6. Dairy, February [?], 1864, John Houston Bills Papers, SHC.

7. Diary, April 30, 1864, reel 1, folder 6, box 1, and June 1, 1864, reel 1, folder 7, box 1, Robert H. Cantrell Papers, TSLA; *New Orleans Times*, May 12, 1864.

8. *Southern Cultivator*, January 1864; *Charleston Mercury*, October 25, 1864.

9. *The Era*, March 23, 1864; *OR*, Series 1, vol. 34, pt. 2, 227–31; Ripley, *Slaves and Freedmen in Civil War Louisiana*, 56.

10. *The Era*, February 27 and June 25, 1864; *OR*, Series 1, vol. 34, pt. 2, 227–31.

11. *The Era*, February 22, 1864; Sitterson, *Sugar Country*, 224–25; *OR*, Series 1, vol. 34, pt. 2, 227–31.

12. *OR*, Series 1, vol. 34, pt. 2, 227–31; Sitterson, *Sugar Country*, 224–26; Rodrique, *Reconstruction in the Cane Fields*, 45–46.

13. Eiss, "A Share in the Land, 55–57; Sitterson, *Sugar Country*, 225–26.

14. Gerteis, *From Contraband to Freedman*, 80; *The Era*, February 22, 1864; Rodrique, *Reconstruction in the Cane Fields* 50; Wiley, *Southern Negroes*, 248–49.

15. Gerteis, *From Contraband to Freedman*, 90; Ripley, *Slaves and Freedmen in Civil War Louisiana*, 57, 59–61.

16. Wiley, *Southern Negroes*, 216; Sitterson, *Sugar Country*, 223.

17. *The Era*, March 23, 1864.

18. Ibid., September 28, 1864.

19. Ibid., October 21 and November 28, 1864.

20. Ibid., December 28, 1864.

21. Wiley, *Southern Negroes*, 184, 222–23.

22. Forbes (Alden Spooner) Diary, March 1, 1864, MDAH; Evans (Dr. Holden Garthur) Diary, March 5 and 22, 1864, MDAH; *The Era*, March 3 and 17, 1864; *New Orleans Times*, March 12 and 30, 1864.

23. *New Orleans Times*, March 10 and April 16, 26, and 28, 1864; *Natchez Daily Courier*, April 18, 1864.

24. Prichard, "The Effects of the Civil War on the Louisiana Sugar Industry," 320; *The Era*, March 18, 1864.

25. Alexander (Robert B.) Diary and Account Book, May 20, 1864, MDAH; *The Era*, February 26 and March 9, 1864.

26. Forbes (Alden Spooner) Diary, March 28, 1864, MDAH; Alexander (Robert B.) Diary and Account Book, April 19, May 14 and 30, 1864, MDAH; *The Era*, April 13, 1864; Bettersworth, ed., *Mississippi in the Confederacy*, 290.

27. Evans (Dr. Holden Garthur) Dairy, May 1 and June 11 and 27, 1864, MDAH; *New Orleans Times*, June 1, 20, and 29, and August 2, 1864; Roberts, "Federal Government and Confederate Cotton," 268; *The Era*, June 9 and 29 and July 29 and 30, 1864.

28. Alexander (Robert B.) Diary and Account Book, January 4 and February 19, 1864, MDAH; Bragg, *Louisiana in the Confederacy*, 196–97; Sitterson, *Sugar Country*, 214; Nimrod Porter Diary and Notebook, January 13 and February 24, 1864, TSLA; OR, Series 1, vol. 39, pt. 3, 788–89.

29. *Nashville Daily Union*, July 22, 1864.

30. *Fort Smith New Era*, February 20 and March 4 and 5, 1864; Gates, *Agriculture and the Confederacy*, 51.

31. *New Orleans Times*, March 12, 1864; Wiley, *The Plain People of the Confederacy*, 22–23.

32. Holcomb, ed., *Southern Sons, Northern Soldiers*, 116, 118, 131.

33. Dear Father and Mother from Elizabeth, July 29, 1864, Beach Letters (Elizabeth Jane), MDAH.

34. Nichols, *The Confederate Quartermaster in the Trans-Mississippi West*, 75; OR, Series 1, vol. 34, pt. 4, 638.

35. OR, Series 1, vol. 38, pt. 4, 481.

36. *The Era*, January 30, 1864; *New Orleans Times*, February 26, 1864; OR, Series 1, vol. 32, pt. 2, 522–23; *Fort Smith New Era*, May 7, 1864; *The Era*, February 6, 1864.

37. *New Orleans Times*, January 30 and February 6, 1864.

38. OR, Series 4, vol. 3, 292–83, 646–48; Ruminski, "'Tradyville,'" 526–27, 531; Powell and Wayne, "Self-Interest and the Decline of Confederate Nationalism," 39, 41–45.

39. Gentry, "White Gold," 237–38; Johnson, *Red River Campaign*, 47, 50, 76–78, 267–70; *The Era*, May 4, 1864; *New Orleans Times*, March 29, 1864; Woodman, *King Cotton and His Retainers*, 223.

40. Woodman, *King Cotton and His Retainers*, 223.

41. *New Orleans Times*, April 4, 5, 11, and 22, and May 27, 1864.

42. *The Era*, September 21, 1864.

43. OR, Series 1, vol. 48, pt. 2, 1049–50; Wiley, "Vicissitudes of Early Reconstruction Farming," 444–45; Roberts, "Federal Government and Confederate Cotton," 270.

44. Nimrod Porter Diary and Notebook, September 15, 1864, TSLA; Roland, "Difficulties of Civil War Sugar Planting in Louisiana," 44–47. Although Johnston made this conscription proclamation, the Confederate Congress did not pass a law authorizing conscription for blacks or army service in "whatever capacity" until March 7, 1865. For a copy of that law see *Harper's Weekly*, March 25, 1865, 179.

45. *The Era*, October 14 and 15, 1864.

46. Nimrod Porter Diary and Notebook, November 28, December 2, 5, and 7, 1864, TSLA; Diary, March 18, 1864, reel 1, folder 6, box 1, Robert H. Cantrell Papers, TSLA; Alexander

(Robert B.) Diary and Account Book, October 10, 1864, MDAH; Gates, *Agriculture and the Civil War*, 52–53; Nichols, *The Confederate Quartermaster in the Trans-Mississippi West*, 105.

47. McPherson, *Battle Cry of Freedom*, 811–15; Pratt, *A Short History of the Civil War*, 354–66.

48. *The Era*, December 9, 1864.

49. Gates, *Agriculture and the Civil War*, 105–7; *The Era*, December 13 and 17, 1864.

50. Vandiver, "Texas and the Confederate Army's Meat Problem," 232; *The Era*, December 4, 1864.

51. Plantation Record and Account Book, June 19, August 16, October 4 and 20, 1864, folder 300, box 26, Rice (Nannie Herndon) Family Papers, MDAH; Receipt for Corn Payment by CSA, September 20, 1864, folder 4, Tom White Crigler Papers, Special Collections, MML; Gates, *Agriculture and the Civil War*, 121, Bettersworth, ed., *Mississippi in the Confederacy*, 213.

52. Ash, *When the Yankees Came*, 94; Gates, *Agriculture and the Civil War*, 21.

53. Evans (Dr. Holden Garther) Diary, November 31, 1864, MDAH; Nimrod Porter Diary and Notebook, December 31, 1864, TSLA.

CHAPTER 8

1. Wiggins, ed., *The Journals of Josiah Gorgas*, 147; Smith, *Starving the South*, 197; Recollections of My Life: An Autobiography by J. B. Killebrew, vol. I, 1866, reel 1, folder 1, box 2, Joseph Buckner Killebrew Papers, TSLA.

2. McWhiney, Moore, and Pace, eds., *"Fear God and Walk Humbly,"* 345–46; Spencer, *The Last Ninety Days of the War in North Carolina*, 29; *OR*, Series 1, vol. 46, pt. 2, 1035, 1143; Sellers, "Economic Incidence of the Civil War in the South," 179–80.

3. *Southern Banner*, January 25, 1865; Otto, *Southern Agriculture during the Civil War Era*, 42–43; Jones, *A Rebel War Clerk's Diary*, vol. 2, 386, 406, 408, 414, 417, 433, 447, 453, 457–58; *Albany Patriot*, February 23, 1865; Plantation Book, January 4, 1865, folder 300, box 26, Rice (Nannie Herndon) Family Papers, MDAH; *Austin State Gazette*, February 1, 1865; Lerner, "Money, Prices, and Wages in the Confederacy, 1861–1865," 24; Lerner, "Inflation in the Confederacy," 163, 171; Gates, *Agriculture and the Civil War*, 53.

4. *Southern Cultivator*, February, 1865; *Southern Confederacy*, February 5, 1865; Otto, *Southern Agriculture during the Civil War Era*, 45.

5. *Southern Confederacy*, February 5, 1865; Ash, *Middle Tennessee Society Transformed*, 88; *Southern Cultivator*, February 1865.

6. *Southern Confederacy*, February 5, 1865; *Prairie Farmer*, April 22, 1865.

7. *Southern Cultivator*, February 1865; Goff, *Confederate Supply*, 17; Taylor, "Rebel Beef: Florida Cattle and the Confederate Army," 31; Vandiver, "Texas and the Confederate Army's Meat Problem," 231; *OR*, Series 1, vol. 46, pt. 2, 1222, 1232–33; William Nalle Diary, April 14, 1865, VHS.

8. *OR*, Series 1, vol. 46, pt. 2, 1, 190–91, 1208; *OR*, Series 4, vol. 3, 1087–89; Ramsdell, "General Robert E. Lee's Horse Supply," 775–77.

9. *OR*, Series 4, vol. 3, 1087–89; *Southern Cultivator*, February 1865; Goff, *Confederate Supply*, 237–38; Ramsdell, "General Robert E. Lee's Horse Supply," 766; *OR*, Series 1, vol. 46, pt. 2, 1232–33, 1242–43.

10. Sharrer, *A Kind of Fate*, 9–10, 17–18; Report of the Commissioner of Agriculture, 1866, 333.

11. Nimrod Porter Diary and Notebook, March 26, April 13, and June 1, 1865, TSLA; Christman, ed., *The South As It Is*, 69.

12. *OR*, Series 1, vol. 46, pt. 2, 1210; *Southern Cultivator*, February 1865; Hay, "Lucius B. Northrop," 19.

13. Ibid., Series 4, vol. 3, 1170–71.

14. Ibid., 1172–73.

15. Ibid., 1169–73; Ramsdell, ed., *Laws and Joint Resolutions of the Last Session of the Confederate Congress*, 151–53; Hay, "Lucius B. Northrop," 19; Goff, *Confederate Supply*, 173–75; Childs, ed., *The Private Journal of Henry William Ravenel*, 211, 214.

16. Crabtree and Patton, eds., *"Journal of a Secesh Lady,"* 691–92.

17. *OR*, Series 1, vol. 47, pt. 3, 83–84; Nimrod Porter Diary and Account Book, January 11, 16, 17, 19, March 27 and April 2, 1865; Forbes (Alden Spooner) Diary, February 28, 1865, MDAH; Alexander (Robert A.) Diary and Account Book, April 29, 1865, MDAH; *OR*, Series 1, vol. 46, pt. 2, 931; *OR*, Series 1, vol. 49, pt. 1, 485–87; Spencer, *The Last Ninety Days of the War in North Carolina*, 43, 174.

18. Roberts, "Federal Government and Confederate Cotton," 266; *OR*, Series 1, vol. 32, pt. 1, 183, 185, 320, and pt. 3, 36.

19. Ramsdell, ed., *Laws and Joint Resolutions of the Last Session of the Confederate Congress*, 113–15.

20. Nimrod Porter Diary and Account Book, March 24, 1865, TSLA; Jones, *A Rebel War Clerk's Diary*, vol. 2, 430; *OR*, Series 1, vol. 46, pt. 2, 445.

21. *Weekly Intelligencer*, April 19, 1865; Diary, October 16, 1865, John Houston Bills Papers, SHC.

22. Diary, June 21, 1865, Robert H. Cantrell Papers, TSLA; *Weekly Intelligencer*, June 7 and July 1, 1865.

23. *OR*, Series 1, vol. 48, pt. 2, 503, 640; *Natchez Daily Courier*, June 27, 1865.

24. *Weekly Intelligencer*, April 19, 1865; Escott, *Many Excellent People*, 66–67; Thomas, *The Confederate Nation*, 300; McPherson, *Battle Cry of Freedom*, 848–51; Pratt, *A Short History of the Civil War*, 383–86.

25. Charles Baker Fields Diary, April 8, 19, 20, 22, 25, 28, June 1, 2, and July 11, 1865, VHS.

26. *Natchez Daily Courier*, May 11, 1865; Sitterson, "Transition from Slave to Free Economy," 224; Cornelius Dabney Diary, August 5, 1865, SHC.

27. Andrews, *The South Since the War*, 36.

28. William Nalle Diary, March 29, April 17 and 18, 1865, VHS; Samuel Henderson Diary, November 20 and 25, 1865, TSLA; Sharrer, *A Kind of Fate*, 31–32; *New York Times*, August 9, 1865.

29. Glatthaar, *General Lee's Army*, 452–53; Diary, January 28, 1865, John Houston Bills Papers, SHC; *Weekly Intelligencer*, July 26, 1865.

30. Coulter, "The Movement for Agricultural Reorganization in the Cotton South," 12; *Austin State Gazette*, February 1, 1865; *Weekly Intelligencer*, April 12 and 19, 1865.

31. Bragg, *Louisiana in the Confederacy*, 219–20.

32. McWhiney, Moore, and Pace, eds., *"Fear God and Walk Humbly,"* 347, 615; Easterby, ed., *The South Carolina Rice Plantation*, 329–30.

33. Younger, ed., *Inside the Confederate Government*, 209, 214; Johns, *Florida during the Civil War*, 212–13.

34. Dattel, *Cotton and Race in the Making of America*, 243–45; Mohr, *On the Threshold of Freedom*, 95–96.

35. Easterby, ed., *The South Carolina Rice Plantation*, 210; Childs, ed., *The Private Journal of Henry William Ravenel*, 219; Woolfolk, ed., *The Journals of Josiah Gorgas*, 175.

36. McWhiney, Moore, and Pace, eds., *"Fear God and Walk Humbly,"* 350–51; *Daily Picayune*, July 4, 1865; Christman, ed., *The South As It Is*, 82–84.

37. Easterby, ed., *The South Carolina Rice Plantation*, 354–55.

38. Sitterson, "Transition from Slave to Free Economy," 221–22; Roland, *Louisiana Sugar Plantations*, 138.

39. Ash, *Middle Tennessee Society Transformed*, 139; Plantation Book, March 28, 1865, folder 300, box 26, Rice (Nannie Herndon) Papers, MDAH.

40. McBride (J. A.) Contract, August 12, 1865, MDAH; Receipts for Labor, folder 123, box 8, McArn (Duncan) and Family Papers, MDAH; Certificate of Indenture, December 26, 1865, folder 3, vol. 1, Humphreys (George and Family) Papers, MDAH.

41. Gerteis, *From Contraband to Freedman*, 94–95.

42. Plantation Book, March 28, 1865, folder 300, box 26, Rice (Nannie Herndon) Family Papers, MDAH; Gerteis, *From Contraband to Freedman*, 164–65, 169.

43. Roland, *Louisiana Sugar Plantations*, 114–15; *OR*, Series 1, vol. 48, pt. 1, 1146–48; Rodrique, *Reconstruction in the Cane Fields*, 51–55.

44. Bragg, *Louisiana in the Confederacy*, 214; Ripley, *Slaves and Freemen in Civil War Louisiana*, 70–73, 75.

45. *OR*, Series 1, vol. 48, pt. 1, 1147–48.

46. Rose, *Rehearsal for Reconstruction*, 337–38.

47. Ibid., 346, 348, 350; see also McKitrick, *Andrew Johnson and Reconstruction*, 49, 146–47.

48. Abbott, "Free Land, Free Labor, and the Freedmen's Bureau," 151–52; Pearson, ed., *Letters from Port Royal*, 314.

49. Rose, *Rehearsal for Reconstruction*, 350–51, 353–54, 357; Pearson, ed., *Letters from Port Royal*, 318; Howard, *Autobiography of Oliver Otis Howard*, 238–40.

50. Pearson, ed., *Letters from Port Royal*, 316–17.

51. Abbott, "Free Land, Free Labor, and the Freedmen's Bureau," 151; Cox, "Promise of Land for the Freedmen," 413; Gates, *Agriculture and the Civil War*, 190–91; *Weekly Intelligencer*, September 9, 1865. The Act to Establish a Bureau for the Relief of Freedmen and Refugees, approved March 3, 1865, mandated that freedmen must be paid for agricultural work, and they could not be subjected to corporal punishment. If full compensation was not made, they would receive half of the crop.

52. *Weekly Intelligencer*, July 26, 1865.

53. Ransom and Sutch, *One Kind of Freedom*.

54. O'Donovan, *Becoming Free in the Cotton South*, 111–13.

55. Ibid., 119–20, 126, 130–33, 136, 143–45.

56. Hahn, Miller, O'Donovan, Rodrique, and Rowland, eds., *Freedom*, Series 3, vol. 1, 309–11.

57. Ibid., 319–20, 222, 324–25.

58. O'Donovan, *Becoming Free in the Cotton South*, 159; Foner, *Reconstruction*, 86, 135, 165–67. For contract examples see Hahn, Miller, O'Donovan, Rodrique, and Rowland, eds., *Freedom*, 341–92.

59. Foner, *Reconstruction*, 53–57, 59–66.

60. Ibid., 173–74.

61. Ibid., 68–69, 71, 134.

62. Ibid., 158–59, 161, 164.

63. Childs, ed., *The Private Journal of Henry William Ravenel*, 248–49; Christman, ed., *The South As It Is*, 13–15; *Weekly Intelligencer*, July 26, 1865.

64. *Weekly Intelligencer*, August 9 and September 6, 1865.

65. Ibid., August 9, 1865; *Weekly Tribune*, August 9, 1865.

66. *New York Times*, August 9, 1865; Diary, May 7, 1865, John Houston Bills Papers, SHC.

67. E. W. Nims to Willie, October 30, 1865, folder 14, Nims, Rankin, and Sprott Family Papers, SHC; Jones, *The Dispossessed*, 13–14.

68. Towbridge, *The South*, 408, 411; Rodrique, *Reconstruction in the Cane Fields*, 63–64, 67; Dattel, *Cotton and Race in the Making of America*, 222; Carter, *When the War Was Over*, 147–75; Garner, *Reconstruction in Mississippi*, 134; Jones, *The Dispossessed*, 28.

69. Wiley, *Southern Negroes*, 236.

70. *New Orleans Price Current*, November 14 and December 22, 1865; James (?) Watt & Co. to Duncan McArn, December 23, 1865, folder 35, box 3 McArn, (Duncan) and Family Papers, MDAH; Rodrique, *Reconstruction in the Cane Fields*, 60.

71. Richard Seargent (?) to C. B. Hamilton, November 27, 1865, Hamilton (Charles B.) and Family Papers, MDAH; Gates, *Agriculture and the Civil War*, 107, 371; Watkins, *King Cotton*, 30.

72. Towbridge, *The South*, 566; Shugg, *Origins of Class Struggle in Louisiana*, 191–93; Nimrod Porter Diary and Account Book, March 17 and 24, and April 6, 1865, TSLA.

73. Roland, *Louisiana Sugar Plantations*, 26–30; Diary, December 31, 1865, folder 12, James Clarence Harper Papers, SHC; Crabtree and Patton, eds., "Journal of a Secesh Lady," 725.

74. Ash, *Middle Tennessee Society Transformed*, 232–33, 239–40; Wiggins, ed., *The Journals of Josiah Gorgas*, 194; Diary, May 11, 1865, John Houston Bills Papers, SHC.

EPILOGUE

1. Easterby, ed., *The South Carolina Rice Plantation*, 216; Crofts, ed., *Cobb's Ordeal*, 283, 285, 289.

2. Pace, "Overwhelmed by the Storm," 8; Rose, *Rehearsal for Reconstruction*, 325.

3. Dethloff, *A History of the American Rice Industry*, 62; *Weekly Intelligencer*, May 2, 1866; *Ninth Census*, vol. 3, *The Statistics of the Wealth and Industry of the United States*, 1870, 83, 87; Tuten, *Lowcountry Time and Tide*, 24–25.

4. Swanson, "Land of the Bright Leaf," 188, 190–201, 234.

5. *Ninth Census*, vol. 3, 83, 88; Hahn, *Making Tobacco Bright*, 76–80; Kerr-Ritchie, *Freedpeople in the Tobacco South*, 5, 15, 94–95, 134, 137.

6. Sitterson, *Sugar Country*, 226, 233; Gates, *Agriculture and the Civil War*, 371; Prichard, "Effects of the Civil War on the Louisiana Sugar Industry," 321–22; Pace, "'It Was Bedlam Let Loose,'" 402; Heitmann, *The Modernization of the Louisiana Sugar Industry*. An arpent is a French measurement of land that equals .85 acre.

7. *Ninth Census*, vol. 3, 85; Pace, "'It Was Bedlam Let Loose,'" 404; Roberts, "Federal Government and Confederate Cotton," 255, 275; Heitmann, *The Modernization of the Louisiana Sugar Industry*, 26–32, 64; Prichard, "Effects of the Civil War on the Louisiana Sugar Industry," 330; Shugg, *Origins of Class Struggle in Louisiana*, 193–94.

8. Lebergott, "Through the Blockade," 883–84; Watkins, *King Cotton*, 30. The cotton crop harvested in 1878–79 produced 5 million bales.

9. Dattel, *Cotton and Race in the Making of America*, 164, 222–23, 244–45; Report of the Commissioner of Agriculture, 1874, 217; Fite, *Cotton Fields No More*, 1–29.

10. Andrews, *The South Since the War*, 36–37; Pace, "Abandoning Self-Sufficiency," 282; Fite, *Cotton Fields No More*, 1–29.

11. *Historical Statistics of the United States, 1789–1945*, 211–24; Watkins, *King Cotton* 30; *Ninth Census*, vol. 3, 83, 88; *Weekly Intelligencer*, January 10 and June 20, 1866.

12. Blevins, *Cattle in the Cotton Fields*, 31; McWhiney, "Revolution in Nineteenth-Century Alabama Agriculture," 21; *Ninth Census*, vol. 3, 75, 82.

13. *Ninth Census*, vol. 3, 75–83, 87; Sellers, "Economic Incidence of the Civil War in the South," 184–89. The 1860 census numbers include the portion of Virginia that became West Virginia in 1863.

14. Sharrer, *A Kind of Fate*, 18.

15. Report of the Commissioner of Agriculture, 1867, 98–100; Sharrer, *A Kind of Fate*, 20–22.

16. Crawford, "Cotton, Land, and Sustenance," 246–47.

17. Ramsdell, *Behind the Lines in the Southern Confederacy*, 40–41.

18. Bryant, *How Curious a Land*, 12–63; *Ninth Census*, vol. 3, 81, 341.

19. *Ninth Census*, vol. 3, 340–41.

20. Report of the Commissioner of Agriculture, 1867, 105–6, 114, 119.

21. Ransom and Sutch, *One Kind of Freedom*, 81–82; *Weekly Intelligencer*, August 8, 1866. For a detailed county breakdown of land values, see Report of the Commissioner of Agriculture, 1867, 102–19.

22. *Ninth Census*, vol. 3, 86, 340–41; Report of the Commissioner of Agriculture, 1871, 49.

23. Shugg, "Survival of the Plantation System in Louisiana," 312, 319, 325; Engerman and Gallman, "Civil War Economy," 237; Shugg, *Origins of Class Struggle in Louisiana*, 236–37, 246, 261; Wright, *Old South, New South*, 49; Recollections of My Life: An Autobiography by J. B. Killebrew, vol. 1, 1866, reel 1, box 2, 191, Joseph Buckner Killebrew Papers, TSLA.

24. Sellers, "Economic Incidence of the Civil War in the South," 182; Woodman, "Post-Civil War Southern Agriculture and the Law," 319–37; Woodman, *King Cotton and His Retainers*, 295–314; McDonald and McWhiney, "South from Self-Sufficiency to Peonage," 1095–1118; Taylor, ed., "Post-Bellum Southern Rental Contracts," 122–23; Wetherington, *The New South Comes to Wiregrass Georgia*, 274, 301–2.

25. Berlin, Miller, and Rowland, "Afro-American Families in the Transition from Slavery to Freedom," 111–12.

26. Ibid., 112–13.

27. Black, "The Railroads of Georgia in the Confederate War Effort," 534; Goff, *Confederate Supply*, 225.

28. Goff, *Confederate Supply*, 234–35; OR, Series 1, vol. 45, pt. 2, 737–38.

29. Sellers, "Economic Incidence of the Civil War in the South," 189–91.

30. Blair, *Virginia's Private War*, 114.

31. Ibid., 109, 117–18.

32. Ibid., 109, 135.

33. Ibid., 115.

34. Brady, *War upon the Land*, 125, 131; Goff, *Confederate Supply*, 242.

Bibliography

ARCHIVAL COLLECTIONS

Georgia State Archives and Libraries, Atlanta
    Adjutant General's Letter Books
    Curry Hill Plantation Records
Library of Virginia, Richmond
    J. D. G. Brown Personal Papers
    Eber Jones Personal Papers
    J. S. Newman Personal Papers
    Levi Pitman Diaries
    Horatio Ross Riddle Diary
    Sally Lyons Taliaferro Diary
    B. H. Walker Diary
Mississippi Department of Archives and History, Jackson
    Alexander (Robert B.) Diary and Account Book
    Allen (James) Plantation Book
    Beach Letter (Elizabeth Jane)
    Downs (Lettie) Collection
    Drennen (William Augustus) Papers
    Evans (Dr. Holden Garthur) Diary
    Fonsylvania Plantation Diary
    Forbes (Alden Spooner) Diary
    Catherine Elizabeth Foster Diary
    Hamilton (Charles D. and Family) Papers
    Hughes (William and Family) Papers
    Humphreys (George and Family) Papers
    McArn (Duncan) and Family Papers
    McBride (J. A.) Contract
    Metcalf Family Papers
    Nutt Family Collection
    Parker (Huston Huling) Papers
    Rice (Nannie Herndon) Family Papers
    Rollins (Mrs. Roy) Papers
    Washington Family Letters
    Wheless (Frederick W.) Plantation Journal
    Worthington Family Letters

Mississippi State University, Special Collections, Mitchell Memorial Library, Starkville
    Bell (Rachel) Letter
    Tom White Crigler Papers
    McRae (Sallie B.) Diary
Tennessee State Library and Archives, Nashville
    Robert H. Cantrell Papers
    John Henry Dent Farm Journals and Account Book
    Samuel Henderson Diary
    Joseph Buckner Killebrew Papers
    Martin Family Memoirs
    Nimrod Porter Diary and Notebook
    Theodore G. Trimmer Papers
University of North Carolina, Southern Historical Collection, Chapel Hill
    John Houston Bills Papers
    Roy Watterson Black Collection
    Cornelius Danby Diary
    Louis M. DeSaussure Journal
    C. D. Epps Papers
    Joseph Espey Papers
    Graves Family Papers
    James Clarence Harper Papers
    Solomon Hilary Helsabeck Papers
    John Kimberly Papers
    William Smith King Papers
    Nims, Ranking, and Sproot Family Papers
    James Jones Philips Papers
    Philip Henry Pitts Papers
    William Porter Letters
    E. H. Riggan Account Book
    John R. Shurley Diary
    Spears and Hicks Family Papers
    Steed and Phipps Family Papers
    David Frank Thorpe Papers
    William Henry Tripp and Araminta Guilford Tripp Papers
    Westover Plantation Journal of John A. Seldon
Virginia Historical Society Library and Manuscript Collections, Richmond
    James Thomas Butler Diary
    Robert Young Conrad Papers
    Charles Baker Fields Diary
    George Bolling Lee Papers
    William Nalle Diary
    Littleton Tazewell Robertson Papers
    Thom Family Papers
    Theodore G. Trimmer Papers
    John Augustine Washington Letter

PUBLISHED DOCUMENTS

Agriculture of the United States in 1860. Washington, D.C.: Government Printing Office, 1864.
Annual Report of the Commissioner of Patents on Agriculture, 1861. Washington, D.C.: Patent Office, Department of the Interior, 1862.
Chandler, Alan D., ed. *Confederate Records of the State of Georgia.* 6 vols. Atlanta: Charles P. Byrd, State Printer, 1909–11; reprint, New York: AMS Press, Inc., 1972.
Historical Statistics of the United States, 1789–1945. Washington, D.C.: Government Printing Office, 1949.
Laws of Congress in Regard to Taxes, Currency and Conscription, Passed February 1864. Richmond: James E. Good State Printer, 1864.
Ninth Census of the United States. 3 vols. Washington, D.C.: Government Printing Office, 1872.
Official Records of the Union and Confederate Armies. 70 vols. Washington, D.C.: Government Printing Office, 1880–1901.
Population of the United States in 1860. Washington, D.C.: Government Printing Office, 1864.
Ramsdell, Charles W., ed. *Laws and Joint Resolutions of the Last Session of the Confederate Congress (November 7, 1864–March 18, 1865) Together with the Secret Acts of Previous Congresses.* Durham, N.C.: Duke University Press, 1941.
Report of the Commissioner of Agriculture for the Year 1866. Washington, D.C.: Department of Agriculture, 1866.
Report of the Commissioner of Agriculture for the Year 1867. Washington, D.C.: Government Printing Office, 1868.
Report of the Commissioner of Agriculture for the Year 1871. Washington, D.C.: Government Printing Office, 1872.
Report of the Commissioner of Agriculture for the Year 1874. Washington, D.C.: Government Printing Office, 1875.
Report of the Secretary of the Treasury. Treasury Department C.S.A., Richmond, November 7, 1864. http://galenet.gale (accessed June 14, 2012).
Richardson, James D. *A Compilation of the Messages and Papers of the Confederacy Including Diplomatic Correspondence, 1861–1865.* 2 vols. Nashville: United States Publishing Company, 1906.

NEWSPAPERS AND PERIODICALS

Alamo Express (San Antonio, Tex.)
Albany Patriot (Ga.)
American Citizen (Canton, Miss.)
Arkansas True Democrat (Little Rock)
Austin State Gazette (Tex.)
Bellville Countryman (Tex.)
Boston Herald (Mass.)
Charleston Mercury (S.C.)
Clarke County Journal (Ala.)
Columbus Enquirer (Ga.)
Columbus Times (Ga.)
Constitutional (Alexandria, La.)
Country Gentleman (Rochester, N.Y.)
Daily Chronicle and Sentinel (Augusta, Ga.)
Daily Constitutionalist (Augusta, Ga.)
Daily Picayune (New Orleans, La.)
Daily Southern Crisis (Jackson, Miss.)
Dallas Herald (Tex.)
Fort Smith New Era (Ark.)
Galveston Weekly News (Tex.)
Genesee Farmer (Rochester, N.Y.)
Harper's Weekly (New York, N.Y.)

Houston Telegraph (Tex.)
Indiana State Sentinel
Louisville Daily Journal (Ky.)
Memphis Daily Appeal (Tenn., and Grenada, Miss.)
Mobile Register and Advertiser (Ala.)
Montgomery Weekly Advertiser (Ala.)
Moore's Rural New Yorker (Rochester)
Nashville Daily Union (Tenn.)
Nashville Dispatch (Tenn.)
Natchez Daily Courier (Miss.)
Natchez Weekly Courier (Miss.)
New Orleans Era (La.)
New Orleans Price Current (La.)
New Orleans Times (La.)
New York Daily Tribune
New York Herald
New York Times
Ranchero (Corpus Christie, Tex.)
Richmond Daily Examiner (Va.)
Richmond Dispatch (Va.)
Richmond Whig (Va.)
San Antonio Herald (Tex.)
Savannah Republican (Ga.)
Semi-Weekly News (San Antonio, Tex.)
Southern Banner (Athens, Ga.)
Southern Confederacy (Atlanta, Ga.)
Southern Cultivator (Atlanta Ga.)
Southern Watchman (Athens, Ga.)
Standard (Clarksville, Tex.)
Texas Republican (Marshall)
Times (New Orleans, La.)
Tri-Weekly Alamo Express (San Antonio, Tex.)
Tri-Weekly Telegraph (Houston, Tex.)
Tyler Reporter (Tex.)
Weekly Columbus Enquirer (Ga.)
Weekly Intelligencer (Atlanta, Ga.)
Weekly Mississippian (Jackson, Miss.)
Wisconsin Farmer

BOOKS AND ARTICLES

Abbott, Martin. "Free Land, Free Labor, and the Freedmen's Bureau." *Agricultural History* 30 (October 1956): 150–56.

——, ed. "A Southerner Views the South, 1865: Letters of Harvey M. Watterson." *Virginia Magazine of History and Biography* 68 (October 1960): 478–89.

Aley, Ginette. "'Uncertainties and alarms': Women and Families on Virginia's Home Front." In *Virginia at War, 1865*, edited by William C. Davis and James I. Robertson Jr., 15–38. Lexington: University Press of Kentucky, 2012.

——. "'We are all good scavengers now': The Crisis in Virginia Agriculture during the Civil War." In *Virginia at War, 1864*, edited by William C. Davis and James I. Robertson Jr., 81–98. Lexington: University Press of Kentucky, 2009.

Ambrose, Stephen E. "Yeomen Discontent in the Confederacy." *Civil War History* 8 (September 1962): 259–68.

Anderson, John Q., ed. *Brokenburn: The Journal of Kate Stone, 1861–1868*. Baton Rouge: Louisiana State University Press, 1955.

Andrews, Sidney. *The South Since the War: As Shown by Fourteen Weeks of Travel and Observations in Georgia and the Carolinas*. Boston: Ticknor and Fields, 1866.

Ash, Stephen V. *Middle Tennessee Society Transformed, 1860–1870: War and Peace in the Upper South*. Knoxville: University of Tennessee Press, 2006.

——. *When the Yankees Came: Conflict and Chaos in the Occupied South, 1861–1865*. Chapel Hill: University of North Carolina Press, 1995.

——. "White Virginians under Federal Occupation, 1861–1865." *Virginia Magazine of History and Biography* 98 (April 1990): 169–92.

———. *A Year in the South: 1865, The True Story of Four Ordinary People Who Lived Through the Most Tumultuous Twelve Months in American History.* New York: Palgrave Macmillan, 2002.

Ayers, Edward L. *In the Presence of Mine Enemies: War in the Heart of America, 1859–1863.* New York: W. W. Norton & Co., 2003.

Ball, Douglas B. *Financial Failure and Confederate Defeat.* Urbana: University of Illinois Press, 1991.

Barnes, Elinor, and James A. Barnes, eds. *Naval Surgeon: Blockading the South, 1862–1866: The Diary of Dr. Samuel Pellman Boyer.* 3 vols. Bloomington: Indiana University Press, 1963.

Berlin, Ira, Barbara J. Fields, Thavolia Glymph, Joseph P. Reidy, and Leslie S. Rowland, eds. *Freedom: A Documentary History of Emancipation, 1861–1865.* Series 1, vol. 1. Cambridge: Cambridge University Press, 1985.

Berlin, Ira, Steven F. Miller, and Leslie S. Rowland. "African American Families in the Transition from Slavery to Freedom." *Radical History Review* 42 (1988): 89–121.

Bettersworth, J. K. *Confederate Mississippi: The People and Policies of a Cotton State in Wartime.* Baton Rouge: Louisiana State University Press, 1943; reprint, Philadelphia: Porcupine Press, 1978.

———, ed. *Mississippi in the Confederacy: As They Saw It.* Baton Rouge: Louisiana State University Press, 1961.

Black, Robert C., III. *The Railroads of the Confederacy.* Chapel Hill: University of North Carolina Press, 1952.

———. "The Railroads of Georgia in the Confederate War Effort." *Journal of Southern History* 13 (November 1947): 511–34.

Blair, William. *Virginia's Private War: Feeding Body and Soul in the Confederacy, 1861–1865.* New York: Oxford University Press, 1998.

Bleser, Carol, ed. *Secret and Sacred: The Diaries of James Henry Hammond, a Southern Slaveholder.* New York: Oxford University Press, 1988.

Blevins, Brooks. *Cattle in the Cotton Fields: A History of Cattle Raising in Alabama.* Tuscaloosa: University of Alabama Press, 1998.

———. "Cattle Raising in Antebellum Alabama." *Alabama Review: A Quarterly Journal of Alabama History* 51 (October 1998): 266–91.

Boritt, Gabor, and Scott Hancock, eds. *Slavery, Resistance, Freedom.* New York: Oxford University Press, 2007.

Brady, Lisa. *War upon the Land: Military Strategy and the Transformation of Southern Landscapes during the American Civil War.* Athens: University of Georgia Press, 2012.

Bragg, Jefferson Davis. *Louisiana in the Confederacy.* Baton Rouge: Louisiana State University Press, 1941.

Brock, Sally A. *Richmond during the War: Four Years of Personal Observation.* New York: G. W. Carleton & Co., 1867.

Bryan, T. Conn. *Confederate Georgia.* Athens: University of Georgia Press, 1953.

Bryant, Jonathan M. *How Curious a Land: Conflict and Change in Greene County, Georgia, 1850–1885.* Chapel Hill: University of North Carolina Press, 1996.

Bushman, Claudia L. *In Old Virginia: Slavery, Farming, and Society in the Journal of John B. Walker.* Baltimore: Johns Hopkins University Press, 2002.

Cameron, Scott, ed. *History of the 90th Ohio Volunteer Infantry in the War of the Great Rebellion in the United States, 1861 to 1865.* Kent, Ohio: Black Squirrel Books, 2006.

Campbell, Randolph B., and Richard G. Lowe. "Some Economic Aspects of Antebellum Texas Agriculture." *Southwestern Historical Quarterly* 82 (April 1979): 351–78.

Carter, Dan T. *When the War Was Over: The Failure of Self-Reconstruction in the South, 1865–1868.* Baton Rouge: Louisiana State University Press, 1985.

Cathey, Cornelius O. "The Impact of the Civil War on Agriculture in North Carolina." *Studies in Southern History* 39 (1957): 97–110.

Chesson, Michael B. "Harlots or Heroines? A New Look at the Richmond Bread Riot." *Virginia Magazine of History and Biography* 92 (April 1984): 131–75.

Childs, Arney Robinson, ed. *The Private Journal of Henry William Ravenel, 1859–1887.* Columbia: University of South Carolina Press, 1947.

Christman, Henry M., ed., *The South As It Is, 1865–1866.* New York: Viking Press, 1965.

Clinard, Karen L., and Richard Russell, eds. *Fear in North Carolina: The Civil War Journals and Letters of the Henry Family.* Asheville, N.C.: Reminiscing Books, 2008.

Connor, Forrest P. "Letters of Lieutenant Robert H. Miller to His Family, 1861–1862." *Virginia Magazine of History and Biography* 70, Part 1 (January 1962): 62–91.

Coulter, E. Merton. "Commercial Intercourse with the Confederacy in the Mississippi Valley, 1861–1865." *Mississippi Valley Historical Review* 5 (March 1919): 377–95.

———. *The Confederate States of America, 1861–1865.* Baton Rouge: Louisiana State University Press, 1950.

———. "Effects of Secession upon the Commerce of the Mississippi Valley." *Mississippi Valley Historical Review* 3 (December 1916): 275–300.

———. "The Movement for Agricultural Reorganization in the Cotton South during the Civil War." *Agricultural History* 1 (January 1927): 3–17.

———. "Planters' Wants in the Days of the Confederacy." *Georgia Historical Quarterly* 12 (March 1928): 38–52.

Coulter, Nate. "The Impact of the Civil War upon Pulaski County, Arkansas." *Arkansas Historical Quarterly* 41 (Spring 1982): 67–82.

Cox, Lawanda. "The Promise of Land for the Freedmen." *Mississippi Valley Historical Review* 45 (December 1958): 413–40.

Crabtree, Beth G., and James W. Patton, eds. *"Journal of a Secesh Lady": The Diary of Catherine Ann Devereux Edmondston, 1860–1866.* Raleigh, N.C.: Division of Archives and History, Department of Cultural Resources, 1979.

Crawford, George B. "Cotton, Land, and Sustenance: Toward the Limits of Abundance in Late Antebellum Georgia." *Georgia Historical Quarterly* 72 (Summer 1978): 215–47.

Crofts, Daniel W., ed. *Cobb's Ordeal: The Diaries of a Virginia Farmer, 1842–1872.* Athens: University of Georgia Press, 1997.

Dattel, Gene. *Cotton and Race in the Making of America: The Human Costs of Economic Power.* Latham, Md.: Ivan Dee, 2009.

DeLeon, Thomas Cooper. *Four Years in Rebel Capitals.* Mobile, Ala., 1890; reprint, New York: Collier Books, 1962.

Dethloff, Henry C. *A History of the American Rice Industry, 1865–1985.* College Station: Texas A&M University Press, 1988.

Duncan, Richard R. *Beleaguered Winchester: A Virginia Community at War, 1861–1865*. Baton Rouge: Louisiana State University Press, 2007.

———. *Lee's Endangered Left: The Civil War in Western Virginia, Spring of 1864*. Baton Rouge: Louisiana State University Press, 1998.

Easterby, J. H., ed. *The South Carolina Rice Plantation as Revealed in the Papers of Robert F. W. Allston*. Chicago: University of Chicago Press, 1945.

Edwards, Laura F. *Scarlett Doesn't Live Here Anymore: Southern Women in the Civil War Era*. Urbana: University of Illinois Press, 2000.

Eiss, Paul K. "A Share in the Land: Freedpeople and the Government of Labour in Southern Louisiana, 1862–65." *Slavery and Abolition* 19 (April 1998): 46–89.

Engerman, Stanley L., and J. Matthew Gallman. "The Civil War Economy: A Modern View." In *On the Road to War: The American Civil War and the German Wars of Unification, 1861–1871*, edited by Stig Förster and Jörg Nagler, 217–47. Washington, D.C.: German Historical Institute, 1997.

Escott, Paul D. *Many Excellent People: Power and Privilege in North Carolina, 1850–1900*. Chapel Hill: University of North Carolina Press, 1985.

———. "Poverty and Governmental Aid for the Poor in Confederate North Carolina." *North Carolina Historical Review* 61 (October 1984): 462–80.

———, ed. *North Carolina Yeoman: The Diary of Basil Armstrong Thomasson, 1853–1862*. Athens: University of Georgia Press, 1996.

Faust, Drew Gilpin. *Mothers of Invention: Women of the Slaveholding South in the American Civil War*. Chapel Hill: University of North Carolina Press, 1996.

Fite, Gilbert C. *Cotton Fields No More: Southern Agriculture, 1865–1880*. Lexington: University Press of Kentucky, 1984.

Fogel, Robert W., and Stanley L. Engerman. "The Relative Efficiency of Slavery: A Comparison of Northern and Southern Agriculture in 1860." *Explorations in Economic History* 8 (Spring 1971): 353–67.

Follett, Richard. *The Sugar Masters: Planters and Slaves in Louisiana's Cane World, 1820–1860*. Baton Rouge: Louisiana State University Press, 2005.

Foner, Eric. *Reconstruction: America's Unfinished Revolution, 1863–1877*. New York: Harper & Row, 1988.

Freehling, William W. *The Reintegration of American History: Slavery and the Civil War*. New York: Oxford University Press, 1994.

Gallagher, Gary W. *The Confederate War*. Cambridge: Harvard University Press, 1997.

———. "The Shenandoah Valley in 1864." In *Struggle for the Shenandoah: Essays on the 1864 Valley Campaign*, edited by Gary W. Gallagher, 1–18. Kent, Ohio: Kent State University Press, 1991.

———, ed. *The Shenandoah Valley Campaign of 1864*. Chapel Hill: University of North Carolina Press, 2006.

Garner, James Wilfred. *Reconstruction in Mississippi*. New York: MacMillan, 1901.

Gates, Paul Wallace. *Agriculture and the Civil War*. New York: Alfred A. Knopf, 1965.

Gemant, Sophie S., and Fanny J. Anderson, eds. "Documents: The Shelby Papers." *Indiana Magazine of History* 44 (June 1948): 181–98.

Genovese, Eugene. "Livestock in the Slave Economy: A Revised View." *Agricultural History* 36 (July 1962): 143–49.

Gentry, Judith F. "White Gold: The Confederate Government and Cotton in Louisiana." *Louisiana History* 33 (Summer 1992): 229–40.

Gerteis, Louis S. *From Contraband to Freedman: Federal Policy toward Southern Blacks, 1861–1865.* Westport, Conn.: Greenwood Press, 1973.

Glatthaar, Joseph T. *General Lee's Army: From Victory to Collapse.* New York: Free Press, 2008.

Goff, Richard D. *Confederate Supply.* Durham, N.C.: Duke University Press, 1969.

Gray, Tom S. "The March to the Sea." *Georgia Historical Quarterly* 14 (June 1930): 111–38.

Greene, A. Wilson. *Civil War Petersburg: Confederate City in the Crucible of War.* Charlottesville: University of Virginia Press, 2006.

Grimsley, Mark. *The Hard Hand of War: Union Military Policy toward Southern Civilians, 1861–1865.* Cambridge: Cambridge University Press, 1995.

Hahn, Barbara. *Making Tobacco Bright: Creating an American Commodity, 1617–1937.* Baltimore: Johns Hopkins University Press, 2011.

Hahn, Steven, Steven F. Miller, Susan E. O'Donovan, John C. Rodrique, and Leslie S. Rowland, eds. *Freedom: A Documentary History of Emancipation, 1861–1867.* Series 3, vol. 1. Chapel Hill: University of North Carolina Press, 2008.

Hamilton, J. G. de Roulhac. *The Papers of Thomas Ruffin.* 4 vols. Raleigh: Edwards & Boughton Printing Co., 1920; reprint, New York: AMS Press, Inc., 1973.

Harper, Roland M. "Development of Agriculture in Lower Georgia from 1850 to 1880." *Georgia Historical Quarterly* 6 (June 1922): 91–121.

———. "Development of Agriculture in Upper Georgia from 1850 to 1880." *Georgia Historical Quarterly* 6 (March 1922): 3–25.

Harwell, Richard, and Philip N. Racine, eds. *The Fiery Trial: A Union Officer's Account of Sherman's Last Campaign.* Knoxville: University of Tennessee Press, 1986.

Hay, Thomas Robson. "Lucius B. Northrop: Commissary General of the Confederacy." *Civil War History* 9 (March 1963): 5–23.

Heard, George Alexander. "St. Simons Island during the War between the States." *Georgia Historical Quarterly* 22 (September 1938): 249–72.

Heitmann, John Alfred. *The Modernization of the Louisiana Sugar Industry, 1830–1910.* Baton Rouge: Louisiana State University Press, 1987.

Hepworth, George H. *The Whip, Hoe, and Sword; or, the Gulf Department in '63.* Boston: Walker, Wise, and Co., 1864; reprint, Baton Rouge: Louisiana State University Press, 1979.

Holcomb, Julie, ed. *Southern Sons, Northern Soldiers: The Civil War Letters of the Remley Brothers, 22nd Iowa Infantry.* DeKalb: Northern Illinois University Press, 2004.

Hurt, R. Douglas. *Agriculture and Slavery in Missouri's Little Dixie.* Columbia: University of Missouri Press, 1992.

———. *American Farm Tools: From Hand Power to Steam Power.* Manhattan, Kan.: Sunflower University Press, 1982.

Iobst, Richard W. *Civil War Macon: The History of a Confederate City.* Macon, Ga.: Mercer University Press, 1999.

James, D. Clayton. "Mississippi Agriculture, 1861–1865," *Mississippi Journal of History* 24 (July 1962): 129–41.

Johns, John E. *Florida during the Civil War.* Gainesville: University of Florida Press, 1963.

Johnson, Ludwell H. "Contraband Trade during the Last Year of the Civil War." *Mississippi Valley Historical Review* 49 (March 1963): 635–52.

———. *Red River Campaign: Politics and Cotton in the Civil War*. Baltimore: Johns Hopkins Press, 1958.
———. "Trading with the Union: The Evolution of Confederate Policy." *Virginia Magazine of History and Biography* 78 (July 1970): 308–25.
Jones, Howard. *Blue and Gray Diplomacy: A History of Union and Confederate Foreign Relations*. Chapel Hill: University of North Carolina Press, 2010.
———. *Union in Peril: The Crisis over British Intervention in the Civil War*. Chapel Hill: University of North Carolina Press, 1992.
Jones, J. B. *A Rebel War Clerk's Diary at the Confederate States Capital*. 2 vols. New York: Old Hickory Bookshop, 1935.
Jones, Jacqueline. *The Dispossessed: America's Underclasses from the Civil War to the Present*. New York: Basic Books, 1992.
Jordan, Weymouth T. *Rebels in the Making: Planters' Conventions and Southern Propaganda*. Tuscaloosa: Confederate Publishing Co., 1958.
Kerr-Ritchie, Jeffrey R. *Freedpeople in the Tobacco South, 1860–1900*. Chapel Hill: University of North Carolina Press, 1999.
Kimball, William J. "The Bread Riot in Richmond, 1863." *Civil War History* 7 (June 1961): 149–54.
Knox, Thomas W. *Camp-fire and Cotton-field: A Southern Adventure in Time of War, Life with the Union Armies and Residence on a Louisiana Plantation*. New York: Blelock, 1865; reprint, New York: Da Capo Press, 1969.
Krug, Donna Rebecca D. "Women and War in the Confederacy." In *On the Road to War: The American Civil War and the German Wars of Unification, 1861–1871*, edited by Stig Föster and Jörg Nagler, 413–48. Washington, D.C.: German Historical Institute, 1997.
Lang, Herbert H. "J. F. H. Claiborne at 'Lorel Wood' Plantation, 1853–1870." *Journal of Mississippi History* 18 (January 1956): 1–17.
Lee, Susan P. *Memoirs of William Nelson Pemberton*. Philadelphia: J. B. Lippincott, 1893.
Lehman, James O., and Steven M. Nolt. *Mennonites, Amish, and the American Civil War*. Baltimore: Johns Hopkins University Press, 2007.
Lerner, Eugene M. "Inflation in the Confederacy, 1861–65." In *Studies in the Monetary Theory of Money*, edited by Milton Friedman, 163–75. Chicago: University of Chicago Press, 1956.
———. "The Monetary and Fiscal Programs of the Confederate Government, 1861–65." *Journal of Political Economy* 62 (December 1954): 506–22.
———. "Money, Prices, and Wages in the Confederacy, 1861–65." *Journal of Political Economy* 63 (February 1955): 20–40.
Lebergott, Stanley. "Through the Blockade: The Profitability and Extent of Cotton Smuggling, 1861–1865." *Journal of Economic History* 41 (December 1981): 867–88.
———. "Why the South Lost: Commercial Purpose in the Confederacy, 1861–1865." *Journal of American History* 70 (June 1983): 58–74.
Lonn, Ella. *Salt as a Factor in the Confederacy*. Tuscaloosa: University of Alabama Press, 1965.
Lunt, Dolly Sumner (Mrs. Thomas Burge). *A Woman's War-Time Journal*. Atlanta: Cherokee Publishing Co., 1894; reprint, Macon, Ga.: J. W. Burke, 1927.
McCurry, Stephanie. *Confederate Reckoning: Power and Politics in the Civil War South*. Cambridge: Harvard University Press, 2010.

McDonald, Forrest, and Grady McWhiney. "The Antebellum Southern Herdsman: A Reinterpretation." *Journal of Southern History* 41 (May 1975): 147–66.

———. "The South from Self-Sufficiency to Peonage: An Interpretation." *American Historical Review* 85 (December 1980): 1095–1118.

McKenzie, Robert H. "Civil War and Socioeconomic Change in the Upper South: The Survival of Local Agricultural Elites in Tennessee, 1850–1870." *Tennessee Historical Quarterly* 52 (Fall 1993): 170–84.

———. "The Economic Impact of Federal Operations in Alabama during the Civil War." *Alabama Historical Quarterly* 38 (Spring 1976): 51–68.

McKinney, Gordon B. *Zeb Vance: North Carolina's Civil War Governor and Gilded Age Political Leader*. Chapel Hill: University of North Carolina Press, 2004.

McKitrick, Eric L. *Andrew Johnson and Reconstruction*. Chicago: University of Chicago Press, 1960.

McPherson, James M. *Battle Cry of Freedom: The Civil War Era*. New York: Oxford University Press, 1988.

———. *The Negro's Civil War: How American Negroes Felt and Acted during the War for the Union*. New York: Pantheon Books, 1965.

McWhiney, Grady. "The Revolution in Nineteenth-Century Alabama Agriculture." *Alabama Review: A Quarterly Journal of Alabama History* 31 (January 1978): 3–32.

McWhiney, Grady, Warner O. Moore, and Robert F. Pace, eds. *"Fear God and Walk Humbly": The Agricultural Journal of James Mallory, 1843–1877*. Tuscaloosa: University of Alabama Press, 1997.

Meier, Kathryn Shively. *Nature's Civil War: Common Soldiers and the Environment in 1862 Virginia*. Chapel Hill: University of North Carolina Press, 2013.

Mobley, Joe A. *"War Governor of the South": North Carolina's Zeb Vance in the Confederacy*. Gainesville: University of Florida Press, 2005.

———. *Weary of War: Life on the Confederate Home Front*. Westport, Conn.: Praeger, 2008.

Mohr, Clarence L. *On the Threshold of Freedom: Masters and Slaves in Civil War Georgia*. Athens: University of Georgia Press, 1986.

Monroe, Haskell, ed. "The Road to Gettysburg: The Diary and Letters of Leonidas Torrance of the Gaston Guards." *North Carolina Historical Review* 36 (October 1959): 476–517.

Moore, Albert Burton. *Conscription and Conflict in the Confederacy*. New York: MacMillan, 1924.

Nichols, George Ward. *The Story of the Great March from the Diary of a Staff Officer*. New York: Harper & Brothers, 1865.

Nichols, James L. *The Confederate Quartermaster in the Trans-Mississippi West*. Austin: University of Texas Press, 1964.

———. "The Tax-in-Kind in the Department of the Trans-Mississippi." *Civil War History* 5 (December 1959): 382–89.

Nieman, Donald G., ed. *The African American Family in the South, 1861–1900*. New York: Garland Publishing, 1994.

O'Connor, Thomas H. "Lincoln and the Cotton Trade." *Civil War History* 7 (March 1961): 20–35.

O'Donovan, Susan Eva. *Becoming Free in the Cotton South*. Cambridge: Harvard University Press, 2007.

Otto, John Solomon. *Southern Agriculture during the Civil War Era, 1860–1880*. Westport, Conn.: Greenwood Press, 1994.

Pace, Robert F. "Abandoning Self-Sufficiency: Corn in the Lower South, 1849–1879." *Southern Studies* 4 (Fall 1993): 271–93.

———. "'It Was Bedlam Let Loose': The Louisiana Sugar Industry and the Civil War." *Louisiana History* 39 (August 1998): 389–409.

———. "Overwhelmed by the Storm: The Atlantic Rice Country, 1849–1879." *Southern Studies* 6 (Summer 1995): 1–23.

Parks, Joseph H. "A Confederate Trade Center under Federal Occupation: Memphis, 1862–1865." *Journal of Southern History* 7 (August 1941): 289–314.

Pearson, Elizabeth Ware, ed. *Letters from Port Royal: Written at the Time of the Civil War*. Boston: W. B. Clarke Co., 1906; reprint, New York: Arno Press, 1969.

Phillips, W. B. "The Correspondence of Robert Toombs, Alexander H. Stephens, and Howell Cobb." In Annual Report of the American Historical Association for the Year 1911. 2 vols. Washington, D.C.: Government Printing Office, 1913, 2:528–672.

Pierce, E. L. "The Freedmen at Port Royal." *Atlantic Monthly* 12 (September 1863): 291–315.

Potter, James E., and Edith Robbins, eds. *Marching with the First Nebraska: A Civil War Diary*. Norman: University of Oklahoma Press, 2007.

Powell, Lawrence N. *New Masters: Northern Planters during the Civil War and Reconstruction*. New Haven: Yale University Press, 1980.

Powell, Lawrence N., and Michael S. Wayne, "Self-Interest and the Decline of Confederated Nationalism." In *The Old South in the Crucible of War*, edited by Harry P. Owens and James J. Cooke, 29–45, 101–3. Jackson: University Press of Mississippi, 1983.

Pratt, Fletcher. *A Short History of the Civil War*. New York: Pocket Books, 1961.

Price, B. Byron. "'Don't Fence Me In': The Range Cattle Industry in the Confederate Southwest." In *Southwestern Agriculture: Pre-Columbian to Modern*, edited by Henry C. Dethloff and Irvin M. May Jr., 59–72. College Station: Texas A&M University Press, 1982.

Prichard, Walter, "The Effects of the Civil War on the Louisiana Sugar Industry." *Journal of Southern History* 5 (August 1939): 315–32.

Putnam, Sallie B. *Richmond during the War*. New York: G. W. Carleton & Co., 1867.

Rabel, George C. *Civil War Years: Women and the Crisis of Southern Nationalism*. Urbana: University of Illinois Press, 1989.

Rainwater, P. L., ed. "Letters of James Lusk Alcorn." *Journal of Southern History* 3 (May 1937): 196–209.

Ramsdell, Charles W. *Behind the Lines in the Southern Confederacy*. Baton Rouge: Louisiana State University Press, 1944.

———. "Captured and Abandoned Property during the Civil War." *American Historical Review* 19 (October 1913): 65–79.

———. "The Confederate Government and the Railroads." *American Historical Review* 22 (July 1917): 794–810.

———. "General Robert E. Lee's Horse Supply, 1862–1865." *American Historical Review* 35 (July 1930): 758–77.

Range, Willard. *A Century of Georgia Agriculture, 1850–1950*. Athens: University of Georgia Press, 1954.

Ransom, Roger L., and Richard Sutch. *One Kind of Freedom: The Economic Consequences of Emancipation.* Cambridge: Cambridge University Press, 1977.

Reidy, Joseph P. *From Slavery to Agrarian Capitalism.* Chapel Hill: University of North Carolina Press, 1992.

Ripley, C. Peter. *Slaves and Freedmen in Civil War Louisiana.* Baton Rouge: Louisiana University Press, 1976.

Roberts, A. Sellew. "The Federal Government and Confederate Cotton." *American Historical Review* 32 (January 1927): 262–75.

Rodrique, John C. *Reconstruction in the Cane Fields: From Slavery to Free Labor in Louisiana Sugar Parishes, 1862–1880.* Baton Rouge: Louisiana State University Press, 2001.

Rogers, William Warren, Jr. *Confederate Home Front: Montgomery during the Civil War.* Tuscaloosa: University of Alabama Press, 1999.

Roland, Charles P. "Difficulties of Civil War Sugar Planting in Louisiana." *Louisiana Historical Quarterly* 38 (October 1955): 40–62.

———. *Louisiana Sugar Plantations during the American Civil War.* Leiden: E. J. Brill, 1957.

Root, L. Carroll, ed. "Private Journal of William H. Root, Second Lieutenant, Seventy-Fifth New York Volunteers, April 1–June 14, 1863." *Louisiana Historical Quarterly* 19 (October 1936): 637–67.

Rose, Willie Lee. *Rehearsal for Reconstruction: The Port Royal Experiment.* Indianapolis: Bobbs-Merrill Co., 1964.

Roser, H. Taylor, ed. "Post-Bellum Southern Rental Contracts." *Agricultural History* 17 (April 1943): 121–28.

Ruminski, Jarrett. "'Tradyville': The Contraband Trade and the Problem of Loyalty in Civil War Mississippi." *Journal of the Civil War Era* 2 (December 2012): 511–37.

Russell, William Howard. *My Diary North and South.* Boston: T.O.H.P. Burnham, 1863.

Saville, Julie. "Grassroots Reconstruction: Agricultural Labour and Collective Action in South Carolina, 1860–1868." *Slavery and Abolition* 12 (December 1991): 173–82.

Scarborough, William Kauffman, ed. *The Diary of Edmund Ruffin.* 3 vols. Baton Rouge: Louisiana State University Press, 1972–89.

Schlebecker, John T. *Whereby We Thrive: A History of Farming, 1607–1972.* Ames: Iowa State University Press, 1975.

Schoen, Brian. *The Fragile Fabric of Union: Cotton, Federal Politics, and the Global Origins of the Civil War.* Baltimore: Johns Hopkins University Press, 2009.

Schuckers, J. W. *Life and Public Services of Salmon Portland Chase.* New York: D. Appleton and Co., 1874.

Sellers, James L. "The Economic Incidence of the Civil War in the South." *Mississippi Valley Historical Review* 14 (September 1927): 179–91.

Sharrer, G. Terry. *A Kind of Fate: Agricultural Change in Virginia, 1861–1920.* Ames: Iowa State University Press, 2000.

Sherman, Rachael Thorndike, ed. *The Sherman Letters: Correspondence between General and Senator Sherman from 1837 to 1891.* New York: C. Scribner's Sons, 1894.

Shugg, Robert W. *Origins of Class Struggle in Louisiana: A Social History of White Farmers and Laborers during Slavery and After, 1840–1875.* Baton Rouge: Louisiana State University Press, 1939.

———. "Survival of the Plantation System in Louisiana." *Journal of Southern History* 3 (August 1937): 311–25.
Sitterson, Joseph Carlyle. *Sugar Country: The Cane Sugar Industry in the South, 1753–1950*. Lexington: University Press of Kentucky, 1953.
———. "The Transition from Slave to Free Economy on the William J. Minor Plantations." *Agricultural History* 17 (October 1943): 216–24.
Smith, Andrew F. *Starving the South: How the North Won the Civil War*. New York: St. Martin's Press, 2011.
Smith, Julia Floyd. *Slavery and Rice Culture in Low Country Georgia, 1750–1860*. Knoxville: University of Tennessee Press, 1985.
Smith, Timothy B. *Mississippi in the Civil War: The Home Front*. Jackson: University Press of Mississippi, 2010.
Spencer, Cornelia Phillips. *The Last Days of the War in North Carolina*. New York: Watchman Publishing Co., 1866.
Stampp, Kenneth M. *The Peculiar Institution: Slavery in the Antebellum South*. New York: Vintage Books, 1956.
Surdam, David G. "The Antebellum Texas Cattle Trade across the Gulf of Mexico." *Southwestern Historical Quarterly* 50 (April 1997): 477–92.
Sutherland, Daniel E. *A Savage Conflict: The Decisive Role of Guerrillas in the American Civil War*. Chapel Hill: University of North Carolina Press, 2009.
Tadman, Michael. *Speculators and Slaves: Masters, Traders, and Slaves in the Old South*. Madison: University of Wisconsin Press, 1989.
Taylor, Robert A. "Rebel Beef: Florida Cattle and the Confederate Army, 1862–1864." *Florida Historical Quarterly* 67 (July 1988): 15–31.
Thomas, Emory M. *The Confederate Nation, 1861–1865*. New York: Harper & Row, 1979.
———. *The Confederate State of Richmond: A Biography of the Capital*. Austin: University of Texas Press, 1971.
Thomas, William G. "'Nothing Ought to Astonish Us': Confederate Civilians in the 1864 Shenandoah Valley Campaign." In *The Shenandoah Valley Campaign of 1864*, edited by Gary W. Gallagher, 222–56. Chapel Hill: University of North Carolina Press, 2006.
Todd, Richard Cecil. *Confederate Finance*. Athens: University of Georgia Press, 1954.
Towbridge, J. T. *The South: A Tour of Its Battlefields and Ruined Cities*. Hartford: L. Stebbins, 1866.
Tuten, James H. *Lowcountry Time and Tide: The Fall of the South Carolina Rice Kingdom*. Columbia: University of South Carolina Press, 2010.
Vandiver, Frank E. "Texas and the Confederate Army's Meat Problem." *Southwestern Historical Quarterly* 47 (January 1944): 225–33.
Wade, Michael G. *Sugar Dynasty: M. A. Patout & Son, Ltd., 1791–1993*. Lafayette: Center for Louisiana Studies, 1995.
Watkins, James. *King Cotton: A Historical and Statistical Review, 1790 to 1908*. New York: Negro Universities Press, 1908; reprint, New York: Greenwood, 1969.
Watson, H. Butler, ed. *Letters Home [by] Jay Caldwell Butler, Captain, 101st Ohio Volunteer Infantry*. Binghamton, N.Y.: self-published, 1930.
Wayne, Michael. *The Reshaping of Plantation Society: The Natchez District, 1860–1880*. Baton Rouge: Louisiana State University Press, 1983.

Wetherington, Mark V. *The New South Comes to Wiregrass Georgia, 1860–1910.* Knoxville: University of Tennessee Press, 1994.

White, Raymond E. "The Texas Cotton Ginning Industry." *Texan* 5 (1967): 344–58.

Whittington, G. P., ed. "Letters from John H. Ransdell to Governor Thomas Moore, dated 1863 Concerning the Loyalty of Slaves in North Louisiana in 1863." *Louisiana Historical Quarterly* 14 (October 1931): 487–502.

Wiggins, Sarah Woolfolk, ed. *The Journals of Josiah Gorgas, 1857–1878.* Tuscaloosa: University of Alabama Press, 1995.

Wight, Willard E., ed. "Some Letters of Lucius Bellinger Northrop, 1860–1865." *Virginia Magazine of History and Biography* 68 (October 1960): 456–77.

Wiley, Bell Irvin. *The Life of Billy Yank: The Common Soldier of the Union.* Baton Rouge: Louisiana State University Press, 1952.

———. *The Life of Johnny Reb: The Common Soldier of the Confederacy.* Indianapolis: Bobbs-Merrill Co., 1943.

———. *The Plain People of the Confederacy.* Baton Rouge: Louisiana State University Press, 1943; reprint, Chicago: Quadrangle Books, 1963.

———. *Southern Negroes, 1861–1865.* Indianapolis: Bobbs-Merrill Co., 1938.

———. "Vicissitudes of Early Reconstruction Farming in the Lower Mississippi Valley." *Journal of Southern History* 3 (November 1937): 441–52.

Wilson, Harold S. *Confederate Industry: Manufacturers and Quartermasters in the Civil War.* Jackson: University Press of Mississippi, 2002.

Wineman, Bradford A. "Trains, Canals, and Turnpikes: Transportation in Civil War Virginia, 1861–1865." In *Virginia at War: 1864*, edited by William C. Davis and James I. Robertson Jr., 65–80. Lexington: University Press of Kentucky, 2009.

Winters, Donald L. *Tennessee Farming, Tennessee Farmers: Antebellum Agriculture in the Upper South.* Knoxville: University of Tennessee Press, 1994.

Wittenberg, Eric J., ed. *Custer's Wolverines: The Civil War Letters of Brevet Brigadier General James H. Kidd, 6th Michigan Cavalry.* Kent, Ohio: Kent State University Press, 2000.

Woodman, Harold D. *King Cotton and His Retainers: Financing and Marketing the Cotton Crop of the South, 1800–1925.* Lexington: University Press of Kentucky, 1968; reprint, Columbia: University of South Carolina Press, 1990.

———. "Post-Civil War Southern Agriculture and the Law." *Agricultural History* 53 (January 1979): 319–37.

Woodward, C. Vann, and Elisabeth Muhlenfeld, eds. *The Private Mary Chesnut: The Unpublished Civil War Diaries.* New York: Oxford University Press, 1984.

Wright, Gavin. *Old South, New South: Revolutions in the Southern Economy since the Civil War.* New York: Basic Books, 1986.

Yates, Richard E. *The Confederacy and Zeb Vance.* Tuscaloosa, Ala.: Confederate Publishing Co., 1958.

Yearns, Wilfred Buck. *The Confederate Congress.* Athens: University of Georgia Press, 1960.

Younger, Edward, ed. *Inside the Confederate Government: The Diary of Robert Garlick Hill Kean.* New York: Oxford University Press, 1957.

Zornow, William Frank. "Aid for Indigent Families of Soldiers in Virginia, 1861–1865." *Virginia Magazine of History and Biography* 66 (October 1958): 454–58.

UNPUBLISHED SOURCES

Basford, Gertha Bass. "Federal Administration of Abandoned Plantations and Negro Labor during the Civil War, 1862–1865." M.A. thesis, University of Texas, 1931.

Ellis, Dorothy Lois. "The Transition from Slave Labor to Free Labor with Special Reference to Louisiana." M.A. thesis, Louisiana State University, 1932.

Gunn, Victoria Reeves. "Jarnell Plantation: A History." State of Georgia, Department of Natural Resources, Historic Preservation Section, Submitted July 1, 1974, Georgia State Archives and Libraries, Atlanta.

Martinez, Jamie Amanda. "For the Defense of the State: Slave Impressment in Confederate Virginia and North Carolina." Ph.D. diss., University of Virginia, 2008.

Swanson, Drew A. "Land of the Bright Leaf: Yellow Tobacco, Environment, and Culture along the Border of Virginia and North Carolina." Ph.D. diss., University of Georgia, 2010.

Index

Act to Regulate Impressments, 143
Act to Suppress Monopolies (Alabama), 43
Adams County, Miss., 23
Adrian County, Miss., 171
Agricultural and Mechanical Committee (Mississippi), 25
Agricultural impressment. *See* Impressment
Agricultural labor: in 1862, 81–85, 108–10; in 1863, 154–56, 181–86; in 1864, 224–30, 232; in 1865, 256–69, 272
Agricultural policy: in 1862, 63, 94, 98–99, 110; in 1863, 118–19, 124, 126, 129, 139, 142–43, 177; in 1864, 10, 191–93, 195, 199, 201–3, 217–20; in 1865, 245, 281; and price fixing, 158. *See also* Impressment
Agricultural population, in 1860, 7
Agricultural power: in 1861, 1–4, 11, 13, 15–17, 30–33, 44–45, 49, 50–51; in 1862, 9, 55, 86, 91–92, 100–101; in 1863, 116, 118, 136, 167; in 1864, 208; in 1865, 252, 255
Agricultural prices: in 1861, 11, 13–14, 16–17, 31, 33, 35, 44–45; in 1862, 55, 58–59, 61–68, 74, 86, 88, 91–92, 97, 100–102, 110–13; in 1863, 115–17, 120–23, 132, 135–38, 140, 143–44, 156–59, 163–65, 168, 187–89, 310 (n. 38), 313 (n. 102); in 1864, 156–57, 192–93, 195, 197, 200, 208, 216–18, 220, 222, 230–31, 234, 317 (n. 11); in 1865, 244, 249, 252, 254, 269–70, 272–73, 275–89
Agricultural problems: in 1861, 49; in 1865, 275–90
Agricultural technology. *See* Implements
Agriculture, impact of Civil War on, 275–89
Aiken, S.C., 62, 209, 250
Alabama: cattle in, 1; cotton burning in, 56; cotton planting regulations in, 57; crops in, 1, 15, 32, 75, 283; distillery prohibition in, 58; food riot in, 90; livestock disease in, 209; and produce loan, 21;

slave hiring in, 80; and tax-in-kind, 198, 311 (n. 50)
Albany, Ga., 135, 192, 244
Albemarle County, Va., 61, 258
Alexandria, La., 37, 223
American Freedmen's Inquiry Commission, 269. *See also* Freedmen's Bureau
American Hoe Company, 60
Anson County, N.C., 150
Arkansas, 1, 15, 234, 282–83; and cotton burning, 94; food prices fixed in, 101; legislature and planting, 98; slaves in, 107
Arpent, defined, 325 (n. 6)
Asheville, N.C., 66, 123, 158, 196
Athens, Ga., 65, 196, 249
Atlanta: agricultural prices in 1861, 33, 36; agricultural prices in 1862, 63, 66, 68, 86, 89; agricultural prices in 1863, 116–17; agricultural prices in 1864, 209; agricultural prices in 1865, 270; slave prices in, 77–78, 150
Augusta, Ga., 55, 60; agricultural prices in, 254; implement manufacturing in, 60
Augusta County, Va., 87
Austin, Tex.: agricultural prices in, 101

Banks, Nathaniel: and agricultural labor, 109–10, 181–84; and cotton seizures, 237–38; and labor policy, 109, 181–86, 226–30; and land policy, 225–30; raiding in Louisiana, 173; and Shenandoah Valley, 70; and sugar planting orders, 239
Barnwell, S.C., 200
Baton Rouge, La., 232
Bayou Lafourche, La., 108, 173
Beaufort, S.C., 34, 39
Beef: in 1861, 16, 36; in Florida, 37; New Orleans prices, 37; price of, 111, 121, 144; shortages of, 166, 169, 194–95, 210; in

[343]

Tennessee, 17, 210; in Upper South, 36; in Virginia, 194. *See also* Cattle; Livestock
Bladenboro, N.C., 90, 130, 200
Blockade: in 1862, 53, 91, 100; in 1863, 119, 125; benefits of, 4, 14–17, 19–20, 27, 29, 44; problems of, 35
Bonham, Tex., 103
Bread riots, 127–32; Atlanta, Ga., 130, 200; Barnwell, S.C., 200; Bladenboro, N.C., 90, 130, 200; Clarke County, Ala., 131; Greensboro, N.C., 130; Greenville, Ala., 90, 130; Milledgeville, Ga., 131; Mobile, Ala., 130, 157; Petersburg, Va., 130; Raleigh, N.C., 200; Richmond, Va., 127–30; Salisbury, N.C., 130; Savannah, Ga., 200; Waco, Tex., 200
Brown, Joseph E.: and agricultural impressments, 143, 159; and bread riot, 130–31; and conscription, 213; and cotton loans, 48; and cotton planting restrictions, 57, 119; and food production, 194; and slave impressments, 214; and soldiers' pay, 153; and trade restrictions, 194; and whiskey distillation, 58, 89
Bureau of Free Labor, 229–30
Bureau of Refugees, Freedmen and Abandoned Lands. *See* Freedmen's Bureau
Butler, Benjamin F., 102, 108

Calhoun County, Ga., 57
Caswell County, N.C., 151
Catherine's Island, Ga., 83
Cattle: in 1861, 1, 5, 13, 17; in 1862, 86–87, 103–4, 111; in 1863, 116, 139–40; in 1864, 168–69, 191, 204, 210, 233; in 1865, 245–46, 272; in Georgia, 6, 36, 280; in Texas, 36–38, 49; trade, 13, 176, 223, 241. *See also* Beef; Livestock
Charles County, Va., 215
Charleston, S.C.: agricultural prices in, 62, 86, 117; bread prices in, 116–17; cattle prices in, 118; lack of beef, 210; rice prices in, 218; slave prices in, 77–78, 147
Chase, Salmon P., 28; and cotton seizures, 81–82; and trade, 28, 62
Chatham County, N.C., 151
Chatham Railroad, 194
Cherokee County, Ga., 143

Christiansburg, Va., 147
Church and Union Hill Humane Association (Richmond), 199
Circular No. 13, 229
Citizen's Relief Committee (Mobile, Ala.), 131
Claiborne County, Miss., 180, 231
Clark County, Ga., 48
Clarke County, Ala., 131
Clarksville, Tenn., 44, 112
Coahoma County, Miss., 110
Columbia, S.C., 123
Columbia, Tenn., 248
Columbus, Ga., 68
Committee of Public Safety (Randolph County, Ga.), 55
Concordia Parish, La., 98
Confiscation Act, 75, 80, 108, 216
Conscription, 10, 146, 164, 211–13, 321 (n. 44)
Conway, Thomas W., 229
Corn: in 1861, 4, 11, 14, 16–17, 47, 49; in 1862, 53, 63–64, 88, 100, 111; in 1863, 117, 122, 137–38, 144, 157, 167, 188; in 1864, 192, 199, 222, 317 (n. 11); in 1865, 244, 248, 270, 272
Corpus Christi, Tex., 112
Cotton, 4–5, 13–14; benefits of, 52–54, 278–79; and blockade, 119; burning, 55–56, 93–95, 97, 171, 173–75, 189, 234–35, 251; committees, 94; Confederate government and planting, 98–99; and currency, 96–97; diplomacy, 9, 20, 23–24, 28–29, 31, 47–48, 52, 55, 74; impressment of, 144, 235; loan program, 74, 110, 168; Mexican buyers, 19, 48–49; planting restrictions, 43, 48, 54, 57, 98, 117–19, 302 (n. 15); postwar production, 326 (n. 8); prices, 11, 97, 189, 232, 252; production in 1860, 13; purchase program, 110, 168; Sea Island, 13–14; trade policy, 19, 27, 62, 95–96, 99, 175–78, 187, 222, 232, 236–43, 252–54. *See also* Trade
Cotton Bureau (Arkansas), 175
Cotton Loan Act (Mississippi), 46
Cotton Planters Bank of Georgia, 48
Crop disease, 66
Crop lien system, 276, 284
Currency: in 1861, 9, 28, 38, 61; in 1862, 9, 59–61, 96–97, 113, in 1863, 137, 160, 163,

168–69, 175; in 1864, 197, 222, 236–37, 240; in 1865, 244–45; reform, 160, 196–97; Tennessee, 299 (n. 39); in West, 317 (n. 15)

Dabney, Thomas S., 23
Dallas, Tex., 37, 91
Davis, Jefferson, 49; and agricultural power, 15, 31; and cotton burning, 95; and cotton diplomacy, 20; and cotton planting, 118; and food distribution, 124; and impressment, 248; and produce loan, 23; and railroads, 286
DeBow, James Dunwoody Brownson, 52
Decatur, Ga., 77
DeKalb County, Ga., 77

Eagle Pass, Tex., 175
Ebenezville, S.C., 54
Edisto Island, 84, 271
Etowah County, Ga., 136
Eufaula, Ga., 54–55
Eutaw, Ala., 136

Fairfax County, Va., 50
Farm equipment. *See* Implements
Fauquier County, Va., 69
Fayetteville, N.C., 245
Fessenden, William Pratt, 215
Fifteen Negro Law, 212, 288. *See also* Twenty Slave Law
Florida, 5, 50, 144, 209; cattle in, 1, 6, 139–40, 210, 246, 280
Flour: in 1861, 4, 14, 17, 33, 44; in 1862, 74, 87, 89–90, 100, 112; in 1863, 123, 136–37, 199, 310 (n. 38), 317 (n. 11); in 1864, 192–94, 197, 199, 202, 216, 225; in 1865, 244, 248, 270
Fluvanna County, Va., 258
Food disturbances. *See* Bread riots
Food prices. *See* Agricultural prices
Food riots. *See* Bread riots
Food security. *See* Hunger
Foraging: Confederate, 69, 74, 104–6, 171, 174–75, 204, 234–35, 250; by guerrillas, 234, 250, 261; for horses, 142
— Union: in Alabama, 142, 146; in Arkansas, 171–72, 234; in Georgia, 204, 218, 247; in Louisiana, 166–67, 173–74, 233;

in Mississippi, 106, 170–71, 232–35; in North Carolina, 251; in Tennessee, 105, 113–14, 170, 172, 189, 204, 224, 233; in Virginia, 32, 71, 142, 146, 204–6, 235; in Texas, 235
Franklin, La., 166
Freedmen's Bureau, 216, 263–67, 269, 285, 324 (n. 51)
Free Labor Order, 225
Frenchburg, Va., 69

General Orders No. 2, 106
General Orders No. 12, 182
General Orders No. 23, 225, 227–28, 262
General Orders No. 57, 186
General Orders No. 91, 109
General Orders No. 138, 239
General Orders No. 141, 178
Georgia: agricultural prices in, 15, 44–45, 64, 66, 68, 192, 194; cattle in, 1, 5–6, 36, 245–46, 280; cotton planting restrictions in, 48, 57, 119; cultivation in, 282–83; food scarcity in, 88, 139; foraging in, 247; hunger in, 88; impressment in, 159; poor relief in, 131; prohibits distilleries, 58–59; provisions in, 193; rice plantations, 275; slave prices in, 147; state banks, 26; tax-in-kind in, 198, 311 (n. 50); wheat in, 199; women, 245
Goliad, Tex., 223
Gonzales, Tex., 223
Gorgas, Josiah, 123, 127, 243, 259
Great Britain, 2, 29, 31, 48; and blockade, 19–20
Green County, Va., 61
Greensboro, N.C., 130
Greenville, Ala., 90
Griffin, Ga., 26

Hampshire County, Va., 69
Hancock County, Ga., 48
Hanover County, Va., 205
Hardin County, Tex., 17
Hardy County, Va., 32
Henrico County, Va., 138
Hill, H. H., 40
Hilton Head Island, S.C., 84
Hogs, 17, 33, 36, 49, 59, 245, 280
Hogsheads, defined, 300 (n. 57)

INDEX [345]

Holly Springs, Miss., 106
Horses: in 1861, 38; in 1862, 70–71, 73–74; in 1863, 140–42, 169–70; in 1864, 210–11, 224; in 1865, 247–49
Houston, Tex., 101, 111, 180, 248–50
Houston County, S.C, 192
Howard, O. O., 264, 267, 271
Hunger: in 1862, 52–53, 88, 100, 106; in 1863, 125, 158, 161–62; in 1864, 192; in Mississippi, 164; in Mobile, 167; in Richmond, 194, 209
Hurlbut, Stephen A., 262

Implements, 35, 60, 91, 153, 271, 283–84
Impressment: in Florida, 50, 144–45; in Georgia, 124, 144, 146, 159, 191–92; Lee orders, 73; in Louisiana, 43; in Mississippi, 50, 164–65; in North Carolina, 151, 160; policy, 9, 42, 201–3, 217–18, 243, 245, 248–50; schedules, 59, 73–74, 159, 208–9, 217–18, 288–89; in South Carolina, 137, 250; in Virginia, 71–74, 121–22, 138, 142, 151, 156–58. *See also* Foraging
Indianola, Tex., 234
Inflation, 42, 60–61. *See also* Currency

Jackson, Miss., 35, 100, 167, 174, 176
Jefferson, La., 187
Jefferson City, Tex., 13, 37, 103, 223, 241, 272
Jefferson County, Ga., 144
Jefferson County, Miss., 17
Jefferson County, Va., 76
Johnson, Andrew, 253, 264, 273

Kean, Robert Garlick Hill, 122
Knoxville, Tenn., 95

Labor: in 1861, 38–39; in 1862, 81–85, 108–9; in 1863, 154–56, 181–86; in 1864, 224–30; in 1865, 256–69, 272, 324 (n. 51)
Ladies Island, S.C., 34
Lafourche, La., 102, 108–9
Land: confiscation of, 154; cultivation losses, 282–83; policy, 154, 215–16; reform, 81–85, 259, 266, 289; and speculators, 186, 189; values, 273, 277, 283
Laredo, Tex., 175, 188
Lawrence County, Miss., 164

Lawton, A. R., 223
Letcher, John, 15, 146
Limestone County, Ala., 142
Lincoln, Abraham: and British neutrality, 19; and trade, 27, 178
Lincoln County, Tenn., 179
Little Rock, Ark., 113
Livestock: in 1861, 17, 36–38; in 1862, 103; in 1863, 139–40; in 1864, 210; in 1865, 245; glanders in, 140–41, 281; and hog cholera, 36, 113, 209, 245, 281; horses, 70–71, 73–74, 140–42, 169, 224, 247–49; postwar, 245, 279–80; and Texas Fever, 280–81. *See also* Cattle
Louisiana, 16, 238; agricultural labor in, 181–84; agricultural prices in, 222; cattle trade in, 223; cotton burning committees in, 94; cotton planting in, 57, 98, 321; cotton trade in, 223; food supplies in, 187–88; foraging in, 233; land values in, 273; slave prices in, 41, 107, 180–81. *See also* New Orleans
Lynchburg, Va., 126, 135, 205

Macon, Ga., 22, 26, 31; agricultural prices in, 44, 125; impressment in, 218; slave hiring in, 80
Madison County, Ala., 142
Madison County, Va., 61
Marshall, Tex., 37
Martin County, N.C., 56
Matamoros, Mexico, 19, 223, 230
McPhersonville, S.C., 85
Mechanics Savings and Loan Association (Savannah, Ga.), 26
Meigs, M. C., 70
Memminger, Christopher G., 24, 27, 51–52, 133–34
Memphis, Tenn.: cotton trade in, 35, 175–78, 189, 241; sugar trade in, 25; Union capture of, 95, 97
Memphis and Charleston Railroad, 64
Meyers, Abraham C., 70, 218
Militia Act, 108
Milledgeville, Ga., 125, 131
Mississippi, 98, 107, 283; agricultural prices in, 17, 100–101, 110, 165, 167; cotton burning in, 97; cotton trade in, 236; currency in, 46–47; drought in, 100, 111;

foraging in, 234–35; implements in, 35; legislature, 25, 45–46, 98; produce loans in, 23; slave prices in, 107, 111; slavery in, 41–42, 107, 180; slave women in, 92; women in, 40, 179, 237
Mississippi River, closure of, 14. *See also* Blockade
Mobile, Ala., 15, 33, 44, 121, 131, 157
Monroe County, Ga., 192
Moore, Andrew Barry, 43
Moore, Thomas O., 45
Murfreesboro, Tenn., 113

Nashville, Tenn., 43, 163; cotton prices in, 252; cotton trade in, 241
Natchez, Miss.: and agricultural prices, 50; beef shortage, 166; and hunger, 100; postwar, 255
Nelson County Va., 259
New Iberia, La., 37, 166
New Orleans: cotton factors in, 22 ; cotton trade in, 178, 222, 230–32, 241; food shortage in, 187–88; slave market, 41, 180; Union capture of, 9, 92, 97
 – agricultural prices: in 1861, 13–14, 32, 35, 37, 44–45; in 1862, 99, 102; 1863, 159; in 1864, 193–94, 197, 202, 222, 225, 232; in 1865, 272
Norfolk, Va., 131
North Carolina: agricultural prices in, 17, 123, 220; bread riot in, 130; cattle in, 280–81; cotton burning in, 56; cultivation loss in, 283; drought in, 75; food shortage in, 115; horses in, 38; impressment in, 159–60; livestock disease in, 209; prohibits whiskey distillation, 58; slave hiring in, 79; slavery in, 77, 79–80, 85; tax-in-kind in, 198; tobacco in, 5; wheat in, 67
Northrop, Lucius B., 73, 88, 119, 221, 246, 248

Opelousas, La., 166–67
Orange County (Va.) Court House, 146
Ossabaw Island, Ga., 83
Oxford, Ala., 139

Panola County, Miss., 21
Pemberton, William Nelson, 87

Petersburg (Va.) City Council, 158
Pettus, John J., 46, 100–112, 171
Phelan, James, 177
Pierce, Edward L., 81–82
Pitt County, N.C., 56
Planters, defined, 1
Point Coupée Parish, La., 237
Port Royal, S.C., 34, 38–39, 81–82, 84; plantations, 155
Price fixing, 157
Prince Georges County, Va., 205
Produce Loan Act, 20
Produce loans: problems with, 22–27, 51–52, 66, 168, 223, 298 (n. 25); terms of, 20–21
Produce Loan Bureau, 219

Raiding. *See* Foraging
Railroads, 6, 66, 122, 125, 210, 286; Chatham, 194; Memphis and Charleston, 64; Virginia and Central, 205; Winchester and Potomac, 30
Raleigh, N.C., 115, 200
Randolph, George W., 71, 74
Randolph County, Ga.: Committee of Public Safety, 55
Randolph County, Va., 31
Rapids Parish, La., 233
Refugio, Tex., 223
Relief of Poor Persons Not in the Poor House (Richmond, Va.), 129
Rice, 1, 4–5, 34, 157; planters, 39, 218, 259, 275–76
Richmond: bread riot, 127–30; food relief in, 129; slave prices in, 41, 77–79, 147, 150; wheat shortage in, 90; whiskey prices in, 195
 – agricultural prices: in 1861, 14, 32–33; in 1862, 62, 65; in 1863, 117, 121, 123, 136–38, 310 (n. 102), 313 (n. 102); in 1864, 156–57, 192–93, 197, 199, 216, 231, 317 (n. 11); in 1865, 192–93, 195, 199–200, 230, 244
 – food shortages: in 1862, 67; in 1863, 124–25, 127, 157–58, 160–61; in 1864, 192–93
Robertson Blacklock and Company, 147
Rockingham County, Va., 150, 207
Ruffin, Edmund, 128, 140, 154, 212

St. Catherine's Island, Ga., 83
St. Landy Parish, La., 233, 237
St. Mary Parish, La., 233, 277–78
St. Simons, Island, Ga., 83
San Antonio, Tex., 49, 91, 101, 175, 223
Savannah, Ga., 26, 135, 200
Saxton, Rufus, 82, 84–85, 109, 155–56, 215
Second Conscription Act, 89
Seddon, James, 73; and impressments, 42, 151, 159; and trade, 96
Selma, Ala., 125–26, 199
Sequestration Commission, 109, 182–83
Sharecropping, 267–69, 276, 279, 284–85
Shelby, Tenn., 178
Shenandoah Valley, 38, 64, 70–71, 87, 205–8
Sheridan, Philip, 10, 206–7
Sherman, William Tecumseh, 10, 204–5, 214–15, 218–20, 269, 313 (n. 98)
Shorter, John G., 119
Shreveport, La., 99, 232
Slaves/slavery: in 1860, 7–8; in Alabama, 80; in Arkansas, 107; and cotton picking rates, 42; and Fifteen Negro Law, 212, 280; and flight, 34–35, 64, 107, 147; in Georgia, 147; hiring of, 40, 80, 107, 180, 213, 258; impressment of, 151, 214, 258; loss of, 285; in Louisiana, 41, 107, 180–81, 258; markets for, 40–41, 77–79; in Mississippi, 40–42, 92, 107, 111, 180, 192; in North Carolina, 77, 79–80, 85; population, 7; rations for, 198–99; in South Carolina, 16, 147, 150; in Tennessee, 107, 256; in Texas, 107, 180; Twenty Slave Law, 75; valuations of, 148–50, 257, 285; in Virginia, 40–41, 79; and women, 42, 92, 96
– prices: in 1861, 41; in 1862, 9, 77–80, 107; in 1863, 147, 150, 180–81; in 1864, 213–14; in 1865, 257
Sopelo Island, Ga., 83
Southampton County, Va., 11, 200
South Carolina, 5, 16, 34–35, 282; and cattle, 280; cotton planting restrictions in, 57, 119; prohibits whiskey distillation, 59; provisions in, 192; rice plantations, 1, 85, 275; slave prices in, 147, 150; wheat, 68; women in, 40
– agricultural prices: in 1862, 59, 62, 66; in 1863, 123, 137, 157; in 1864, 192, 209

Southern Agricultural Implement Factory (Jackson, Miss.), 35
Special Field Orders No. 15, 259, 269, 313 (n. 98)
Special Orders 63, 165
Stanton, Edwin M., 70
Starvation. *See* Hunger
Staunton, Va., 87–88
Sugar: in 1861, 34–35; in 1862, 86–87, 102; in 1863, 166, 310 (n. 38); in 1864, 231; in 1865, 270; planters, 34–35, 109, 181, 222, 229, 262, 277–78

Tax-in-kind: in 1863, 10, 132–34, 151, 160; in 1864, 197–98, 202, 211, 240–43, 251–52, 270, 282, 311 (n. 50)
Technology. *See* Implements
Tennessee: agricultural prices in 1861, 16–17; beef in, 17; cattle in, 5; cotton production in, 1; cotton trade in, 236; horses in, 224; slaves in, 107, 256; tobacco in, 5, 276, 302 (n. 15); Union foraging in, 113–14, 172–73, 224; wheat in, 15; women in, 179
Texas: cotton planting regulations in, 57; cotton production in, 1; currency in, 168; slave prices in, 180; slavery in, 107; wheat in, 15, 105
– cattle: in 1861, 5, 13, 36–37; in 1862, 103–4; in 1863, 116, 140; in 1864, 168, 210, 223, 241; in 1865, 246
Thomas, Lorenzo, 185–86
Tishomingo County, Miss., 242
Tithe. *See* Tax-in-kind
Tobacco: 5, 13–14, 22–23, 55, 58; and military market, 90; opposition to, 118, 120; planters' optimism, 117; postwar, 276; and produce loan, 26, 219; and tax-in-kind, 133, 198, 276; Virginia planting restrictions, 302 (n. 15)
– prices: in 1861, 14; in 1862, 68, 112; in 1863, 117–18, 120, 276–77
Toombs, Robert, 48, 54
Trade: in 1865, 252–54; across boundary lines, 27–28, 62, 96, 176–78, 236–39, 242–43; federal supervision of, 95; Grant opposes, 252; with Great Britain, 286–87; Lincoln prohibits, 27; and Mississippi River, 14, 187–89

[348] INDEX

Twenty Slave Law, 75, 152
Tyler, Tex., 103

Union City, Tenn., 35
Union County, Miss., 235

Vance, Zebulon B., 43, 119, 151, 160
Vicksburg, Miss., 101, 140, 168, 174, 234, 241
Virginia: cattle in, 5–6, 17, 86, 280; cultivation decline in, 283; drought in, 209; impressment in, 247–49; slavery in, 40–41, 79; tobacco in, 5, 276, 302 (n. 15); whiskey in, 59. *See also* Richmond
Virginia and Central Railroad, 205

Waco, Tex., 175, 200
Warren County, Miss., 30, 49
Warwick Courthouse, Va., 17
Washington, D.C., 14
Washington County, Miss., 100, 104, 170
Washington County, N.C., 56
Watts, Thomas H., 201–2
West Virginia, 326 (n. 13)

Wheat: in 1861, 5, 15, 31, 45, 47, 49; in 1862, 55, 63, 67–68, 88, 101; in 1863, 122–23, 125, 137–38, 144; in 1864, 192–93, 242; in 1865, 244, 248, 270
Whiskey prohibition, 58–59, 89, 115, 159, 209, 281
Wigfall, Louis T., 43
Wilcox, John A., 103
Wilder, Charles B., 82–83
Wilmington, N.C., 252
Winchester, Tenn., 105, 207–8
Winchester, Va., 30, 69, 71, 87,
Winchester and Potomac Railroad, 30
Winstead, Ga., 60
Women: and bread riots, 90, 127–31, 157, 200; as farm operators, 39–40; free black, 227, 285–86; in Mississippi, 40, 179; planter, 76–77, slave, 10–11, 92, 96, 152, 179; in South Carolina, 40; in Tennessee, 179; and wages, 182, 185, 226–27, 258, 260; and white field work, 9–10, 152–53, 178–79, 225, 245

Yancey, William Lowndes, 19

www.ingramcontent.com/pod-product-compliance
Lightning Source LLC
Chambersburg PA
CBHW021352290426

44108CB00010B/212